Faculty Guidebook

A Comprehensive Tool for Improving Faculty Performance

First Edition

Project Directors

Steven W. Beyerlein
University of Idaho

Daniel K. Apple
Pacific Crest

Pacific Crest

Faculty Development Series

Faculty Guidebook
First Edition
second printing, July 2004

Copyright © 2004

Pacific Crest

906 Lacey Avenue, Suite 211

Lisle, IL 60532

630-737-1067

www.pcrest.com

ISBN 1-878437-00-3

Preface

Project Overview

Pacific Crest is pleased to announce its newest, most impressive, most dynamic publication to date—the *Faculty Guidebook*. The product of more than fifteen years worth of accumulated knowledge, experience, research, and collaborative efforts, this valuable reference is a tool that individual faculty members and those responsible for faculty development will treasure. More than 60 faculty members and administrators and over 50 colleges and universities are already contributing to this resource, providing an effective blend of theory and practice in a highly usable format.

Topics are wide ranging, covering the areas of educational philosophy, learning and developmental theory, facilitation and quality of learning environments, teaching practices and learning tools, assessment, evaluation and performance measurement, instructional design, and program assessment. During the next two years, more content will be added to each successive edition. For the next edition, modules are under development in the following areas:

Educational Philosophy	Learning Tools	Performance Measurement & Tasks
Learning Theory	Program & Course Design	Faculty Development
Mentoring	Activity Design	Institutional Effectiveness
Enriched Learning Environments	Assessment	Educational Research
Facilitation	Program Assessment	Annotated Bibliography
Teaching Practices	Evaluation	

How to Use this Book

The *Faculty Guidebook* is a practical document, meant to be used much like one might use an encyclopedia. Individual modules are short (either two or four pages in length) and summarize, in concise form, what is essential about any given topic. Despite the many diverse sources and contributors, the guidebook has a consistent format and a uniform, easy-to-read style. The material is well-researched, distilled for quick access, yet modules also provide ample bibliographic references which one can use to access original material if one wants to find out more. Frequent references within modules point users to related entries elsewhere within the guidebook (bold italicized is the notation referring to other modules in the *Faculty Guidebook*), minimizing overlap and needless repetition. In addition to being an excellent, concise background resource on a wide variety of topics, the guidebook is application-oriented, suggesting ways that educators may integrate methods into their current practices.

The *Faculty Guidebook* is designed to be used in the following contexts:

- a preferred reference for individual faculty desiring to improve their performance inside and outside of the classroom.
- a resource for higher education institutions to guide faculty development efforts.
- a coaching tool to help faculty mentor colleagues.
- a textbook to enhance graduate student training.
- a vehicle for moving classroom innovations to conferences and publications (rapidly converting new teaching/learning knowledge into an accessible, peer-reviewed reference).
- a digital library to support "on-line" and distance learning environments.

Obtaining Additional Copies

Single copies of the *Faculty Guidebook* are available for individual purchase at $75. Discounts may be applied to quantity orders (of fifty or more). Contact Pacific Crest at 800-421-9826 for more information about ordering.

Pacific Crest also offers a generous site license arrangement to institutions that is priced according to the number of full-time faculty. The site license allows for duplication and distribution of guidebook content to all full-time and part-time faculty, staff, and administrators. Both hardcopy and softcopy masters are provided to licensed institutions as well as on-line access. More information about the benefits and costs associated with a site license can be found on the Pacific Crest web site: www.pcrest.com

Editorial Team

Project Directors:	Steven Beyerlein, University of Idaho
	Daniel Apple, Pacific Crest
Project Administrator:	Deirdre Brennan, Pacific Crest
Layout/Graphic Designer:	Karl Krumsieg, Pacific Crest
Technical Editors:	Carol Nancarrow, Sinclair Community College
	Linda Spoelman, Grand Rapids Community College
	Suzanne Ashe, Cerritos College
First Edition Section Editors:	
Educational Philosophy	Mark Schlesinger, University of Massachusetts Boston
Learning and Developmental Theory	Cy Leise, Bellevue University
Facilitation in a Quality Learning Environment	Peter Smith, Saint Mary's College
Effective Teaching Practices and Learning Tools	Kathleen Burke, SUNY Cortland
	Carol Nancarrow, Sinclair Community College
Assessment, Evaluation and Performance Measurement	Marie Baehr, Elmhurst College
	Sandy Bargainnier, Pennsylvania State University
Instructional Design	Chris Davis, Baker College
Program Assessment	Kelli Parmley, SUNY New Paltz
Annotated Bibliography	Carol Nancarrow, Sinclair Community College

How to Become an Author

The *Faculty Guidebook* is a valuable way to access a tremendous amount of what has been gathered and gained in recent efforts in higher education. However, the guidebook is a work in progress. Over the next two years, much content will be added to the book, making it even more comprehensive. There's room for you if you'd like to be part of this personally rewarding effort. If you'd like to be involved in creating future modules, contact Project Director, Steve Beyerlein at sbeyer@uidaho.edu, or Pacific Crest at inquiries@pcrest.com.

Contents

Daniel Apple, President and founder of Pacific Crest
Pacific Crest, Lisle, IL   email: dan@pcrest.com

Vita highlights:

1. Facilitated more than 200 Institutes since 1991, including three-day Process Education Teaching Institutes, Curriculum Design Institutes, Advanced Teaching Institutes, and Learning-to-Learn Camps.

2. Author of faculty resources such as the *Process Education Teaching Institute Handbook, Curriculum Design Handbook*, and *Program Assessment Handbook* as well as student texts such as *The Learning Assessment Journal* and *Learning Through Problem Solving*.

3. Served as a facilitator and coach in transformational change at more than 25 colleges during the past ten years.

4. Collaborated on more than ten research grants in areas including technological innovations, curriculum reform, science and engineering reform, and new educational approaches to advance student success.

Richard Armstrong, Chemistry Instructor
Madison Area Technical College, Madison, WI   email: armstrong@matcmadison.edu
Favorite course: College Chemistry II

Vita highlights:

1. Thirty five years of teaching chemistry at the high school, Associate degree and College levels.

2. Written 25-30 "guided inquiry" activities for General Chemistry.

3. Worked with colleagues to plan and conduct several Learning-to-Learn Camps for under-perfoming students.

4. Four years of teaching fire fighter courses including hydraulics, pump operation, hazardous materials, fire-fighter safety, Level I and Level II certification programs and Driver-Operator Certification. Wrote a manual: "Live Fire Training Standard Operating Procedure."

Suzanne Ashe, Professor of English, Coordinator of First-Year Experience Program, Director of Writing Center
Cerritos College, Norwalk, CA   email: sashe@cerritos.edu
Favorite courses/activities: Learning Communities, Composition (basic skills through advanced), Writing Centers and Labs, Critical Thinking/Argumentation, Drama, Shakespeare

Vita highlights:

1. Ten years combined experience in learning communities and First-Year Experience programs; extensive experience in related faculty and staff development at local and national levels.

2. Established campus-wide cross-curricular writing lab and web site, including faculty development component.

3. Selected for Distinguished Faculty Award at Cerritos College (2002) and Outstanding Faculty of the Year Award from Center for the Study of Diversity in Education (De Anza College, California) in 2001.

Carol Atnip, Educational Consultant – Developmental Mathematics
Former coordinator of Developmental Mathematics, University of Louisville   email: carolatnip@hotmail.com

Vita highlights:

1. Actively involved with issues in developmental education. Presented workshops and sessions at state and national conferences on faculty development and alternative ways to serve academically at-risk students.

2. National service includes a two-year term as secretary on the board of the National Association for Developmental Education and the NADE representative on the AMATYC National Advisory Committee for the revision of the *Crossroads in Mathematics: Standards for Introductory College Mathematics Before Calculus*. Was co-chair of the NADE national conference in 2001.

3. Served on the board of the Kentucky Association for Developmental Education since 1989, holding numerous offices, including current position as archivist.

4. Co-authored two developmental mathematics texts for Pacific Crest. Collaborated extensively on curriculum development using the Process Education philosophy and adapting active learning techniques for use in the developmental mathematics classroom.

Marie Baehr, Associate Dean of the Faculty and Professor of Physics
Elmhurst College, Elmhurst, IL   email: marieb@elmhurst.edu
Favorite courses/activities: New Faculty Orientation, Assessment of General Education, General Physics, and Chaos Theory

Vita highlights:

1. Co-author of *Foundations of Learning* and *Foundations of Learning Activities Book* (Pacific Crest, 2000) and *Laboratory Manual for Liberal Arts Physics*, 2nd Edition (Prentice Hall, 2003).

2. Member of North Central Association's Higher Learning Commission's Assessment of Student Learning Think Tank whose purpose is to define the Commission's role and programming and services that can further improve student learning in schools under their oversight.

3. Creator of several handbooks for Elmhurst College, including Adjunct Faculty Handbook (1999), Assessment Handbook (2002), General Education Handbook (2003), and Department Chair's Handbook (in progress).

Sandy Bargainnier, Assistant Professor, Department of Kinesiology
The Pennsylvania State University, University Park, PA   email: ssb5@psu.edu
Favorite courses: Curriculum Design, Program Planning, and Health Education Concepts

Vita highlights:

1. Scholarship includes rubric development, documenting problem-based learning with a course portfolio and designing professional development activities to improve classroom assessment and student learning.

2. Active in peer-reviewed conference presentations on the use of Readiness Assessment Tests (RATs), Rubric Design, Classroom Assessment, and Group Process. Conferences include the American Alliance for Health, Physical Education, Recreation, and Dance, the American School Health Association, and the Pennsylvania State Association for Health, Physical Education, Recreation and Dance.

3. Conducts faculty development workshops at Penn State University on the use of Readiness Assessment Tests (RATs), Classroom Assessment, and group work.

4. Consultant/Grant writer for a $400,000 Carol M. White Physical Education Program Federal Grant.

Steve Beyerlein, Professor of Mechanical Engineering
University of Idaho, Moscow, ID   email: sbeyer@uidaho.edu
Favorite courses: Sophomore Design, Senior Design, and Combustion Engine Systems

Vita highlights:

1. Research interests include testing catalytic engine systems, conducting action research in college classrooms, teaching and documenting open-ended problem solving, and designing professional development activities.

2. Active in the Transferable Integrated Design Engineering Education (TIDEE) consortium that produced and field-tested a three component Design Team Readiness Assessment.

3. During a 2001-2002 sabbatical year, collaborated with a broad range of *Faculty Guidebook* authors to create the design for the project.

4. Co-PI of the NSF Enriched Learning Environment grant with primary responsibility for the formation and ongoing development of a community of research-based classroom practitioners at the University of Idaho.

Paula Bobrowski, Associate Professor and Chair of Marketing and Management
State University of New York at Oswego   email: bobrowsk@oswego.edu
Favorite courses: Technology Management, International Marketing, and Advertising and Promotion

Vita highlights:

1. Research interests include: technology management, international business, healthcare management, and marketing.

2. PI of a Department of Education Title VIB—International Business Grant.

3. Recipient of the 2003 Chancellors Award for Excellence in Teaching and the Presidents Award for Teaching Excellence.

4. Fulbright Research Fellow, Japan 1996-1997.

5. Co-Author of the textbook *Gateway to Business* (3rd edition).

6. Fifteen years of experience in the healthcare industry.

Kathleen Burke, Assistant Professor of Economics
SUNY Cortland, Cortland, NY   email: burkek@cortland.edu
Favorite courses: Econometrics, Statistics, and Mathematical Economics

Vita highlights:

1. Research interests include issues in public education in New York State, household decision making and its influence on health care and education in developing countries, and salary analysis in higher education.

2. Received a 2004 Excellence in Teaching award for the Incorporation of Technology in Teaching.

William Collins III, Associate Professor of Neurobiology and Behavior and Director of Undergraduate Biology
Stony Brook University, Stony Brook, NY   email: william.collins@sunysb.edu

Vita highlights:

1. Has extensive experience in the use of computer hardware and software in research and teaching.

2. Developed instructional laboratory courses in physiology, computer modeling, and introductory biology.

3. Recipient of a SUNY Merit Award for Excellence in Teaching and Course Development and the President's and Chancellor's Award for Excellence in Teaching.

4. Actively involved in faculty development and the use of real-time assessment to grow student performance in laboratory and research process.

Pamela Cox, Assistant Professor of Management
State University of New York at Oswego   email: pcox@oswego.edu
Favorite courses: Organizational Behavior, Cultural Environments of International Business, and Human Resource Staffing

Vita highlights:

1. Research interests include developing effective teamwork models, improving first-year college retention, and integrating writing and critical thinking across the university curriculum.

2. Developed and implemented (with Paula Bobrowski) a critical thinking course for first-year business students that has significantly improved first-year retention rates and first-year grade-point-averages.

3. Co-authored (with Paula Bobrowski) *Gateway to Business* (3rd edition).

4. Published articles on curriculum design and assessment in *Journal of Management Education*, *Business Communications Quarterly*, *Decision Sciences Institute Journal of Innovative Education*, and *Journal of Behavioral and Applied Management*.

Chris Davis, Director of Instructional Technology
Baker College, Flint, MI   email: chris.davis@baker.edu

Vita highlights:

1. Works with the faculty and administrators of the Baker College campuses on the integration of technology to enhance teaching and learning.

2. Leads the Baker College Center for Teaching Excellence.

3. Previously was Dean of CIS and Technical programs at Baker College of Muskegon.

4. Academic interests evolve from his Ph.D. work from the University of Michigan in Urban, Technological, and Environmental Planning: Sociotechnological Planning.

Denny Davis, Professor of Bioengineering
Washington State University, Pullman, WA   email: davis@wsu.edu
Favorite courses: Multidisciplinary Capstone Engineering Design, and Freshman Design

Vita highlights:

1. Research interests include teaching, learning and assessing engineering design; teaching professional skills and attributes; student retention in engineering.

2. Project leader for the NSF Transferable Integrated Design Engineering Education (TIDEE) consortium that produced and field-tested instructional and assessment resources for design education. www.tidee.cea.wsu.edu

3. Founding member of Washington State University's President's Teaching Academy, focused on improving teaching and learning on campus.

4. Collaborator with NSF Enriched Learning Environment grant at the University of Idaho that focused on the development of a community of research-based classroom practitioners.

Victor Harms, Assistant Professor of Psychology and Human Services
Bellevue University, Bellevue, NE   email: harms@bellevue.edu
Favorite courses: Introductory Psychology, Mental Health Diagnosis and Treatment, and Internship

Vita highlights:

1. Research interests are influence of home environment and parenting on self-esteem, and problem solving of adolescents.

2. Ten years experience as the president of a full service outpatient mental health practice.

3. Extensive experience as a counseling educator at the University of Nebraska-Omaha, Grace University, and Bellevue University.

4. Experienced at being an active learning facilitator and with creating a positive learning environment (use the curriculum *Process Education Activities for Introduction to Psychology*).

Wendy Duncan-Hewitt, Assistant Dean for Education
Auburn University Harrison School of Pharmacy, Auburn, AL   email: duncawe@auburn.edu
Favorite activities: Synthetic educational research, facilitation of educational quality improvement, and problem-based learning facilitation

Vita highlights:

1. Research interests include cognitive/moral development, leadership in learning communities, professionalization.

2. Produced a framework that links a social model of cognitive/moral development to optimal teaching methods that faculty can use to facilitate growth and empowerment.

3. Developed a modified problem-based learning format that can be used in large classes with one facilitator.

Sharon Jensen, Instructor, College of Nursing
Seattle University, Seattle, WA   email: sjensen@seattleu.edu
Favorite courses: Advanced Pharmacology and Critical Care Senior Practicum

Vita highlights:

1. Research interests include effectiveness of learning strategies and facilitating high level reflection practices.

2. Beginning work on a first edition of a medical surgical nursing book in collaboration with faculty from the University of Washington.

3. Ten years of experience teaching at the university level and four years of continuing education in the hospital setting.

4. Use technology, active learning strategies, and integrate the philosophy of Process Education in teaching practices and curriculum design.

Cy Leise, Professor of Psychology and Director of the M.S. in Human Services
Bellevue University, Bellevue, NE   email: cleise@bellevue.edu
Favorite courses: Introductory Psychology and Making Positive Life Choices (online)

Vita highlights:

1. Research interests include learning and self-growth theory, especially how educators can facilitate these.

2. Author of *Process Learning Activities for Introduction to Psychology* (3rd edition).

3. Facilitated, as a change agent, the incorporation of program assessment within the Bellevue University community.

4. Presented at the North Central 2003 meeting and at other assessment conferences on the use of active learning rubrics as a guide for both students and instructors.

Vicky Minderhout, Associate Professor of Chemistry
Seattle University, Seattle, WA   email: vicky@seattleu.edu
Favorite courses: Undergraduate Research, Biochemistry, and General Chemistry

Vita highlights:

1. Research interests include biochemical signal transduction processes as they relate to atherosclerosis; analyzing effective teaching for open-ended problem solving; and designing professional development activities for high school instructors.

2. Facilitator at national workshops for the NSF Process-Oriented Guided Inquiry Learning (POGIL) project. Co-designer and facilitator for a professional development series for local physical science teachers.

3. Presented at several chemical education conferences on coaching problem solving skills in the classroom.

4. Co-author of process oriented activities for biochemistry (in development).

Jim Morgan, Associate Professor of Civil Engineering
Texas A&M University, College Station, TX   email: jim-morgan@tamu.edu
Favorite courses: Solid Mechanics, Structural Analysis, and Dynamics and Vibrations

Vita highlights:

1. The father of two daughters and the spouse of an engineer.

2. A licensed professional engineer in Texas.

3. Facilitated workshops (in a dozen states plus Denmark and Puerto Rico) on active-cooperative and collaborative learning, and the use of teams in and out of the classroom.

4. Taught the first year engineering course at Texas A&M University during all of the past thirteen years, serving as freshman engineering coordinator from 1993-1997. Was an active member of the NSF Foundation Coalition team that changed the course to an ACL team-based format (offered to all TAMU engineering students starting in the fall of 1998).

Temba Bassoppo-Moyo, Assistant Professor, School of Education
Illinois State University, Normal, IL   email: tcbasso@ilstu.edu
Favorite courses: Instructional Systems Design and Technology, Instructional Media and Technology, Designing Computer-Based Instructional Software, and Project Management

Vita highlights:

1. Has done extensive research in online instruction, eLearning, multi-media interactive delivery systems, electronic performance support systems, and evaluation of distance learning environments.

2. A former Fulbright scholar.

3. Has a telecommunications engineering background.

4. Selected for Who's Who in Instructional Technology. Is a member of the Association for Educational Communications and Technology (AECT) as well as several international organizations that represent distance education and eLearning.

Eric Myrvaagnes, Professor of Mathematics and Computer Science
Suffolk University, Boston, MA   email: eric@mcs.suffolk.edu
Favorite courses: Freshman Problem Solving, Freshman Interdisciplinary Course, and Operating Systems

Vita highlights:

1. Designed and taught for ten years Suffolk's first computer course for non-science majors, using a student-centered, Process Education approach.

2. Principal author of *Foundations of Problem Solving*, published by Pacific Crest and now the primary text in the course mentioned above.

3. Authored the book *Trust in Learning: A Practical Guide to Student-Centered College Teaching*.

Carol Nancarrow, Associate Professor of English
Sinclair Community College, Dayton, OH   email: cnancarr@sinclair.edu
Favorite courses: Writing Lab, Research Paper, and English Composition

Vita highlights:

1. Research interests span the effective use of technology, professional development practices, and writing theory and practice.

2. Practices her profession in a wide-range of mediums and formats, such as a traditional structure, online-learning, interactive television, and within a writing lab.

3. Facilitates faculty development at Sinclair in process learning, distance learning, and Learning-to-Learn Camps.

4. Presented at the League for Innovation in the Community College on faculty development at Learning-to-Learn Camp and active learning in interactive television.

Marta Nibert, Chairwoman of the Occupational Therapy Assistant Program
James A. Rhodes State College, Lima, OH   email: nibert.m@RhodesState.edu
Favorite courses: Human Development, Psychosocial Dysfunction, and Human Anatomy

Vita highlights:

1. Serve as the project leader for Process Education at James A. Rhodes State College which involves: writing grants for initial funding, collaborating with Dr. Dan Apple in institution-wide consultation and training sessions, and serving as a faculty mentor. Successfully written additional grants for other projects receiving more than forty thousand dollars.

2. Presented at more than 20 professional conferences. Consulted with many institutions on occupational therapy and educational topics.

3. Founded the Occupational Therapy Assistant Program at James A. Rhodes State College, receiving both initial accreditation and reaccreditation.

4. Served on the Roster of Accreditation Evaluators for Occupational Therapy Education. Is Chairwoman of the Ohio Occupational Therapy Program Director's Council. Is the Educational Liaison for the Ohio Occupational Therapy Association Board and was appointed Alternate to the American Occupational Therapy Association's Commission on Education.

Kip Nygren, Colonel, U.S. Army, Professor and Head, Department of Civil & Mechanical Engineering
United States Military Academy, West Point, NY   email: kip.nygren@us.army.mil
Favorite courses: Dynamics and Controls, Senior Design, and Astrodynamics

Vita highlights:

1. Research interests include issues associated with the development and integration of new technology for the military, classroom research on the use of technology to enhance learning, and the history of technology.

2. Served as the Director, Interim Research, Development and Engineering Command, and special assistant to the Commanding General, U.S. Army Materiel Command (AMC) in 2002.

3. During a 2001-2002 sabbatical year, conducted a study regarding the military potential and perils of future technologies for the Deputy Assistant Secretary of the Army.

4. Chair of the Mechanical Engineering Department Heads Committee, American Society of Mechanical Engineers, 2001 to 2003, and assisted in the organization of the 2004 Annual ME Education Conference.

Kelli Parmley, Director of Institutional Research
State University of New York at New Paltz   email: parmleyk@newpaltz.edu
Favorite course: Introduction to Public Speaking

Vita highlights:

1. Actively promoted, over the course of four years, Institutional Research as a resource for translating data into information for decision-making, consulting for gathering information through survey development, administration, and analysis, and acting as a problem-solving interface with Computer Services.

2. Actively involved in the profession of Institutional Research as president-elect in 2003-04 for a SUNY wide organization of professionals and local arrangements chair for the 2005 regional conference for Institutional Research professionals.

3. Key leader of campus-wide efforts to identify a plan for moving forward with assessment, identifying and offering key professional development opportunities for faculty and staff through Pacific Crest, and supporting the implementation of assessment systems in academic programs, general education, and administrative departments.

4. Knowledgeable of the broader policy and financial context of public higher education in New York State, through a combination of advanced education in public administration and higher education administration as well as professional budgeting experience at the State and System SUNY level.

Duncan Quarless, Jr., Associate Professor of Chemistry
State University of New York, College at Old Westbury   email: quarlessd@oldwestbury.edu
Favorite courses: Freshman Chemistry and Advance Inorganic Chemistry

Vita highlights:

1. Research interests include bio-inorganic approaches to environmental remediation; creating models for the Lewis acid catalysis and coordination chemistry of cysteinate metalloproteins; exploring structure-reactivity relationships for secondary non-covalent intra-molecular interactions in coordination complexes; and improving the integration of research-based methodology into laboratory instruction in natural science.

2. Program Director for a Science and Technology Entry Program (STEP) grant from the NYS Education Department to develop inquiry-based guided discovery activities for both formal and informal science education at the secondary school level; and to improve learning outcomes for STEP students.

3. Engaged in a number of pro-active mentorship activities as the Chair of the Minority Affairs Committee for the NY Section of the American Chemical Society (ACS), as the PD for STEP and as the Assistant Campus Director for the NSF sponsored SUNY Louis Stokes Alliance for Minority Participation (LSAMP).

4. Member of the Teaching for Learning Center committee and co-organizer for the interconnected learning project in natural sciences at the College.

Virginia Romero, Professor of Counseling
Cerritos College, Norwalk, CA   email: vromero@cerritos.edu
Favorite courses/activities: Career guidance, Athletic-academic counseling, Aerobics instruction

Vita highlights:

1. Ten-year commitment to learning communities program, with emphasis on team-teaching career guidance taught in conjunction with basic writing/composition; extensive experience in related faculty and staff development at local and national levels.

2. Received Distinguished Faculty Award at Cerritos College for outstanding service in counseling, especially in program serving 500 athletes; Outstanding Faculty of the Year Award from Center for the Study of Diversity in Education (De Anza College, California) in 2001.

3. Named Counselor of the Year in 2001 by 3C4A faculty association for college athletic academic advisors.

Mark Schlesinger, Associate Professor and Director of Communication Studies
University of Massachusetts Boston   email: mark.schlesinger@umb.edu
Favorite courses: Analyzing Media, Information Technology and Human Communication, and Seminar on Media Effects

Vita highlights:

1. Research interests include teaching and learning (especially problem solving), communication issues in information technology, mass media).

2. Pioneered distance learning at UMass Boston, developing teleconferencing courses in the mid 1990's and online courses thereafter.

3. Co-editor of the text *Learning through Problem Solving*.

4. Academic Advisor, Center on Media and Society, McCormack Graduate School of Policy Studies, University of Massachusetts Boston.

Peter Smith, Professor Emeritus of Mathematics and Computer Science
Saint Marys College, Notre Dame, IN   email: psmith@saintmarys.edu
Favorite projects: old house renovation, caring for grandkids, promulgating war tax resistance, and traveling

Vita highlights:

1. Research interests include improving facilitation in the classroom.

2. Ten years teaching all courses following Process Education philosophy.

3. Attended and mentored at many Process Education events.

4. Presented at several ASCUE Conferences papers on teaching Computer Science using Process Education principles.

Jack Wasserman, Professor of Mechanical Engineering
University of Tennessee at Knoxville   email: wasserma@utk.edu
Favorite courses: Introduction to Biomedical Engineering, Biomechanics, and Applied Biomechanics

Vita highlights:

1. Research interests include determination of spinal response to vehicle vibration, development of aquatic exercise program that actively promotes a decrease in osteoporosis, orthopaedic biomechanics.

2. Active in web based Engineering Education for the College of Engineering.

3. Co-PI of several University of Tennessee grants on interactive technology related to realistic problem solving for upper division students.

Kenneth Wesson, Executive Assistant to the Chancellor; Educational Consultant: Neuroscience
San Jose/Evergreen Community College District, San Jose, CA   email: Kenneth.Wesson@sjeccd.org
Favorite courses and speaking topics: Neuroscience of Learning, Early Brain Development, Emotional Intelligence, and Neuropsychology of Prejudice

Vita highlights:

1. International presenter (South America, Asia, Eastern Europe, the Middle East, Northern Africa, and sub-Saharan Africa) and keynote speaker on the topics of Neuroscience of Learning, Early Brain Development, Emotional Intelligence and the Neuropsychology of Prejudice to audiences ranging from pre-school and early childhood specialists to college-level administrators, faculty members and counseling organizations.

2. Served as a researcher and science writer for Science IQ contributing articles on brain research.

3. Worked as an Educational Consultant for Stanford Research Institute (SRI).

4. Worked on the development and marketing of several of the nation's leading mathematics, science and reading programs, including coordinating the efforts of one of the nation's major publishers with America's largest school systems and the National Science Foundation's (in mathematics and science).

Section One
Educational Philosophy

Modules in this section:

Overview of Process Education

by Steven Beyerlein, University of Idaho; Mark Schlesinger, University of Massachusetts Boston; and Daniel Apple, Pacific Crest

Process Education is an educational philosophy that focuses on the development of broad, transferable learning skills. It has evolved over the course of ten years, supported by research done by college and university faculty from a wide range of disciplines across the country. Implementation of this philosophy means using processes and tools to create new types of environments in which students take center stage and discover how to improve their learning and self-assessment skills within a discipline. This philosophy also supports the current institutional reform movement that calls for a shift in emphasis from an agenda driven by teachers' desires and designs to one focused on students' needs. It consistently seeks answers to the question, "How do students learn most effectively and enduringly?"— and then works to translate the answer into teaching practice and, ultimately, institutional policy. This module analyzes this transformational movement, defines the cornerstones of Process Education, and presents its underlying principles so that individual faculty members, as well as departments, divisions, and school administrators, can understand the philosophy and explore its potential for their institutions.

Context for Process Education

Over the last half-century, as our economy has shifted from a regional, manufacturing base to a global, information base, institutions of higher education have been faced with significant new challenges. Some of these challenges relate to changing student demographics. For example, there is a greater diversity among students today, including greater numbers of nontraditional students, many of whom have part-time or full-time jobs as well as family responsibilities. There are now many students entering higher education who are not adequately prepared to succeed in college-level courses. Other challenges relate to the accelerating rate at which knowledge is added to academic disciplines, preventing comprehensive presentation and mastery within a four-year span. Furthermore, the changing world of work demands that college graduates be both technically skilled and broadly educated so that they can readily construct and apply new knowledge that is yet to be discovered. Reflecting on these challenges, Peter Drucker noted that "it is a safe prediction that in the next fifty years schools and universities will change more and more drastically than they have since they assumed their present form 300 years ago when they organized themselves around the printed book."

During the last decade, a series of change processes have occurred on hundreds of campuses to respond to these challenges. They include the following:

- Creating a culture of student-centered learning (Barr & Tagg, 1995).
- Accepting responsibility for teaching skills as well as content (SCANS, 1991).
- Broadening the diversity of learners served (Rosser, 2000).
- Restructuring dialogue in the classroom (Johnson et al, 1991).
- Expanding the temporal and spatial boundaries of the classroom (Batson & Bass, 1996).
- Continuously improving student learning outcomes (Huba & Freed, 2000).
- Aligning institutional, program, and course systems (Boyer Commission, 1998).

Schools at all levels are taking these actions to transform themselves into high-performance organizations with a focus on a new set of competencies (information processing, resource management, systems thinking, and technology) and basic skills (communication skills, teamwork skills, thinking skills, and personal qualities). With new accreditation criteria, institutional success is now measured by the quality of student learning produced. This theme is introduced in ***Methodology for Designing a Program Assessment System***. As more active learning approaches are adopted, schools are investing in learning environments that better support discovery and construction of knowledge beyond transfer of disciplinary content. This focus is summarized in ***Overview of Creating a Quality Learning Environment***. Perhaps the most significant change underway is in the educational philosophy of individual faculty members as they move away from the traditional teacher-centered "instruction paradigm" and begin to explore a student-centered "learning paradigm."

What is Process Education?

Process Education is an educational philosophy focusing on improving students' learning skills in the cognitive, social, affective and psychomotor domains, with the ultimate goal of creating self-growers. Learning skills are aptitudes, abilities, and techniques used to acquire new knowledge and skills. These skills are distinct from disciplinary content. They are associated with particular process areas (e.g., the construction of understanding, problem solving, and both personal development and interpersonal development); skills in these areas can be developed to progressively higher levels of performance. Self-growers demonstrate a high level of performance across a spectrum of learning skills, continually growing their capabilities by using strong self-assessment to enrich and enhance their future performance. While self-growers can usually cite many significant mentors in their lives, they are not dependent on mentors for ongoing personal development.

Principles of Process Education

The principles of Process Education outlined in Table 1 offer a vision for quality learning and teaching. They are based on a belief that students' potential for learning is in no way based upon their developmental position. This premise is underscored by Principles #1 and #2. Taken together, the principles suggest new roles and responsibilities for teachers and learners that differ from traditional practice. These relate to four broad areas of faculty performance:

- assessment (principles #3 and #4)
- facilitation (principles #5, #6, and #7)
- mentoring (principles #7 and #8)
- curriculum improvement (principles #9 and #10)

Assessment is the process of measuring and analyzing a performance or product to provide feedback that can help improve future performance or products. *Overview of Assessment* presents assessment as a powerful tool for focusing attention on learning skills. Facilitation is the set of thoughtful and appropriate actions associated with a learning activity taken to ensure that individuals and groups best meet the criteria set out for the activity. *Overview of Facilitation* presents guidelines for becoming a quality facilitator. Mentoring provides support and challenge to learners so that they experience personal growth in addition to acquiring new knowledge. *Overview of Mentoring* and the *Personal Development Methodology* contain many insights for mentors. Curriculum design at the program, course, and activity level helps to reinforce

Table 1   ***Process Education Principles***

1. Every learner can learn to learn better, regardless of current level of achievement; one's potential is not limited by current ability.

2. Although everyone requires help with learning at times, the goal is to become a capable, self-sufficient, life-long learner.

3. An empowered learner is one who uses learning processes and self-assessment to improve future performance.

4. Educators should assess students regularly by measuring accomplishments, modeling assessment processes, providing timely feedback, and helping students improve their self-assessment skills.

5. Faculty must accept fully the responsibility for facilitating student success.

6. To develop expertise in a discipline, a learner must develop a specific knowledge base in that field, but also acquire generic, life-long learning skills that relate to all disciplines.

7. In a quality learning environment, facilitators of learning (teachers) focus on improving specific learning skills through timely, appropriate, and constructive interventions.

8. Mentors use specific methodologies that model the steps or activities they expect students to use in achieving their own learning goals.

9. An educational institution can continually improve its effectiveness in producing stronger learning outcomes in several ways:
   - by aligning institutional, course, and program objectives,
   - by investing in faculty development, curricular innovation, and design of performance measures, and
   - by embracing an assessment culture.

10. A Process Educator can continuously improve the concepts, processes, and tools used by doing active observation and research in the classroom.

intended personal development that occurs over multiple courses and activities. Principles for continuously improving curriculum are examined in the sections about instructional design and program assessment.

Discussion in the Guidebook modules referenced above stresses movement away from traditional teaching models to more innovative ones. In the former, communication is didactic, with information flowing from expert speakers to novice listeners; in the latter, it is more collaborative, with learners getting more involved in their learning process. As a result, they learn to use multiple resources for information, guidance, challenge, and feedback.

Classification and Learning Skills for Educational Enrichment and Assessment

The *Classification of Learning Skills* is an essential resource for Process Educators (Krumsieg and Baehr, 2000). In its initial development, the Classification started simply as a list of learning skills students needed to successfully learn content. Over the years, the list has assumed a more complex, methodically ordered form—largely because many educators dealing with both general education and discipline-specific programs have come to a new awareness. The list now identifies 15 key processes and more than 200 specific skills from four domains: cognitive, social, affective, and psychomotor. These processes and skills are outlined in the modules *Cognitive Domain* and *Social Domain* (the affective domain and psychomotor domain will be presented in a later edition of the *Faculty Guidebook*).

Many faculty use the Classification to design skill development more systematically into their curricula. This includes crafting learning outcomes that relate to transferable *skills,* not just to the academic *content* of their courses. Many faculty also use the Classification to structure a collection of assessment data that examines specific skill development and to provide assessment reports tailored to specific skill sets. The modules *Assessment Methodology* and the *SII Method for Assessment Reporting* provide insights into how to use the Classification effectively for these purposes.

A significant number of faculty have discovered value in the Classification of Learning Skills for their own professional development. Their heightened awareness of the transferable learning skills identified here has guided them in identifying skills critical to their teaching success. Improving teaching on the basis of that analysis can enhance opportunities for tenure, promotion, and further academic achievements for all faculty committed to the process.

Implementation of Process Education

There is no one way to implement Process Education. Instead, each teacher must customize an approach, drawing from a diverse set of concepts, processes, tools, and techniques to find those most suited to his or her instructional context and objectives. The module *Framework for Implementing Process Education* serves as a pathfinder to many of these. Elements from the knowledge table are valuable in a broad range of teaching and learning activities, including:

- clearly defining and articulating course goals that can be supported by measurable learning outcomes;

- creating challenging, student-centered learning environments that promote high levels of performance;

- enhancing students' learning skills in all domains (cognitive, social, affective, and psychomotor) by creating and using active, cooperative learning activities;

- checking on the effectiveness of those situations by engaging students in self-assessments that provide useful feedback for improvement;

- designing course assessment systems (separate and distinct from course evaluations) that are timely, systematic, and effective in helping students identify strengths and areas for improvement;

- using these assessments to help students achieve higher-level performance in future learning situations;

- investing in faculty and staff development activities that support continuous improvement of key professional activities essential to institutional effectiveness: teaching, learning, mentoring, curriculum design, assessment, advising, and educational administration.

Faculty who choose to adapt a Process Education approach face significant challenges in how they perceive their relationship to students, in how they design courses and prepare materials, and in how they assess and evaluate the effectiveness of their instruction. For instance, they must illustrate respect for students' learning potential and challenge them to perform at an optimal level. They must allow students more ownership of their learning and learn to assess more and evaluate less. They must revamp the classroom environment, recognizing the need to solicit student buy-in for the alternative teaching/learning methods and conventions they will employ. In terms of course design, interested faculty must commit to a disciplined system of writing measurable learning outcomes that are tied to clear performance criteria. Both elements need to be correlated to an evaluation system that reflects upon and incorporates them. Within their courses, faculty must be willing to redesign activities for greater effectiveness, as well as provide timely interventions to assist student learning. They must also regularly check the effectiveness of their instruction through appropriate assessments. Similarly, they need to provide opportunities for students to assess their own performance—and then review those assessments to give students the clarity and insight they seek. Finally, they must thoughtfully design performance measures for their instructional programs to ensure that objectives are truly being met and evidenced through systematic data collection.

Concluding Thoughts

Process Education responds to a societal need for students to be well prepared to apply their expertise and to be self-directed learners, capable of learning new concepts and abilities on their own, no matter what type of challenging situations they encounter. Faculty and graduate students, in turn, can no longer rely on discipline-specific expertise to fulfill their teaching obligations. For these individuals, there is a growing need to develop skill in the "second discipline" of educating students with the kind of learning that can sustain them in and outside of the classroom. The new scholarship of teaching "requires a kind of 'going meta' in which faculty frame and systematically investigate questions related to student learning: the conditions under which it occurs, what it looks like, and how to deepen it" (Hutchings & Schulman, 1999). Important questions for classroom research include:

- How much time should be dedicated to skill development versus content?

- How can I measure added value from different class activities and courses?

- What impact does my teaching style have on student learning?

- When should students be held accountable for skills learned in other classes?

- What is the proper balance between assessment and evaluation?

The modules in this Guidebook are offered as a framework for obtaining answers to questions about teaching and learning. Readers will find that self-assessment is a key ingredient in the inquiry process and that thoughtful attention to "process" when implementing solutions can make a profound difference in their professional development, as well as in the growth of their students.

References

Barr, R., & Tagg, J. (1995). From teaching to learning: A new paradigm for undergraduate education. *Change, 27*, 13-25.

Batson, T., & Bass, R. (1996). Teaching and learning in the computer age. *Change, 28*, 42-47.

Boyer Commission. (1998). *Reinventing undergraduate education: A blueprint for America's research universities.* Menlo Park, CA: Carnegie Foundation.

Drucker, P. (1992). *Managing for the future.* New York: Plume Books.

Huba, M., & Freed, J. (2000). *Learner-centered assessment on college campuses.* Boston: Allyn and Bacon.

Hutchings, P., & Shulman, L. (1999). The scholarship of teaching: New elaborations, new developments. *Change, 31*, 11-15.

Johnson, D., Johnson, R., & Smith, K. (1991) *Active learning: Cooperation in the college classroom.* Edina, MN: Interaction Book Company.

Krumsieg, K., & Baehr, M. (2000). *Foundations of learning.* Lisle, IL: Pacific Crest.

Rosser, S. (2000). *Women, science, and society: The crucial union.* New York: Teacher's College Press.

Secretary's Commission on Achieving Necessary Skills (SCANS). (1991). *What work requires of schools: A SCANS report for America 2000.* Washington, DC: Department of Labor.

Faculty Development Series

Knowledge Table for Process Education

by Mark Schlesinger, University of Massachusetts Boston and Daniel Apple, Pacific Crest

Educators introduced to Process Education in faculty workshops often want to begin implementing a wide range of best practices in their courses. This module highlights central concepts, processes, and tools that support the educational philosophy presented in the module ***Overview of Process Education***. This module also highlights the broad range of institutional and instructional environments where these can be applied, as well as a mindset for facilitating deep learning and personal growth. Faculty will find that many items appearing in the knowledge table can help strengthen their own professional development.

The Knowledge Table

Knowledge tables communicate the infrastructure that supports an area of knowledge. This includes key concepts, processes, tools, contexts, and ways of being. Table 1 presents a knowledge table for Process Education. Items appearing in Table 1 are ordered thematically to facilitate discussion in each of the sections that follow.

Key Concepts

The concepts highlighted in this module provide a shared language for understanding teaching/learning, promoting transformation, reflecting on success/failure, and communicating results, methods, and discoveries to other like-minded educators. These concepts are grouped into three areas: developing knowledge, growth and development, and measuring results.

Knowledge construction

As clarified in Pacific Crest's ***Learning Process Methodology***, learning is not a magical happening, but a very disciplined set of actions that are more effective if done in sequence. These purposeful actions bring about construction of knowledge to reach intended learning outcomes—precise statements of what students will learn and will be able to do. If learners, educators, and institutions assure that strong learning outcomes are met after each learning experience, a quality learning process will exist. Learning outcomes for a course should span multiple levels of knowledge, ranging from awareness to working expertise.

The relationship between educators and learners plays a major role in how efficiently and effectively outcomes are met. Modern research on how people learn confirms that knowledge must be constructed within the mind of the learner (Bransford, 2000). Realization of the importance of learner ownership underlies a variety of recent movements in math, physics, and writing instruction that feature active learning (Tagg, 2003). This is in marked contrast to more traditional approaches to teaching/learning that center on faculty performance (focusing on the instructor's responsibility for effectively presenting material).

Growth and development

There is much more to education than mastery of subject matter. A cornerstone of Process Education is that transformational change (growth) within an individual is valued as highly as the knowledge which that learner constructs (learning). Thus it is important to address both learning and growth in our classrooms and degree programs. A barrier for some educators is their inability to believe that learning rate can be improved through advancing learning skills. Learning rate is a function of the aggregate of current performance with the learning skills. There is one threshold level of learning skills needed to be a lifelong, self-directed learner. Another important threshold is that of becoming a self-grower. The key differentiation between a life-long learner and a self-grower is that while both can fluently construct their own knowledge, self-growers can assess their own performance and are able to mentor their own growth.

In this guidebook, an important distinction is made between teaching and mentoring. Teaching is defined as the facilitation of the quality of learning, while mentoring is the facilitation of personal growth. To engage in quality teaching as well as quality mentoring, faculty and students must develop a relationship characterized by mutual shared respect. This respect should incorporate a mutual belief in potential for growth, a shared commitment to the learner's success, and a willingness to undergo temporary failures on the way to that success. Learning, teaching, and mentoring are most effective if they support the learner's life vision.

Measuring results

To be an effective educator, one must develop the critical ability to measure, assess, and evaluate learning and its associated learning outcomes (Huba & Freed, 2000). Fundamental to this ability is the educator's understanding of the separate and distinct purposes of assessment and evaluation. Assessment involves improving future performance, while evaluation measures performance against standards to determine level of quality. Fundamental to quality assessment and quality evaluation are well thought-out performance measures that can gauge both

Table 1

Knowledge Table for Process Education

Concepts	Processes	Tools	Contexts
learning process	designing a program	cooperative learning	community colleges
learning outcomes	designing a course	structured activities	liberal arts colleges
levels of knowledge	designing an activity	methodologies	technical schools
learner ownership	creating methodologies	reflection time	professional schools
active learning	facilitating learning experiences	*Learning Assessment Journal*	research universities
learning versus growth	constructive intervention	peer assessment	high schools
learning skills	measuring performance	self growth paper	summer camps
learning rate	mentoring	learning communities	lecture courses
lifelong learner versus self-grower	creating a learning environment	*Classification of Learning Skills*	general education courses
teaching vs. mentoring	assessing learning	course management system	laboratory courses
shared respect	evaluating learning	foundations course	academic advising
life vision	communicating	capstone course	living groups
assessment vs. evaluation	professional development	profiles	developmental education
performance criteria	modeling quality learning	portfolios	on-line learning
	conducting action research	rubrics	faculty committees

Way of Being
A process educator...
wants to see growth in others.
trusts and respects students.
is a risk-taker.
is willing to shift control to students.
can handle and adapt to change.
has the desire to be a self-grower.
enjoys assessment and is open to feedback.
utilizes self-assessment to improve future performances.
works well with others, and uses time efficiently and effectively.

the level of learning (knowledge) and growth in learning skills. To determine what these performance measures need to be, learning experiences need to be measured against strong performance criteria that communicate essential elements of quality.

Key Processes

Integrating the concepts discussed above requires a number of fundamental educational processes that can be deployed with ever-increasing complexity and creativity. This guidebook is full of methodologies to help you become more proficient in your use of academic processes. These processes are grouped into four major areas:

designing a learning experience, managing a quality learning experience, continuous quality improvement of the learning experience, and professionalism of the educator.

Designing a learning experience

A quality educational experience is a product of conscious design, informed by the concepts described above (Krumsieg & Baehr, 2000). There are several processes that can be used to help design and improve differently-scaled learning experiences. The first process is designing a program, including its intentions, learning outcomes, performance expectations, broad structure, means for determining outcomes, and the underlying philosophy supporting the program. The second process is designing a course to produce a portion of the program learning outcomes. This involves course-level learning outcomes, performance criteria, sets of activities, a knowledge table, and assessment and evaluation systems. The third process is designing an activity to maximize student-centered learning during each class period. Within courses and activities, key processes can be learned much more effectively if the faculty member invests in creating methodologies. As you progress through this guidebook, you will learn about key methodologies for learning, assessment, facilitation, curriculum design—and even a methodology to create methodologies. The goal of a methodology is to take expert knowledge and make it accessible to the learner in the form of a step-by-step model.

Managing a quality learning experience

Faculty accustomed to more traditional courses and classroom sessions find that a process learning environment presents new time performance challenges. Attention to the learning process, rather than merely topics, student work products, and submission deadlines, provides a deeper and more immediate sense of what is happening at every moment (Hanson, 2000). Therefore, the primary role of the Process Educator is facilitating learning experiences. This includes setting high expectations associated with clear performance criteria and then engaging in constructive intervention. This type of intervention involves a few key steps: identifying when a student is in difficulty, isolating the key skill that is impeding the learning performance, and presenting the student with an appropriate learning challenge to help him or her advance the use of that skill. Teaching also includes creating a learning environment. Starting with respect and shared commitment to learning, this environment involves ongoing student-instructor rapport. Through it, learners discover the means to accept learning challenges, reflect on discoveries, and analyze failures. Mentoring is the term used to describe the teacher/learner relationship that makes possible profound personal development. It is important that mentors be role models as well as effective advocates for their mentees.

Continuous quality improvement of the learning experience

Building quality in teaching/learning requires the instructor to develop a clear sense of the level of student learning, as well as his or her growth in learning skills. If we have clear expectations of what performances we require from the student at the end of the learning experience (performance criteria), we are in a much better position to accurately measure performance. Measuring performance is the basis for both assessing learning and evaluating learning. When we assess, we use measurement to improve future performance. When we evaluate, we compare measurements to standards to determine level of quality. Creating and maintaining separate course assessment and evaluation systems is as important as assembling curriculum materials. Aligning individual course assessment and evaluation systems with those of an entire program and institution greatly facilitates strategic planning and accreditation initiatives.

Professionalism of the educator

Many academic performances are based on processes that are used on a daily basis. Communicating is fundamental to learning, teaching, and mentoring. This includes active listening, rephrasing, articulating, perception checking, and formal presentation skills. Another critical area involves ongoing professional development through assessing past efforts, formulating a strong annual plan, pursuing continuing education, and constantly assessing current efforts to improve both knowledge and performance skills. Many would say we learn best by teaching. It follows that modeling quality learning in the presence of students and colleagues is good practice. It reminds us that learning is not restricted to the boundaries of the classroom. Educators can also dramatically expand their influence by coaching students to serve as apprentice teachers and mentors. Likewise, educators in different contexts and locations can join in an extended learning community in which all academic activity becomes the fodder for action research which often involves qualitative methods. Dynamic in nature, this type of inquiry is done with the knowledge that system behavior may change during the course of the research.

Key Tools

An educator's effectiveness depends on proficient use of academic processes, as well as the size of his or her toolkit for teaching/learning. This guidebook provides a multitude of general-purpose and special-purpose tools that provide valuable prompts for both students and teachers. These tools are designed to strengthen teaching/learning processes, as well as to improve work products. They fall into three broad categories: classroom tools, organizational tools, and program tools.

Classroom tools

Cooperative learning promotes the development of shared performance expectations, individual accountability, positive interdependence, social skills, and group processing to support a wide range of learning outcomes (Johnson et al., 1991). Efficient use of learning time can be increased through structured activities and methodologies (Krumsieg & Baehr, 2000). In a high-level performance environment, it is important to bring closure to past learning and growth experiences. This can be accomplished in several ways, including oral and written reflection. A learning assessment journal helps students assess their learning and create action plans for future activities. Many learning activities can also be enriched through peer assessment of various work products. In so studying the work of others, students come to see strengths and areas for improvement in their own work. On the other hand, producing a self-growth paper can help students develop a panoramic view of a semester or term's achievements. By analyzing such cumulative data as journal entries, team reports, and other academic accomplishments, they can create a portfolio of evidence documenting their growth and development over time. An examination of the assembled data can then be used to effect their own transformational change.

Organizational tools

Establishing cohorts of learners spanning multiple classes and grade levels through formal and informal learning communities is a very effective strategy for advancing student success (Johnson et al., 1991). Course management systems such as Blackboard and WebCT provide a convenient and instantaneous method for disseminating updated course materials and a forum for real-time discussion about course content and assignments. The classification of learning skills is a powerful instrument for parsing human performance across different domains, right down to specific skills. Visualizing this organizational structure can both help faculty make constructive interventions and help students self-assess their learning performance (Krumsieg & Baehr, 2000).

Program tools

Many colleges and universities have instituted foundations courses and programs, often based on the First-Year or Freshman-Year Experience Programs modeled by the National Resource Center for the First-Year Experience and Students in Transition at the University of South Carolina. These college-orientation courses prepare incoming students for academic life at the post-secondary level. In so doing, they promote buy-in to institutional and program objectives and produce a powerful shared experience that sets cultural norms for course achievement within specific disciplines. Analogously, capstone courses document the gains made within a program; they also serve to transition students from the classroom to the modern workplace. Ideally, graduate and alumni performance should match the learning and thinking profiles typical of professionals in their chosen fields. These expected behaviors can also be assessed and evaluated by assembling portfolios of student work that document their growth and development over time, space, and performance areas. Students' academic achievements can also be accurately measured by applying a variety of rubrics to the work products they assemble (Huba & Freed, 2000).

Context

Heightened interest in Process Education accompanies the growing realization among educators and policy makers that the educational process needs to focus more explicitly on the needs and development of the student. This realization traverses all educational institutions and instructional environments, including those beyond the 12th grade, which have traditionally been least susceptible to student-centered concerns. A number of exciting institutional changes have emerged from leading community colleges around the nation (O'Banion). Conventional notions of "scholar" and "research," for example, have been challenged and have been supplanted by a new vision emphasizing scholarship not in the content area but in the secondary discipline of teaching and learning (Boyer, 1997).

Way of Being

The more your values and belief system align with the ways of being in the Knowledge Table, the easier it will be for you to implement a process-oriented approach to teaching/learning. You will most likely find some of these to be easier than others. The ones that you find difficult should be taken to heart and analyzed against your educational philosophy. Thoughtfully responding to this list is likely to produce a transformation in your own learning and could pave the way for doing things in the classroom that you never dreamed before. The attitudes that you carry with you in halls of your institution and within the walls of your classroom are just as important as what you know.

Concluding Thoughts

This module, along with the glossary, defines a vocabulary for building and sharing understanding about teaching and learning. As such, section editors and authors contributing to the guidebook have made a concerted effort to define and use items from the knowledge table in a consistent manner. In doing so, we hope our readers will be better able to connect educational theory with best practices in teaching/learning. At times, the lifelong journey to become a more effective educator can seem daunting. The guidebook team encourages you to use this module as a compass, checking your bearings often to remind yourself what you have accomplished and to seek out fruitful areas for future focus.

References

Boyer Commission. (1998). *Reinventing undergraduate education: A blueprint for America's research universities.* Menlo Park, CA: Carnegie Foundation.

Bransford, J., Brown, A., & Cocking, R. (2000). *How people learn: Brain, mind, experience, and school.* Washington, DC: National Academy Press.

Hanson, D., & Wolfskill, T. (2000). Process workshops—a new model for instruction, *Journal of Chemical Education, 77,* 120-130.

Huba, M., & Freed, J. (2000). *Learner-centered assessment on college campuses.* Boston: Allyn and Bacon.

Johnson, D., Johnson, R., & Smith, K. (1991). *Active learning: Cooperation in the college classroom.* Edina, MN: Interaction Book Company.

Krumsieg, K., & Baehr, M. (2000). *Foundations of learning.* Lisle, IL: Pacific Crest.

O'Banion, T. (1997). *A Learning college for the 21st century.* Phoenix: Oryx Press.

Tagg, J. (2003). *The learning paradigm college.* Boston: Anker Publishing.

Framework for Implementing Process Education

by Wendy Duncan-Hewitt, Auburn University

This module integrates five major themes in the *Faculty Guidebook*, bringing them together in a "Process Map for Process Educators." This Process Map communicates the inter-relationship and natural sequencing of different teaching/learning processes that support the philosophy of Process Education. It includes actions of both teachers and learners surrounding constructive intervention at "teachable moments." Like *Overview of Process Education* and *Knowledge Table for Process Education*, this module also serves as a pathfinder to other resources in the *Faculty Guidebook*.

Themes of Process Education

Process Education occurs when educators, learners, and curriculum interact in a system that produces continuing growth, empowerment, and improvement of students, teachers, and learning organizations. Five common themes for collaboration between Process Educators appear in the Process Map for Process Educators shown in Figure 1 at the end of the module. The location of each of these themes in the Process Map is noted in Table 1. Bolded items in the Process Map refer to specific sections in the *Faculty Guidebook*. These are areas educators can study to improve their effectiveness. Unbolded items in the Process Map refer to outcomes produced at different stages in the teaching/learning process. Verbs appear in hexagonal boxes. The large box with dashed lines shows a natural grouping of distinct, but interdependent teaching/learning tools.

Table 1

Location of Process Education Themes in Process Map

Theme	Location
Learner Growth	lower left
Bridge for Growth	upper left
Assessment	top
Outcomes Oriented Curricula	middle right
Student-Centered Facilitation	middle left

The Process Map shows three developmental pathways, all of which lead to empowerment. One pathway involves the stepwise growth of mentors' and students' knowledge in an enriched learning environment. The second pathway also uses an enriched learning environment but focuses on measurable growth of transferable learning skills and processes from the cognitive, affective, social, and psychomotor domains. The third pathway involves the comprehensive assessment of all aspects of the system, leading to a scientific approach to the design of learning systems that aligns with institutional effectiveness. Note that the third pathway indirectly influences the first two pathways.

Learner Growth

The goal of Process Education is stepwise growth of knowledge and skills that are supported by a supportive learning environment, real-time assessment that informs curriculum and facilitation decisions, and meaningful collaboration between teachers and students in various learning activities. Personal and professional growth can be tracked through behaviorally-anchored stages of self-growth (Collis, 1980). A framework for tracking this development is presented in *Performance Levels for Self-Growers*. Process Education also produces growth in mastery of disciplinary knowledge and skills, a subject examined in *Performance Levels for Learners*. In a traditional classroom, growth is not assured with the sole emphasis being on disciplinary content. However, growth can be accelerated when learning skills and methodologies are integrated with the teaching of disciplinary material at an appropriate level of challenge. *Learning Processes through the Use of Methodologies* discusses this topic in great detail and includes a rubric for measuring internalization of steps in a process. As people climb through levels of knowledge, performance, and institutional alignment, they are able to see the world—and themselves—in a different way (Mezirow, 1991).

Bridge for Growth

A fundamental premise of Process Education is that everyone's performance and abilities can improve if given proper support and challenge in the learning process (Perkins, 1995). However, growth activities are often risky for the learner. Raven (1978) found that these perceived risks could be dramatically reduced if:

- learners conclude with relative certainty, that the learning will result in achievement of valued and personally relevant knowledge (cognitive goal);

- learners conclude with relative certainty that they are capable of achieving the learning goal (affective goal);

- the behavior is consistent with the kind of person he or she wants to become (affective goal); and

- the more he or she is motivated by social expectations regarding the behaviors in question (social goal).

Overview of Mentoring and *Methodology for Creating a Quality Learning Environment* outline how a motivational bridge for growth can be constructed by honoring and respecting a learner's current knowledge, needs, abilities, and attitudes while upholding high expectations for achievement and personal transformation. Mentors can add tremendous value to the teaching/learning process by taking time to discuss cognitive, social, and affective goals of learning activities with their mentees. Enriched learning environments can further support cognitive, social, and affective dimensions of learning by:

- growing a set of problem-solving and reasoning capabilities which encourage intelligent thinking by formulating questions, get information, and analyze ideas (Tishman, 1995);

- providing a toolkit of social strategies that enable students to know how, why, and when to ask questions, get help, and how to help others (Bruffee, 1983); and

- reinforcing the belief that everyone has a right and obligation to understand and make sense of the world, given sufficient time (Dweck, 1999).

Assessment

Assessment is a major component of process education because it is the process that determines whether growth has occurred and provides the data required to initiate strategic changes. Its prominence is indicated by its location at the top of the diagram and the fact that all teaching learning activities are "processed" by assessment. It is through self-assessment and metacognition that individuals can be taught to regulate their behaviors using strategies such as predicting outcomes, planning ahead, apportioning one's time, explaining to one's self in order to improve understanding, noting failures in comprehension, and activating background knowledge (Bransford et al, 1999).

Overview of Assessment outlines guiding principles as well as a productive mindset for assessment activities. *Assessment Methodology* highlights four distinct stages in the assessment process and provides case studies in its use. Incorporation of quality measures such as holistic and analytic rubrics can enrich the assessment process by triggering data collection and analysis of desired performance characteristics or work products. Studying the level at which distinct learning skills from the *Cognitive Domain* and *Social Domain* are applied during the teaching/learning process provides a meaningful focus for assessment efforts. Separation of the process of assessment from the process of evaluation as clarified in *Distinctions between Assessment and Evaluation* improves the likelihood that assessment feedback will be adopted.

The assessment camera can and should be used to improve teaching and program effectiveness as well as learner performance. *Performance Levels for Assessors* provides a way for mentors to gage their abilities and to understand what they need to do to move to the next level. *Mid-term Assessment* is an effective means for soliciting student feedback in the middle of a course to surface changes that can be made before the end of the course. *Assessing Program Assessment Systems* describes an annual process for establishing institutional priorities and preparing for accreditation visits.

Outcomes Oriented Curricula

Process Education advocates instructional design with long-term behaviors and performance measures in mind. This approach is advocated by Wiggins (1998) and is featured in *Methodology for Designing a Program Assessment System* and *Methodology for Course Design*. As discussed in *Learning Outcomes*, five different types of measurable learning outcomes can result from educational activities and each of these naturally align with different types of assessment instruments. Learning activities for achieving learning outcomes should be well-informed by learning theory. *Overview of Learning Theory* supplies a set of practitioner-oriented principles that follow from the education, psychology, and brain research literature.

An efficient approach to learning activity development is creating a Knowledge Table that classifies different types and levels of knowledge within a course. Concepts, processes, tools, contexts, and way of being are five types of knowledge identified in *Forms of Knowledge and Knowledge Tables*. Five different levels of knowledge are identified in *Blooms Taxonomy—Expanding Its Meaning*. *Elevating Knowledge from Level 1 to Level 3* and *Developing Working Expertise* explain how tasks within learning activities can be structured to maximize cognitive growth at different stages of development. To assure formation of correct schema, attention should also be given to knowledge construction and deconstruction in creating learning activities (Larochelle, 1998). The *Learning Process Methodology* is offered as a user-friendly tool for doing this. Finally, balancing emphasis on transferable learning skills with disciplinary content in the design of learning activities makes for richer and more engaging learning experiences where the level of challenge can be continually increased (Bransford, 1999). The *Classification of Learning Skills*, *Cognitive Domain*, and *Social Domain* contain a variety of prompts for specific skill development within learning activities.

Student-Centered Facilitation

Teaching and learning is a social process that involves interaction within a community (Wenger, 1998). As emphasized in *Profile of a Quality Facilitator* and supported by Bransford (1999), facilitation is most effective when it responds to student needs in real-time. Chances for successful facilitation are improved if one has a repertoire of teaching techniques and learning tools, however success in practice depends on how these are implemented. *Facilitation Methodology* and *Creating a Facilitation Plan* offer advice on scripting the flow of activity in an active learning classroom and the best responses to anticipated difficulties in achieving desired outcomes. *Getting Student Buy-In* provides tips on using students' needs to generate connection with course content. *Designing Teams and Assigning Roles* provides tips on structuring cooperative learning activities to promote social learning.

A large part of facilitation is managing affective issues (Dweck, 1999). As discussed previously, learner growth is maximized when learning challenges exceed existing knowledge and skill sets. The development of the affective domain helps students visualize and become committed to learning goals and overcome emotional barriers to learning. The development of the psychomotor and cognitive domains provides students with ever-increasing confidence that they are capable of achieving more and more ambitious learning goals. The development of the social domain provides a network of support, both for the learning process and for the goal itself. *The Accelerator Model* integrates these developmental processes and provides a rationale for regulating challenge and support during facilitation.

Concluding Thoughts

A fundamental strength of Process Education is its scientific, systems perspective. Whenever an educational problem is encountered, Process Educators (a) define the scope of the problem in the context of programmatic needs, (b) generate appropriate learning outcomes, (c) validate understanding with colleagues, (d) design methodologies to help learners master relevant procedural knowledge, (e) identify qualitative and quantitative indicators of change, (f) refine systems for continual improvement in implementing problem solutions. It is the intense collaboration of many minds around five themes embodied in the Process Map that makes Process Education robust, transforming personal knowledge into "true knowledge" (Popper, 1965). The Process Map also represents a tool for rooting out the source of poor teaching/learning performance, separating out environmental issues, errors in knowledge construction, or deficiency in learning skills and suggesting theory, techniques, and tools closely related to the poor performance.

References

Bransford, J. D., Brown, A. K., & Cocking, R. R. (2000). *How people learn: brain, mind, experience, and school.* Washington, DC: National Academy Press.

Bruffee, K. (1983). *Collaborative learning: higher education, interdependence, and the authority of knowledge.* Baltimore, MD: Johns Hopkins University Press.

Collis, K. F. (1980). *Levels of cognitive functioning and selected curriculum areas.* In J. Kirby and J. Biggs (eds.), Cognition, development and instruction (eds.). New York: Academic Press, p 65-89.

Dweck, C. (1999). *Self-theories: their role in motivation, personality, and development.* Philadelphia, PA: Psychology Press.

Larochelle, M., Bednarz, N., & Garrison, J. (1998). *Constructivism and education.* Cambridge: Cambridge University Press.

Mezirow, J. (1991). *Transformative dimensions of adult learning.* San Francisco: Jossey-Bass.

Perkins, D. (1995). *Outsmarting IQ: The emerging science of learnable intelligence.* New York: Simon and Schuster.

Popper, K. (1965). *The logic of discovery.* New York: Basic Books.

Raven, J., & Dolphin, T. (1978). *Toward value-expectancy measures of human resources.* Edinburgh: Competency Motivation Project.

Tishman, S., Perkins, D., & Jay, E. (1995). *The thinking classroom: Teaching and learning in a culture of thinking.* Needham, MA: Allyn & Bacon.

Wenger, E. (1998). *Communities of practice: Learning, meaning, and identity.* Cambridge: Cambridge University Press.

Wiggins, G., & McTighe, J. (1998). *Understanding by design.* Alexandria, VA: Association for Supervision and Curriculum Development.

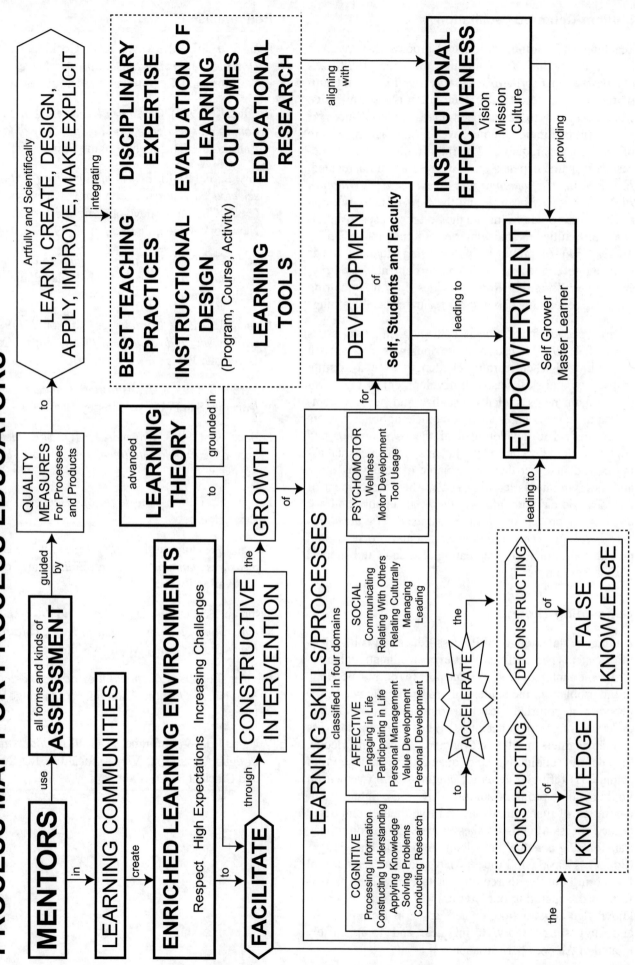

Figure 1

PROCESS MAP FOR PROCESS EDUCATORS

Performance Levels for Learners

by Eric Myrvaagnes, Suffolk University

Two important missions of higher education are to produce the highest level of learning possible as well as individuals who are sufficiently strong in self-assessment to be able to self-mentor their own growth. This module focuses on how to measure levels of learner performance while the companion module, *Performance Levels for Self-Growers*, focuses on how to measure levels of self-growth. Three widely accepted categories for examining learner performance are knowledge base, skills, and attitudes. Knowledge base consists of facts, concepts, and procedures that can be readily applied. Skills control how effectively one's knowledge base can be transferred to related contexts. Attitudes ultimately determine how closely a learner's actual performance approaches the learner's potential.

Distinction between Learning and Growth

Learning and growing involve two different, though closely related, developmental paths. The learner's path deals with content—that is, increasing mastery of factual, conceptual, and procedural knowledge (Anderson and Krathwohl, 2001). Results of learning can be classified using the scheme described in *Bloom's Taxonomy— Expanding its Meaning*. The grower's path focuses on internalization of assessment skills that fundamentally change the learner and unlock higher levels of performance in each of the domains of human performance described in *Classification of Learning Skills*. Differences between the learner's path and grower's path are highlighted further in *Performance Levels for Self-Growers*.

Rubric for Performance Measurement

As educators we need to be able to tell whether our students are learning, and what degree of understanding they have of our course material. The rubric presented in Table 1 provides a yardstick for judging the progress of a learner within a discipline. (For a discussion of rubrics, see *Fundamentals of Rubrics*). This rubric can help refine methods of assessment so that they will more accurately indicate the quality of a student's learning. The rubric can also help educators design curricula and teaching methods to reach students at various levels. And finally, the rubric can help us improve the quality of our own self-assessments in disciplines and research areas in which we feel we "know something."

This rubric was developed over several years by college faculty in Teaching Institutes conducted by Pacific Crest (Krumsieg and Baehr, 2000). It describes important stages in the development of a learner. The first column gives a descriptive name for individuals at each level with the highest level at the top of the table. The other three columns describe the knowledge base, skills, and attitude of learners at those levels.

Organization and Use of the Rubric

At the lowest level are Trained Individuals, who have developed a specific knowledge base, with specific skills, for a specific context, such as a typist who is very familiar with one version of a word-processing software package. Such individuals must have new things explained to them. The typical first-year college student may operate at this level. At the second level are Learned Individuals. They have acquired a broad base of general knowledge which they can apply to related contexts. They feel comfortable learning, within their base of experience. All college graduates should have reached this level. At the third level are Lifelong Learners. They have developed the skills and motivation to self-facilitate their ongoing learning and can apply them to a variety of contexts. They are able to tackle a reasonable percentage of learning requirements in a changing environment. These individuals make good graduate students. At the fourth level are Enhanced Learners. They have developed performance skills expected of a professional in the field and are comfortable applying their skills in different environments. At the top level are Master Learners. These individuals use a set of refined and integrated skills to identify and tackle inter-disciplinary learning challenges within complex systems. They are recognized as experts in their fields.

As with any measuring device, the number of levels in the rubric is somewhat arbitrary. One could make finer distinctions, but the rubric makes sufficiently fine distinctions for one to go beyond the gross measurement implied by the frequent question, "Have my students learned the material?" It encourages us to ask just what kind of learners we are trying to produce in a particular course. Do we want to produce something beyond simply Trained Individuals? The rubric also encourages us to look beyond the purely cognitive goals for the course, suggesting questions such as "Once my students know the content of my course, will they know how to apply it in new situations? Mentor others who want to learn it? Do original research in the field?"

Concluding Thoughts

Moving from one level of learner to the next requires development of a great variety of skills. It is important to look at the learner's performance and characteristics through several different cameras to get an accurate assessment. One person may be able to function as an "enhanced learner" in History, while functioning barely as a "trained individual" in Mathematics. Is such a person truly an enhanced learner? Probably not. A fruitful research question might be to determine whether one person can truly function at different levels in different disciplines. Alternatively, someone may have functioned for quite some time recently as a "lifelong learner," but then suddenly may revert to the level of a trained individual, having a "bad day" for no visible reason. With some familiarity with this rubric, class discussions and even off-hand remarks can be seen to give clues about what level a person is operating on at a particular moment.

References

Anderson, L. W., & Krathwohl, D. R. (Eds.) (2001). *A taxonomy for learning, teaching, and assessing.* New York: Longman.

Krumsieg, K., & Baehr, M. (2000). *Foundations of learning.* Lisle, IL: Pacific Crest.

Table 1

Performance Levels for Learners

	Knowledge Base	Skills	Attitude
Level 5 Master Learners	Understand the research paradigm and posses insights that are valued by experts in many different fields.	Have highly developed learning and research skills that enable them to learn or teach on many subjects with ease.	Create their own challenges and control their own destiny defining highest levels of performance for a community or organization.
Level 4 Enhanced Learners	Have many highly-developed schema that can be readily deployed in a multi-disciplinary setting.	Able to analyze the learning process and to construct new knowledge and cultivate new skills in unfamiliar areas.	Proactively seek out greater challenges, responsibilities, and problems to solve. Seek to push the boundaries of their own performance.
Level 3 Lifelong Learners	Have a variety of well-developed schema that can be readily deployed within a discipline.	Able to learn from how other people function in a particular discipline. Can construct new knowledge in a well-defined area.	Willing to tackle challenges in new areas of knowledge. Accept responsibility for team tasks that exceed their personal expertise.
Level 2 Learned Individuals	Have wide, but shallow, knowledge that can be invoked within a variety of disciplines.	Have enough critical thinking and analytic skills to perform low-level problem solving within a narrow base of experience.	Willing to train others in the areas of knowledge they know best. Accept responsibility for new tasks within their areas of expertise.
Level 1 Trained Individuals	Have minimal information about areas to which they have been exposed.	Posses rudimentary information processing skills.	Must have explicitly defined rules, procedures, and policies. Need to be prompted to ensure task completion.

Performance Levels for Self-Growers

by Eric Myrvaagnes, Suffolk University

Self-growers are valued in society because of their ability to leverage their strengths and to rapidly address areas for improvement, mentoring their own development. These individuals continually raise the bar on their own as well as the performance of others. They are responsible for significant innovations across a spectrum of disciplines (Gardner, 1998). A companion module, ***Performance Levels for Learners***, focuses on how to measure learner performance at levels from novice to master learners. This module presents a rubric for measuring potential for self-growth in four domains of performance—cognitive, social, affective, and psychomotor. This progression involves increasingly sophisticated use of assessment and self-management to embrace bigger challenges and associated opportunities for growth.

The Need for Self Growth

Although some talented individuals can become strong learners unconsciously without a high degree of self-awareness and without highly developed self-assessment skills, these attributes are essential for unlocking one's full potential (Bransford et al, 2000). In this regard, the development of a special way of being is needed to insure that students have the resources to continue their growth as learners beyond formal education (SCANS, 1991). As educators, the more you help students learn how to become self-growers, the more they will be able to process life, move toward their career goals, and execute a quality academic career plan.

Mindset of a Self-Grower

Self-growers have an enduring interest in their processes, especially assessment and self-assessment, in order to maximize performance in every aspect of life. They have a well thought-out personal and professional vision that they use to guide their lives. They also have a high degree of self-confidence and emotional maturity that allows them to take risks to put themselves in challenging situations that require increased levels of performance. They have an ability to define motivating and meaningful outcomes for every learning experience, eagerly seeking the personal and professional growth that results from these experiences. Self-growers are adept at clarifying issues and critical assumptions associated with problems that are important to themselves and others. They can be counted on to apply themselves and serve as a role model to others in producing high quality results.

Rubric for Self Growth

The rubric presented in Table 1 was initially created as a tool to help students visualize progress toward achieving a way of being exemplified by highly successful individuals (Myrvaagnes, 1999). The first column contains a descriptive name for individuals at each level, extending from regressive individuals to star performers. The next remaining columns sketch out self-growth behaviors

associated with the domains of performance defined in the ***Classification of Learning Skills***. Across each level there is parallelism in the use of assessment skills to transform future performance.

At the lowest level are "regressive individuals" who can be bitter about their lives, but who have little interest in self-improvement and who are often paralyzed by change. They have little confidence in their cognitive, social, affective, and psychomotor abilities, often blaming their lot in life on actions of others rather than themselves. At the second level are "stagnant individuals" who are content with the status quo. They have some self-assessment and personal development skills that support low-quality feedback, but they tend to view these skills as a poor investment in time and energy. At the third level are "responsive individuals" who like to be assessed by others and are eager to implement feedback that can bolster performance. These individuals are enjoyable and productive team members. They are willing to accept responsibilities for tasks and be accountable for timely, high-quality completion. At the fourth level are "self-starters." They actively seek assessment by others, listen carefully to their ideas, and are attuned to personal strengths that they can effectively and efficiently use to implement change. "Star performers" occupy the highest level in the rubric. These individuals are unusually observant. They are always aware of what is going on around them and how they are interfacing with their environment. They hold themselves and their associates to high standards, and they are constantly looking for ways to grow their own and others performance.

Concluding Thoughts

Having reached the level of competence that one's natural ability permits, individuals can become stuck at that level, unable to make further progress. The high-level self-grower, on the other hand, is both motivated and able to use his or her life vision, self-assessment skills, self-control in the face of challenging situations, positive orientation toward growth, and aptitude for servant leadership to move to the next level. As teachers we naturally want to help our students master knowledge at the highest possible levels in Bloom's Taxonomy. However, the biggest legacy we can leave to our students may be to help them take one step closer to becoming a "star performer."

References

Bransford, J. D., Brown, A. L., & Cocking, R. R. (2000). *How people learn: Brain, mind, experience, and school*. Washington, DC: National Academy Press.

Gardner, H. (1998). *Extraordinary minds*. New York: Basic Books.

Myrvaagnes, E., with Brooks, P., Carroll, S., Smith, P., & Wolf, P. (1999). *Foundations of Problem Solving*. Lisle, IL: Pacific Crest.

Secretary's Commission on Achieving Necessary Skills (SCANS). (1991). *What work requires of schools: A SCANS report for America 2000*. Washington, DC: Department of Labor.

Table 1

Performance Levels for Self-Growers

	Cognitive	Social	Affective	Psychomotor
Level 5 Star Performers	Understand the reasons for deficiencies in the current paradigm, and readily construct more appropriate paradigms.	Create movements and organizations that often become self-perpetuating.	Control their emotions in challenging situations while managing the affect of others.	Outperform others because of reserves in strength and endurance.
Level 4 Self-Starters	Respond to needs of research communities, adding incrementally to knowledge in their discipline.	Initiate and manage social structures to accomplish more out of every hour of their time.	Feel frustrated when not being challenged about their performance.	Engage in a rigorous physical routine, providing resources for dealing with stress.
Level 3 Responsive Individuals	Use their problem-solving, learning, and thinking skills to get better performance and higher quality results.	Are positive people whom others enjoy and want to have on their team.	React to challenges with improved performance rather than complaints, feeling good about accomplishment.	Exercise regularly and pay attention to nutrition because they want to perform better than expectations.
Level 2 Stagnant Individuals	Satisfied with their modest levels of effort in learning, thinking, and problem-solving.	Interact freely with family and friends, but don't seek more diverse contacts and more challenging relationships.	Feel like a cog in machinery, doing little more than is asked feeling their contributions are not very significant.	Want to maintain current health and fitness but unable to realize much visible progress.
Level 1 Regressive Individuals	Try to minimize or avoid effort needed to think, learn, or solve problems.	Limit their social interactions to like-minded individuals who complain about what they are not getting out of life.	Feel that whatever they do will have little impact, that most things are not worth the effort.	Must conserve energy to deal with frequent health issues.

Pacific Crest

Faculty Development Series

Classification of Learning Skills

by Daniel Apple, Pacific Crest; Steven Beyerlein, University of Idaho; Cy Leise, Bellevue University; and Marie Baehr, Elmhurst College

The Classification of Learning Skills for Educational Enrichment and Assessment is an organizational scheme created by a team of process educators over a ten-year period. The Classification helps educators and learners identify and understand the nature of transferable learning skills that apply to multiple disciplines. The four distinct but interconnected domains that comprise this scheme—cognitive, social, affective, and psychomotor—are further developed in their own respective modules. (Though the authors acknowledge the existence of a fifth domain, the spiritual one, they have elected not to include it in this discussion.) Language development provides a common platform for all of the domains. Assessment provides a common core for improving performance in all domains. This module describes the educational philosophy behind the Classification and the rationale used to identify learning skills within it, as well as the features of this scheme that enhance teaching/learning effectiveness.

Need for the Classification

Educators committed to applying learning theory to educational practice have long needed a shared language to use in discussing learning skill development. This is especially important among faculty engaged in general education classes, designers of active learning curricula, and members of accreditation committees striving to connect course-level learning outcomes with program-level outcomes. The Classification is introduced as a framework for advancing understanding about the nature and inter-relationships of learning skills across all academic disciplines. It integrates key findings in pedagogical research, including the following:

1. Learning involves building a tapestry of conceptual, procedural, and meta-cognitive knowledge (Bransford et al., 2000).

2. Learning results in subject matter mastery, transferable long-term behaviors, and mature perspectives that can be both measured and elevated (Dewey, 1936).

3. Subject matter mastery (conceptual development in an area of knowledge, joined with fluency in applying it) can be planned, cultivated, and assessed, using modern derivatives of Bloom's taxonomy (Anderson and Krathwohl, 2001).

4. Focusing on a small set of life skills at one time helps learners integrate these skills in their lives and elevate their daily performance (Covey, 1989).

The developers of the Classification began by recognizing that each discipline has its own special concepts, tools, language, and performance rubrics. However, they decided not to attempt a lengthy compilation of many overlapping skills. Instead, they chose to highlight a smaller listing of general learning skills that appear in multiple learning contexts (Krumsieg and Baehr, 2000).

The Classification has evolved into a comprehensive model of transferable procedural knowledge that can be used to address a number of educational research questions of interest to higher education. Which learning skills are most critical for a well-rounded education? How do individual learning skills relate to each other? How can they best be taught, especially in concert with the content-mastery skills essential to specific disciplines? How should these learning skills be measured and documented? How can these skills be best communicated to support transfer from one discipline to another?

Anatomy of a Learning Skill

Learning skills are discrete entities that are embedded in everyday behavior and operate in conjunction with specialized knowledge. They can be consciously improved and refined. Once they are, the rate and effectiveness of overall learning increases. They can be identified at an early stage of a learner's development. No matter what the person's age or experience, learning skills can be improved to higher levels of performance through self-reflection, self-discipline, or guidance by a mentor. This growth in learning skill development is usually triggered by a learning challenge of some kind and is facilitated by actions built on a shared language between mentor and mentee. Finally, the growth and development of a learning skill is sustained by quality assessment and feedback. These factors underlie the rubric for learning skill development presented in Table 1. Note how these change incrementally as one progresses from the rudimentary (Level 1) to the sophisticated (Level 5).

Table 1   *Stages of Learning Skill Development*

Level 5 **Transformative** **Use**	The skill is expanded and integrated with other skills so that it can be applied in new contexts that inspire other comparably skilled people to investigate its use for their own purposes and possible emulation.
Level 4 **Self-reflective** **Use**	The skill can be self-improved and adapted to unfamiliar contexts with occasional advice from a mentor.
Level 3 **Consistent** **Performance**	The skill is routinely called upon and effectively applied in multiple contexts by the user, who is consciously directing the effort, frequently with the help of a mentor.
Level 2 **Conscious** **Use**	The skill can be used proactively by a learner, but its use needs to be constantly encouraged and supported by a mentor.
Level 1 **Non-conscious** **Use**	The skill appears on a reactive basis in response to an immediate need, but without the awareness of the learner or of those surrounding him.

Assumptions about Learning Skills

The Classification of Learning Skills is based on several assumptions. First, by focusing on a small set of transferable, mutually exclusive learning skills, educators have an opportunity to build shared language about learning performance. Admittedly, there are many more learning skills than those featured in the Classification; in addition, the labels educators use to describe these often differ from one person to the next and from one discipline to the next. So, in order to work more productively across classroom and temporal boundaries, it is helpful to have a broadly recognized system for naming these skills. Second, a rubric for learning skill development helps educators and learners to understand and assess individual skills. However, it is important to keep in mind that learning skills are developed through practice and feedback; they cannot be elevated through conceptual knowledge alone. Third, a person only recognizes the need to learn a new learning skill when he or she cannot perform a task at a certain level—in other words, when the current skill level is less than that required for the task. If the learner perceives a task to be less challenging than his or her level of competence, he or she will not seek higher-level skills to do it.

Organization of the Classification

The Classification of Learning Skills embodies a deliberately selective grouping of essential, yet discrete, learning skills. Each one is assigned only to the domain where it is most commonly applied; that placement is determined by a decision as to where it first becomes most critical to learning performance. While skills related to thinking processes are "housed" within the *cognitive* domain, those related to interpersonal processes can be found under the *social* domain. Similarly, skills related to attitude and emotional development are located in the *affective* domain, and those connected with body development and control, under the *"psychomotor"* domain.

The Classification of Learning Skills can be visualized using a four-sided pyramid situated on a base plate (see Figure 1), with each side of the pyramid representing one of the domains. Language development lies at the base of this pyramid because this is essential for conscious development of any learning skill in any domain. Assessment is a unifying feature that integrates learning skill improvement at all levels of learning skill use and development. Along each side, the processes associated with each domain are listed in hierarchical order. High-level learning skills associated with processes at the top of the

Figure 1   *Domains and Process Areas in the Classification of Learning Skills*

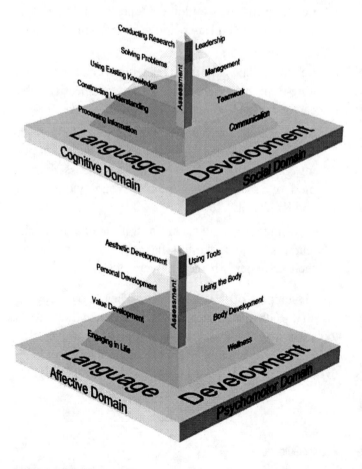

pyramid rely on lower-level learning skills associated with processes at the bottom of the pyramid. For example, within the cognitive domain, processing information should be addressed before tackling skills associated with the processes of constructing understanding, applying knowledge, solving problems, and conducting research.

Within each process area, learning skills are organized into clusters, as illustrated in Table 2. This example explores one of the five skill clusters that support information processing. Unlike the process areas, the skill clusters associated with a particular process area and the specific skills associated with each cluster do *not* follow a hierarchy. A listing of skill clusters and specific skills in the process areas that make up the cognitive, social, affective, and psychomotor domains are shown in companion modules.

Table 2   ***Example of a Skill Cluster***

Domain	cognitive	
Process	processing information	
Cluster	collecting data (from disorganized source)	
Skills	observing	*seeing details in an object/environment*
	listening	*purposeful collection of aural data*
	skimming	*inventorying using key prompts*
	memorizing	*active mental storage of information*
	recording	*transcripting key information*

The development of this Classification scheme has evolved over time, with infusions from several different traditions of scholarly research. Initial work on this system, guided by Bloom's taxonomy (Bloom, 1956), focused on the cognitive domain—specifically focusing on comprehension, critical thinking, and problem solving. Later, research projects such as the SCANS Report (Secretary's Commission on Achieving Necessary Skills), focusing on communication and teamwork skills (SCANS, 1991), inspired much of the work on the social domain. Work on the affective dimension of the pyramid was shaped by current self-improvement and leadership literature that highlighted the role emotional skills play in personal and professional life (Goleman, 1997). It should also be noted that this Classification system has been debated, discussed, and developed extensively in a variety of educational institutions. By dialoguing about the design, implementation, and measurement of general education courses, educators across the nation have helped refine this approach. Even now, the Classification remains a work in progress, subject to new insights derived from classroom and clinical research.

Selection and Placement of Learning Skills

Each of the skill listings in the Classification was brainstormed, located, and validated by several cross-disciplinary teams consisting of up to a half-dozen faculty members working in Pacific Crest institutes. This typically began by writing short definitions of potential ("candidate") skills that were then placed within a process area and assigned key attributes. Table 2 shows examples of the learning skills involved with the skill cluster "collecting data."

To be considered for the classification, each learning skill was then tested against all of the following criteria:

- improvement in this skill had to lead to enhancement of learning performance,
- the skill had to be accessible and usable at all times,
- performance in this learning skill had to be unbounded (i.e., it could be "grown" to progressively higher performance levels),
- the skill had to be transferable across disciplines and contexts,
- the skill could apply to multiple forms of knowledge (see the module "Forms of Knowledge"),
- the skill had to be a holistic element which could not be subdivided (i.e., it could not be either a label for a cluster of skills or a label for a process), and
- the skill was not a process consisting of multiple steps.

Once a skill passed all of the above tests, it was associated with a predominant domain and linked with the appropriate skill cluster. The skill cluster was then examined to insure that it formed a compact, complete, and non-overlapping set—in other words, that nothing essential was left out or shared with another cluster. In this process, the following conditions had to be met:

- each of the skills had to be distinct and provide unique added-value to the set;
- the skills had to be worded concisely, congruently, and completely so that there could be no room for improvement in the definition; and
- the skills could not be critical to learning performance at the next lower process level.

As "candidate" skills were considered for the Classification, definitions were refined so that they represented something unique and essential. This continued until all redundant learning skill components had been parsed out and nothing new remained.

Using the Classification

By incorporating the transferable learning skills found in the Classification into instructional design and delivery, process educators have found ways to make subject matter mastery more authentic (Hanson and Wolfskill, 2000). They have also developed ways to accelerate learning by using appropriate follow-on activities, based on the skill levels they have identified. *(See Developing Working Expertise (Level 4 Knowledge), Overview of Facilitation, and Overview of Assessment.)* Thus, optimal instruction blends discipline expertise (i.e., *applied* knowledge, such as solving an algebraic equation or critiquing a play) with performance in general learning skills (i.e., *process* knowledge, such as critical thinking, teamwork, problem solving, and language development.)

Process educators have also noted that learning skill growth in one domain can leverage growth in other domains (Krumsieg and Baehr, 2000). For instance, growth of learning skills in the affective and social domains can occur relatively quickly and can have a positive impact on skill development in the cognitive domain, where growth occurs more slowly. *(See Overview of Creating a Quality Learning Environment, and Introduction to Learning Communities.)*

Instructors who see the essential connections between skill development and subject matter mastery will find the Classification of Learning Skills to be a useful tool for course design and delivery. Yet, they are wise not to address too many of these learning skills at once. Instead, they are well advised to focus on those skills that are best matched to their students' developmental and disciplinary needs. The Classification can help determine which lower-level skills should be cultivated before addressing the more sophisticated ones. These choices are critical to effectively tailoring learning activities to different student populations; they are also key to articulating learning outcomes at different points in a program. *(See Methodology for Designing a Program Assessment System.)*

Concluding Thoughts

The Classification of Learning Skills for Educational Enrichment and Assessment is an important tool for facilitating learners' growth and development, measuring and documenting growth, self-assessing performance, and improving instructional design for skill development. It builds upon and continues to incorporate a wide range of theories to improve life-long learning skills to increase subject-matter mastery. Finally, the generation of this Classification has sparked interest in new kinds of questions related to the identification and understanding of learning skills. Research issues have arisen regarding the measurement of learners' growth and development, the role of faculty in mentoring, and the importance of skill development to learning (as opposed to exclusively focusing on content mastery.) Faculty who use this Classification to strengthen their own skills will find they can significantly enhance their teaching, research, and service to the profession.

References

Anderson, L. W., & Krathwohl, D. R. (Eds.). (2001). *A taxonomy for learning, teaching and assessing.* New York: Longman.

Bloom, B. S., Engelhart, M. D., Furst, E. J., Hill, W. H., & Krathwohl, D. R. (1956). *Taxonomy of educational objectives: The classification of educational goals. Handbook 1: Cognitive domain.* New York: David McKay.

Bransford, J. D., Brown, A. L., Cocking, R. R., & Pellegrino, J. W. (Eds.). (2000). *How people learn: Brain, mind, experience, and school.* Washington, DC: National Academy Press.

Covey, S. (1989). *Seven habits of highly effective people.* New York: Simon & Schuster.

Dewey, J. (1938). *Experience & education.* New York: MacMillan.

Goleman, D. (1997). *Emotional intelligence.* New York: Bantam Books.

Krumsieg, K., & Baehr, M. (2000). *Foundations of learning.* Lisle, IL: Pacific Crest.

Secretary's Commission on Achieving Necessary Skills (SCANS). (1991). *What work requires of schools: A SCANS report for America 2000.* Washington, DC: Department of Labor.

Worldwide Instructional Design Systems. (2002). *WIDS Learning Design System.* Waunakee, WI: Wisconsin Technical College System Foundation.

Cognitive Domain

by Denny Davis, Washington State University; Steven Beyerlein, University of Idaho;
Cy Leise, Bellevue University; and Daniel Apple, Pacific Crest

The cognitive domain contains learning skills predominantly related to mental (thinking) processes. Learning processes in the cognitive domain (Table 1) include a hierarchy of skills involving processing information, constructing understanding, applying knowledge, solving problems, and conducting research. These processes enable performance at five different levels of learner knowledge that parallel levels of educational objectives originally defined by Bloom (1956) and elaborated in *Bloom's Taxonomy—Expanding its Meaning*. However, as suggested by Krathwol (2002), Bloom's taxonomy focused on describing levels of attainments rather than process skills, and did not substantially address the manner in which the learner proceeds from one level to the next. The Cognitive Domain includes skill clusters that organize a complete, concise, and complementary listing of the learning skills most critical for each process. The cognitive domain learning skills presented here are a valuable reference for curriculum design, classroom observation, and assessment of learning outcomes.

Role of the Cognitive Domain

The cognitive domain encompasses thinking skills that are independent of context and discipline. In contrast to other domains of learning, the cognitive domain addresses development that is individual rather than interpersonal, focuses on content rather than context, and is independent of emotion. The organizational framework given in Table 1 is intended to support learner-centered knowledge acquisition as well as learner-centered growth in cognitive performance.

Cognitive skills can be evidenced at many levels of proficiency (Bransford et al, 2000). Five distinct levels that apply to all learning skills are suggested in the *Classification of Learning Skills*. Cognitive skill development is best sequenced following the levels that parallel educational objectives laid out in Bloom's taxonomy because learning skills from lower-level processes are embedded in learning skills associated with higher-level processes (Anderson & Krathwohl, 2001).

In the cognitive domain, skilled professionals typically utilize a set of specific, highly developed skills along with discipline-specific knowledge in conjunction with a broad spectrum of less-developed skills (Wenger, 1998). Methodologies provide tools for novices as well as experts to strengthen these complex performances *(see Learning Processes through the Use of Methodologies)*. Strengthening underlying learning skills can accelerate mastery of important methodologies *(see Learning Process Methodology, Facilitation Methodology, and Assessment Methodology)*.

Cognitive Domain Processes

As illustrated in Table 1, five thinking processes comprise the cognitive domain. These processes are sequenced and identified as: (1) processing information, (2) constructing understanding, (3) applying knowledge, (4) solving problems, and (5) conducting research. Processing information includes collecting data, generating data, organizing data, retrieving data, and validating information. Constructing understanding includes analyzing, synthesizing, reasoning, and validating understanding. Applying knowledge includes performing with knowledge, modeling, being creative, and validating results. Solving problems includes identifying the problem, structuring the problem, creating solutions, and improving solutions. Conducting research includes formulating research questions, obtaining evidence, discovering, and validating scholarship.

Critical thinking is purposely not identified with a single process area in the cognitive domain. Instead, critical thinking is considered a super-process that draws from all process areas in the cognitive domain during the creation of new knowledge or the improvement of existing knowledge. This viewpoint is consistent with principles of the National Council for Excellence in Critical Thinking (Paul, 2003). Further exploration of the holistic nature of critical thought is given in *Overview of Critical Thinking*.

Cognitive Domain Clusters

Clusters of learning skills are identified under each of the cognitive domain processes. As many as five clusters support each process area. Each skill cluster contains up to a half-dozen unique, but closely related, learning skills. Skill clusters are given labels that communicate their role within each process area. In Table 1, skill clusters are arranged left-to-right in a progression of increasing sophistication. There is no special significance in the order in which the learning skills appear within a cluster.

Table 1   **Cognitive Domain Learning Skills**

Processing Information

Collecting Data *(from disorganized source)*
Observing – seeing details in an environment/object
Listening – purposeful collection of aural data
Skimming – inventorying using key prompts
Memorizing – active mental storage of information
Recording – transcripting key information
Measuring – obtaining data using a predetermined scale

Generating Data *(to fill a void)*
Predicting – forecasting from experience
Estimating – approximating from mathematical models
Experimenting – inferring from empirical study
Brainstorming – gathering ideas from previous experience

Organizing Data *(for future use)*
Filtering – selecting data based on criteria
Outlining – identifying primary and subordinate groupings
Categorizing – associating data with established groups
Systematizing – designing an organizational framework

Retrieving Data *(from organized source)*
Recognizing patterns – perceiving consistent repetitive occurrences
Searching – locating information within a system
Recalling – retrieving from memory
Inventorying – retrieving from collective memory

Validating Information *(for value)*
Testing perceptions – verifying based on interpretations
Validating sources – verifying based on credibility
Controlling errors – verifying based on procedures
Identifying inconsistency – detecting outliers/anomalies
Ensuring sufficiency – verifying data quantity/quality for context

> **Process**
> *Skill Cluster*
> Specific skill

Constructing Understanding

Analyzing *(characterizing individual parts)*
Identifying similarities – recognizing common attributes of parts
Identifying differences – recognizing distinguishing attributes of parts
Identifying assumptions – examining preconceptions/biases
Inquiring – asking key questions
Exploring context – seeing relationship of parts to environment

Synthesizing *(creating from parts)*
Joining – connecting identifiable parts
Integrating – combining parts into new whole
Summarizing – representing whole in a condensed statement
Contextualizing – connecting related parts to environment

Reasoning *(revealing meaning)*
Interpreting – bringing meaning for better understanding
Inferring – drawing conclusions from evidence and logic
Deducing – arriving at conclusions from general principles
Inducing – arriving at general principle by observing specific instances
Abstracting – describing essence of an idea, belief, or value

Validating Understanding *(for reliability)*
Ensuring compatibility – testing consistency with prior knowledge
Thinking skeptically – testing against fundamental principles/schema
Validating completeness – checking for missing aspects
Bounding – recognizing limits of application of knowledge

Applying Knowledge

Performing with Knowledge *(in real context)*
Clarifying expectations – defining proficiency level
Strategizing – planning how to use knowledge
Using prior knowledge – integrating unprompted knowledge
Transferring – using ideas in a new context

Modeling *(in abstract context)*
Analogizing – representing similar elements in dissimilar contexts
Exemplifying – showing by example
Simplifying – representing only primary features
Generalizing – transferring knowledge to multiple contexts
Quantifying – representing with numbers or equations
Diagramming – clarifying relationships through visual representation

Being Creative *(in new contexts)*
Challenging assumptions – exploring possibilities by relaxing constraints
Envisioning – imagining desired conditions
Linear thinking – generating new ideas from previous ideas
Divergent thinking – taking variety of positions to stimulate ideas
Transforming images – manipulating images to gain new insight
Lateral thinking – generating new ideas from associations

Validating Results *(for appropriateness)*
Complying – comparing results with accepted standards
Benchmarking – comparing with results from best practices
Validating – using alternative methods to test results

Table 1   **Cognitive Domain Learning Skills** *(continued)*

Solving Problems

Identifying the Problem *(to establish focus)*
Recognizing the problem – stating what is wrong or missing
Defining the problem – articulating a problem and need for solution
Identifying stakeholders – naming key players/audiences
Identifying issues – inventorying key stakeholder desires and concerns
Identifying constraints – recognizing limitations to solutions

Structuring the Problem *(to direct action)*
Categorizing issues – grouping by underlying principles
Establishing requirements – articulating solution criteria
Subdividing – separating into sub-problems
Selecting tools – finding methods to facilitate solution

Creating Solutions *(for quality results)*
Reusing solutions – adapting existing methods/results
Implementing – executing accepted solution practices
Choosing alternatives – selecting alternatives using criteria
Harmonizing solutions – fitting components into holistic solution

Improving Solutions *(for greater impact)*
Generalizing solutions – modifying for broader applicability
Ensuring robustness – modifying to fit more contexts
Analyzing risks – identifying external sources/impacts of error
Ensuring value – testing against requirements and constraints

Conducting Research

Formulating Research Questions *(to guide inquiry)*
Locating relevant literature – searching out seminal sources
Identifying missing knowledge – determining gaps in community understanding
Stating research questions – asking empirically answerable questions
Estimating research significance – forecasting value/impact to community
Writing measurable outcomes – specifying deliverables from research

Obtaining Evidence *(to support research)*
Designing experiments – specifying observable parameters and sampling
Selecting methods – determining research procedures
Extracting results – analyzing data to produce quality characterizations
Replicating results – duplicating experiments and findings

Discovering *(to expand knowledge)*
Testing hypotheses – discerning significant effects
Reasoning with theory – explaining data with accepted knowledge
Constructing theory – formulating new conceptual structures
Creating tools – adapting knowledge for practitioners

Validating Scholarship *(for meaningful contribution)*
Defending scholarship – presenting within disciplinary performance expectations
Responding to review – elevating scholarship from community input
Confirming prior work – adding credibility to body of knowledge
Judging scholarship – evaluating scholarship against criteria

Cognitive Domain Skills

Learning skills are inseparable entities that can be consciously elevated and refined with proven potential to increase the rate and capacity for learning. As explained in *Overview of Learning Theory*, these are the mortar for building schema to which learners can connect new knowledge. Each learning skill is given a brief explanation that visualizes its use.

Two different learning skills from the cognitive domain are analyzed in Table 2—listening and identifying assumptions. These two examples illustrate how a specific skill used for basic processing of information and another skill used in constructing understanding can be demonstrated at very low levels (without conscious effort) and at very high levels (impressing and inspiring others). Monitoring learning skill proficiency along a common developmental continuum can be a tremendous motivator for learners. Similarly, recognizing which skills are underdeveloped in different learning situations can be used to plan interventions that accelerate desired cognitive development.

The cognitive domain presented in Table 1 includes over 90 transferable learning skills relevant to undergraduate education, graduate education, and professional practice. These were selected using the methods described in the *Classification of Learning Skills* and worded in a manner intended to appeal to users in all academic disciplines. Enough specificity has been retained to insure that well-defined cognitive domain learning skills can be traced to most course and program learning outcomes. Explicit attention to targeted learning skills in classroom activities, instructor interventions, and assessment sessions can increase the probability that these outcomes are achieved and the likelihood that they can be transferred to other settings *(see Learning Outcomes and SII Method for Assessment Reporting)*.

Table 2   **Illustration of Cognitive Domain Competency Levels**

Level of Competency	Description of Individual Response	Examples: (a) Listening (b) Identifying assumptions
Level 5 **Transformative use**	Skill is expanded and integrated with other skills for creative, productive application in novel contexts; inspires others to emulate use.	(a) Purposefully listens and observes nuances and contextual details that deepen understanding of information and its application to a clearly stated need (b) Clearly articulates own and others' assumptions, enabling all to understand impacts on interpretations and conclusions on matters involving a wide variety of disciplines and perspectives
Level 4 **Self-reflective use**	Effective use of skill by learner; skill can be self-improved and adapted to unfamiliar contexts with occasional advice from a mentor.	(a) Carefully listens and reflects on success to gain maximum understanding relevant to a specific need (b) Analyzes and recognizes relative impacts of assumptions made by self and others across a variety of disciplines and perspectives
Level 3 **Consistent performance**	Skill used routinely and effectively in multiple contexts through learner self-direction; not able to advance without external coaching.	(a) Carefully listens to understand key points useful to address a specific need (b) Looks for impacts of assumptions by self and others in discussing interpretations and conclusions within areas of specialty
Level 2 **Conscious use**	Skill used knowingly, possibly proactively, by learner, but skill needs to be constantly challenged by a mentor.	(a) Actively listens; identifies information thought important to general need (b) Aware of some assumptions underlying personal interpretations and conclusions, but often unaware of assumptions made by others
Level 1 **Non-conscious use**	Use of skill initiated by a prompt or influence external to the learner; unintended use of skill.	(a) Passively listens; notes only information highlighted by others (b) Unaware when assumptions are made by self or others, often leading to erroneous conclusions

Concluding Thoughts

Teachers and learners need to understand the hierarchy of processes and skills within the cognitive domain so they appreciate prerequisite skills for learning as well as the way these skills need to be transformed to master more complicated elements of discipline-specific concept inventories. Development of learning skills should never be taken for granted in teaching or learning new content. Skills associated with lower-level processes should be introduced in foundation courses and elevated in intermediate-level coursework. Skills associated with higher-level processes should be thoughtfully introduced and reinforced in upper-division courses. Methodically invoking key learning skills from different process areas and clusters across the cognitive domain also provides a method for infusing richness in course activities while strengthening life-long learning skills. Like the *Social Domain*, this module serves to remind us that improved cognitive domain performance is always possible, no matter what one's state of learning skill development.

References

Anderson, L. W., & Krathwohl, D. R. (Eds.). (2001). *A taxonomy for learning, teaching and assessing*. New York: Longman.

Bloom, B. S., Engelhart, M. D., Furst, E. J., Hill, W. H., & Krathwohl, D. R. (1956). *Taxonomy of educational objectives: The classification of educational goals. Handbook 1: Cognitive domain*. New York: David McKay.

Bransford, J. D., Brown, A. L., Cocking, R. R., & Pellegrino, J. W. (Eds.). (2000). *How people learn: Brain, mind, experience, and school*. Washington, DC: National Academy Press.

Krathwohl, D. (2002). A revision of Bloom's taxonomy: An overview. *Theory into practice*. Autumn 2002 v41 i4 p212 (8).

Paul, R. (2003). Draft statement of principles. *National Council for Excellence in Critical Thinking*. Retrieved on May 28, 2004 from <www.criticalthinking.org/ncect.html>

Wenger, E. (1998). *Communities of practice: Learning, meaning, and identity*. Cambridge: Cambridge University Press.

Social Domain

by Cy Leise, Bellevue University; Steven Beyerlein, University of Idaho; and Daniel Apple, Pacific Crest

The learning processes in the Social Domain of Learning (Table 1) include a hierarchy of skills related to communication, teamwork, management, and leadership. It is distinct from the Cognitive, Affective, and Psychomotor domains in that all of its process areas and specific skills involve interpersonal performance in the large range of social contexts where learning occurs. Traditionally, educators (e.g., Bloom) have subsumed the social domain mostly under the Affective Domain but with some crossovers to the Cognitive Domain (e.g., critical thinking about a communication performance). However, with the emergence of newer learning theories that take fuller account of the social and cultural contexts of learning, educators have become aware of the unique types of learning in the social domain and of interdependence among the four domains of learning for all complex performance goals. Some of the benefits of learning about Social Domain skills include greater awareness that communicating and teaming skills support management and leadership skills, that context greatly influences selection and uses of knowledge, and that integration of social domain processes into any learning process will enhance transfer potential.

Role of the Social Domain

Bloom *(see **Bloom's Taxonomy—Expanding its Meaning**)* did not author a social domain of learning skills to complement his Cognitive, Affective, and Psychomotor taxonomies. However, sociocultural and constructivist philosophies of education strongly incorporate social domain learning skills. Cobb and Yachel (1996) provide an overview of these theories.

The socio-cultural approach is associated with theorists such as the Russian psychologist Lev Vygotsky (1934/1962) and the American philosopher/educator John Dewey (1916) who assume that learning is a developmental process that starts with "external" stimulation and emerges as "internalized" abilities. In process education, this approach is used in the "scoping" of learning activities to assure that the learning expectations are within the present capabilities of the learners and compatible with the time and other resources available. Before a learner can internalize knowledge it is essential to provide appropriately designed, guided experiences *(see **Methodology for Course Design**)*.

The emergent/constructivist theories are often associated with Jean Piaget's (1970) developmental theory. These theories assume that the physically maturing brain contributes equally with environmental stimulation to an individual's ability to construct knowledge. A general similarity to the socio-culturalists is the principle that learning is maximized if opportunities stimulate emergence of new "schemas" (knowledge patterns or units). An assumption of process education is that learners not only continually construct knowledge but that the quality of construction can be facilitated as suggested by the five levels of skill competency presented in Table 2.

Description of the Social Domain

The learning processes included in the Social Domain feature performances involving social skills as a direct focus (e.g., being courteous) as well as uses of social skills to manage a situation or problem (e.g., improvising). There are general rules of thumb for identifying key distinctions among the four domains *(see **Classification of Learning Skills**)*. The Cognitive Domain involves reasoning-related skills that need not be connected to a concrete context, the Affective Domain involves valuing skills related to ways of being, the Psychomotor Domain involves physical skills involving tool use or movement coordination in specific contexts, and the Social Domain involves communication-related skills in goal-oriented contexts.

The five process areas of the Pacific Crest Social Domain include communicating, relating to others, relating culturally, managing, and leading. As with the other domains, the Social Domain processes consist of a hierarchy of complexity from the more basic or foundational (i.e., communicating) to the more complex (e.g., managing and leading).

Within each of the five Social Domain processes are four to six clusters of skills whose titles indicate how specific skills are related to each other. The combination of clusters for a process identifies the skill types for that process; the skills identified within a cluster have no further subdivisions because they are assumed to occur holistically in natural settings. There is no significance to the order in which the specific skills are listed under each skill cluster.

Table 1   **Social Domain Learning Skills**

Communicating

Receiving a Message

Attending – mindful focusing by a listener

Reading body language – gathering information from nonverbal cues

Responding – giving appropriate and timely responses

Checking perceptions – feeding back implied meaning

Preparing a Message

Defining purpose – specifying outcomes for a message

Knowing the audience – predicting background and interests of receivers

Organizing a message – sequencing elements for best impact

Selecting word usage – using language that matches audience background

Formatting a message – selecting a mode or style that fits the purpose

Illustrating – enhancing a message with images, tables, drawings

Delivering a Message

Selecting a venue – deciding when and where to present a message

Generating presence – authoritative delivery of a message

Sharing knowledge – effective presentation of relevant facts and interpretations

Persuading – using information selectively to convince

Story telling – relating what happened

Managing transitions – using planned techniques to lead an audience

Relating Culturally

Accepting Constraints

Obeying laws – complying with rules meant for the common good

Inhibiting impulses – delaying reaction until aware of situation

Noticing social cues – recognizing situational signs of how to behave

Recognizing conventions – behaving politely within a context

Living in Society

Sharing traditions – participating in mutually meaningful rituals

Supporting institutions – upholding important organizations

Valuing communities – recognizing the worth and needs of a group

Reacting to history – responding with knowledge of past events

Being a citizen – participating in the political process

Demonstrating Cultural Competence

Clarifying stereotypes – checking assumptions about people in different cultures

Appreciating culture differences – enjoying the learning of cultural knowledge

Generalizing appropriately – validly acknowledging cultural differences

Using culture-specific expertise – possessing detailed knowledge about a culture

Relating with Others

Inviting Interaction

Taking interest in others – enjoying personal differences

Initiating interaction – approaching and engaging others

Hosting – using social events to build social cohesion

Expressing positive nonverbals – accurately projecting feelings

Assisting others – being kind without expecting reward

Being non-judgmental – responding with an assessment mindset

Relating for Meaning

Belonging – gaining acceptance in a group

Befriending – initiating a supportive relationship

Empathizing – taking another's emotional perspective

Collaborating – working together for mutual benefit

Parenting – guiding social-emotional development of children

Mentoring – encouraging growth through an advisory relationship

Performing in a Team

Goal setting – formulating shared outcomes

Achieving consensus – agreeing on decisions based on shared values

Planning – deciding how to use resources to achieve goals

Cooperating – respecting role boundaries and responsibilities

Compromising – modifying positions to achieve common ground

Performing in an Organization

Accepting responsibility – demonstrating initiative and persistence

Being assertive – advocating strongly on the basis of reason and evidence

Making proposals – presenting plans for consideration

Documenting – creating a record of activities, work products, and processes

Influencing decisions – using assessment data to support decision paths

Process
Skill Cluster
Specific skill

Table 1
Social Domain Learning Skills (continued)

Managing

Managing People

Building consensus – developing goals and plans that are well-accepted

Motivating – arranging rewards that fit individual aspirations

Modeling performance – demonstrating high quality in action

Assessing performance – providing feedback for improving performance

Evaluating performance – judging whether a performance standard has been met

Building and Maintaining Teams

Defining team roles – deciding on roles that support a goal

Setting rules – defining ethical and professional expectations

Delegating authority – authorizing others to manage selected tasks

Confronting poor performance – requiring specific change

Recruiting – selecting qualified personnel for specific functions

Mediating – resolving interpersonal conflicts

Managing Communication

Connecting with stakeholders – involving key individuals at appropriate times

Networking – developing relationships with internal and external advocates

Marketing – initiating messages to persuade clients of the value of something

Sustaining change – promoting creative proposals for ongoing improvement

Managing Resources

Negotiating – making agreements with other stakeholders to advance position

Politicking – advocating positions with external stakeholders

Securing resources – assuring appropriate funding, scheduling, and staffing

Creating productive environments – arranging for essential resources in a setting

Leading

Envisioning

Projecting the future – visualizing future status based on trends/logic

Seeing implications – describing operational impacts of future trends

Balancing perspectives – maintaining the vision while working within constraints

Responding to change – being flexible in strategic thinking

Building a Following

Inspiring – being positive in the face of negative challenges

Sharing a vision – using empathy and imagery to help others see a vision

Generating commitment – asking for specific signs of willingness to tackle challenges required for a vision

Maintaining integrity – responding to personal issues with clear criteria/principles

Maintaining Commitment

Meeting individual needs – responding to evidence of needs with relevant resources

Taking meaningful stands – publicly articulating principles

Thinking opportunistically – using positive strategies to predict and reduce risks

Being charismatic – displaying confidence in action

Empowering

Giving credit – publicly and equitably acknowledging performance

Encouraging ownership – engaging others in important tasks for a vision

Grooming subordinates – developing future leaders to take over key roles

Being a servant leader – placing interests of others before personalinterests

Social Domain Skill Competency Levels

Table 2 presents five levels of competency that potentially can be achieved in any skill in the Social Domain. From the lowest to the highest, these five levels are "nonconscious use" [of a skill], "conscious use," "consistent performance," "self-reflective use," and "transformative use." These level descriptors provide a way to identify how much competence an individual has with any social domain skill. Brief examples are presented in Table 2 to illustrate how varying levels of competency in the skills of "attending" and "sharing a vision" look at each of the five levels.

Table 2

Social Domain Competency Levels

Level of Competency	Description of Individual Response	Examples: (a) attending (b) sharing a vision
Level 5 **Transformative Use**	Highly skilled in timely use of the skill to improve others' engagement or commitment.	(a) discerning of subtle changes in audiences and stakeholders (b) updating of vision to improve "capture" of real future potential of the organization.
Level 4 **Self-Reflective Use**	Uses the skill within a planned strategy for organizational change, e.g., when running meetings.	(a) noticing effectiveness of meetings on basis of own criteria for effective meetings (b) designing organizational teams to implement vision through action projects
Level 3 **Consistent Performance**	Uses the skill to make a difference in real-time, e.g., cooperatively or collaboratively.	(a) task-oriented listening, questioning and paraphrasing (b) volunteering to be a member of a college committee on vision; presenting personal and peer perspectives effectively
Level 2 **Conscious Use**	Uses the skill passively but with awareness of need to grow; limited in confidence, social smoothness, and timing.	(a) actively selecting information from team comments (b) questioning a college president's vision in discussions with peers
Level 1 **Non-Conscious Use**	Responsive if prompted by others; attentive but not consciously identifying social domain processes and skills.	(a) passively present; able to respond if asked a question (b) noting the main features of a new college president's vision

Concluding Thoughts

This module presents the processes, skill clusters, and skills of the Social Domain of learning (Table 1) and differentiates these from the processes and skills in the cognitive, affective, and psychomotor domains. A five-level rubric is presented in Table 2, analogous to Bloom's Taxonomy for Cognitive Learning Objectives, for assessing the level of competence with any skill in the Social Domain. The socio-cultural and constructivist philosophies of learning and development are briefly discussed in order to demonstrate how skills in the Social Domain fit into educational theory and practice. As a systematic approach to education, process education emphasizes the significance of social domain learning skills which often in the past have been considered peripheral to learning. By identifying the relevant skills from the Social Domain that are likely to make a difference in a learning context, educators will be able to integrate these skills with those from the other domains to create truly integrated learning experiences.

References

Anderson, L. W., Krathwohl, D. R., Airasiari, P. W., (Eds.) & Bloom, B. S. (Contributor). (2000). *A taxonomy for learning, teaching and assessing: A revision of Bloom's taxonomy of educational objectives*. New York: Longman Publishing.

Apple, D. K., Duncan-Hewitt, W., Krumsieg, K., & Mount, D. (2000). *A handbook on cooperative learning*. Lisle, IL: Pacific Crest.

Cobb, P., & Yachel, E. (1996). Constructivist, emergent, and sociocultural perspectives in the context of developmental research. *Educational Psychologist, 31*, 175-190.

Dewey, J. (1916/1967). *Democracy and education*. New York: Free Press.

Piaget, J. (1970). *Science of education and the psychology of the child*. New York: Orion.

Vygotsky, L. S. (1934/1960). *Mind in society: The development of higher psychological processes*. Cambridge, MA: Harvard University Press.

Annotated Bibliography — Educational Philosophy

by Steven Beyerlein, University of Idaho and Mark Schlesinger, University of Massachusetts Boston

Acting on an educational philosophy makes one's teaching more than an organization of subject matter or a sequencing of disjointed learning activities. This annotated bibliography exposes assumptions associated with learning and personal growth, articulates a variety of thoughtful and uplifting visions for teaching and learning, and provides many illustrations of how others have translated these into daily practice. The selections appearing below are a sampling of educational philosophy congruent with Process Education. We do not propose them as a comprehensive bibliography of educational philosophy in general.

Books

Dewey, J. (1997). *Experience & education.* New York: Touchstone. (Originally published in 1938. New York: MacMillan.)

In this classic work that has inspired a variety of educational reform movements, John Dewey addresses a long-standing controversy: whether the focus of formal education should be development from within or formation from without. He bases his thoughts on lessons learned through several decades of experimentation with "progressive schools" that emphasized personal freedom and self-directed learning. These institutions were set up as alternatives to "traditional schools" that stressed transmission of pre-ordered information and competency in pre-defined skills. Dewey recognizes that not all experience is educative, but that transformational teaching/learning moments involve attention to personal life-experiences as well as purposeful facilitation. This work outlines criteria for experiential learning that ensures construction of transferable knowledge and personal ownership of enlarged learning skills.

Friere, P. (2000). *Pedagogy of the oppressed.* New York: Continuum.

Originally published in 1970 (New York: Continuum), this modern classic flows from the author's commitment to relieve the burden of both the oppressed and their oppressors, which can occur only when the former perceive oppression "not as a closed world from which there is no exit, but as a limiting situation which they can transform." The pedagogy of liberation requires reflection linked to action, and it places the chief agency for growth with the learners. Friere decries education that regards students as "containers" and educational institutions as "banks." In Friere's pedagogy, teachers and students engage in "co-intentional" education: both dedicate themselves not simply to illuminating reality or knowledge, but to re-creating it. Rather than inculcating solutions, Friere's prototype teacher collaborates with the learner in a process of "problem-posing education."

Gardner, H. (1999). *Multiple intelligences for the 21st century.* New York: Basic Books.

This book describes the characteristics of eight very different intelligences that operate within our classrooms and society. These intelligences include: verbal-linguistic (word smart), logical-mathematical (logic smart), spatial (picture smart), physical-kinesthetic (body smart), musical (music smart), natural (nature smart), interpersonal (people smart), and intra-personal (self smart). The text provides a platform for students and instructors to reflect on "how" they are smart, not "if" they are smart. By identifying personal strengths and areas for improvement, readers get a clearer view of themselves and their life-vision. Readers also gain an appreciation of how they can contribute and benefit from interacting with team members who possess complementary intelligences.

Krumsieg, K., & Baehr, M. (2000). *Foundations of learning.* Lisle, IL: Pacific Crest.

This text introduces entering college students to the principles and culture of process education. It includes a large number of multi-disciplinary examples of guided discovery activities featuring cooperative learning groups. These activities possess a common format that begins with a statement of purpose/significance; includes criteria for performance, supportive models and learning resources, and implementation plan; and ends with a strategy for assessing how well learning outcomes are achieved. Each activity also features up to three transferable learning skills from the Classification of Learning Skills. Activities are grouped by process area (i.e. information processing, teamwork, personal development, and problem solving) and are supported by methodologies that can be used by both novice and advanced learners.

O'Banion, T. (1997). *A learning college for the 21st century.* Phoenix: Oryx Press.

Jointly published by the American Council on Education and the American Association of Community Colleges, this book outlines how colleges can become a place where learning comes first and the right educational experiences are routinely facilitated for the right learners, at the right time, and the right place. Drawing on significant innovation within America's community colleges, the author illustrates how institutions at different stages of reform can pursue six principles of a learning college. The book challenges the reader to distinguish between major advances in learning culture and major social changes in the use of information technology, governance and control, student demographics, funding and resources, alliances and partnerships, and classroom innovations that will happen whether championed or not.

Palmer, P. (1999). *The courage to teach: Exploring the inner landscape of a teacher's life*. San Francisco: Harper and Row.

Herein lies a place of contemplation for teachers overwhelmed by novel accreditation requirements, institutional reorganization, rapid evolution of instructional technology, pressure to respond to a variety of educational reform movements, and increasing expectations for research and service activities. The author reminds us that because "we teach who we are" all enduring changes in the teaching learning/dynamic must begin in the heart of teachers, not in external mandates for change. Teaching and learning is interpersonal, and the richness of this interaction depends on connectivity to the subject matter, to specific populations of learners, to colleagues, and most importantly, to oneself. The text offers a number of excellent ideas for expanding self-knowledge leading to more genuine and more transformational dialogue with students as well as communities of practitioners.

Rosser, S. (2000). *Women, science, and society: The crucial union*. New York: Teachers College Press.

Based on her experience at two large research universities, the author suggests cultivating alternative ways of knowing in science, mathematics, engineering, and technology (SMET) classrooms. Through integrating more interactive teaching methods as well as connecting subject-matter with more open-ended, holistic problems, the book hypothesizes that a larger number of individuals with more diverse learning styles can be attracted and retained in technical fields. Deeper and more frequent dialogue between SMET faculty and humanities/social science faculty is the catalyst for this enlarged vision of scholarship. As an added benefit, the author also theorizes that more intense inter-disciplinary cooperation in the area of pedagogy is likely to enrich all aspects of academic life, including research and service.

Senge, P., Cambron-McCabe, N., Lucas, T., Smith, B., Dutton, J., & Kleiner, A. (2000). *Schools that learn: A fifth discipline fieldbook for educators, parents, and everyone who cares about education*. New York: Doubleday.

This anthology thoroughly examines five disciplines essential for effective learning organization: personal mastery, mental models, shared vision, team learning, and systems modeling. A central theme of the book is that deep, enduring learning occurs when new skills and capabilities, new awareness and sensibilities, and new attitudes and beliefs reinforce each other. Learning is presented as the key ingredient to sustaining change at the individual, team, and institutional level. To support learning within organizations, several systems modeling tools are offered for conceptualizing and constructively responding to change. These tools are presented in a way that is easily accessible to the non-mathematical reader, but also thought-provoking for those with more quantitative backgrounds. Practices in each of the five disciplines are comprehensively illustrated through case studies drawn from a broad spectrum of primary, secondary, and post-secondary schools. Linkages to supporting material in other sections of the book and to other sources are prominently displayed in the sidebars.

Article

Barr, R., & Tagg, J. (1995). From teaching to learning: A new paradigm for undergraduate education. *Change, 27,* (6), 13-25.

This article examines ongoing reform in higher education in terms of a paradigm shift from a teacher-centered "instruction paradigm" to a student-centered "learning paradigm." Significant differences are noted in the mission and purpose of education, criteria for success, teaching/learning structures, nature of roles, and underlying learning theory. The "instruction paradigm" focuses on enrollment growth, high participation rates, revenue growth, curriculum expansion, and enhancement of physical resources. The "learning paradigm" is closely aligned with the principles of Process Education and focuses on identifying learning goals, facilitating student success, and documenting learning outcomes. The "instruction paradigm" stresses the quality of entering students while the "learning paradigm" stresses the quality of exiting students and the value-added to their learning skills.

Web Sites

American Association of Colleges and Universities. <http://www.aacu.org>
This organization promotes new paradigms for general education as well as political support for education funding.

American Association for Higher Education. <http://www.aahe.org>
This organization's mission, guiding principles, and strategies for action include the scholarship of teaching/learning. AAHE advocates a strong assessment component.

Section Two
Learning and Developmental Theory

Modules in this section

Overview of Learning Theory

by Cy Leise, Bellevue University

Learning involves continuously increasing one's capacity to process, connect, and create knowledge that supports skillful performances in any area of life. This module reviews key principles of learning from a process education perspective. It also provides background for answering questions about (a) the forms and structures of knowledge, (b) the factors that influence variations in learning outcomes, (c) the role of different brain processes in learning, and (d) processes involved in learning-to-learn.

Elements of Learning Theory

Knowledge exists when a learner, with the necessary "learning skills" *(see Classification of Learning Skills)* gains competency in manipulating and applying relevant concepts, processes, and tools for a learning goal and can do so in varying contexts and in ways consistent with his or her "way of being." These five forms of knowledge are described and analyzed in *Forms of Knowledge and Knowledge Tables*.

Learning outcomes can vary according to factors such as learner competency levels and buy-in, quality of the learning environment, and level of challenge provided by the educator. These issues are examined in *Getting Student Buy-In*, *Bloom's Taxonomy—Expanding its Meaning*, and *The Accelerator Model*. As discussed in *Methodology for Creating a Quality Learning Environment*, strengthening learning processes requires well-designed learning opportunities that are embedded in continuous assessment activities.

Progress in the brain sciences during the past 20 years has yielded clear evidence that educational methods must be consistent with the way the brain is organized and how it processes knowledge. This history is recounted in *A Brief History of Neuroscience* and *From Synapses to Learning*. The physiological make-up of the brain requires that educators present learning opportunities related to a knowledge goal at appropriate developmental times. Furthermore educators need to be prepared to deliver a full-range of interventions to ensure the establishment of long-term memory as well as metacognition about content and about personal growth. *Creating a Facilitation Plan* provides prompts for improving facilitation skills in these areas.

As emphasized in the *Overview of Process Education*, knowledge cannot be fully mastered without the learner "knowing how to learn." Designing learning challenges in steps that appropriately increase the challenge and complexity helps learners elevate their knowledge. As learners improve they can add additional elements such as transfer of their knowledge and problem solving in new contexts. This transition is evident by comparing *Elevating Knowledge from Level 1 to Level 3* and *Developing Working Expertise*. A framework for guiding this process is the *Learning Process Methodology*.

Principles of Learning

Table 1 summarizes ten principles of learning that are well-founded in the educational psychology literature and are essential to a vibrant process education classroom. The modules identified in the previous paragraphs provide detailed information about educational psychology, teaching techniques, and facilitation tools that align with these principles. Discussion of each principle is followed by an introduction to two methodologies that are central to good learning.

Table 1　　　**Principles of Learning**

1. Learners need solid schemas or frameworks to which they can connect new knowledge.

2. The learning process is more powerful if it is systematic and disciplined.

3. Learner empowerment increases proportionally with improvements in effective use of a set of learning tools and strategies.

4. Learning is a frustrating process that requires strong affective skills.

5. Language, learning, and memory are highly dependent upon brain functions.

6. Quality learning is based on a hierarchical set of cognitive learning skills that include language, information processing, critical thinking, and knowledge application.

7. Learning-to-learn, a metacognitive competency, increases in proportion to improvements in reflection, self-assessment, and mentoring.

8. Long-term growth in learning requires that learners assess and improve upon current learning styles and preferences rather than seek accommodation for them.

9. Learners who have ownership of their learning processes will be highly motivated and will set high, but realistic, standards.

10. Strong learners strive to learn in ways that will enable them to reuse and generalize their knowledge in multiple contexts.

1. **Learners need solid schemas or frameworks to which they can connect new knowledge.**

Quality learning cannot occur without adequate motivation and effort, which are related to affective domain skills. Learners need to establish a life vision that includes values and goals related to learning, and they need to learn to use skills from the *Social Domain*. Once they do that, they are better able to acquire the specific *Cognitive Domain* skills that will enable them to consciously and systematically build knowledge. The constructivist view of learning emphasizes that knowledge must be constructed by the learner; it is not possible to "deconstruct" knowledge and give it to someone else. See *Forms of Knowledge and Knowledge Tables* for a useful framework that distinguishes between different types of schemas.

2. **The learning process is more powerful if it is systematic and disciplined.**

It is essential that understanding precede application. Various methodologies offered by the *Faculty Guidebook* provide guidance for logical—but very flexible—sequencing of steps in learning a process. The better a learner understands the knowledge table for a given area of knowledge, the stronger the schema structure for adding new knowledge. A common thread for all of learning is that only the learner can "own" the learning process—no one else can do it. In addition to commitment to a growth path, learners must also develop strong and systematic ways to proceed along their chosen path.

3. **Learner empowerment increases proportionally with improvements in effective use of a set of learning tools and strategies.**

Among the process education tools for learners are knowledge tables, methodologies, assessment techniques and measures, a comprehensive skills classification, and self-growth strategies. Ownership of the learning process is incomplete until the individual becomes skilled at selecting and using the full range of tools and strategies that are needed to challenge self-growth in learning. Constraints to self-growth are examined in *Becoming a Self-Grower* and a proven process for enhancing self-growth is given in *Personal Development Methodology*.

4. **Learning is a frustrating process that requires strong affective skills.**

Learning challenges affect in many ways: (a) thinking is a very hard process that often makes one feel inferior, (b) incompleteness of knowledge, while something always to recognize, makes learners feel inadequate, and (c) the constant need to "deconstruct" false knowledge requires humility and openness if one's false assumptions are ever to be identified. Learners must acquire, and own, affective self-management skills that will enable them to rise to the challenges created by internal (e.g., self-handicapping thoughts) or external (e.g., low grades) evaluations as well as from unpredictable internal (e.g., emotional over-reactions, cognitive distortions) or external (e.g., competing priorities) influences on learning. Frustration often increases at junctures in the learning process for complex knowledge where the learner's process skills require significant improvement. *Performance Levels for Self-Growers* provides a rubric for monitoring learner empowerment.

5. **Language, learning, and memory are highly dependent upon brain functions.**

Learners must understand that their approach to learning must take into account how the brain, as well as other physiological processes of the body, define learning potential. Language, the foundation for all the learning domains, develops in concert with the physical maturing of the brain in early childhood. No other species has language with the symbolic range of human speech and language. Basic principles of learning derived from extensive behavioral research with animals demonstrate that the genetic and other biological characteristics of each species directly control what specific types of learning are possible. Although there are highly general behavioral models (e.g., Pavlovian and operant conditioning) that show the evolutionary inheritance in common between humans and other species, the greatest differences between humans and other animals are in language and in the flexibility of human learning capabilities. Memory is an area of brain research in which it is abundantly clear that there are definite patterns of input and output controlled by brain structure. Part of every learning strategy must include an accounting for how the brain works for that process and whether influences on the brain (e.g., fatigue, illness, drugs, or damage) will change brain capacity (Bloom, Nelson, & Lazerson, 2001).

6. **Quality learning is based on a hierarchical set of cognitive learning skills that include language, information processing, critical thinking, and knowledge application.**

Learning is based on a set of cognitive processes with a hierarchical pattern or structure. Language is a prerequisite for all domains of learning, but it is especially crucial for the symbolic representations common in the cognitive domain. Information processing refers to broad patterns of attention to the location, general structure, and content of knowledge resources (e.g., the layout of professional articles). *Critical Thinking* involves an array of analytical and argumentative skills that must be selected and applied, depending upon requirements of purposes and contexts. Therefore, there is no one "methodology" for critical thinking, although the basic considerations and criteria involved across all approaches to critical thinking have been clearly defined. (Paul and Elder, 2001). Typically, the first really new challenge for college learners is to actually apply knowledge systematically and usefully for some real purpose or product. After this large application step is mastered, the potential for growth as a quality learner expands exponentially.

7. **Learning-to-learn, a meta-cognitive competency, increases in proportion to improvements in reflection, self-assessment, and mentoring.**

Generalized learning capability, known as learning-to-learn, involves conscious awareness of the processes implicated in each learning experience. With experience, this meta-cognitive competency can become highly flexible in the ways exemplified by experts. Regular reflection on processes leads to improved insights about the types of skills involved in complex learning across varied contexts. It also leads to personal insights about learning styles and attitudes that must be assessed and managed. Several tools for cultivating metacognition are found in the *Overview of Assessment*, *Assessment Methodology*, and *SII Method for Assessment Reporting*. When learners have learned to accurately and reliably use basic techniques for their own learning they can expand to helping or mentoring others in the same processes *(see Overview of Mentoring)*.

8. **Long-term growth in learning requires that learners assess and improve upon current learning styles and preferences rather than seek accommodation for them.**

Each individual has a "way of being" or personal approach to learning that puts a unique twist or perspective on all knowledge learned by the individual. There is substantial educational research *(see Annotated Bibliography—Learning Theory)* on "learning styles." Some of these are learned preferences based on extensive experiences while others are unchangeable sensory, perceptual, or cognitive differences or deficits related to brain function. Current federal law requires all educational institutions to provide appropriate adaptations to support learning if someone has a diagnosed learning disability. The *Mindset for Assessment* advocated by process education encourages every learner to engage in active learning and self-awareness to escape as much as possible from an attitude of accommodation that permeates many high schools. Regardless of learner style or preference, all learners benefit from identifying their strengths, analyzing their ability to improve despite some limitations, and generating deeper insights about themselves.

9. **Learners who have ownership of their learning processes will be highly motivated and will set high, but realistic, standards.**

Researchers in social learning have concluded that those whose learning is intrinsically motivated also tend to know how to set goals and standards that are challenging but realistic (Bandura, 1986). They take the initiative in establishing goals and standards that are important for their own purposes. The key problem is how to facilitate learning improvement so that initially externally motivated learners (e.g., those who work for grades) become intrinsically motivated. Process education philosophy and teaching materials are resources for helping learners with this transition from "extrinsic" to "intrinsic" motivation.

10. **Strong learners strive to learn in ways that will enable them to reuse and generalize their knowledge in multiple contexts.**

Ultimately knowledge exists to help people address problems in many life contexts. A strong learner does not learn just for the present context; he or she will take the time to generalize the form and meaning of the knowledge so it can fit multiple contexts—including those presently unpredictable. *Performance Levels for Learners* provides a convenient rubric for measuring this progress.

Methodologies Related to Learning

1. Learning Process Methodology

Good learners prepare for learning by assessing their current knowledge and setting specific goals for the new learning they have in mind. Effective strategies must be used to accomplish the learning, and the results must be assessed afterwards. An important standard of success is the ability to transfer knowledge to other contexts. Effective facilitation of the use of this and other methodologies requires careful attention to setting objectives that are focused on a substantial outcome that can be accomplished within a practical time limit. Initially learners find methodologies confusing so they typically start using them in a step-by-step manner until the purpose and nature of the isolated steps become "internalized". A rubric for internalization of methodologies is given in ***Learning Processes through the Use of Methodologies***.

2. Problem Solving Methodology

The ultimate purpose of knowledge is to provide the basis for solving new problems. This methodology helps learners to specify a problem in a form that can be worked on in logical and systematic ways. The steps in the methodology provide a clear guide for moving toward solutions and, at the same time, provide criteria for assessing whether the problem has been properly defined. Like the learning process methodology, the problem solving methodology is as valuable for teachers as it is for learners.

Effective use of learning principles and supporting methodologies will be facilitated by:

- Becoming familiar with process education through Teaching Institutes,

- Learning to use methodologies as learning facilitation guides,

- Setting challenging standards for performance processes and outcomes,

- Keeping a focus on learner empowerment,

- Developing activities that actively engage learners,

- Using assessment and facilitation to promote growth, and

- Providing role modeling and mentoring for others to help them learn how to learn.

Concluding Thoughts

Adopting the ten principles of learning given here should stimulate many ideas for designing more effective learning environments as well as actions you might consider to be a more effective facilitator of learning. Increasing the percentage of our students who have "learned-to-learn" will generate self-growth and increased motivation that is likely to be passed on to other students through peer mentoring. But these benefits don't extend only to your students. Incorporating the principles of learning into your own professional development is likely to have a major impact on research and service aspects of your job.

References

Bandura, A. (1986). *Social foundations of thought and action.* Englewood Cliffs, NJ: Prentice-Hall.

Bloom, F. E., Nelson, C. A., & Lazerson, A. (2001). *Brain, mind, and behavior* (3rd ed.). New York: Worth Publishing.

Paul, R., & Elder, L. (2001). *A miniature guide for students on how to study and learn a discipline using critical thinking concepts and tools.* Dillon Beach, CA: Foundation for Critical Thinking.

A Brief History of Neuroscience

by Kenneth Wesson, San Jose/Evergreen Community College District

This module presents historical background for understanding "brain-considerate learning." *(See From Synapses to Learning—Understanding Brain Processes.)* Educators will benefit in two important ways from learning about the historical milestones that have made contemporary neuroscience possible. First, they will recognize the difficulties, as well as the triumphs, in the search to understand the brain, and this knowledge will help them better understand the challenges of higher-order learning. Second, they will recognize the physical limitations of the human brain, as well as the impressive potential that it has for learning. Five significant myths will provide a storyline for the ways people have viewed the brain throughout history, progressing from misconceptions and false assumptions to increasingly accurate data and sound theories. Today the invention of new research methods makes it possible to ask and answer important questions in neuroscience. All of these questions are of interest to educators because the answers impact the teaching and learning equation. Despite this progress, however, full answers to questions about how neuroscience theory and methods can enhance the way educators approach learning remain in the future. For now, educators can best use information from neuroscience to re-evaluate their assumptions about the brain as they construct models of learning and classroom performance.

Overview

The significant problems facing us today cannot be solved at the same level of thinking that we were at when we created them.—Albert Einstein

The human brain is the most complicated and adaptable single object residing in the known universe. Despite the brain's complexity, however, scientists have been able to make progress in understanding it. Their findings have enabled educators to deploy more powerful pedagogies and construct a brain-considerate system of education. Developing a respectable knowledge base of "how the brain works" is necessary for boosting achievement and maximizing the potential of each and every student in our classrooms. All educators need to understand the inner workings of the human brain so that they can put the research findings from neuroscience to the most profitable classroom advantage.

In one manner or another, investigations into the mammalian brain from centuries past have paved the way for our contemporary knowledge reservoir. Five notions which set the stage for our current understanding of the brain will be covered in this module.

1. Early evidence of brain investigations
2. The cardiocentric view of behavior
3. Phrenology
4. Localization of function
5. The theory of mass action

Early Evidence of Brain Investigations

In early civilizations throughout the world, most notably in South America, there is abundant evidence of brain investigations (Bishop, 1995). Skulls from these civilizations indicate frequent trepanation, a crude method of brain surgery. As early as 5,000 B.C., Pre-Inca and other early practitioners bored holes into the skulls of individuals suffering ailments that ranged from migraine headaches, epileptic seizures and mental disorders to possession by evil spirits. Skulls uncovered with several holes indicate that large numbers of patients received multiple treatments for on-going mental health difficulties. Equally important, in several locations trepanized skulls have been unearthed with revealing signs of post-operative recoveries, indicating that patients survived well beyond the time of these surgical procedures. This high volume of trepanized crania found worldwide points to early awareness of the human brain's central role in orchestrating behavior, an understanding which pre-dates similar thinking in European civilizations.

Early Egyptians, in contrast, could attribute nothing of significance to the human brain. During their elaborate mummification process, they extracted the brain with gross indifference via the nostrils and disposed of it unceremoniously, even though they preserved the heart, liver, kidneys, and lungs for service in the afterlife. Interestingly, their medical texts do talk about the brain. An ancient Egyptian surgical papyrus from 3,000 B.C. records twenty-six cases of brain trauma along with corresponding procedures for treating specific injuries. Moreover, the term "brain" has been found on a surgical papyrus dating from 1,700 B.C.

The father of Western medicine, Hippocrates (460-379 B.C.), contended that the human brain was the principal organ responsible for intelligence. In contrast, Aristotle (384-322 B.C.) and the leading thinkers of his day advocated the cardiocentric position which supported the notion that the human heart was the seat of all cognitive abilities, as well as the human soul. The brain was relegated to more humble undertakings comparable to a radiator designed exclusively to cool the hot blood circulated by the heart. The brain's relationship to behavior and cognitive functioning was significantly and consistently overshadowed by a focus on the heart. Throughout the first millennium and a half, written records in the Western world mistakenly pointed to the heart as the center of human behavior, consciousness, and cognition. Our contemporary language still reflects vestiges of this perspective. Today, we refer to successfully memorized facts as information that we know "by heart."

The church sanctioned the cardiocentric underpinnings of philosophy, medicine, and science. Moreover, the church made it clear that one's longevity and his or her support for church positions intersected. Science, medicine, and education safely mirrored the church.

Electricity and the Brain

In 1791, Italian scientist Luigi Galvani demonstrated that electrical forces not only exist in the body, but that electricity also plays a dynamic role in the operation of nerves and muscles. Galvani's experiments showed that it was possible to activate the motor nerves connected to a frog's leg muscles by introducing a mild electrical current. He concluded—erroneously—that muscle movements were proof of electricity flowing between the nerves and the muscles. His research, however, took the emerging study of the electrochemical basis of neural activity and pointed it in the right direction. Galvani's astonishing discoveries inspired "Frankenstein," Mary Shelley's 1818 novel. The novel's popularity served as a testament to the torrent of public curiosity in scientific research that was unleashed by Galvani's fascinating research findings.

In the early 1900's, teams of researchers, notably Adrian, Erianger, and Gasser (Finger, 2000) discovered electrical pulses traveling through brain cells. Today, it is common knowledge that motor and cognitive functions rely on a combined electro-chemical neural process. Neurons, the "network communicators" inside the brain, transmit messages to one another by sending electrical signals down the neuron's elongated axon. The electrical signal triggers the release of neurotransmitters which carry chemical messages to adjoining neurons along a neural circuit.

Phrenology

Throughout the 19th and 20th centuries, a steadily growing list of investigations provided increasingly greater detail on how particular brain regions were responsible for producing specific skills, behaviors, and human faculties. The most reliable theories were born in the error-riddled pseudo science of Phrenology.

Phrenology was the result of work by an Austrian medical student, Franz Joseph Gall, who identified twenty-seven personal traits, talents and predilections. He selected a corresponding brain region for each trait. The fundamental premise of phrenology, the "brainchild" of Gall, was that (a) the human mind was indeed like other muscles in the body, and (b) exercising any of the twenty-seven personality traits, skills or mental functions would produce a corresponding increase in the quantity of brain tissue in that brain area.

According to Gall's theory, high levels of activity would eventually cause the brain tissue to swell just beneath the surface of the cranium, producing detectable bumps on the skull of an individual. These excessively used regions would ultimately alter the external contours of the cranium. Affluent members of society and prominent businessmen had their skulls measured and analyzed. Favorable phrenology results were illustrated on personal busts which they proudly displayed in homes and offices. The crowns of walking canes, designed to impress others, were similarly adorned with detailed reproductions of a phrenologist's assessments.

The primary sources for Gall's research were sculptors' busts of highly accomplished individuals and the cadavers of criminals and the mentally insane. There was, however, nothing scientific about phrenology. Among the earliest clues rendering the very foundation of phrenology questionable was the fact that few "experts" ever reached the same scientific conclusions, generating growing and well-founded suspicions. Detractors, including French experimentalist Marie-Jean-Pierre Flourens, referred to phrenology as "Bumpology."

Nevertheless, phrenology was wildly popular, widely accepted, and extremely profitable during the 1800's and the early 1900's, both in Europe and the United States, despite a) it's enormous methodological deficiencies, (b) its arbitrary selection of primary characteristics, and (c) its unscientific assumptions and conclusions. Few psychologically-based schemes have ever generated the level of attention or the revenues of phrenology during its heyday.

Although phrenology was completely incorrect with respect to its behavioral attributions, the theory serendipitously suggested that there were indeed structural, functional, and regional correlations in the human brain. The true legacy of Franz Joseph Gall and the theory of phrenology was setting the stage for more scientifically-based and dependable theories related to the localization of brain function.

The Localization of Function

Finger (2000) describes a series of experiments from the 19th and early 20th centuries which investigated functioning in mammalian brains. These experiments by Marie-Jean-Pierre Flourens, Hermann Munk, and John Hughlings Jackson ranged from examining which areas of the brain were responsible for coordinated voluntary movements to the specific effects of localized brain damage in the cerebrum, the spinal column, and the cerebellum.

In hundreds of well-documented experiments, Gustav Fritsch, Eduard von Hitzig, and David Ferrier selectively removed various parts of mammalian brains, producing focal lesions (precise regional brain damage) to study the responsibilities associated with particular areas of the cerebral cortex and the brain's sub-cortical structures. Their investigations included applying an electrical stimulation to one side of the brain to produce a response on the opposite side of the body (contralateral motor cortex). This principle turned out to be true for all mammals including human beings.

The systematic investigations of Paul Broca, a young French neurologist who worked with institutionalized stroke victims, helped to locate the region of the cerebral cortex that plays a central role in language production. In 1861 when one of his patients died, the autopsy showed a lesion in the area of the brain (the third gyrus of the pre-frontal cortex) known today as Broca's area.

Broca's research paved the way for subsequent research by a German neurologist, Carl Wernicke. While also working with institutionalized patients, Wernicke located the cortical region most responsible for understanding language. The location that converts speech sounds into meaningful language is known today as Wernicke's area, positioned adjacent to the primary auditory cortex. Combined, Broca's area and Wernicke's area are considered the region of the brain where critical human language functions reside.

Surgeon Wilder Penfield is credited with making a significant contribution in charting the motor cortex. In the mid-20th century, Penfield startled the world by performing brain surgery on conscious patients who could report sensations or memories, depending on the precise areas of the brain that were being electrically stimulated by Penfield. Mapping the "homunculus," which represents the sensory and motor cortices, was possible only through the daring surgical procedures first attempted by Penfield.

Until the latter half of the 20th Century, most discoveries about the human brain came by way of research opportunities that were made available only through human tragedies.

Mass Action

Memory storage in the cerebral cortex mystified brain researchers including Karl Spenser Lashley, who probed into the localization of memory (Kandel, Schwartz, & Jessell, 2000). Using rats as his original subjects, Lashley researched the specific neural components of memory. Like Flourens, Fritsch, and his numerous predecessors, Lashley tested maze-running memories in rats while gradually eliminating selective portions of the rats' cerebral cortex.

Lashley correctly theorized that no single place exists where all memories are stored in the brain. Instead, he found numerous components and connections that make specific, but simultaneous (parallel), contributions to the final memory product. Lashley authored a theory of "mass action" describing how the entire brain, as opposed to a particular module or neuronal component, is responsible for both memory and all other complex behaviors.

In the 20th century, the work of Lashley and others challenged the concept that a single area is exclusively responsible for a given cognitive function. Researchers, including Nobel prize-wining researcher Ramon y Cajal, began promoting the idea of a more holistic brain. Their theory described a rich variety of neurons arranged into functional networks that execute a specific action, although just one key brain region plays a central role in the final collective action. For example, the discrete elements of language are processed in the brain's left hemisphere, while the right hemisphere provides meaning, humor and the Gestalt. These elements and functions, in tandem, make a process such as reading comprehension possible. Like a symphony orchestra, there are numerous contributors to the final single product—the observable manifestations of complex thinking and behavior.

Concluding Thoughts

The collective work of scientists pursuing answers to the question "how does the brain work?" has led us to the contemporary field of cognitive neuroscience, how the brain learns. We have moved from a cardiocentric view of learning to contemporary theories of learning based on sound, reproducible scientific findings. Although erroneous notions (phrenology, electricity, cardiocentrism, etc.) may have impeded the general public's understanding of human behavior, early scientists were taking the first steps on the way to today's insights into the learning brain. We now understand that the body-brain connection governs behavior, with the brain as the conductor of the cerebral symphony.

Table 1   ***The Evolution of Concepts***
                 Driving Early Neuroscience

Incas	Earliest evidence of brain surgery.
Egyptians	Viewed the brain as an insignificant organ.
Hippocrates	Thought the brain influenced behavior and intelligence.
Aristotle	Supported the cardiocentric view of the church.
Galvani	Demonstrated that electricity had a role in neural functioning.
Phrenology	A serendipitous pseudoscience that reduced the human brain to a limited number of "faculties" housed in precise regions.
Localization of function	Key regions of the brain are central to behavioral functioning.
Mass action	The entire brain (not just specific modules) is responsible for orchestrating all complex human behavior.

References

Bishop, W. J. (1995). *The early history of surgery.* New York: Barnes & Noble.

Finger, S. (2000). *Minds behind the brain: A history of the pioneers and their discoveries.* Oxford: Oxford University Press.

Kandel, E. R., Schwartz, J. H., & Jessell, T. M. (2000). *Principles of neural science.* New York: McGraw-Hill.

Thorne, M. T., & Henley, T. B. (2001). *Connections in the history and systems of psychology.* Boston: Houghton Mifflin.

Wesson, K. A. (2001). What recent research tells us about learning. *Independent School Magazine, 61,* 58-71.

From Synapses to Learning — Understanding Brain Processes

by Kenneth Wesson, San Jose/Evergreen Community College District

The human brain has been quite secretive about the operating principles and prioritizing strategies that it uses to organize, store, and retrieve information. Although neuroscientists know far more today about how the brain grows, changes, and develops, the long journey to fully understanding the human mind is barely under way. The most recent advances in neuroscience and brain-imaging, however, permit us to conduct a much closer and more informed examination of the structural, chemical and functional aspects of just *how* the human brain actually works.

The most effective methods of pedagogy (the theory and practices related to teaching the young learner) and andragogy (specialized strategies for adult learning) should not take place without an understanding of the human brain. Educators should be intimately familiar with important principles of cognitive science. If they are not, they will try to force 4.2 million years of brain development into the practices and assumptions of the 140 year-old model used in contemporary education. This model is not working well and warrants the exchange of older components with more brain-considerate practices.

A Macroscopic View of the Human Brain

The human nervous system is composed of two major parts—the *peripheral nervous system* and the *central nervous system*. The sensory receptors of the peripheral nervous system (PNS) receive stimulation from the outside environment and forward it to the central nervous system (CNS) where the incoming information is systematically processed. The CNS is made up of the spinal column and the brain, forming the central command station. Typically, the spinal column sends information to the brain for sophisticated processing, decision-making, and other deliberate actions.

The human brain is divided into three interconnected anatomical components or regions—the *cerebrum*, the *cerebellum* and the *brain stem*.

The cerebrum makes up the largest part of the brain and has changed very little over the past 130,000 years. It is divided into distinctive asymmetrical left and right hemispheres which oversee specialized brain functions. The most striking feature of the cerebral cortex, home to all higher human brain processes, is the wrinkled two-millimeter thick surface of the cortex. These folds permit the fixed interior volume of the human skull to house a fairly large amount of cortical surface tissue. If the human brain were "unfolded" and stretched out, its surface area would be approximately the size of a desktop (2.5 square feet or 2500 cm²). Six paper-like layers are neatly stacked together as the arranging principle underlying the cerebral cortex. The interactions of these neuron-rich layers foster the biological basis of all human behavior.

Normal human brains are lopsided, the left hemisphere being generally larger and more active than the right.

Paula Tallal, of Rutgers University, and others have noted that whenever the two sides more closely approximate symmetry, the left hemisphere is usually somewhat underpowered. This symmetry is suspected as a leading cause in incidences of male language deficits and disorders. In females, the left hemisphere is typically larger than the right. However, the male brain appears slightly more symmetrical, as the average male brain comes equipped with a larger right hemisphere than would be typically found in females.

The second brain component is the cerebellum, a cauliflower-like structure that sits immediately behind and below the cerebrum. The cerebellum facilitates tasks such as balance, movement and coordinating the body's senses. It orchestrates many of our automatic behaviors. Every time we get up in the morning, stand at a podium, or walk down the corridor, our cerebellum deserves an immense amount of the credit. The third brain component, the brain stem, controls the body's vital processes (heart rate, breathing, etc.).

Three Critically Important Brain Processes

Synaptic proliferation

Neurons constitute the basic building blocks of the mammalian brain and the spinal column, transmitting commands and information to muscles and glands and other neurons. Neurons are separated by *synapses*, the microscopic contiguous gaps between brain cells. These junctions form tiny synaptic gaps that are approximately 0.02 microns (8 millionths of an inch) wide. Synapses link the cells inside the brain through the process of *synaptogenesis*, which organizes those cells into the all-important operating circuits. Following birth, most new synapses come by way of new experiences or through pre-programmed genetic instructions. Billions of synapses form in utero, while trillions more will develop as a result of postnatal stimulation and learning experiences. Physically, synaptic connections build the neural networks that make the vast catalogue of human behaviors and all learning possible.

During *neurogenesis*, there is an overproduction of synapses, *synaptic proliferation,* which does more than just ensure that enough connections are available for the awakening body to "turn on" and operate the heartbeat, muscles, lungs, eyes, and other organs. This connectivity excess provides its owner with a neural insurance policy for the young brain. Synaptic proliferation guarantees that the young brain is capable of adapting to virtually any environment into which a child is born. Thanks to this overabundance of synapses, the growing brain eventually has the neurological wherewithal to blend itself comfortably and seamlessly with a specific external environment.

A toddler's brain has twice as many synapses among its 100 billion neurons as the brain of a fully matured adult. His brain also operates at 225% the adult's energy levels. This is a result of "wiring up" the neurons in his developing brain as he responds to the local environment. A single neuron may have as many as 50,000 *dendrites*, which are the short threadlike fibers that extend themselves away from the neuron's cell body in order to receive electro-chemical signals from other active neurons. With new learning, dendrites respond by reaching out to one another in an elaborate branching process that bonds previously unaligned brain cells with one another, thereby creating complex neural circuits. The outcome of these extensions *(dendritic trees)* is the formation of dense neural forests *(dendritic density)* that are the neurophysiological byproducts of learning within a stimulating environment. Synapses reach the peak of their postnatal production levels at approximately the fifth year of life, during kindergarten.

Neurons communicate when the chemical composition of a *pre-synaptic* or sending neuron's cell body is modified by the in-coming chemical signals transmitted from another neuron. An electrical impulse or signal is sent down a neuron's axis at speeds up to 270 miles per hour. The electrical impulse causes the tiny chemical reservoirs (synaptic vesicles) at the end of the neuron to rupture, sending neurotransmitters, the chemical messengers, across the synaptic gap to the *post-synaptic* or receiving neuron. The molecules released by one neuron traverse

the synaptic gap and bind at the receptor sites of the next neuron, causing a chain reaction along a neural pathway. Neurons send messages to and from one another permitting vital information to travel from one part of the brain/body to another. These chemical communications sponsor all human thinking, learning and behavior.

Neurotransmitters can be excitatory or inhibitory, sending signals for cells to communicate or explicitly instructing them *not to* communicate at all. When the lightning-fast electrical impulse flashes and prompts the discharge of its chemicals, the process mimics the sequence of events taking place during a winter's storm, giving rise to a unique neurophysiological interpretation of the term *brain-storm*.

Neural pruning

All efficient organisms need a method by which unused or damaged cells are discarded. Even healthy brain cells will perish through *neural pruning* if they fail to find a job to perform during the critical or sensitive periods of development. There is no neuronal welfare agency operating inside the cranium that is designed to sustain non-working neurons. Controlled cell death, *apoptosis*, is a merciless process that occurs by *necrosis,* deliberately killing brain cells. Each neuron must connect to a functioning neural pathway or it will be subjected to programmed neural cell death.

As the twentieth week of fetal life approaches, nearly 200 billion neurons have already been created. During the third trimester, the process of neural pruning occurs to reduce the dangerously excessive numbers of brain cells. Following this pruning period, only fifty percent of the original cells remain. The surviving 100 billion neurons are ready for assignment to a functional neural circuit at birth. The appropriate number of postnatal neurons is critical in forming highly functional networks that will aid the growth and development of a thriving newborn.

Following birth, billions of synapses are nourished while others are eliminated over time, changing the nature of *how* information gets communicated among the neurons. Future cortical adaptations will come by way of further synaptic pruning to reduce the numbers of synapses. Some neural pruning results from healthy environmental stimulation, while the balance typically occurs from the lack of stimulation, poor nutrition, reduced physical activity, minimal social interaction, or abuse. Under these adverse conditions, there will often be (1) a decrease in neurons, (2) a correlative decrease in the thickness of the cerebral cortex, (3) lower numbers of synapses, and (4) accelerated synaptic pruning in cases of extreme impoverishment.

Apoptosis, the regulated destruction of a cell, may be triggered by either external or internal factors. If a child does not hear words by the age of nine or ten, he or she will encounter enormous difficulty in ever learning to speak any language and may not speak at all. The lack of any visual stimuli reaching the visual cortex for processing during infancy can rob a healthy eye of the gift of sight. Only those brain cells with important linkages to active neural circuits are permitted to survive the ongoing pruning-down and linking-up processes to which most neural networks are subjected.

Cortical Plasticity

Brain growth and development are immensely influenced by *cortical plasticity,* the brain's remarkable ability to allow different regions, structures, and connections to change physically as a consequence of experiences and input from the external environment. Connections among the one trillion brain cells are consistently impacted by incidents processed consciously and unconsciously. Synapses are also changed by experience as the neurotransmitters released by a particular synapse are modifiable. Neurons release multiple neurotransmitters and/or neuromodulators and are capable of altering their chemical messages over time.

As new behaviors, skills, and learning tendencies emerge, there are neurophysiological correlates representing each of them. They largely determine how much cortical growth will take place, in what regions the growth will take place, and where subsequent development will occur or become delayed. The very architecture of each human brain is adjusted as a result of all newly acquired competencies. Even the corpus callosum, the neural super highway connecting the two corrugated hemispheres of the brain, is modified by skills development. There is recent evidence that literacy can impact the thickness of this connecting structure. These processes pave the way for a uniquely structured brain within every individual.

Neurophysiological processing does not change from the early pre-school learner to adults, although the brain continues to reorganize itself. Neural patterns with the greatest likelihood of developing elaborate neural connections are those emerging talents and capabilities that (1) an individual devotes significant amounts of time and attention to, (2) those that have key emotional, personal or survival value, and (3) those that are often repeated. These neural patterns are nearly impervious to destruction short of disease or regional brain trauma. Substantial amounts of nerve growth factors, vital for brain cell growth and survival, are regularly carried to these essential regions and circuits, assuring their continued healthy existence.

A high level of dense neural connections represents one's acquired knowledge, abilities, and skills. Thus, it is easier to expand concept understanding by tapping into the existing fertile networks that correspond to a person's strengths. A comparatively large number of neural pathways must exist to support proficiency or mastery. These efficient circuits are subsequently used in skill enhancement or refinement and play a vital role in the comprehension of newer, but related, concepts or events. We use stored knowledge bases to dissect, process, and make sense of novel experiences in order to understand and act upon them. The absence of an adequate neuronal investment is often responsible for talent deficits, conceptual misunderstandings, and learning difficulties.

Unfortunately, schools spend an inordinate amount of time identifying academic deficiencies and devote even greater numbers of hours to subsequent remediation by concentrating on a student's problem areas. Instead, schools should focus on further cultivation of a student's strengths which indicate the presence of healthy, efficiently working neural networks. This focus will result in far more cognitive resources to work with in any plan for performance improvements or skill level enhancements in the classroom. A disproportionate level of cortical real estate gets devoted to proficient skills, and an abundance of complex learning networks are dedicated to supporting those manifested competencies.

There is an interesting method by which the brain oversees and modifies the distribution of cortical real estate. There are more neurons and more cortical space designated for certain areas of the body. The undemocratic assignment of cortical territories is initially based on the degree of importance that a given area of the body has in relation to one's survival. However, the brain is not a static organ. Later, the allocations are, gradually but regularly, reallocated as a consequence of *how frequently* a particular area of the brain is used, how its related functions are valued in one's specific environment, and its importance to survival and emotional fulfillment.

For example, if a region of the motor cortex responsible precisely for right-hand movement in a human is damaged, the use of his right hand will be substantially diminished or lost completely. Conversely, if movement in the right hand is grossly limited, the cortical regions of the brain responsible for movement in that hand will atrophy. Interestingly, the cortical areas representing the opposite (left) hand will often *increase* to compensate for the loss of right-hand use, and a marked improvement in left-hand dexterity and proficiency will take place. This phenomenon, *compensatory hypertrophy*, is how all brains physically reorganize themselves in such a way that the opposite hand (or leg, or eye, etc.) gets stronger as a response to the lost service of its counterpart. Thus the brain adapts to life's changing conditions—always looking towards survival and the future.

Many "facts" in the field of neuroscience continue to change based on new research. It is now a widely accepted fact that neural plasticity takes place in the sensory-motor cortex at all ages, and the brain continues to re-wire itself as it responds to new input, permitting new learning, new skills, and new behaviors throughout a lifetime. There is also evidence that the human brain actually does grow *new* neurons in the cerebral cortex throughout our lives. This discovery has forced us to re-write our "brain facts," and it is revolutionizing our understanding of postnatal neural regeneration.

Concluding Thoughts

Through its elastic power to undergo physical and chemical changes as it responds to its environment, the human brain may either expand or shrink based on the quality, quantity, and richness of the learning experiences encountered. Neural plasticity is one of the chief cognitive enablers of all formal education benefits. The latest findings in neuroscience leave little doubt that the human brain grows and feeds on consistently healthy stimulation. Unfortunately, the very same healthy cerebral cortex can also exercise its flexible nature and be molded by severely negative events. But when the brain is (1) properly nourished, and (2) allowed to grow and develop in a positive, reassuring, and encouraging atmosphere, it responds favorably to that rich supportive environment. Under these conditions the probability of maximizing the brain's remarkable potential increases dramatically. When the opposite conditions prevail (whether early in life, later in life, or consistently during one's life), there is a frightful price to pay. The neurophysiological costs are seldom cheap and rarely short term.

With the latest discoveries, the human brain is regaining its rightful place as the centerpiece for all conversations about learning. Understanding how the brain processes information can assist kindergarten through university-level educators in crafting instructional practices and designing classroom environments that are consistent with the brain's natural inclinations for learning. Devising methodologies that accommodate the brain's processing techniques will enhance the prospects of academic success for any student, regardless of age.

References

Black, I. (2002). *The changing brain: Alzheimer's disease and advances in neuroscience.* Oxford, UK: Oxford University Press.

Byrnes, J. (2001). *Minds, brains, and learning: Understanding the psychological and educational relevance of neuroscientific research.* New York: The Guilford Press.

Clifton, D. O., & Anderson, E. (2002). *StrengthsQuest: Discover and develop your strengths in academics, career, and beyond.* Princeton, NJ: The Gallup Organization.

Goldblum, N. (2001). *The brain-shaped mind: What the brain can tell us about the mind.* Cambridge, UK: Cambridge University Press.

LeDoux, J. (2002). *Synaptic self: How our brains become who we are.* New York: Viking Press.

Kotulak, R. (1996). *Inside the Brain: Revolutionary discoveries of how the mind works.* Kansas City, MO: Andrews McMeeley Publishing.

Kovalik, S. J., & Olsen, K. D. (2001). *Exceeding expectations: A user's guided to implementing brain research in the classroom.* Covington, WA: Susan Kovalik & Associates, Inc.

Nathanielsz, P. (2001). *The prenatal prescription.* New York: Harper Collins Publishers.

Bloom's Taxonomy — Expanding its Meaning

by Paula Bobrowski, SUNY College at Oswego

Faculty Development Series

This module expands the usefulness of Bloom's taxonomy beyond its original intent of clarifying educational objectives to help faculty prepare better-designed courses, achieve more student-centered implementation, and establish outcomes-oriented evaluation criteria. Bloom's taxonomy is explored from a historical perspective and examined for its applications in process education. A Pacific Crest adaptation of Bloom includes five different "levels of learner knowledge." Each of these is defined and illustrated with key words and questions for use in designing curriculum and instructional materials.

Significance and a Description of Bloom's Taxonomy

Educational objectives indicate what students should attend to and put effort into learning; they are "explicit formulations of the ways in which students are expected to be changed by the educative process" (Bloom, 1956, p. 26). Bloom's taxonomy provides a well-accepted pedagogical framework for classifying vast numbers of educational objectives into useful structures. Benjamin Bloom's pioneering work on learning was initiated in 1948, when he headed a team of educators and psychologists investigating three major learning domains: cognitive, affective, and psychomotor. Over the last half-century, the theoretical framework produced by this team has facilitated analyses of learning objectives classification, criteria for performance-based learning, and levels of mastery in learning (Simon, 2000).

To the extent that the goal of education is the diffusion of knowledge through learning, a description of Bloom's taxonomy represents a seminal work in developing and implementing high quality instruction. There are six different levels of factual and conceptual knowledge progressing from elementary to complex in the cognitive domain. The levels include knowledge, comprehension, application, analysis, synthesis and evaluation as demonstrated in Table 1.

Evolution of Bloom's Taxonomy

Over the past 40 years Bloom's work has been translated into more than twenty languages and has provided a basis for test design and curriculum development. Many modern interpretations of Bloom's taxonomy are found in the literature. Recently Anderson and Krathwohl (2001) expanded the single dimension of the original taxonomy into a two-dimensional framework consisting of factual/conceptual knowledge and cognitive processes. High quality educational objectives combine both elements as seen in the following example: "The student will learn to distinguish (cognitive process) among confederate, federal, and unitary systems of government (knowledge)." Apple and Krumsieg (2001) clarified some of

Table 1   **Description of Bloom's Taxonomy of Educational Objectives**

> **Knowledge** of terminology, specific facts, ways and means of dealing with specifics, conventions, trends and sequences, classifications and categories, criteria, methodology, abstractions in a field, principles and generalizations, and theoretical structures.
>
> **Comprehension** in translation, interpretation, extrapolation.
>
> **Application** of concepts in the use of abstraction in particular and in concrete situations.
>
> **Analysis** of elements, relationships, and organizational principles.
>
> **Synthesis** of ideas in the production of unique communications and plans.
>
> **Evaluation** leading to judgments about the value of materials and methods for given purposes.

the definitions found in the original taxonomy by viewing it in terms of transferable knowledge that progress in complexity through the six levels. The most basic level, using Apple and Krumsieg's labels, involves information (knowledge in Bloom), followed by knowledge (comprehension), knowledge skill (application), problem solution (analysis), new knowledge (synthesis), and finally evaluation (peer-reviewed knowledge). This model of learning has supported development of a learning process methodology for efficiently and effectively advancing the level of student knowledge (Krumsieg and Baehr, 2000).

There is also extensive educational research aimed at moving beyond the cognitive domain in formal education by focusing more attention on the affective and psychomotor domains (Shank, 1994; Tinto, 1993; Bobrowski and Molinari, 1992). Although this is not the focus of this module, it is important to be aware of these developments. Tinto (1993) and Shank (1994) have published significant works in this area, arguing that academics must change the way teaching is performed, by paying special attention to the intra-personal and inter-personal contexts of learning. Tinto examined learning communities in depth, while Shank promotes the perspectives that the only way learning occurs is "by doing."

Levels of Learner Knowledge

Bloom's taxonomy has been adapted and transformed by Apple and Krumsieg (2001). According to their Learning Process Methodology, five levels of learner knowledge are observable in college classrooms. These are defined in Table 2 and represent increasing complexity in the way students formulate, connect, and present their thoughts. Information acquisition occupies the lowest level and is typified by memorization of information. Conceptual Understanding represents the next higher level and is the result of combining information elements to achieve understanding and meaning. Application is the ability to apply knowledge in a new context. Working Expertise is the ability to understand the logical constructs and apply knowledge without expert prompting. Research is the goal of graduate study and is the ability to create novel discoveries from basic elements and logical constructs. The "Evaluation Level" in Bloom is considered separately as part of assessment, which can take place at any level.

Brookfield (1987) argues that learning is promoted by asking questions that challenge students' understanding at the appropriate level. Good questions can also stimulate students' curiosity and allow the teacher to probe current understanding as well as assess effectiveness of past instructional activities (Eggen and Kauchak, 1988). Inquiry as a learning method requires active participation both by the students and teachers. For this reason, Table 2 integrates Barton's (1997) hierarchy of critical thinking questions with the levels of learner knowledge. The combination of these two concepts creates a useful tool for teachers to use in classroom applications. It provides key words and questions that are appropriate to ask students at each level of learning and demonstrates the link with Blooms taxonomy of educational objectives.

Classroom Application

Questions and key words in Table 2 can be used to set performance criteria for learning activities, to verify prerequisite knowledge, and to measure achievement against learning outcomes. Prompts in this table also provide guidance on which thinking skills are most developmentally appropriate for cultivation and suggest possible avenues to challenge students at the next higher-level of knowledge. For example, introducing methodologies and studying their elements at levels one and two is a particularly effective way to accelerate the creation of transferable knowledge at levels three and four.

Fundamental to all aspects of educational processes is the knowledge that results from experiencing applications of knowledge. To gain additional insights into the connections between the learning process and Bloom's taxonomy, see the modules *Classification of Learning Skills*, and *Learning Processes through the Use of Methodologies*. These modules clarify the role of educators in building stronger transferable skills at increasingly higher levels of learning.

Concluding Thoughts

This module provides an overview of Bloom's taxonomy and subsequent work, which offers a rational and holistic approach to defining *academic quality*. Table 2 is designed around Bloom's levels of knowledge model to help illuminate appropriate teaching/learning processes for different performance capabilities and to focus attention on the detail that is expected of students in order to accomplish learning objectives. The related components of the table will help faculty ask better questions, define clearer expectations for assignments, and compose exam questions that are matched to specific levels of learning outcomes.

References

Anderson, L. W., & Krathwohl, D. R. (Eds.). (2001). *A taxonomy for learning, teaching and assessing.* New York: Longman.

Apple, D. K., & Krumsieg, K. (2001). *Teaching institute handbook.* Lisle, IL: Pacific Crest.

Barton, L. G. (1997). *Quick flip questions for critical thinking.* San Clemente, CA: Edupress.

Bloom, B. S., Engelhart, M. D., Furst, E. J., Hill, W. H., & Krathwohl, D. R. (1956). *Taxonomy of educational objectives: The classification of educational goals. Handbook 1: Cognitive domain.* New York: David McKay.

Bobrowski, P. E., & Molinari J. (2000) Empirical study of simulation: The pedagogical value in marketing education? *Journal of Business Education, 1,* 80-96.

(continued)

Table 2

Levels of Learner Knowledge

Level I Information Bloom's Level 1: Knowledge	— The learner can talk about a concept, process, tool, or context in words and can provide definitions or descriptions. — The learner has some sense of what information is relevant and not relevant. — Limited comprehension makes it difficult for the learner to carry on an extensive dialog.
Key Words	*who, what, where, when, which, find, choose, define, list, label, show, spell, match name, tell, recall, select, organize, outline*
Questions	What is…? Where is…? When did…? What facts or ideas show…? Who were the main…? Which one…? Can you recall…? Can you select…? Can you list the three …? Who was…?
Level II Conceptual Understanding Bloom's Level 2: Comprehension	— The learner is able to construct a strong degree of comprehension about a concept, process, tool, or context. — Information and relationships have been processed so that the learner can construct an appropriate model in his/her mind pertaining to the particular item of knowledge. — The learner can process answers to critical inquiry questions and articulate what he or she understands as well as what remains confusing. — The learner also has some understanding as to how the item of knowledge is linked to other forms within his/her knowledge base.
Key Words	*relate, compare, contrast, how, illustrate, translate, infer, demonstrate, summarize, interpret, show, explain, classify, select, rephrase, why*
Questions	How did… happen? How would you compare or contrast…? How would you describe…? How would you summarize…? How would you show an understanding of…? How would you state or interpret in your own words…? What is the main idea of…? Which statements support…? Can you explain what is happening…? What is meant by…?
Level III Application Bloom's Level 3: Application	— The learner has the skill to apply and transfer the particular item of knowledge to different situations and contexts. — The learner has taken the time to generalize the knowledge to determine ways to apply it, testing boundaries and linkages to other information. — The learner can recognize new contexts and situations to skillfully make use of this knowledge. — The learner is able to teach this knowledge to others; "knowing he or she knows" rather than just "thinking he or she knows."
Key Words	*apply, construct, make use of, plan, build, develop, model, interview, experiment with, identify*
Questions	How would you use…? What examples can you find to…? What would result if…? Can you make use of the knowledge to…? What approach would you use to…? How would you apply what you learned to develop…? What other way would you plan to…? How would you structure an argument to show…? What elements would you choose to change…? What questions would you ask in an interview with…?

table continues on next page

Table 2 (continued)

Level IV Working Expertise Bloom's Levels 4 & 5: Analysis and Synthesis	— The learner has the ability to integrate application knowledge with other skills to perform in an expert fashion. — The learner is able to solve complex problems by applying and generalizing multiple concepts, processes, and tools to produce a quality problem solution. — The learner has the ability to produce a general problem solution which can be reused and transferred to similar situations with minimal adjustments. — Defines an "expert" in a particular field.
Key Words	*analyze, dissect, inspect, model relationships, divide, simplify, solve, test for, connects function, making and testing assumptions, examine, applying a design, creating themes, improving*
Questions	What motive is there...? What inference can you make...? What ideas justify...? What conclusions can you draw...? What changes would you make to solve...? What is the function of...? What would happen if...? How would you solve....using what you've learned....? Can you propose an alternative...? Can you construct a model that would change...?
Level V Research Bloom's Level 6: Evaluation	— The learner has innovative expertise which can be used to develop new understanding. — Through the use of lateral thinking the learner makes new linkages among concepts and problem solutions, which have not been seen before. — The learner knows how to validate and test his/her assumptions and hypotheses to build reliability in the knowledge structure. — The learner knows how to communicate this understanding to others so it can be shared as common knowledge.
Key Words	*theorize, design, formulate, discover, make up, hypothesize, prove, disprove, invent, create an original work*
Questions	Can you formulate a theory for...? How feasible is the plan to...? Can you think of an original way to ....? Can you create a design to...? How would you prove...? Disprove...? Can you predict the outcome if...? Should you accept the hypothesis that...? Can you publish your findings...? How would you estimate the results for...? What is necessary to discover...?

References *(continued)*

Braxton, J. M., & Nordvall, R. C. (1996). An alternative definition of quality of undergraduate college education: Toward usable knowledge for improvement. *Journal of Higher Education, 67,* 483-498.

Brookfield, S. (1987). *Developing critical thinkers: Challenging adults to explore alternative ways of thinking and acting.* San Francisco: Jossey Bass.

Eggen, P., & Kauchak D. (1988). *Strategies for teachers.* Englewood Cliffs, NJ: Prentice-Hall.

Krumsieg, K., & Baehr, M. (2000). *Foundations of learning.* (3rd ed.). Lisle, IL: Pacific Crest.

Simon, N. (2000). Managing the CI department: Cognition and performance. *Competitive Intelligence Magazine, 3,* 53-56.

Tinto, V. (1993). *Leaving college: Rethinking the causes and cures of student attrition.* Chicago: University of Chicago Press.

Overview of Critical Thinking

by Paula E. Bobrowski, SUNY College at Oswego and Pamela L. Cox, SUNY College at Oswego

Critical thinking is the ability to use and manage intelligence and skills for tasks or goals across all four domains of knowledge. Although many strategies and models of critical thinking are available to educators and learners, the degree of success in application usually depends upon the user's level of awareness of what strategy will fit what problem in what context. This module examines definitions of critical thinking and addresses questions such as whether it is beneficial to provide specific training in such skills. Examination of the meta-cognitive skills required for critical thinking within any discipline is followed by a set of tactics for enhancing critical thinking performance in the classroom. A holistic rubric for assessing critical thinking skills concludes the module.

Importance of Critical Thinking

There is an intimate interrelation between knowledge and thinking. Knowing that something is so is not simply a matter of believing that it is so; knowledge is justified belief. There are general as well as domain-specific standards for the assessment of thinking. Critical thinking supports the creation of new knowledge, or improved quality of knowledge, in any field or application (Paul, 2003).

Edward DeBono (1995) believes that, "…many highly intelligent people are bad thinkers. Intelligence is like the horsepower of a car. A powerful car has the potential to drive at any speed. But you can have a powerful car and drive it badly" (p. 8). He discusses how critical thinking is the "driving skill" with which each individual manages his or her intelligence. Critical thinking activities need to be sequenced in ways that elevate learner use *(see Elevating Knowledge from Level 1 to Level 3)*, and learners must be meta-cognitively aware of how their use of critical thinking strategies fits requirements of different problems.

Critical thinking is also connected with employers' desires for college graduates who are curious, analytical, reflective thinkers and problem-solvers, and critical thinking skills are vital for maintaining effective workplace relationships. Employers are demanding their new hires have more than textbook knowledge and technical skills; they want problem solvers who can be effective in today's work environments (Pithers & Soden, 2000). McEwen (1994) presents additional evidence that the ability to think critically is important to job performance and career mobility.

Despite the importance of critical thinking, many educational analysts and researchers report that students leave higher education with an underdeveloped ability to think critically because undergraduate curricula in general do not emphasize the teaching of these skills. Critical thinking must be based on articulated intellectual standards that are used to assess quality of critical thinking in context.

Multiple Definitions of Critical Thinking

Glock (1987) argues that there is *no* definitive way to define critical thinking and that some of the differences between definitions cannot easily be reconciled. Some authorities contend that critical thinking is a way to think about subject matter; others think it is a kind of knowledge or a skill or a habit; still others insist that it is a way of thinking about thinking. Glock describes critical thinking as diverse cognitive processes and associated attitudes critical to intelligent action in diverse situations and fields that can be improved by instruction and conscious effort. A Chaffee College (1988) statement about critical thinking asserts that it cannot be reduced to *one skill* or even to *one set* of skills because it involves intelligent actions that enable students to comprehend, communicate, or engage in problem-solving or strategy-building techniques. In other words, critical thinking plays a strong role in problem solving, in synthesizing of hypotheses or alternative solution strategies, and in assessing quality or success of results. Because it is used in these, as well as in many other uses and contexts, critical thinking remains difficult to fully capture in any one definition. It also cannot easily be broken into standard steps in a process methodology as has been done in the *Learning Process Methodology*. Educators such as Paul (2003) help to guide use of critical thinking by providing frameworks, models, and criteria as flexible, universal tools.

Practices for Critical Thinking

Across universities and disciplines, one finds multiple definitions for critical thinking and different approaches to practicing it. In reality, critical thinking "looks" different in different contexts because the focus must be adapted for each purpose. The following definition is broad in scope; rather than being prescriptive, it embraces multiple approaches to critical thinking.

Critical thinking can be significantly enhanced or diminished by social, affective, psychomotor, and spiritual influences. Critical thinking includes a healthy skepticism about sources of information, one's internal thinking and self-assessment processes, and the quality of the resulting solutions, conclusions, decisions, or new knowledge. It fundamentally involves meta-cognition: i.e., thinking about thinking while thinking. A quality learning environment

Critical thinking is the synergistic process of constructing and applying knowledge efficiently and effectively to select strong, relevant logic and evidence; to draw accurate conclusions from logic and data, to make strategic decisions; to support problem solving, and to produce higher quality insights in scholarship and research processes, i.e., in the creation of new knowledge. Critical thinking spans skill areas such as information processing, reasoning, analysis, synthesis, and creativity. It is the ability to make linkages across contexts with thoughtful purpose and flexibility.

*(see **Overview of Creating a Quality Learning Environment**)* enhances learners' growth in critical thinking by providing instruction, facilitation, and assessment that lead to increasing internalization of the processes involved *(see **Learning Processes through the Use of Methodologies**).*

Critical Thinking in the Curriculum

"To define critical thinking skills is to restate many of the traditional goals of higher education; that is, to provide a program of instruction that enables students to become independent learners, to be capable of exercising informed and balanced judgment, and to contribute as mature citizens in their society" (Chaffee College, 1988).

The notion of teaching critical thinking in separate "add-on" courses has been largely abandoned because of evidence that these skills can be developed more effectively when integrated with the teaching/learning of subject-matter content (Bonnett, 1995). Deepened understanding and use of disciplinary or professional knowledge occurs when students explore multiple perspectives, ask penetrating questions, critique the quality of their available information, and link their own and other's information to relevant questions (Langer, 1997).

Paul (2003) argues that instruction in all subjects should result in the progressive disciplining of the mind with respect to the capacity and disposition to think critically within that domain and should contribute to a self-chosen commitment to a life of intellectual and moral integrity. Hence, instruction in science should lead to disciplined scientific thinking; instruction in history should lead to disciplined historical thinking; and in a parallel manner to every discipline.

The exploration of what critical thinking is suggests some principles relevant to its integration into curricula and programs. Educators most clearly agree that high-quality critical thinking requires the development or growth in the following skills and capabilities:

1. Identifying and pursuing questions, problems, and assumptions through research (Ennis, 1993; Pithers & Soden, 2000).

2. Presenting evidence to support arguments persuasively (Pithers & Soden, 2000).

3. Judging the validity of data, evidence, arguments, and assumptions (Ennis, 1993).

4. Proposing opinions as alternatives to one's own opinions and know what evidence would support these opinions (Pithers & Soden, 2000).

5. Recognizing errors in thinking so as to make reasonable decisions about what one believes (Norris & Ennis, 1989).

6. Applying critical thinking skills within the discipline and generalizing one's thinking to life outside the discipline (Cowan, 1994).

Designing critical thinking into courses and curricula requires considering how to evaluate the effectiveness of the desired learning outcomes, e.g., those in the above list, and to incorporating measurement tools into curriculum and activity designs (Critical Thinking Consortium, 2003).

Tools and Techniques for Facilitating Critical Thinking Skills

To enhance how critical thinking is addressed in any curriculum, the following examples and tools are useful starting points. The central logic of each discipline must be considered in deciding which tools and techniques can best help students to successfully confront the core components of any discipline. For example, integrating critical thinking with writing is one technique that is relevant to all disciplines.

Tsui (1999), in her extensive study of the integration of critical thinking in college classrooms, found that the development of these skills is linked to an emphasis on writing and rewriting, classroom discussion, and active, hands-on learning. Writing assignments must emphasize analysis, synthesis, and evaluation *(see **Bloom's Taxonomy—Expanding its Meaning**).* Rewriting should be encouraged to stimulate students to think more deeply about what they have written and to utilize feedback to improve it *(see **Overview of Assessment**).* Tsui (p. 26) argues, "Writing is likely to exert a greater impact on student cognitive outcomes when it is stressed throughout the curriculum....Success in fostering critical thinking is in part contingent upon the degree to which faculty utilize writing assignments in their teaching." She recommends that instructors rely less on lecturing and emphasize classroom discussion because students are more likely to comprehend and retain ideas when they participate in a discussion or debate on them (p. 29). Shaw (2000) similarly recommends the development of student's reading, writing, and presentation skills as a way to stimulate critical thinking in the classroom.

Strum (1998) describes how a well-designed "first-year experience" can provide a stimulating environment for intellectual growth, a firm grounding in inquiry-based learning, and improved communication of information and ideas. Pacific Crest's *Foundation of Learning* curriculum is another example of how to facilitate the growth of basic critical thinking skills.

Some classroom facilitation *(see Overview of Facilitation)* tactics that encourage active learning are presented in Table 1.

Assessing Critical Thinking Performance

Educators (e.g., Tsui, 1999), recommend that writing assignments involving critical thinking should include a step-wise assessment process to raise the level of performance. The *Bellevue University Critical Thinking Rubric* provides a holistic way to set standards for assessment of critical thinking *(see Fundamentals of Rubrics)* and also can be used to analyze classroom activities and assignments for potential for raising the level of critical thinking performance.

Concluding Thoughts

Because multiple definitions of critical thinking are necessary to address the wide range of applications across disciplines and problem contexts, special care must be exercised in building models to fit specific uses of critical thinking. The meta-cognitive requirements for both learners and educators are substantial, which means that gaining expertise in critical thinking will take extended practice and assessment across many contexts and problem types. Educators often use written and oral responses to evaluate student critical thinking, so special attention has been paid in this module to how to enhance such responses. The limited clarity of definition and the many strategies needed to enhance critical thinking make it a continuing challenge, but clearly critical thinking is at the heart of the higher-education experience.

References

Bonnett, M. (1995). Teaching thinking and the sanctity of content. *Journal of Philosophy of Education, 29,* 295-309.

Cowan, J. (June, 1994). Research into student learning—Yes, but by whom? In Tornkvist, S. (Ed.), *Teaching Science and Technology at Tertiary Level: Proceedings of the Conference of Royal Swedish Academy of Engineering Sciences* (p. 51-59). Stockholm, Sweden.

Table 1   **Tactics that Encourage Active Learning**
Source: Critical Thinking Consortium

Use the following tactics during class to ensure that students are actively engaged in thinking about the content. When students do not know when they will be called on, they are much more likely to remain alert and engaged in the learning process. Students should be routinely called upon to:

1. Summarize or put into their own words what the teacher or another student has said.

2. Elaborate on what they have said.

3. Relate the issue or content to their own knowledge and experience.

4. Give examples to clarify or support what others have said.

5. Make connections between related concepts.

6. Restate the instructions or assignment in their own words.

7. State the question at issue.

8. Describe to what extent their point of view on the issue is different from or similar to the point of view of the instructor, other students, the author, etc.

9. Write down the most pressing questions on their minds. The instructor then uses the above tactics to help students reason through the questions.

10. Discuss any of the above with partners and then participate in a group discussion facilitated by the instructor.

Critical Thinking Consortium (2003). Foundation for Critical Thinking (n.d.). *Tactics that encourage active learning*. Retrieved November 17, 2003 from <http://www.criticalthinging.org/K12/k12class/tactics.html>

DeBono, E. (1995). *Mind power*. NY: Dorling Kindersley Publishing, Inc.

Education Policies Committee. (1997/1998). Critical thinking skills in the college curriculum. Retrieved November 17, 2003 from Chaffee College <http://www.academicsenate.cc.ca.us/Publications/Papers/Downloads/CriticalThinkingSkills.doc>

Ennis, R. H. (1993). Critical thinking assessment. *Theory into Practice, 32,* 179-186.

Glock, N. C. (1987). *Public Policy and Educational Reform*. Paper presented at the 1987 Fall Conference of the Academic Senate of the California Community Colleges, Los Angeles.

Langer, E. (1997). *The power of mindful learning*. New York: Addison-Wesley.

McEwen, B. (November/December, 1994). Teaching critical thinking skills in business education. *Journal of Education for Business, 70,* 99-103.

continued

Paul, R. (2003). National Council for Excellence in Critical Thinking. *Draft statement of principles.* Retrieved November 17, 2003 <http://www.criticalthinking.org/ncect.html>

Paul, R., & Elder, L. (1999). *Miniature guide to critical thinking.* Dillon Beach, CA: Foundation for Critical Thinking.

Pithers, R. T., & Soden, R. (2000). Critical thinking in education: A review. *Educational Research, 42,* 3, 237-249.

Shaw, V. N. (2000). Reading, presentation, and writing skills in content courses. *College teaching, 47,* 4, 153-157.

Strum K. S. (1998). *Reinventing undergraduate education: A blueprint for America's Universities.* Presented at the 1998 AACSP Continuous Improvement Symposium, Dallas, TX.

Tsui, L. (1999, November), *Critical thinking inside college classrooms: Evidence from four institutional case studies.* Presented at the 24th Annual Meeting of the Association for the Study of Higher Education, San Antonio, TX.

Table 2   **Bellevue University Critical Thinking Rubric***

5. Master Thinker

a. Risks trying to answer intractable, perplexing, and complicated questions.

b. Reinterprets the history of thought in the relevant area.

c. Redefines the assumptions and premises from which all valid reasoning must proceed in the relevant area.

d. Creates an original synthesis of diverse perspectives.

e. Reaches conclusions that others acknowledge as foundational for all subsequent reasoning in the relevant area.

4. Advanced Thinker

a. Tackles questions that arise from profound cognitive dissonance.

b. Challenges conventional, received wisdom responsibly in search of new perspectives.

c. Reaches original conclusions through creative and imaginative lines of reasoning; draws vital distinctions and creates new categories.

d. Internalizes contrary positions; makes the arguments of opponents for them.

e. Actively cooperates or collaborates with others to test and expand the universe of knowledge.

3. Practicing Thinker

a. Seeks the most reasonable among the several reasonable answers possible.

b. Delays judgment until a substantial range of relevant information is known and assessed; able to admit ignorance or inability to resolve an issue on the basis of evidence.

c. Constructs sound lines of reasoning based on a fair and accurate assessment of the evidence; examines his or her own presuppositions and assumptions.

d. Demonstrates full understanding of opposing positions.

e. Is aware that the community of skillful thinkers will value attempt to be reasonable and fair.

2. Beginning Thinker

a. Seeks to justify his or her position rationally, but with a limited sense of perspective.

b. Selects information that supports a particular perspective.

c. Reasons on the basis of personal goals or needs with limited assessment of personal bias.

d. Discounts opposing points of view after only cursory examination.

e. Believes that, given the same evidence, most people would arrive at the same conclusions.

1. Egocentric Thinker

a. Assumes that knowledge is perceived by everyone from a purely personal perspective.

b. Accepts limited facts and information as adequate for present purposes.

c. Uses reasoning only within the context of communicating personal opinions as valid.

d. Takes no interest in alternative points of view and is unaware of their significance.

e. Believes merely stating his or her position is persuasive in itself.

*Based, in part, on Paul & Elder (1999)

Profile of a Quality Learner

by Carol Nancarrow, Sinclair Community College

Quality learners exhibit definable behaviors that optimize their learning. These behaviors can be classified and assessed. By recognizing these behaviors, learners and faculty members can work toward the ideal behaviors, and instructors can design instruction to foster growth in learning behaviors. Quality learning behavior is a good predictor of successful performance.

The Learner's Affect

Very young children are motivated to learn as a survival instinct. The joy of persevering through failure to reach success shines on every toddler's face as he or she takes first steps or puts together a simple puzzle. A quality learner brings that same joy to calculus formulas, Russian grammar, or medieval art. Almost everyone can recount experiences where very bright youths with great potential have not achieved their potential through formal education. In other cases, students overcome significant barriers to achievement. The difference may well lie in their learning behaviors. The good news is that quality learning behavior can be defined, measured, and taught.

What is a Quality Learner?

Quality learners are intrinsically motivated to learn and grow, with or without external rewards. Learning is as natural and necessary a part of life for them as is breathing. Learning is an integral part of daily experience, not limited to external structures, such as classes. Quality learners consciously use the opportunities in their personal experiences and learning environments to meet their personal learning objectives. They exhibit learning behaviors that lead to success.

Learning behaviors are more complex than the learning skills as introduced in the module *Classification of Learning Skills*. A learning behavior involves choosing and using appropriate combinations of learning skills from across domains, aligning cognitive skills with values and attitudes. For the quality learner, learning behaviors are fully integrated into the personality and routine of daily life. One can possess a skill and not use that skill in a given context. A quality learner not only has a high level of learning skill, but also chooses and uses the right combinations of skills in the right circumstances.

Research Studies on Learning Behavior

Educational psychologists have researched behavior that affects learning, though there is still much work to do in this area. Albert Bandura's cognitive theory of personality asserts that individuals can and do control their own motivation and thought processes, using observation and self-assessment to change their behaviors to accomplish their own goals. Bandura uses the term "self-regulation" to refer to the individual's cognitive control of his or her behavior. He found that "self-efficacy,"—belief in one's own ability—is a greater influence on self-regulated behavior than any other single factor (1999). In a sense, the "Little Engine That Could" is right about the power of belief in one's ability to succeed. By implication, then, successful learners believe they can succeed, motivate themselves, and see failure as a temporary condition that they can overcome. Those who lack adequate self-efficacy belief are likely to attribute failure to outside forces beyond their control.

Researchers have found a positive correlation between student's ability to self-regulate and academic success. In this context, self-regulation refers to "active management by students of their motivations, cognitions, and behaviors to achieve their goals" (Garavilia and Gredler 2002). Self-regulation occurs in the planning, performance, and assessment phases of a process (Zimmerman 2002). While Bandura's concept of self-regulation is largely cognitive and involves such specific learning skills as rehearsal, self-testing, and active reading, Schapiro and Livingstone have extended the concept to include "dynamic self-regulation." Dynamic self-regulation is a way of being that provides a drive for learning, including curiosity, enthusiasm, and risk-taking. Dynamic self-regulated students look for new applications and connections, persist despite difficulties, and apply learning in new contexts (2000).

The best news from these studies is that self-regulation can be consciously embedded in courses and produce significant growth in these essential behaviors (Garavilia and Gredler 2002; Schapiro and Livingstone 2000; Zimmerman 2002). Schapiro and Livingstone, for example, studied 342 students before and after the course Methods of Inquiry for freshmen and sophomores and found significant growth in dynamic self-regulation, with nearly half of the low-quadrant students moving into the high quadrant by the end of the course (2000).

Table 1   **Profile of a Quality Learner**

Information Processing	• Accesses information quickly. • Distinguishes relevant from irrelevant information. • Engages all senses to access information. • Uses appropriate tools and technology. • Learns new tools and technologies to facilitate learning. • Attributes results to causation.
Values	• Creates a vision for life and articulates goals and objectives with measurable outcomes. • Uses learning to clarify personal value system. • Responds ethically to strong challenges. • Respects and values the difficulty and importance of learning. • Approaches tasks with confidence in his or her ability to master new learning.
Learning Skills	• Takes responsibility for his or her own learning process. • Demonstrates interest, motivation, and desire to seek out new information, concepts, and challenges. • Validates his or her own growth and understanding, without the need for outside affirmation. • Actively seeks out ways to improve his or her learning skills. • Integrates new concepts within a general systems perspective and grasps instructions as part of a logical structure. • Develops stronger learning skills by modeling the learning process itself.
Interpersonal Skills	• Interacts easily with other people on productive teams. • Seeks models and mentors to enhance learning. • Understands and appreciates the values of others.
Intrapersonal Skills	• Focuses energy on the task at hand. • Perseveres through difficult tasks, making good decisions about when to seek help. • Judiciously takes risks to advance personal growth. • Uses failure as a frequent and productive road to success. • Prioritizes tasks to effectively live a balanced life. • Assesses goals and makes appropriate changes to reach goals. • Structures physical and social environment to facilitate goal attainment.
Thinking Skills	• Uses inquiry, questioning, and critical thinking to gain new insights. • Clarifies, validates, and assesses understanding of concepts. • Applies concepts to new contexts. • Transfers and synthesizes concepts to solve problems. • Continually assesses his or her own performance. • Clarifies, validates, and asseses understanding of concepts. • Takes corrective actions to get "on track" when the planned path is blocked or ineffective.

This research has two crucial implications for college faculty. The first is that teaching students how to be successful learners is both possible and essential. The second is that faculty need to assess the student's beliefs about learning and their self-efficacy to help them realize their greatest potential as lifelong learners.

Profile of a Quality Learner

Through ten years of evolution, Pacific Crest has developed a profile that provides a description of a quality learner based on positive behaviors in the learning function. The advantage of such a description is that faculty can have students use these behaviors to set goals for improving their own learning behavior, and thereby grow in taking responsibility for their own success and growth as learners. In Table 1, the areas of learner performance include information processing, values, learning skills, interpersonal skills, intrapersonal skills, and thinking skills. These common behaviors in quality learners are valued and appreciated by students and faculty.

Attempts at Measuring Changes in Learning Behavior

Barbara A. Schaefer and Paul A. McDermott (1999) have been studying the correlations of learning behaviors and scholastic achievement in K-12 students, using a Learning Behavior Scale designed for teacher observations. They report that learning behavior accounts for about one-third of the variance in scholastic performance as measured by grades. They conclude, "Given roughly comparable levels of ability, students trained in optimum levels of learning behavior will have a distinct advantage over those not so trained" (1999). It follows, then, that educators at all levels should be teaching learners how to learn and rewarding learning behaviors that are associated with high achievement. However, for the purpose of defining optimum learner behaviors, the Learning Behavior Scale used by Schaefer and McDermott is limited by its focus on negative behaviors, such as "reluctance to tackle new tasks" and "unwilling to accept needed help," and by its design for use with young students.

Two other instruments are also in use to measure some of the behaviors of learners. The Learning and Study Strategies Inventory (LASSI) from the University of Texas, Austin, is a self-report questionnaire that measures motivation, self-management, and cognitive strategies. The cognitive scales for LASSI derive from the premise that successful learning depends upon integrating new learning into the framework of previous knowledge. This is consistent with current explanations of how people learn in such books as *How People Learn* (Bransford, Brown, Cocking 2000).

The National Center for Research in Improving Post-Secondary Teaching and Learning at the University of Michigan produced another instrument, the Motivated Strategies for Learning Questionnaire (MSLQ). Also self-reporting, the MSLQ measures goal-orientation, intrinsic/extrinsic motivation, and task value. It also includes a measure of the students' belief that they are in control of their own learning and their level of expectation of success.

LASSI and MSLQ are useful instruments for measuring subsets of the learning behaviors in the Profile and could be repeated to show growth over time. Neither of them gives a complete picture of the complex set of behaviors of the quality learner.

Strategies for Using the Profile to Improve Learner Performance

Choosing and Assessing Learning Outcomes

Recognizing the ideal qualities of a learner is helpful for choosing a portion of the learning outcomes to embed in a course design to move toward the ideal and for assessing the targeted areas of improvement. Learning environments can be designed to provide learners opportunities to move toward the ideal and to leverage the qualities that are already present in learners to maximize learning in any discipline. These qualities can be used to assess learning performance across disciplines.

The Learning-to-Learn Camp Experience

Students are very receptive to information about how to learn better. In a Learning-to-Learn Camp, students are introduced to the profile of a quality learner, and quality learning behavior is deliberately rewarded and reinforced. Students use self-assessment to deliberately set achievable goals for improving their learning behavior in the short term and set long-term goals in their Life Vision Portfolios. After three years of experience with Learning-to-Learn Camps at Sinclair Community College, the students who attended the week-long camps are continuing to show significantly better success in college, as measured in grade averages and in retention, than the general college population.

The activities in a Learning-to-Learn Camp address all the areas in the Profile. With respect to information processing, learners are introduced to tools such as the Reading Log and methodologies such as the Writing Process Methodology. With respect to values, the Life Vision Portfolio fosters an examination of personal values and goals through writing a personal mission statement. One of many examples of learning skills is the use of a self-paced computer-based math review in which students validate their own learning. Instruction in the interpersonal skills includes using roles in cooperative learning and using coaches and assistant coaches as mentors. Activities in time management and a climate of challenging performance develop intrapersonal skills. Many camp activities, ranging from problem-solving challenges to games, incorporate thinking skills.

Advancing Learner Performance through Instruction Design

Student-centered learning activities give students opportunities to improve their skills as learners. Students who are working in groups on guided discovery activities with critical thinking questions will have to practice skills in all five areas. When designing a guided-inquiry activity, specific learning skills can be selected and improved in the context of an activity. Building specific learning skills enables students to improve their learning behaviors. When students are aware that it is largely their own learning behavior that determines how successful they will be at learning, they are motivated to grow their own skills.

Concluding Thoughts

Yogi Berra said, "You've got to be very careful if you don't know where you are going, because you might not get there." The module *Profile of the Quality Learner* maps out a destination for a life-long journey. Along with their students, quality faculty members are on this journey as mentors, travel guides, and fellow learners. True learning is not, then, measured in credits and grade points and diplomas, but in the practice of continuing to move toward the ideal.

References

Bandura, A. (1999). The cognitive theory of personality. In D. Cervone and Y. Shoda, (Eds.). *The coherence of personality: Social-cognitive bases of consistency, variability, and organization.* New York: Guilford Press.

Bransford, J. D., Brown, A. L., & Cocking, R. R., (Eds.) (2000). *How people learn: Brain, mind, experience, and school.* National Research Council. Washington, DC: National Academy Press.

Garavalie, L. S., & Gredler M. E. (2002). Prior achievement, aptitude, and use of learning strategies as predictors of college student achievement in college. *Student Journal, 36,* 616-25.

Garcia, T., & Pintrich, P. R. (1996). Assessing student's motivation and learning strategies in the classroom context: The motivated strategies for learning questionnaire. In M. Birenbaum and F. Dochy, (Eds.) *Alternatives in assessment of achievements, learning processes and prior knowledge.* Boston: Kluwer Academic.

Krumsieg, K., & Baehr, M. (2000) *Foundations of learning* (3rd ed.). Lisle, IL: Pacific Crest.

McDermot, P. (1999). National scales of differential learning behaviors among American children and adolescents. *School Psychology Review, 28,* 280-91.

Schaefer, B. A., & McDermott, P. A. (1999). Learning behavior and intelligence as explanations for children's scholastic achievement. *Journal of School Psychology, 37,* 299-313.

Schapiro, S. R., & Livingstone, J. A. (2000). Dynamic self-regulation: The driving force behind academic achievement. *Innovative Higher Education, 25* (1) 59-76.

Weinstein, C. E., Zimmermann, S. A., & Palmer, D. R. (1988). Assessing learning strategies: The design and development of the LASSI. In C. E. Weinstein & E. T. Goetz, (Eds.) *Learning and study strategies: Issues in assessment, instruction, and evaluation.* San Diego, CA: Academic Press.

Zimmerman, B. J. (2002). Becoming a self-regulated learner: An overview. *Theory into Practice, 41.*

Elevating Knowledge from Level 1 to Level 3

by Kip Nygren, United States Military Academy at West Point

The process of elevating knowledge from level 1 to level 3 can be described in terms of Bloom's taxonomy beginning with level 1, terminology and related information; moving to level 2, comprehension and understanding; and then to level 3, transferring and applying knowledge in new contexts. A methodology for elevating knowledge provides guidance to faculty as they facilitate the movement of learners to level 3. A special matrix provides descriptions of how five types of knowledge vary as learners progress up the levels. Ten specific techniques are discussed for helping to improve learning performance. Finally, the focus of inquiry for each level, from both faculty and student perspectives, is provided to guide formulation of critical thinking questions relevant for learning and assessment at each of the three levels of knowledge construction.

Transferable Knowledge

"All new learning involves transfer." (Bransford 2000). This statement defines the essence of education as opposed to training. A broad education allows individuals to effectively respond in new situations instead of simply being trained to perform explicit tasks in consistent conditions. Because transfer of learning involves generalizing concepts that can be applied in a variety of contexts, measuring students' ability to transfer knowledge represents a true indication of the quality of a learning experience. However, the ability to transfer knowledge (level 3) first requires preparation for learning and the attainment of knowledge levels 1 and 2. *(see Bloom's Taxonomy—Expanding its Meaning.)* The focus of this module is on the elevation of knowledge from level 1 to level 3.

Preparation for Learning

Before knowledge can transfer successfully, educators must initially establish favorable conditions to support the attainment of knowledge at level 3. Three steps of the Learning Process Methodology (Why, Orientation, and Prerequisites) do just that *(see The Learning Process Methodology).* With both the student and teacher primed for success, pre-class preparation can proceed. Level-one knowledge (information) requires obtaining definitions, facts and information. The LPM divides this acquisition into two steps—Vocabulary and Information.

The next goal is to obtain level 2 knowledge which is comprehending and understanding the concept. At this level, the learner should be able to pose and attempt to answer critical thinking questions as well as explain the topic effectively to someone else. Successful attainment of level 3 means the ability to generalize the new knowledge and transfer it for application in new contexts.

Elevating Knowledge

Knowledge is not dispensed by a teacher; rather it is constructed by the student. As previously discussed, the construction of knowledge requires a firm informational base which the facilitator can validate with directed questions. The foundation also requires cornerstones of prior knowledge to which the new knowledge can be connected. Understanding and comprehension of new knowledge emanates directly from the student's pre-existing knowledge. Teachers can help connect new concepts to the preconceptions that learners bring to the classroom with level 2 (comprehension) links that correct, enlarge and organize the knowledge structure. Once this model of the new concept is in place, its reliability can be assessed with critical thinking questions that focus on the assumptions or logic of the model.

The new knowledge structure or model can be turned into "knowledge skill" for the learner through problem solving in a familiar context to reinforce the framework and to initiate the generalization and transfer of the knowledge. The knowledge expertise becomes stronger as the learner transfers and applies the skill in slightly different contexts. Eventually the learner will be able to use the skill in a completely new and unfamiliar context with the teacher acting as a consultant. The ultimate achievement of knowledge level 3 occurs when the new knowledge can be generalized to apply in any appropriate context. Shown below is a formal methodology for elevating knowledge to level 3.

Methodology for Elevating Knowledge

1. Establish and solidify an informational base. (level 1)

2. Identify the cornerstones for the knowledge. Knowledge is built upon a foundation of prior knowledge. (level 2)

3. Identify the key inquiry questions for comprehension and key issues for constructing the knowledge. (level 2)

4. With the framework in place, test the conditions of the structure—use critical thinking to explore the assumptions or logic of the knowledge model. (level 2)

5. Transfer and apply the knowledge to a familiar context to enrich understanding. (low level 3) *continued*

6. Transfer and apply the knowledge to another context that is similar. (low level 3)

7. Transfer and apply the knowledge to a context that is some distance from the original context. (level 3)

8. Transfer and apply the knowledge in a totally unfamiliar context with teacher as consultant. (level 3)

9. Independently make a generalization of the new knowledge. (level 4)

Simple Example of the Methodology – Change Car Oil

1. **Establish and solidify an informational base.** Identify the tools required to change the oil, three possible facilities at which to change the oil, how to add and measure engine oil, the type of oil filter required, etc.

2. **Identify the cornerstones for the knowledge.** Determine the student's prior knowledge about the need for lubricants in any type of machine, the basics of engine oil systems, and the purpose of the filter.

3. **Identify the key inquiry questions for comprehension.** What are the reasons for the order of the steps involved in changing oil? What would happen if a particular step were left out of the process? What happens to the old oil?

4. **With the framework in place, test the conditions of the structure.** What will happen if there is less oil than recommended? More oil?

5. **Find a context you are familiar with and transfer and apply the knowledge to that context.** Demonstrate or explain in detail how to change the oil in your own car.

6. **Transfer and apply the knowledge to another context that is similar.** Demonstrate or explain in detail how to change the oil in a pickup truck.

7. **Make a transfer and apply the knowledge to a context that is some distance from the original context.** Demonstrate or explain in detail how to change the oil in a riding lawn mower.

8. **Pick a totally unfamiliar context and, transfer and apply the knowledge with teacher as consultant.** Explain why there is no need to change the oil in a chain saw engine.

9. **Generalize the new knowledge.** Discuss possible means to provide lubrication in a wide range of machines from air-conditioner units to turbo-jet engines.

Knowledge Forms

Knowledge forms include the following:

- **Concept** — an idea that represents a set of relationships.

- **Process** — a sequence of activities.
- **Tool** — an instrument to accomplish a task.
- **Context** — conditions relevant to performance.
- **Way of Being** — a set of attitudes, actions, or values.

The summary table on the next page illustrates levels of knowledge based upon each of the knowledge forms from level 0.5 to level 4.

The Most Difficult Steps in the Method

1. *The Pre-Learning phase*, steps 1-5 in the LPM. The learner and the teacher must reach agreement on why the learning objective is important, gain mutual orientation to the learning issues and context, and resolve any barriers related to prerequisite knowledge.

2. *Achievement of level 2.* Comprehension of the principles, theories, and models that have developed in an area of knowledge facilitates and enhances successful application. However, learners vary in their needs for exposure to simple application opportunities as a way to clarify their level 2 understanding and to motivate deepening of their understanding. Authentic learning is a constructivist education theory that emphasizes the connection of content to learner experience as the solution to achievement of usable level 2 knowledge.

3. *Generalization of the knowledge* to higher level 3. Extensive experience with using knowledge in varied contexts is the basis for increasingly sophisticated internalization of both theoretical knowledge and problem solving expertise.

Techniques for Helping Learners Improve

Make sure that the cornerstones to learning are in place. There are many ways to make sure that these foundational blocks of information are in place. Ask directed questions that require linking personal experiences, prior knowledge, informational readings, or key aspects of examples that are provided. Use a reading log or reading quiz to assess the preparation for learning. Before starting a discussion in class, ask a couple of inquiry questions or have certain students summarize what they understand currently about the concept. Finally, ask the students to inventory what they think the key cornerstones are for this learning exercise.

Connect to previous knowledge by inventorying learner experience. Conduct a learning assessment survey to determine the level of student content knowledge, create tasks that will reveal preconceptions, and facilitate the organization of preexisting understanding into conceptual frameworks.

Table 1   **Levels of Knowledge Across Knowledge Forms**

Levels of Knowledge	All Forms of Knowledge	Concept	Process	Tool	Context	Way of Being
Level 0.5 Pre-Informational (Language)	Structures in own words.	Knows meaning of words.	Follows grammar and syntax.	Recognizes key symbols.	Decodes acronyms.	Recognizes critical words within disciplines and cultures.
Level 1.0 Informational	Memorizes and repeats information. Assesses quality of data.	States facts and definitions. Draws pictures and diagrams.	Describes steps in a method. Initiates use of a method.	Uses step-by-step instructions. Recognizes purpose and intended use.	Repeats stories. Describes events.	Follows social conventions. Responds to traditions.
Level 2.0 Comprehension & Understanding (Why, significance, implications, meaning)	Produces good inquiry questions. Analyzes models effectively.	Articulates understanding. Describes relationships and linkages.	Rationalizes use of steps. Knows criteria for quality outcomes.	Comprehends instruction sets. Knows full range of use.	Condenses a story. Shares implications.	Values well-reasoned arguments. Values accepted models and theories.
Level 3.0 Application, low level	Applies in a familiar context. Analyzes results.	Combines with related ideas. Links principles and practices.	Documents use of steps in a method. Links the steps together.	Locates instructions. Uses basic features and functions.	Requires guidance. Able to serve as a trainee.	Notices mismatch of a principle and its application. Accepts expected results.
Level 3.5 Application, high level	Applies in new contexts. Synthesizes new solutions.	Clarifies boundaries. Understands why a theory will work.	Internalizes use of a theory. Links methods together.	Uses hidden features. Adapts instructions.	Responds to subtle prompts. Able to serve as a teacher.	Harmonizes theory with practice. Collaborates for better outcomes.
Level 4.0 Working Knowledge (Expertise)	Efficient in producing quality results. Proposes criteria to define quality.	Evaluates alternative models. Generalizes understanding.	Customizes methods for future use. Monitors quality in real time.	Debugs fluently. Creates customized tools.	Provides prompts for others. Serves as a consultant.	Serves as a role model. Interacts with a larger community.

Discipline the process. The most efficient and least frustrating learning occurs with a step-by-step process. This can be facilitated by testing understanding and having learners involved in judging when they can move to the next step. Be prepared to move back a level if the knowledge structure is not strong enough to add the next "floor."

Test the robustness of understanding with critical thinking questions. Step 4 requires that learners test the quality of their own learning before going to application. Is the frame strong enough?

Develop learner participation. Ultimately, students must take control of their own learning and monitor their own learning progress *(see Persistence Log)*. A powerful metacognitive strategy is to have students track their progress and use reflective essays to ask and answer their own critical thinking questions.

Understand the knowledge forms. Use the descriptions and guidance in Table 2 to clarify and assess the learner's current understanding and performance level.

Generalize understanding. Ask students to write a paragraph about applying their knowledge in a familiar context, then in another paragraph about applying their knowledge in an unfamiliar context, and finally in a paragraph that generalizes their knowledge by describing similarities and differences between the two contexts and identifying common underlying principles.

Transfer knowledge to a far context. For example, after learning about using oil in a familiar context like a door hinge and a slightly less familiar context like a riding lawn mower, discuss how an airplane pilot might monitor the oil in the jet engines of an airliner to ensure the engines operate efficiently in flight.

Motivate and inspire the learner while maintaining high expectations. Persistence to achieve learning goals is clearly affected by the student's motivation to learn. Pay close attention to the first five steps in the LPM to assure that the learner understands and is committed to the learning challenge. Assess prerequisite knowledge (step 5 in the LPM) to ensure that the challenge is at the proper level of difficulty to avoid frustration that is beyond what is optimal for motivation. The usefulness of the knowledge skill and the social consequences of application are strong contributors to motivation. Authentic problems that are important in the learner's community or related to career goals are particularly stimulating.

Control the affective domain to limit frustration. As discussed above, learner frustration, or boredom, is closely related to the level of the learning challenge and the time allotted to achieve it. Increase or decrease the allocated time to adjust the challenge. Let students assess the class at periodic intervals throughout the semester to vent frustrations and suggest changes to improve future performance.

Essential Inquiry at Each Step

Critical thinking requires a healthy level of skepticism and a set of skills to validate sources of information, to monitor one's internal process, and to assess the quality of the resulting solutions, conclusions, decisions, or new knowledge. Critical thinking questions are central to the validation of new knowledge and can be differentiated as to the level of difficulty in both formulation and response. The scale below, which is based on the first three levels of Bloom's taxonomy, provides examples of the role inquiry plays in the achievement of knowledge levels.

Level 1 – Informational

1. Inquiring about a specific fact in a specific context.

2. Inquiring about a set of facts related to a specific area.

Level 2 – Comprehension & Understanding

3. Asking about an inferential relationship between two facts or a fact to a context.

4. Determining the similarities or differences between things.

5. Asking to clarify the meaning of implicit relationships in a model or a discussion.

6. Making indirect inferences and connections (e.g. $a \rightarrow b$ and $b \rightarrow c$ then $a \rightarrow c$).

Level 3 – Application

7. Identifying explicit assumptions when using this knowledge.

8. Identifying implicit assumptions when using this knowledge in varying contexts.

Concluding Thoughts

Faculty and students can become familiar with knowledge elevation for each type of knowledge by using the descriptors and suggestions in Table 1. Consistent use of the Methodology for Elevating Knowledge will enable them to facilitate learning that leads to level 3. The concepts, processes, and tools described in this module will help faculty and students cooperate in raising learning levels to achieve the fundamental aim of education: the transfer and application of knowledge in new, unfamiliar contexts.

Reference

Authentic Learning. (n.d.). Retrieved July 12, 2004 from <http://chd.gse.gmu.edu/immersion/knowledgebase/strategies/constructivism/authentic.htm> (George Mason University Instructional Technology Program).

Bransford, J. D., & Brown, A. L., et al. (2000). *How people learn: Brain, mind, experience, and school*. Washington, DC: National Academy Press.

Developing Working Expertise (Level 4 Knowledge)

by Kip P. Nygren, United States Military Academy at West Point

Faculty in many kinds of programs, especially those designed for professional careers, need to articulate outcomes and curriculum features that will produce Level 4 knowledge, also referred to as working expertise. Failure to do so results in graduates with knowledge deficiencies that impede successful practice in work settings. Developing higher-level knowledge requires careful instructional design to build both learner capacity for handling more interacting elements of knowledge and learner ability to transfer knowledge to multiple contexts. This module includes a description of Level 4 knowledge, a profile of the characteristics of Level 4 learners, and an educational model for developing Level 4 knowledge that is theoretically sound and also practical for the classroom educator. A basic assumption is that learning performance assessment and evaluation *(see **Distinctions between Assessment and Evaluation**)* must be based on clear understanding of a learner's problem solving capacity in relation to the complexity of the problems and contexts involved in learning experiences, whether in the classroom or in life situations.

Characteristics of Level 4 Knowledge and Level 4 Learners

The original resource for defining levels of knowledge is Bloom (1956). However, Pacific Crest's adaptation of Bloom's taxonomy introduces changes in the levels beyond Level 3, "application," by using new terminology that emphasizes a problem solving and research focus *(see **Bloom's Taxonomy—Expanding its Meaning**)*. In Pacific Crest's adaptation, Level 3 remains similar to Bloom's application level, i.e., ability to apply knowledge to new contexts. Level 4, working expertise, is defined as ability to use knowledge flexibly in multiple contexts. Level 5, "research," and Level 6, "assessment," are additional knowledge levels in the Pacific Crest model that enhance Bloom's "synthesis" and "evaluation" levels.

The most substantive indication of Level 4 knowledge is attainment of greater capacity for learning in complex contexts. Building knowledge beyond Level 3 includes careful regulation of problem complexity, usually by an expert, to provide predictable increases in difficulty and context that best meet the developmental needs of students.

Level 4 learners demonstrate the following characteristics:

- Ability to integrate knowledge with learning skills to produce a *generalized* problem solution.

- Ability to solve complex problems by applying many kinds of knowledge and integrating these with processes and tools to produce a *quality* problem solution.

- Ability to produce general solutions that can be reused and *transferred* to similar situations with minimal adjustments.

An "expert" in a particular field will demonstrate all of the above characteristics within his or her discipline or field. This expertise is the goal for most educational programs, but the concept of even more generalized types of expertise is valid as well. Some of the greatest minds have produced striking changes in the paradigms of knowledge used by experts across many fields.

A Model of Level 4, Working Knowledge

The capacity to solve problems at Level 4 is a complex topic that is receiving increasing amounts of attention from cognitive and educational researchers (e.g., Van Merriënboer et al., 2003; Renkl & Atkinson, 2003). In order to facilitate students' ability to achieve working expertise. Educators must recognize two significant interactions: (a) interdependence of problem complexity and learner capacity, and (b) interdependence of learner capacity and the problem context.

The level of difficulty of a problem solving task is a function of three major, interacting variables that are discussed in the following sections. These variables are:

- problem *complexity,*
- individual *learning capacity* of the learner, and
- problem *context.*

Problem Complexity and Levels of Difficulty

The complexity of a problem is characterized by the following criteria:
- number of knowledge items involved,
- number of schemas crossing discipline boundaries,
- how recently the knowledge area has been practiced,
- extent of direction or guidance provided,
- clarity of problem definition and of key issues,
- subtlety of the assumptions,
- availability of information or misinformation,
- resource constraints,
- difficulty in validating solutions either through estimation or alternative solutions,

- large scale integration of information,
- complexity of the relationships among aspects of the problem,
- ease of partitioning the problem into sub-problems,
- extent of history of efforts to resolve a problem, and
- level of emotional commitment or involvement.

Table 1 contains a classification of the levels of difficulty of problem solving tasks. This general rubric is a guide for selection or design of learning tasks that fit the current level of knowledge and experience of learners in a course or program.

Table 1

Levels of Difficulty of Problem Solving Tasks

Difficulty Level		Description
1	automatic	Performance of a task without thinking.
2	skill exercise	Consciously involved, but minimal challenge using specific knowledge.
3	problem solving	Challenging, but possible with current knowledge and skills through a strong problem solving approach.
4	research	Requires additional knowledge that currently doesn't exist within current learner capacity to effectively accomplish the task.
5	over-whelming	Cannot be accomplished without a significant increase in capacity, most likely by bringing in additional expertise.

Learner Capacity

Capacity refers to an individual's ability to solve problems. It represents a combination of traits, including the following:

- past problem solving and critical thinking experience,
- ability to apply a variety of concepts across boundaries,
- internalization of the problem solving process,
- portfolio of problem solving techniques and models,
- a personal attitude that includes persistence, coping, recovering from failure, etc.,
- adventurousness, including playfulness, creativity, open-mindedness, etc.,
- access to additional capacity as needed to expand beyond the learner's current limits,
- ability to remain objective, and
- understanding of the significance of the problem.

Problem Context

The context in which a problem is presented also influences the ability of a learner to address it. Bransford et al. (2000) comment that "Learners do not always relate the knowledge they possess to new tasks, despite its potential relevance" (p. 237). Therefore, a learner's familiarity with the context significantly enhances his or her ability to effectively and efficiently employ conceptual knowledge in concert with appropriate processes and tools to produce an intended outcome. Moving a problem to an unfamiliar context will make it more challenging for learners, even if no new tools are needed.

An example illustrates how perceptions of context can change problem solving success for learners at lower levels of capacity. Transferring the principles from a statics problem, initially illustrated with trusses, frames, and simple tools, to the skeletal system of a living organism is a change of context that many students will find disorienting at first. Once the transferable elements and principles are recognized, however, they are much more ready to apply the laws of mechanics to other situations. The educator's goal is to expand learner ability to recognize the universality of principles that first were learned and applied in a narrower context.

Interdependence of Problem Complexity and Learner Capacity

Figure 1 illustrates how, at a low level of problem complexity and high individual capacity, the problem solving experience is merely a skill exercise without any additional development towards working expertise. As the complexity of the situation increases, a boundary is crossed and a skill exercise develops into a problem solving situation that can assist in the development of working expertise. However, if the complexity continues to increase further, additional boundaries are crossed, and the problem solving challenge can become utterly overwhelming for the student and fruitless as a learning experience.

Figure 1

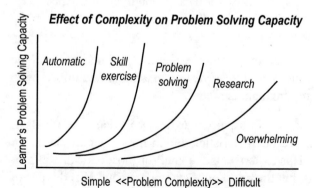

Effect of Complexity on Problem Solving Capacity

Interdependence of Learner Capacity and Problem Context

Figure 2 represents the interdependence between problem complexity (ranging from simple skill exercises to challenging research) and problem context. Although the success and speed of the solution (i.e., capacity) of a learner may be very strong for familiar contexts, the addition of more varied contexts will create challenges that will require substantial growth, especially in ability to integrate knowledge in more complex ways. Often, direct experience in varied contexts is the most effective way to facilitate growth from using mainly lower level knowledge to consistent use of Level 4 knowledge.

Figure 2

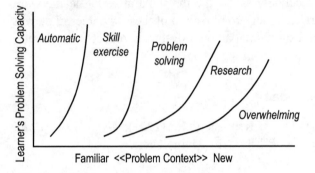

Effect of Context on Problem Solving Capacity

Generalizing Knowledge

A critical issue in Level 4 knowledge development is facilitation of the learning process so it will generalize across multiple contexts. Typically, learners first need to explore a series of examples in order to build a conceptual model that allows them to recognize that it is possible to apply knowledge in varied contexts. Experts must recognize when knowledge should not be transferred—even if it is technically possible.

Classroom Application

Educators can use the concepts and tools presented in this module to adjust the level of complexity in problem solving to provide sufficient challenge to elevate student knowledge to Level 4. By controlling the factors of problem complexity and context, educators can design the learning experience so that it is more than simply a skill exercise but not overwhelming for individual learners. A specific example follows to illustrate the ways in which a problem can be modified to adjust its level of complexity.

Problem Statement: *You are visiting a car dealership with a friend who is ready to purchase a car. The dealer and your friend have agreed upon a purchase price of $10,000. As your friend is completing the purchase agreement, the sales manager offers a choice between a $1,000 rebate and a 3.9% interest rate. Your friend asks for your expert problem solving assistance to decide which is the better choice. What advice would you give?*

This is a complex problem with some missing information that must be filled in by the learner. For example, some assumptions will have to be made about current and future inflation rates, the time period of the loan, how and when the interest charges are calculated, and the size of any initial payment. Complete solution of this problem for multiple situations covering a wide range of variables would be a significant undertaking. However, depending on the learning level and experience of the students, an instructor might make the following modifications to reduce the complexity, rendering the problem tractable for less experienced learners:

complex	Specify only the time period for the loan.
difficult	Provide an example of a comparison loan including a repayment schedule that has already been fully worked out
medium	Specify what comparison to calculate.
easy	Define the problem fully and ask for a computational solution.
simple	Define the problem, provide the formula, and ask for a computation.

Table 2   **Levels of Problem Complexity**

Complexity Level	Description
complicated	Minimal or no assumptions and constraints provided.
difficult	Provide an example of the solution to a similar problem.
medium	Specify the assumptions and constraints to be placed on the problem.
easy	Define the problem fully and ask for a solution.
simple	Define the problem, provide a detailed problem-solving method, and ask for a solution.

Table 2 suggests how the level of learning challenge can be adjusted to fit overall learner capacity. By starting with the most complex problem statement, and then simplifying it step by step, educators can guide learners to recognize how the difficulty level is being scaled back as more information and structure is provided. Students should be continuously challenged to work at the most difficult level they can manage.

Techniques for Shaping Growth to Level 4, Expert Knowledge

General techniques are offered below for facilitating the movement of learners to the level of working expertise:

1. **Generalize understanding**. Ask learners to write paragraphs about (a) applying their knowledge in a familiar context (e.g. current and voltage analysis of an electric circuit in a homework problem), (b) applying their knowledge in an unfamiliar context (e.g., flow and pressure analysis of a fluid piping network, or series and parallel combinations of mechanical spring elements), and (c) generalizing their knowledge by describing similarities and differences between the two contexts, identifying common underlying principles.

2. **Categorize problems**. Develop proficiency in problem classification by asking colleagues, mentors, and students to tackle problems in a variety of contexts. Have faculty and students rank these problems in level of difficulty, justifying their reasoning. This activity can give insight about the range of problem solving capacity present in the classroom and give students a better idea how a particular course builds toward the working expertise of a professional.

3. **Practice formulation and estimation**. Instead of having learners to invest time in implementing a single, formal solution, ask them to explain alternate solution paths and provide an estimate of the answer.

4. **Use self-assessment**. Grow self-awareness and self-control of problem solving skills by having learners document and assess their problem solving performance by identifying strengths, areas for improvement, and insights *(see **SII Method for Assessment Reporting**)*.

5. **Use a problem solving methodology**. Unquestionably, the best means for a learner to tackle a potentially overwhelming problem is through the use of a methodology. A solution is more likely when learners move through the necessary steps of a problem solving process.

6. **Assess use of problem solving methodology**. Examining how well a methodology for a complex process is employed, in contrast to evaluation of the solutions themselves, provides links with complementary teaching and learning processes such as information processing, critical thinking, teamwork, and communication.

7. **Validate problem solutions**. Ask students to write a paragraph describing how to validate their solutions. The paragraph should identify the most important assumption made and how the result might change if that assumption were changed.

8. **Holistic development**. In order to fully build Level 4 proficiency or working expertise, other aspects of personal development should also be considered. Particularly, enhancement of the learner's affective skills is needed to counter learner frustration as the complexity of the problem solving situation goes up and the comfort level decreases.

Concluding Thoughts

Educators who can recognize and assess Level 4 knowledge, i.e., working expertise, will be in a better position to create effective learning experiences to facilitate growth to this level. Three major variables interact to create the complexity involved in expert knowledge: learner capacity, problem complexity, and variations in context. If educators accurately assess the threshold at which learners are frustrated by any combination of these variables, they will avoid a substantial amount of the unproductive frustration that impedes learning.

References

Apple, D., & Krumsieg, K. (2001). *Teaching institute handbook*. Lisle, IL: Pacific Crest.

Bloom, B. ,et.al. (Eds.). (1956). *Taxonomy of educational objectives*. New York: D. McKay.

Bransford, J. D., et al. (Eds.). (2000). *How people learn*. Washington, DC: National Academy Press.

Krumsieg, K., & Baehr, M. (2000). *Foundations of learning* (3rd ed.). Lisle, IL: Pacific Crest.

Renkl, A., & Atkinson, R. K. (2003). Structuring the transition from example study to problem solving in cognitive skill acquisition: A cognitive load perspective. *Educational Psychologist, 38,* 15-22.

Van Merriënboer, J. J. G., Kirschner, P. A., & Kester, L. (2003). Taking the load off a learner's mind: Instructional design for complex learning. *Educational Psychologist, 38,* 5-14.

Woods, D. R. (2000). An evidence based strategy for problem solving. *Journal of Engineering Education, 89,* 443-459.

Pacific Crest

Faculty Development Series

Learning Processes through the Use of Methodologies

by Cy Leise, Bellevue University and Steven Beyerlein, University of Idaho

Methodologies are multiple-step models for complex processes. Their purpose is to systematically guide learners through a full series of steps that must be internalized in order for growth in a process to occur. Although methodologies are quite helpful, some experts discount methodologies because they are concerned about the potential effects on creativity, along with a number of other sound reasons. This module analyzes the role of methodologies in learning with particular emphasis on how learners go about internalizing these tools. Tips for teaching with methodologies and a rubric for assessing levels of internalization of methodologies are also included.

Need for Methodologies in Teaching/Learning

An educator's most difficult challenge is to become more effective in facilitating rapid development of performance in learners (Bransford et al., 2001). This involves facilitating growth of procedural knowledge, which is the sequence or series of steps needed to produce or change something. For example, the writing process involves distinct steps that result in a written product (e.g., Bean, 1996). Analogously, there are widely recognized steps in problem solving (e.g., Wood, 2000). Procedural knowledge is distinct from conceptual knowledge that cannot be analyzed into steps but can be described by using concept maps and other organizational tools. This module focuses on how methodologies can guide the learning of processes that have four or more steps. Application may be special-purpose, such as writing research papers or designing software, as well as general-purpose, such as assessment and problem solving. Many processes build on transferable learning skills that involve less than four steps. A framework for identifying, measuring, and enhancing these is presented in *Classification of Learning Skills*. The *Faculty Guidebook* presents many methodologies that have been implicitly, if not explicitly, used for many years by faculty across disciplines.

Challenges in Growing Process Knowledge

Performance of a process requires that the conceptual understanding be put into action through some application. *(See Elevating Knowledge from Level 1 to Level 3.)* Most student problems link back to incomplete process knowledge or inability to draw upon the process knowledge that is needed within a specific context. Examples include completing a proof, constructing a free-body diagram, doing a self-analysis, and classifying biological specimens. Many specialized disciplinary processes draw upon transferable process knowledge. This is the reason many evaluations of educational methods (e.g., SCANS, 1991) focus attention on critical thinking, problem solving, and other transferable processes that are difficult to grow.

Historical Use of Methodologies

Experts have always guided the learning of novices by using methodologies, explicitly or implicitly. For example, Aristotle and other philosophers recommend specific steps in the syllogistic method for checking the "truth" of the logic between varying types of statements. John Dewey (1938) argued that logic is only one component of inquiry and that an "inductive-deductive" cycle of processes is involved in any inquiry. His inquiry methodology included: (a) recognition of an "indeterminate situation," (b) conceptual specification of the problem, (c) determination of a hypothetical solution, (d) reasoning to check meaning and relevance of the hypothesis, (e) collection and interpretation of "facts-meanings," and (f) judging whether outcomes attained resolve the problem situation. Basically, Dewey's inquiry methodology involves a pattern similar to that of the Pacific Crest Problem Solving Methodology. Methodology examples could be added from literally centuries of experience in every culture with arts, crafts, mechanical, management, and professional applications of many kinds. Examples are works on thinking (e.g., DeBono, 1994), nursing procedures for effective stroke unit procedures (e.g., Langhorne & Pollock, 2002), and engineering methodologies for safety evaluation of chemicals (e.g., Smith, Janfunen, & Goldstein, 2002). Methodologies have universal features that are presented in Table 1.

Reasons for Currently Limited Use of Methodologies

Educators rightly express concerns about using methodologies for at least four good reasons. First, it is realistic to be concerned that novices may use methodologies as rulebooks that limit their growth and ownership of the learning processes. Novices tend to want to take shortcuts when they are challenged in new arenas requiring complex performances that are difficult to learn. This can easily occur if learners use methodologies as directive shortcuts that reduce their engagement in the thinking and problem solving essential for achieving the desired internalization of the process. Novices want a "silver bullet" solution rather than a full, deep mastery of the process.

Table 1   **Distinctive Features of Methodologies**

1. Are logical and practical rule-of-thumb (i.e., heuristic) guides for complex processes.
2. Involve set-up, performance, and reflection.
3. Are self-help tools.
4. Are a "bridge" for guiding learners from incomplete, tacit knowledge to systematic, assessed knowledge.
5. Involve at least four steps, each of which is essential for completion of a quality process.
6. Involve integration of skills from multiple domains.
7. Require flexibility about the amount of attention each step receives in a given task context.
8. Facilitate meta-cognitive understanding of a process from repeated assessment of steps and outcomes.
9. Speed communication between learners and educators or between advanced learners.
10. Internalization of several methodologies will greatly increase the ease of learning additional ones.

Second, experts already have internalized a stronger, richer process than the methodology. Experts want to transfer this richness to the learner and may believe that they can produce a better version of the methodology. In addition, experts are usually concerned more about helping novices learn several methods for approaching a task than in establishing steps for only one basic process.

Third, educators may assume, on the basis of experience and from observation, that processes work mainly in specific contexts. Experience with learners tends to support the hypothesis that they often do not transfer knowledge from course to course or from courses to work settings. Belenky et al. (2000) provide extensive interview evidence of this difficulty, especially in adults without growth-enhancing opportunities.

Fourth, some educators may prefer to work on processes without the constraints of system or outcome specifications, timing, and criteria. Negroponte (2003), for example, argues that the narrow focus of some discipline-based research reduces the creativity and efficiency of the innovation process. Educators and researchers value the originality that results from use of multiple perspectives.

Arguments for Increased Use of Methodologies

For each of the four reasons or barriers to the use of methodologies presented in the preceding section, there are equally compelling counter arguments to consider.

First, although learners often do use the prescribed steps in methodologies as a crutch, this is a learning facilitation issue rather than an inherent flaw of these tools. When used to introduce novices to a complex process, methodologies serve as a conceptual "bridge" for a complex process. Novices need to realize that skilled performers use an essential set of steps that includes some the novices don't use yet.

Second, although a methodology is less rich than an expert's approach, it is essential to have a way to lead novices through the initial learning in a reliable way so that they can proceed to learn the more subtle aspects. This suggests the significance of the differences in perspective and learning needs of experts versus novices. The educational process will produce stronger knowledge and performance outcomes if novices are guided through the details that experts have long ago internalized.

Third, although it is common to create methodologies to fit specific tasks, a stronger approach is to create them for generalizable processes such as problem solving. Many educators believe that methodologies cannot cross boundaries such as those between humanities and the sciences. Woods (2000), however, identified 150 ways that the basic problem solving methodology is used across disciplines.

Fourth, although methodologies can inhibit creativity and innovation, it is easy to underestimate the significance of establishing correct patterns. Schön (1987) provides a series of detailed professional teaching/learning examples—e.g., from architectural design, musical performance, counseling—that demonstrate the importance of starting with a disciplined method, protocol, recipe, algorithm, procedure, or technique to assure proper attention to main principles before trying to resolve the special or detailed problems related to a current context. Architecture students described by Schön hit barriers in their designs when they paid attention too soon to a later stage in their methodology, e.g., by trying to design the shape of a building to fit the landscape before ascertaining all the needs, functions, and features.

All disciplines, in producing curriculum and associated learning resources, use methodologies as educational tools to help novices become more practiced and professional. An essential purpose of methodologies is to direct learners' attention to the criteria and assessment steps that help to define useful outcomes from a process. With a sound foundation they can progress to internalized, meta-cognitive uses of methodologies.

Internalization of Methodologies

Internalization is the psychological process of moving one's ability to perform from reliance on external cues or guidance (e.g., from a parent or teacher) to reliance on a "mindful" personal representation of a process that can be used flexibly across contexts.

The internalized process skills of individuals need little mental attention unless a challenging situation arises. This type of knowledge is also known as "implicit" or "procedural" knowledge. "Natural genius" is a higher level use of internalized process knowledge but the natural genius may not be metacognitively aware of the learning history that has produced his or her effortless performance. Both novices and experts can increase their growth in process knowledge through cycles of assessment and reflection. Until such conscious efforts are made, individuals' flexibility will be restricted and their metacognitive understanding limited (see the levels of competency in Table 1 of the *Social Domain*).

Table 2 presents five pairs of factors related to internalizing methodologies as well as techniques or assignments that facilitate learning for each of the factors.

Levels of Development in Internalizing a Methodology

Five levels describe growth and development in learning and internalizing a methodology (see next page). Descriptively, the five levels are (a) Rule-governed users, able to perform step-by-step, (b) Task-focused users, able to perform in easy contexts, (c) Explorers, able to self-assess use of a methodology and to affect others' performance, (d) Generalizers, able to internalize a methodology and capable of mentoring others, and (e) Developers, able to engage in creative development of new methodologies to fit new needs or contexts. These five levels are incorporated into the Rubric for Internalization of Methodologies.

Concluding Thoughts

This module introduces methodologies as essential Process Education tools. Educators who avoid methodologies as too rigid or simplistic overlook their considerable benefits. The Rubric for Internalization of Methodologies provides a succinct model of the main factors and levels of competency involved in learning a methodology. Using the tips provided, educators can work toward new levels of learning in both themselves and their students.

Table 2   *Methodology Internalization Factors and Related Tips for Educators*

Factors Related to Internalization of Methodologies	Examples and Tips for Educators
(a) Understanding the methodology	
Awareness of learning factors and issues	*Use team activities to support learning how to apply a methodology to a specific assignment.*
Fluency of process area language	*Assign an oral presentation of how a methodology was used and why each step was essential.*
(b) Translating into practice	
Fluency in translating instructions into effective actions; versatility	*Put learners into a competition for speed and versatility in applying a methodology to a challenging task.*
Discipline in use to obtain a planned outcome	*Request self-assessment of the validity of the reasoning related to each step in application of the tool to a task.*
(c) Valuing the process for which the methodology is a tool	
Belief in the tool as a valid representation of a process	*Put learners into a performance arena that is too challenging in order to increase reliance on the tool.*
Belief in personal ability to gain effectiveness in application of the tool	*Challenge the accuracy of a learner's self-efficacy as part of the performance assessment process.*
(d) Meta-cognitive abilities	
Awareness of the whole; ability to proactively assess "fit" to purpose	*Ask learners to predict (and later assess) which steps will be most critical for a specific context. Request journal descriptions of using a process at a level above current ability.*
Ability to communicate purposes and benefits for multiple contexts	*Request journal reflections addressing purpose and benefits of recent uses of methodologies.*
(e) Creative adaptation	
Creative customization and adaptation	*Challenge to develop several valid outcomes for the same learning task or problem.*
Willingness to take to new challenge levels	*Challenge to use a process at a higher level on the Internalization Rubric.*

Rubric for Internalization of Methodologies

5. Developer

a. Has high level of "knowledge skill" that can be applied universally.

b. Is able to facilitate growth in the use of methodologies with skilled individuals.

c. Demonstrates strong self-efficacy in influencing increased educator competence with methodologies.

d. Is aware of issues and principles related to the way learners achieve metacognitive awareness of whole methodologies.

e. Can facilitate growth in experts to improve their creative customization and adaptation of methodologies in any context.

4. Generalizer

a. Flexibly uses "knowledge skill" to deepen learner insights.

b. Diagnoses misdirection or irrelevancies when observing others use any methodology.

c. Has strong self-efficacy in facilitating any use of methodologies.

d. Is metacognitively aware of the whole; able to identify learning issues on the basis of the "flow" across all steps for any learner.

e. Is able to facilitate self-assessment in any learner in order to enhance his or her creativity in adapting methodologies.

3. Explorer

a. Is conceptually comfortable with methodologies; growing in knowledge skills.

b. Fluently translates the steps into effective actions that result in planned outcomes.

c. Starts in a disciplined way because of strong self-efficacy beliefs regarding benefits.

d. Is aware, when moving to a new step, of the need to assess and integrate results from previous steps.

e. Notices the potential to creatively customize known methodologies and often achieves valid results.

2. Task-focused

a. Understands purpose and benefits of methodologies for self but unable to communicate to others.

b. Demonstrates some independence of use for simple tasks; easily distracted from disciplined sequence.

c. Shows some self-efficacy beliefs about future ability to use specific methodologies for familiar problem contexts.

d. Is aware that the best results will occur if all steps are attended to.

e. Notices some variations in benefits from using methodologies but unable to take advantage of this knowledge.

1. Rule-governed

a. Has limited awareness of purpose or features of methodologies.

b. Follows steps accurately only if directly guided.

c. Has no sense that using a disciplined approach will improve performance.

d. Is aware only of own efforts to learn how to handle a current step.

e. Is unable to adapt a methodology; may randomly attempt to do so.

References

Bean, J. C. (1996). *Engaging ideas: The professor's guide to integrating writing, critical thinking, and active learning in the classroom.* San Francisco: Jossey-Bass.

Dewey, J. (1938). *Logic: The theory of inquiry.* New York: Holt, Rinehart and Winston.

De Bono, E. (1994). *De Bono's thinking course.* International Center for Creative Thinking.

Langhorne, P., & Pollock, A. (2002). What are the components of effective stroke unit care? *Ageing, 31,* 365-371.

Negroponte, N. (February, 2003). Creating a culture of ideas. *Technology Review.* 34-35.

Schön, D. A. (1987). *Educating the reflective practitioner.* San Francisco: Jossey-Bass.

Secretary's Commission on Achieving Necessary Skills. (1991). *What work requires of schools: A SCANS Report for America 2000.* Department of Labor.

Smith, K. R., Janfunen, M., & Goldstein, B. D. (Eds.). (2002). Proceedings of the Scientific Group on Methodologies for the Safety Evaluation of Chemicals. *Chemosphere, 49,* (9).

Woods, D. R. (2000). An evidence-based strategy for problem solving. *Journal of Engineering Education, 89,* 443-459.

Pacific Crest

Faculty Development Series

The Learning Process Methodology

by Cy Leise, Bellevue University; Steven Beyerlein, University of Idaho; and Daniel Apple, Pacific Crest

The Learning Process Methodology (LPM) is a guide for learners who wish to improve their efficiency and depth of learning and for educators who wish to help learners achieve these goals. Implementing each of the steps in the LPM can add value to any learning activity. The LPM flexibly supports the construction of knowledge in any field and its elevation from basic information to applications. It also supports the creation of new knowledge. The steps in the methodology have validity across disciplines and are consistent with the tenets of major learning theories. Examples are provided to demonstrate use of the LPM at novice and at expert levels.

Universality of the LPM

Learning is a complex process involving multiple steps (see Table 1) which are usefully modeled as a methodology. Learning also requires simpler processes which are identified in the *Classification of Learning Skills*. For fully developed knowledge in a specific topic or application, learners will need several other process methodologies to complement the LPM, such as those for information processing, reading, writing, and assessment. Although created from the constructivist perspective of process education, the LPM approach is consistent with virtually all models of learning (e.g., Grow, 2003; Lorsbach, 2003; NCREL [North Central Regional Educational Laboratory], 2003; Epsilon Learning Systems, 2003; Dufresne, Leonard, & Gerace, 2003).

Every learning theory or model includes elements or implications related to each step in the LPM. The authors of the sample of models cited above exemplify, argue, or describe why learning occurs best when the learner is motivated, is aware of current personal level of knowledge, has set specific learning objectives and related performance criteria, has a plan for finding, remembering, and managing information, can transfer the learning to new situations and problems, and can create new knowledge through research if desired. The LPM provides additional value because it is a generalized model of the learning process and is a basis for evaluating the pros and cons of any specific model of learning because it integrates and is consistent with tenets of major learning theories.

Using the LPM to Elevate the Level of Knowledge

Because learning is a process that is characterized by the distinct steps in the LPM, it is possible to add value to learning activities in any discipline through its use. Bloom *(see **Bloom's Taxonomy—Expanding its Meaning**)* pioneered the concept of a hierarchy of knowledge levels which should guide curriculum design and learning facilitation *(see **Elevating Knowledge from Level 1 to Level 3** and **Developing Working Knowledge (Level 4 Knowledge)**).*

Halpern (2003) argues, consistent with process education principles, that the essential purpose of learning is its transfer to new situations and problems. She provides the following set of scientifically supported principles and propositions that support this position.

1. Long-term transfer requires a series of learning opportunities that involve varied "cues" for use of the learning, e.g., in different contexts.

2. Long-term transfer also requires that learning episodes be spaced over time, i.e., the learner must use "spaced practice."

3. Varying cues and contexts make learning more challenging, which is essential for improved probability of transfer.

4. Using multiple kinds of models and representing knowledge in multiple ways enhances construction of knowledge so that it will transfer.

5. Learner assumptions (e.g., that they are innately incapable of certain kinds of learning), experiences (e.g., of anxiety or pleasure with certain kinds of learning), and expectancies (e.g., that learning certain subjects is easy) must be assessed in order to help them build effective models of knowledge that will transfer.

6. Performance assessment and evaluation must focus on the main learning objectives in order to avoid learner misperceptions and forgetting essential knowledge as a result of attending to the wrong knowledge for the purpose at hand (e.g., learning to pass a test rather than learning to perform in a real context).

7. In-depth knowledge is usually needed for effective transfer. The amount of information to be learned at Bloom's levels 1 and 2 must support the goal of transfer.

8. Learning strategies must be validated with empirical evidence that they actually produce desired outcomes in learner transfer of knowledge.

Table 1   **Assessment Criteria for Learning Process Methodology (LPM) Steps**

Description of LPM Steps	Learning Plan Criteria
1. **Why:** Motivation to learn depends upon the relevance of learning to personal, educational, career, and life goals. State why learning about this topic is important and how it is relevant to your interests, needs, or concerns. Think beyond immediate needs.	(a) Reason is personally meaningful. (b) Reason indicates a practical benefit.
2. **Learning Objective:** State a knowledge or skill outcome or result that you intend to achieve. It should be personally meaningful, relevant, valuable, motivating, and supportive of your larger learning goals.	(a) Outcome specified as a positive achievement. (b) Medium "scope" or range of learning described.
3. **Performance Criteria:** Indicate two or three general areas of performance (e.g., writing quality) and what standard you intend to meet (e.g., level 3 on a writing rubric) in each area to demonstrate that the learning outcome has been met. These should be measurable, observable, fair, and challenging.	(a) Indicates qualities or types of performance that will indicate achievement of the objective. (b) Describes how learning outcome will be measured, e.g., by a rubric or exam. (c) Sets a standard that must be met for success, e.g., level, grade, number of items completed. (d) Method of documenting results is clear, e.g., in a Recorder Report or from an exam grade.
4. **Orientation:** Review the instructions, materials, and main focus of what is to be learned about the topic. Usually a subset of knowledge is needed but one must be aware of the whole topic area and how the knowledge is used.	(a) Statement indicates the context, e.g., a course assignment or a research project. (b) Statement demonstrates awareness of the overall topic or area of knowledge, e.g., factoring problems in algebra or hormone systems in biology.
5. **Prerequisites:** Identify what prior learning or skills are necessary as background or foundation for new learning about this topic. Review this issue again after setting a specific learning objective.	(a) Required entry or background knowledge is described briefly. (b) Personal limitations in background knowledge specified.
6. **Study Plan:** Identify resources to use, concepts to study, models and examples to apply, questions that must be answered, a study schedule, and what to assess about your learning process in steps (a) through (f).	Record elements of your study plan in the cells below as specified in steps (a) through (f).
(a) **Information:** Follow the IPM (Information Processing Methodology) to identify a list of relevant resources, e.g., readings, library items, notes, Internet.	(a) List of useful resources compiled. (b) List validated by reviewing the IPM steps.
(b) **Vocabulary:** Identify essential concepts that must be understood and remembered. Use analysis techniques, e.g., concept mapping, and memory techniques, e.g, chunking, to deeply learn concepts.	(a) List of concepts collected from all relevant information resources, e.g., text, notes, articles. (b) Categorization or organization techniques used before memorizing or using terms. (c) Effective memorization technique chosen.

Description of LPM Steps	Learning Plan Criteria
(c) **Models and Examples:** Identify simpler models/examples to study first (e.g., easy or worked-out problems); then plan more complex or varied ones.	(a) Collect and rank-order models/examples from easy to complex. (b) Time management plan (step 6e) includes spaced practice of problems in order of difficulty.
(d) **Critical Thinking Questions:** State the most important questions that relate background knowledge to the learning objective. Questions should be open-ended, logical, and challenging.	(a) Questions are open-ended. (b) Questions raise important issues. (c) Questions suggest connections between the learning objective and background or prerequisite knowledge.
(e) **Time Management:** Schedule enough time, and space the time over a number of days to benefit from "spaced practice." Allot time for each step in your plan. Make use of brief time periods to review.	(a) Include enough time to realistically complete all learning steps. (b) Include spaced practice spread over days or weeks. (c) Calendar record is not too detailed or general.
(f.) **SII (Strength, Improvement, Insight):** Use to assess your performance in terms of your study plan steps and in terms of the performance criteria for your learning objective.	(a) Assessments focus on processes in the study plan used to achieve the learning objective. (b) SII statements answer "Why?" for strength, "How?" for improvement, and "So What?" for insight.
7. **Transfer/Application:** To enhance your learning, change the context/situation to demonstrate flexibility in applying knowledge related to the learning objective. This step may require a new learning objective and related plans.	(a) State a related learning objective for a new context or situation. (b) SII assessments indicate generalization of the original learning to the new context or situation.
8. **Problem Solving:** To enhance application of knowledge related to the learning objective, challenge yourself to solve more complex types of problems that are closer to those worked on by experts in the field.	(a) Document use of knowledge to analyze and solve a problem in an "unstructured" context. (b) Document awareness of perspective and skills used by experts in the problem type.
9. **Research:** Increase the creative aspects of your learning by designing new ways to investigate knowledge or applications related to the topic. Expand your range of artistic expression or interpretation.	(a) Design a study that investigated a challenging question related to the learning or problem area. (b) Share results and interpretation to an appropriate audience.
10. **Self-Assessment of Growth:** Document improvements in "knowing you know" that will change your future "learning style." Steps 7, 8, & 9 involve challenges that demonstrate growth.	(a) Use appropriate rubric(s) related to growth in learning skills. (b) Identify new ways to challenge still further growth in learning skills and meta-cognition.

By facilitating systematic use of the LPM, educators can help learners at any level to elevate their learning. The initial steps in the methodology engage learners and educators in considering the rationale for specific learning objectives, in assessing readiness to learn, in planning of effective study methods, and eventually in learning to transfer and problem solve with the new knowledge. Initially users of the LPM struggle to understand how to respond to the requirements of each step, but over time the purpose and potential become more apparent. The "Rubric for Internalization of Methodologies" from

Learning Processes through the Use of Methodologies provides a guide for expected levels of progress in using the LPM. New users of a methodology typically move from a step-by-step (level 1) or outcome-oriented (level 2) approach to a task before achieving a true level of comfort at level 3 ("Explorer"). Meta-cognitive awareness must be developed through exposure of learners to increasingly challenging learning tasks that they achieve with decreasing amounts of guidance. Extensive assessment *(see **Overview of Assessment and Assessment Methodology**)* is essential for progress.

Applying the Learn Process Methodology

Example 1: Novice Learner's use of the LPM

Students in an introduction to psychology course are engaged in an activity designed to facilitate learning about Piaget and Vygotsky's theories of development. The LPM was introduced in the previous class session as a framework to use to guide their learning process. In that "guided tour" of the LPM, the students readily found that these theories of development are important because they could easily imagine themselves as future—or present—parents. The stated objective is for them to provide a model that they can learn from for future independent work. They are to "Identify three insights that Piaget and/ or Vygotsky propose in their theories about the developmental basis for 'internalization' of learning styles." The orientation process is assisted by reviewing the Critical Thinking Questions in the activity. This review helps the students realize that internalization is a basic feature of all development and that their own learning style is a good example. There are no academic prerequisites, but the students find that having read the assignments is important once they move into teams and address the objective. The performance criterion is to identify three insights about developmental internalization that are related to learning style. The steps in the Study Plan section of the LPM are reviewed so the students recognize that various components and strategies are part of effective studying. At this point the students are ready to do the work to prepare for the cooperative teamwork on the objective during the next class. Assessment of their insights helps them realize the quality of their insights and provides the instructor with an opportunity to discuss potential ways to transfer and problem solve with the knowledge attained.

Example 2: An Expert Learner's use of the LPM

A curriculum designer wishes to produce an integrated set of learning activities for an introductory course in psychology. It is clear from previous knowledge and experience that courses are much more effective if the knowledge to be learned is properly analyzed to identify a realistic set of concepts, processes, and tools that are related to the context and the "way of being" of the learners. Curriculum design steps are an essential resource that must be well-internalized; the educator must also have at least level 3 (application) and preferably level 4 (working) knowledge *(see **Bloom's Taxonomy—Expanding its Meaning**)* of the topic at hand. For the expert, the setting of a clear objective with challenging performance criteria takes special attention and care. The critical thinking questions and models in the Study Plan section are also significant because of the need to identify assumptions, discover inconsistencies, and to articulate the model

one is using. The transfer and problem solving steps are essential as indicators of the level of expertise and ongoing assessment of growth in the processes of curriculum design. These are of extreme importance because of their career and employment implications.

Concluding Thoughts

The LPM supports educational process from both the learner and the educator perspectives. Using the LPM, learners increase their meta-cognitive awareness; as a result, they can self-assess and expand the learning skills and strategies that they use. Educators "leverage" their influence through effective curriculum design in combination with thoughtful planning and facilitation. They raise the level of challenge so that learners become more active, independent, and self-directed. The examples illustrate how to facilitate use of the LPM with novices and how it can serve as a guide for an expert. Novices are unaware of the process of knowledge construction that should be at the heart of their learning efforts. Experts have internalized the LPM so well that all the steps occur without need for much direct attention once the objective has been established.

References

Dufresne, R. J., Leonard, W. J., & Gerace, W. J. (1995, February). Model of knowledge, cognition, and learning: A qualitative model for the storage of domain-specific knowledge and its implications for problem-solving. *Physics Education Research Group. University of Massachusetts-Amherst.* Retrieved May 25, 2004 from <http://umperg.physics.umass.edu/perspective/model/>

Learning objects. (2003). *Epsilon Learning Systems.* Retrieved May 25, 2004 from <http://www.epsilonlearning.com/ objects.htm>

Grow, Gerald O. (1996). A Cognitive model of learning. *Gerald Grow's Home Page.* Retrieved May 25, 2004 from <www.longleaf.net/ggrow/StrategicReader/StratModel.html>

Halpern, D. F., & Hakel, M. D. (July/August, 2003). Applying the science of learning. *Change.* 36-41.

Lorsbach, A. W. (2003). The learning cycle as a tool for planning science education. *Illinois State University Science Education Laboratory.* Retrieved May 25, 2004 from <http://www.coe.ilstu.edu/scienceed/lorsbach/ 257lrcy.htm>

North Central Regional Educational Laboratory (NCREL). (2003). *Incorporating assessment into the learning process.* Retrieved May 25, 2004 from <www.ncrel.org/sdrs/ areas/issues/content/cntareas/science/sc3asses.htm>

Forms of Knowledge and Knowledge Tables

by Duncan Quarless, SUNY College at Old Westbury

The definition of knowledge from a process education perspective includes both breadth and depth. Breadth is indicated by five forms of knowledge—concepts, processes, tools, contexts, and taxonomy. Depth is indicated by levels of knowledge use as represented by Bloom's taxonomy. The five forms of knowledge are the components of a "knowledge table" that can be assembled around any complex knowledge focus or application. The principles for constructing such a table are presented and exemplified to show the flexibility that emerges from this systematic approach to the analysis of knowledge.

Knowledge Forms

Donald (2002) proposes that knowledge occurs in two stages: an initial declarative (information) stage and a subsequent procedural (application) stage. There is, however, a growing body of evidence that suggests there is both the declarative and procedural in all of the forms of knowledge that ultimately facilitate knowledge construction. Krumsieg and Baehr (2000) and Apple (1998) argue that learner growth is exhibited in a movement between forms, and this movement creates some subjectivity (variance) in the classification of knowledge forms. Forman's (2000) discussion of knowledge-building communities provides strong insights about the social dimensions of the forms and how these social aspects impact the interpretative flexibility between the forms (see the section "Principles for Constructing a Knowledge Table" later in this module). The five basic forms of knowledge are defined and illustrated in Table 1. Also included is a sixth form, rule knowledge. Rule knowledge is perhaps the most trivial but is included for completeness. All knowledge can be classified as being one of these forms.

Knowledge Construction and the Knowledge Table

Knowledge is dynamic and flexible if the learning process produces growth in the level of knowing *(see Bloom's Taxonomy—Expanding its Meaning)*. Additionally, the five forms of knowledge span the four learning skill domains: cognitive, social, affective and psychomotor. The implication is that any knowledge table represents substantial complexity even if constructed for beginning learners.

Process education uses a learner-oriented philosophy of education in which construction of knowledge requires the implementation of learning principles *(see Overview of Learning Theory)* as guided by the Learning Process Methodology *(see The Learning Process Methodology)*. Piaget and other developmental psychologists have recognized that learners must actively develop knowledge within the framework of their cognitive organizational schemes (Liben, 1983), a perspective consistent with process education principles. A knowledge table (sometimes referred to as a "knowledge map") is a tool that guides the process of analyzing specific cognitive schemes or frameworks within any particular area of knowledge.

Fisher, et al. (2000) illustrate why knowledge tables are an important and useful tool in a learner-centered pedagogy. They enable educators to identify aspects of knowledge that are externally valid, e.g., facts, theories, models, and also aspects that are unique because of context and way of being. Knowledge mapping produces several significant consequences that include promoting active learning, facilitating conceptual change, and interconnecting and deepening understanding. All of these are important for elevating learner knowledge *(see Elevating Knowledge from Level 1 to Level 3)*. Use of the LPM is facilitated or enhanced if a knowledge table is used to present the five forms of knowledge that are relevant to a particular area of knowledge being learned (Krumsieg & Baehr, 2000). Without the knowledge table, it is easy for learners to set learning objectives with only one dimension, e.g., to memorize conceptual facts for a test.

Educators need to be aware of several practical limitations in the way that knowledge tables have sometimes been constructed and applied

1. If there is excessive ambiguity in the distinctions among the five forms of knowledge within a map, e.g., by overlapping of concepts with processes, learning activities may also lack appropriate focus.

2. If the descriptions and details used to represent the five forms of knowledge within a knowledge map are disjointed, e.g., lacking in integration or parallelism, multiple problems in learning and assessing performance are likely.

3. If there is not enough detailing or complexity in how the forms in the map are represented, learners may not fully recognize relevant exemplars or models, and educators may find it difficult to provide clear assessments (Fisher, 2000).

4. If educators falsely assume a difference between "knowledge maps" and "knowledge tables," they may create ambiguity in their understanding that impedes curriculum design. Apple (1998) argues that the term "knowledge table" is more intuitively relevant for practical pedagogical concerns.

Table 1   **Types of Knowledge and Examples**

Knowledge Form	Definition	Examples
Concept	an idea that connects a set of relationships; a generalized idea about something or a classification label such as process methodologies	chemistry – the mole
Process	a sequence of steps, events, or activities that results in a change or produces something over a period of time	using chemical equations to interconvert and predict masses, moles and number of particles
Tool	any device, implement, instrument, or utensil that serves as a resource to accomplish a task	chemical equation
Contexts	the whole situation, background, or conditions relevant to the process	atomic theory (laws of conservation of mass-energy, definite composition, multiple proportion; classification of matter; use of various representations, e.g., chemical formulas, structural formulas, empirical formulas, molecular formulas)
Way of Being	the set of behaviors, actions, and use of language associated with a particular discipline or knowledge area; a culture	specificity in use of language; use of representations; application of skills, e.g., visualizing, problem-solving; validating solution
Rule	memorized fact or set of facts that govern performance in a knowledge area; may be thought of as a convention that is required within the knowledge construction	the units that are reported as part of the solution when unspecified in the question. In chemistry bond length would be an illustration, specified typically either in angstroms (e.g., in the U.S.) or picometers (e.g., in Europe)
	Additional examples: driving on the left-hand side of the street in European countries; hand signaling with European cars which have steering wheels on the right-hand side; spelling certain words with the addition of a "u", e.g., valor – valour	

Constructing a Knowledge Table

The various knowledge forms move from the basic, declarative kinds of knowledge to procedural or application (skill) types of knowledge. The methodology for facilitating the elevation of knowledge along this continuum is treated in ***Elevating Knowledge from Level 1 to Level 3***. Table 2 contains a knowledge table related to home remodeling in which the five forms of knowledge are described for each knowledge level from "Information" to "Research."

The knowledge table is best thought of as the systematic framework that interlocks the forms. In the example presented in Table 2, it should be recognized that the forms generally interconnect within the exemplified knowledge area of home remodeling. What may not be as clear is the fact that a particular learner may not demonstrate full integration of these interconnections. For example, an apprentice carpenter might be able to measure and saw straight cuts under supervision but not have an adequate understanding of building plans to make his or her own determinations of how to make the cuts. The apprentice's process is at a low level of application, and the conceptual understanding is only at the information level. The plan exists and has certain features that the apprentice is aware of, but it does not yet serve as a guide for steps in the building process.

Principles for Constructing a Knowledge Table

1. **Planning and Preparation**. It is important that particular learning outcomes and behaviors be incorporated in the planning. What variations in levels of knowledge must be assessed? How must the assessments address variations in forms of knowledge? What are the targeted behaviors and outcomes for a good performance?

2. **Context and Way of Being**. The knowledge-building community establishes the predominant elements of the learning environment that are relevant to the "culture" of each particular discipline. It is important to be mindful of these elements as they impact on the forms. As an example, argumentation may be a context for dealing with a concept in one knowledge building community, while consensus building may be a context in another learning community. Consequently, the way of being associated with knowledge building in each of these communities will likely be different as well.

3. **Strengthening the Existing Knowledge Base**. The process of constructing the table should activate and strengthen the learner's prior knowledge base. The learner(s) should be encouraged (motivated) to explore their existing knowledge. This is done in light of the steps that follow.

Table 2

Constructing Levels of Knowledge

Knowledge Levels for "Remodeling"	Concepts	Processes	Tools	Contexts	Way of Being
Information	facts, definitions, number codes on materials to be used	able to identify steps in the plan	safety rules, list of materials	description of lot where home will be built	personal preferences about home features
Conceptual Understanding	model, plan, or blueprint for house	analyze own or builder's work on basis of the plan	use city permit standards to analyze construction plan	features of site that will require adaptations to the plan	understanding of reasons for recommended adaptations
Application	match of model to work in progress	follow plan step-by-step, imitate an expert builder	use appropriate tools and measures while building	use adapted plan to build a specific house	open to required adaptations
Working Expertise	match of model to construction codes	efficiently integrate all elements and make adaptations during construction	create "jigs" or unusual solutions to solve unexpected problems	adapt plan in ways that make it easy to use in varied sites	collaboration with builder to achieve maximum outcomes
Research	propose construction models for varied climates	test new procedures or products for general improvement of home construction	use testing devices related to new home building methods	develop principles for adapting construction plans to varied sites	long-term self-assessment of ability to collaborate in varied projects

4. **Critical Thinking Questions**. It is important to determine and detail the key questions related to the various knowledge forms. In the example above on home remodeling, the idea becomes somewhat different if the house is Victorian versus Ranch style. What differences in processes and tools would be required if the remodeling construction plan were to be prepared for an older house that doesn't meet current code requirements? Can a relatively inexperienced, but well-trained, carpenter handle the new requirements? How will the electrical and plumbing requirements be different? How will costs be affected? Will the design be suitable if the owner is physically disabled?

5. **Classification Variance**. It is important to recognize the flexibility and relationship between forms. Returning to the current illustration, "Victorian" style can also be classified as a context, since it also describes conditions that are relevant to the construction. Similarly, the building materials can be classified either as tools (instruments used to accomplish the construction) or context (part of the relevant conditions for the construction).

6. **Facilitating both Content and Process Development**. It is important to emphasize both the learning process and learning outcome(s) during the construction of the table. The framing of such an exercise should involve a mindful process to perform the task. That is, both the means and the end are important. This can be done by establishing learning outcome and learning process criteria for the performance.

7. **Guidelines for Classifying Forms of Knowledge**. Table 3 provides a matrix of guidelines for deciding what form of knowledge one is working with. The classification of knowledge forms involves a series of judgments that must remain consistent with the learning purpose and outcomes. In the example of "home remodeling" (Table 2), each column represents varying levels of complexity of that form. The information in Table 3 includes criteria and standards to support assessment of classification accuracy.

Table 3   **Criteria for Classifying Forms of Knowledge**

	Concepts	**Processes**	**Tools**	**Contexts**	**Way of Being**
Examples	ideas, definitions synthesis, model; set of relationships	sequence of activities; producing or changing something; can continue to improve quality	method; instrument; reach a level of skill usage	conditional, will change; environmental; grows with experience	set of values; culture/beliefs; growing appreciation over time
Distinctions to Make	thinking you know versus knowing you know	actual performance— not just understanding what to do	selection/use of tool— not just concept of tool or of its use	adaptation to varied conditions—not a change in basic processes	preferences, tacit assumptions—not concepts or processes
Criteria	representational; abstract	active; continuous	instrumental; increases quality	type of environment; change in conditions	clarity of interests, values, feelings, thoughts
Standards	relevant to the area of knowledge	defines actions done to reach a goal	enhances process and outcome	used as basis to redefine other forms for best fit	able to articulate how personal factors influence knowledge

8. **Classification Example**. Consider the electrical components of a house. The plan of the electrical grid is conceptual. An electrician must perform many processes and use many tools to carry out the plan. Knowledge forms "feed back" in a sense because the plan is a "tool" for the electrician as well as a conceptual representation of an electrical layout. Each type of building plan involves context variations and home owners make many decisions to fit their personal needs and preferences.

Concluding Thoughts

This module presents the theory of forms of knowledge and relates these forms to Bloom's levels of knowledge. Creation of a complete knowledge table is a powerful technique for analyzing all aspects of knowledge related to a specific learning goal and relevant performance criteria. The forms are "linked" to each other in real practice, but assessment of performance will be enhanced if a fully worked out knowledge table is developed. An extended example is worked out in Table 2 and several principles are provided that help in building such tables. Table 3 provides criteria for differentiating and accurately classifying forms with a knowledge table. Using knowledge tables will enhance the design of curriculum and improve the ability to provide effective performance assessment.

References

Apple, D. K., & Krumsieg, K (1998). *Teaching institute handbook*. Lisle, IL: Pacific Crest.

Christen, W. L., & Murphy, T. J. (1991). Increasing comprehension by activating prior knowledge. Indiana. *ERIC Digest*.

Krumsieg, K., & Baehr, M. (2000). *Foundations of learning* (3rd ed.). Lisle, IL: Pacific Crest.

Forman, E. A. (2000). Knowledge building in discourse communities. *Human Development, 43,* 364-368.

Dijkstra, S. (1997). The integration of instructional systems design models and constructivistic design principles. *Instructional Science, 25,* 1-13.

Liben, L. S. (Ed). (1983). *Piaget and the foundations of knowledge*. Mahwah, NJ: Lawrence Erlbaum Associates.

Donald, J. (2002). *Learning to think: Disciplinary perspectives*. San Francisco: Jossey-Bass.

Kolb, D. A. (1984). *Experiential learning: Experiences as the source of learning and development*. Englewood Cliffs, NJ: Prentice-Hall.

Fisher, K. M., Wandersee, J. H., & Wideman, G. (American Association for the Advancement of Science, Annual Meeting). (2000). *Enhancing cognitive skills for meaningful understanding of domain specific knowledge*. Washington, D.C.

Overview of Mentoring

by Cy Leise, Bellevue University and Steven Beyerlein, University of Idaho

Mentoring involves a trusting, but clearly bounded, relationship entered into by an experienced mentor and a mentee who can benefit in terms of personal or career change and growth. Effective mentoring relationships involve clear definition of the purpose and goals of a mentee who is willing to challenge himself or herself in an area of performance that will produce future benefits. Mentors use challenging strategies that facilitate learning, decision making, and growth in real time contexts. Key skill areas include communication, information processing, problem solving, and servant leadership. The mentor-mentee relationship adds meaning and value to both parties in terms of immediate goal attainment and in valuable deepening of insights about performance and growth processes.

Why Mentoring is Important

Any person concerned about and motivated to achieve personal or professional growth faces the challenge of articulating a substantive direction or area of change that currently is incompletely understood. In addition the person must plan and implement specific action steps that have potential to lead to the desired growth. Future success of mentees is a practical goal that should be the outcome of effective mentoring, which is the facilitating of movement from unclear development goals to independence in self-growth *(see Becoming a Self-Grower, Personal Development Methodology, and Performance Levels for Self-Growers)*.

Relationships between more experienced or expert individuals and those near the beginning of the growth process are always unequal in terms of status and power so mentoring involves carefully planned relationships involving openness and trust that can "sideline" these differences for a time. The relationship must be a "hands-on" one that is focused on the mentor staying "along-side" the mentee. Mentors must avoid influencing on the basis of authority or power and mentees must take risks by engaging in real performance learning that is improved by use of assessment by the mentor and by others. It is not the mentor's job to remediate problems of the mentee; the role is to be an honest and open sounding board and a source of wisdom for assessing and planning.

Principles of Effective Mentoring

The ten principles provided in Table 1 define effective mentoring and provide a framework for all the modules related to mentoring.

Main Issues Related to Mentoring

For the mentoring process to be maximally effective, certain issues and barriers must be predicted and handled with forethought.

Table 1   *Ten Principles of Effective Mentoring*

1. Mentoring requires a trusting, confidential relationship based on mutual respect.

2. Mentoring involves a clearly bounded relationship that is close and uncoerced (unlike friendship or parenting).

3. Mentoring involves a definite time commitment.

4. A mentoring relationship is planned for enhancing specific growth goals of a mentee—not for organizational requirements such as employee evaluation.

5. The purpose of mentoring must be mutually established and clearly defined by clear goals/outcomes.

6. Mentors should model performances for mentees thereby providing opportunities for observation and insight development.

7. Mentors provide quality performance assessments, especially of mentee's self-assessment.

8. Mentees must show progress by "raising the bar" for themselves as their insights and skills increase.

9. The mentoring relationship ends when the mentee is able to operate independently.

10. Mentors follow a servant leadership model by providing much value to another without extrinsic rewards.

First, both parties must be willing to enter the relationship with an agreement that coercion will never be used. Consideration of the differences between assessment and evaluation is essential for avoiding coercion. (*See Distinctions between Assessment and Evaluation*.)

Mentors and mentees vary widely in personality styles, purposes, and assumptions about how to achieve improvements in performance and growth. The relationship between the individuals must have clear boundaries that are identified through careful discussion between the parties.

In many cases mentees have significant life barriers that have an influence on success of the mentoring process and relationship. The module *Becoming a Self-Grower* provides assessment suggestions and resources for working with preliminary barriers to growth such as work on a *Life Vision Portfolio* or referral to a mental health professional.

Because it is not possible to predict how a mentor-mentee relationship will evolve, mentors must facilitate an appropriate level of challenge and mentees must accept the challenge with honesty and openness, especially when things are not going as well as hoped.

Because they already have experienced the type of growth that their mentees need to attain, it is important to consider the benefits of the relationship for mentors. The results for the mentor must be motivating both intrinsically, e.g., be experienced as "servant leadership," and extrinsically, e.g., recognition as an effective mentor. Similarly, mentees must experience intrinsically motivating results such as enhanced self-esteem and extrinsically motivating results such as improved performance.

Key Skills of Mentors

The following list of skills describes essential skills that mentors must have in order to be effective with mentees and with the process itself. Additional skills that may be important for certain circumstances can be identified in the *Classification of Learning Skills*, especially in the *Social Domain* and the affective domain. This set of performance skills in combination with other tools such as those found in *Performance Levels for Self-Growers* will be valuable for mentors' self-assessments.

1. Listening
2. Being positive
3. Identifying assumptions
4. Taking other's perspective
5. Appreciating other's values
6. Ethical reasoning
7. Resource identification and access
8. Setting criteria
9. Challenging
10. Assessing against criteria
11. Respect of diverse talents and interests
12. Affective availability
13. Servant leadership values

Mentoring Contexts

The purpose of mentoring is to facilitate growth in already well-functioning individuals. Many authors address the various forms of mentoring (e.g., Holliday 2001; Fritts, 1998) and discriminate between mentoring and other forms of learning or growth facilitation. The phrases "life coaching," and "learning leader" appear to have a meaning more similar to mentoring than to learning assessment, peer coaching, or training. In higher education contexts the major opportunities for mentoring of students occur in advising and independent project contexts.

Faculty growth can be facilitated by mentoring from more experienced colleagues who have a "servant leadership" attitude and themselves are open to change and growth. Part-time faculty have substantial professional experience but need mentoring in order to become effective educators. New faculty often need a mentor in order to move ahead quickly in gaining expertise as teachers and in establishing a research program that results in publications and grants. All faculty are experiencing new challenges as their roles are changing due to external influences such as funding and accreditation requirements.

Concluding Thoughts

Mentoring is an important strategy for enhancing specific areas of growth that are not yet required but are likely to support future success in career or personal life. In this overview module the basic principles, issues, processes, skills, and contexts of mentoring have been identified and described. It is clear that the meta-cognitive insights gained during mentoring, from using many processes and tools, will substantially improve transfer of learning by both the mentor and the mentee. Benefits to mentors include opportunities for servant-leadership experiences that can add meaning and purpose to their lives as experienced professionals. For mentees the process opens a window on their future, and on themselves, by making it possible to experience growth that may not have happened if left to their own devices. Mentoring is an essential process, especially in the fast-changing world of higher education.

References

Fritts, P. J. (1998). *The new managerial mentor: Becoming a learning leader to build communities of purpose.* Palo Alto, CA: Davies-Black Publishing.

Holliday, M. (2001). *Coaching, mentoring, & managing.* (2nd ed.). Franklin Lakes, NJ: The Career Press, Inc.

Wadsworth, E. M. (2002). *Giving much/gaining more: Mentoring for success.* West Lafayette, IN: Purdue University Press.

Becoming a Self-Grower

by Cy Leise, Bellevue University

Faculty Development Series

Parents have many hopes and dreams for their children, but one of the most common is that their children get what they value in life. In addition, they hope that their offspring will make conscious decisions and stay in control of their lives rather than having life "process" them. But this goal can only be achieved through a life-long process called self-growth, one that involves learning to improve a person's performances and values through effective self-assessment of his behavior. Table 1 below outlines the ideal characteristics of such an individual and illustrates how they all relate to five essential life goals: life vision, self-assessment, control, growth, and servant leadership. The sequence or ordering of these behaviors is meaningful but individuals frequently vary in their actual "way of being" in regard to the growth process. The goal of this module is to assist faculty who are mentoring students by describing the kinds of behaviors related to each life goal, identifying common barriers to achieving those goals, and suggesting appropriate strategies and tools to help students address their difficulties. Table 2 presents an analytical view of typical impediments to goal achievement and the resources and tools one can use to overcome them. An application case example suggests how the self-growth model may be used in a mentoring relationship.

Table 1

Profile of a Self-Grower

	A self-grower...	associated with:
1.	thinks critically in different contexts so as to be efficient while producing quality results from the processes utilized.	control/ self-assessment
2.	uses information in an efficient manner to limit "overload" by maximizing consistency of choices with values.	self-assessment/ life vision
3.	seeks to improve his or her own performance with every experience.	control/ self-assessment
4.	puts him or herself into challenging environments that require an increased level of performance.	growth/control
5.	self-assesses and self-mentors to facilitate his or her own growth.	self-assessment/ life vision/growth
6.	takes positive action in responding to external challenges that are personally critical or important to society.	control/ servant leadership
7.	has a strong desire to grow and develop in all aspects of his or her life.	growth
8.	creates his or her own challenges in order to take control of his or her own destiny.	life vision/control
9.	has a high degree of self-confidence and emotional maturity reflected in abilities to set realistic priorities and to take meaningful risks.	life vision/growth/ servant leadership
10.	serves as a mentor to others and is a model of service.	servant leadership

Behaviors that Support Self-Growth

1. Life Vision

Self-growth occurs only if a "critical mass" of developmentally relevant self-knowledge is learned over a period of time. An important resource that can support such self-analysis is found in the *Life Vision Portfolio* (Mettauer, 2002). Individuals must test new insights against the consistency and value they have for creating a meaningful life. Individuals need to know about the variables that influence their abilities, motives, opportunities, and personal development. The *Life Vision Portfolio* is designed to help individuals gain some perspective about their lives. However, assistance from a mentor will also significantly enhance this process *(see Overview of Mentoring)*.

2. Self-Assessment

Self-growers often learn how to use assessment skills in their quest for self-growth by working interactively with a mentor. This guide needs to use a consistent strategy *(see Personal Development Methodology)* over a sufficiently long period of time to influence self-growers, not only in the realm of values, but in terms of specific life goals. If they are to learn the skills of self-assessment and self-mentoring in a manner that influences growth, they must have a clear life vision—one that includes commitment to realistic goals. And if the self-growth is to continue, it must be rooted in individuals' ability to sustain the process *(see Assessment Methodology)*.

3. Control

Those individuals who show strong "control" behaviors are most likely to demonstrate assertiveness in the face of challenge. They are likely to use assessment to gain valuable information for themselves, which they then use to maintain, improve, or control their performance. Research in positive psychology (e.g., Seligman, 1991), cognitive development (e.g., Baxter Magolda, 2000), and social learning theory (e.g., Bandura, 1997) indicates that early experiences involving performance mastery and effective coping skills greatly enhance an individual's sense of control. Growth occurs when individuals learn how to maintain conscious control of their lives at increasingly mature and effective levels by using all available resources and abilities to fully "process" significant life experiences.

4. Growth

Individuals focused on growth find it to be the most compelling motive in their lives. As they gain in maturity and wisdom, they learn to set priorities for themselves. They find that focusing excessively on externally imposed values, such as social status, can distract them from more important tasks. By contrast, when they learn how to stay motivated to improve in high-priority performance areas, such as servant leadership, they find balance in their lives. Csikszentmihalyi (1997) discusses "flow"—the satisfying experience that comes from a deep sense of involvement in a task, without conscious concern for the superficial definitions of success. He sees it as a key indicator of exceptional growth. Self-growers experience this state of flow as they self-assess their behavior and values. Doing so on a regular basis helps them establish clear "benchmarks" for their growth across all domains of performance.

5. Servant Leadership

Servant leadership can be thought of as the culmination of adult developmental processes. It results from increasing in self-awareness and growth throughout life from conscious, empathic engagement with others. Maslow's (1971) theory of self-actualization, one model for examining maturity and wisdom, emphasizes individuals' movement from focusing on personal needs and goals to focusing on community or world concerns. Servant leaders focus on enhancing quality of life for others through creative change. They put a high value on enhancing other's empowerment as a measure of whether change was successful. Mentoring and other helpful relationships have an increasingly important priority for those who fully internalize servant leadership.

Contextual Variables that Strongly Influence Self-Growth

This section addresses some of the cultural, family, and other contextual factors that create or increase barriers to self-growth. These contextual factors exist or occur on a continuum from "external" (influences from the outside world) to "internal" (influences within a person). Mentors must keep in mind that, typically, the external barriers to growth must be dealt with before a person can manage to internalize self-growth processes.

1. Effects on Life Vision

To persist in the self-growth process, a person must commit to a full and deep understanding of his or her own preferences, personality, values, goals, and commitments. Creation of a Life Vision Portfolio is useful for examining how well one's behaviors, attitudes, relationship skills, and decisions correspond to deeper values and ideals. In order to be successful, an individual must continue this development process into adulthood as he or she develops not only performance skills but also growth-related competencies, such as wisdom.

2. Effects on Self-Assessment

In order to set priorities that are consistent with self-growth, individuals need to employ self-assessment skills of many kinds. One critical set of these skills relates to their discovering how their own cognitive and emotional dissonance relates to cultural norms and expectancies. La Fromboise and Low (1989), for example, describe the difficulties Native Americans often experience in learning to negotiate between the individualism found in "majority culture" and the interdependence typical of tribal culture. Mussweiler (2000) found that two powerful behaviors, individuals' reliance on impulsive emotional reactions (i.e., use of information in short-term memory that is associated with negative feelings) and a dependence on negative comparisons with others, inhibit their developmental progress in adulthood. To break out of these patterns of thinking and behavior, individuals often need a supportive mentor for the key role of sustaining motivation and focus for the complex self-assessment aspect of the growth process.

3. Effects on Control

Individuals' ability to control their destinies can be heavily influenced by one or more conditions or life experiences: being a member of an oppressed group, being imprisoned for political stands, experiencing severe family disruptions and dysfunctional parenting, having a mental illness, being addicted, being unenlightened about coping with a disability, developing an antisocial or impulsive personal style, and many other life conditions or states. Self-growth for individuals with these backgrounds frequently requires "external" assistance, such as counseling, support groups, work skills programs, medical services, and advocacy assistance. Fortunately, even individuals who have faced significant life challenges exhibit "resilience" (e.g., Masten, 2001) that enables them to return to a positive path of growth, despite the negative experiences and conditions they have had to confront.

4. Effects on Growth

Individuals who are caught up in negative emotions like anxiety, fear, and depression tend to resort to instant gratification in order to feel better. As a result, they assume that luck or fate controls their destiny; they do not see the part their decisions play in keeping them stuck in a non-productive mode. These attitudes significantly interfere with growth potential and are difficult to change—at least, until the person is motivated by some life challenge or crisis.

Table 2

Self-Growth Behavior, Barriers, and Resources

Types of Behavior	Psychological Competencies	Developmental and Cultural Resources	Internal Barriers	External Barriers	Strategies/Tools for Growth
Life Vision	motivation to examine life patterns, continuous reflection	published biography & autobiography models, ethics & values, social codes/norms/ideals, spiritual experiences	discomfort with self-discovery process, lack of priority with respect to searching for meaning	lack of mentoring, peer discounting of search for meaning	*Life Vision Portfolio*, *Learning Assessment Journal*, *Foundations of Learning*, goal setting, mentoring
Self-Assessment	self-monitoring skills, self-analysis skills, ability to perceive the "big picture," planning & goal-setting habits	mentors, college advisors, spiritual advisors, discussion groups, counseling/therapy	inability to accept feedback, focus on evaluation, lack of assessment skills, impulsiveness	lack of mentoring, limited experience with performance challenges	self-assessor profile, Assessment Meth., Personal Development Methodology, skill rubrics and other measures, growth hypotheses from dev. theories
Control	learned optimism, self-efficacy (accurate prediction of performances), well-formed identity, self-management	early mastery learning, supportive family, educational opportunities, supportive mentoring, positive work experiences, properly processed life crises	avoidance, lack of life awareness and perspective, lack of belief in oneself, low self-esteem, self-destructive behaviors	prejudice, ineffective support systems, abuse, addiction, unprocessed life crises	strengthening of affective skills, opportunities to practice and assess performances, increasing assertiveness
Growth	flow, assumption of continuous growth process, ability to prioritize wisely, interest in integration of life, wisdom	well-processed challenges & "hits" in life, openness of family & close friends to growth, exposure to growth-oriented spiritual & philosophical models	unenlightened assumptions about disabilities, learned pessimism	overly focused on tasks, job, or grades, lack of growth challenges	profile of a self-grower, annual benchmarking and growth analysis, reflection on "flow" experiences, integration of significant past experiences
Servant Leadership	self-actualization, empathy, maturity, accurate "theory of mind"	citizenship values, positive role models, commitment to spiritual & philosophical ideals, experience with service-oriented organizations	lack of service values, low empathy, alienation from society	absence of role models, peer rejection of service ideals	mentoring, life vision, exploration of values, tutoring and other college service, community involvement, internships

Prochaska, DiClemente, and Norcross (1992) found that individuals typically progress through a series of stages before attaining a sense of commitment to self-change goals. It takes experience, time, and external support before individuals stuck in non-growth life paths are likely to make a conscious commitment to overcoming barriers to their self-growth. Once they are in motion toward self-change, specific "growth plans" developed with a mentor can help individuals become more conscious of how to overcome or manage impediments and of how to enhance their skills in achieving goals in a positive, pro-active manner that is consistent with their values.

5. Effects on Servant Leadership

Many people who have experienced severe problems or setbacks in life emerge with a stronger sense of their own identity, filled with resolve to help others like themselves—such as the founders of Alcoholics Anonymous in the 1930's. But, more often, stereotyping or prejudice create a sense of victimization or at least of "stereotype vulnerability" (Steele, 1997), an anxiety about being able to compete in the dominant culture or context. This stigmatizing can make people feel rejected, thereby eroding their sense of inclusion in the larger social order and even encouraging a sense of irresponsibility towards it. These and other serious barriers mean that servant leadership is likely to emerge only after progress with the other four self-growth components (life vision, self-assessment, control, and growth). As suggested in the previous section (on barriers to growth behaviors), a predictable pattern of change takes time, even with effective mentoring.

Application of the Self-Growth Model

The fictional case that follows is intended to illustrate how to nurture the self-growth process in an individual with substantial internal and external barriers to growth. It includes direction both in assessing and facilitating these developmental changes.

Randall, a Native American who transferred to a four-year university from a community college, has missed many classes because he spends a lot of time helping members of his family deal with daily problems related to their adjustment to city life. Randall was encouraged to work closely with his faculty advisor when his failing grades brought him to the attention of a student services staff member. After several discussions with his advisor he decided to take on the challenge of working on self-growth as a positive way to deal with his academic and life issues. Through the initial task, completing a Life Vision Portfolio, he was able to discover that his tribal values included taking on life's difficulties; he could see how his problems with college could be related to this cultural dictate. He began to plan a more realistic balance between his family and college responsibilities as he increasingly understood the long-term value of learning for life as well as for work. He also discovered that he had learned as a

child how to interpret the qualities and skills others had. What he learned to do with his family he could apply to the new community in which he found himself. Randall learned he could develop his talents without threatening the traditional role he had played in his family. Having found a way to blend his new role as student without betraying his loyalty to complex tribal traditions, Randall then felt free to focus on his learning. He was able to use the specific tools provided by the *Foundations of Learning* in order to improve his academic work.

Concluding Thoughts

This module provides faculty mentors with concepts, processes, and tools for working with students on their self-growth. The behaviors related to five types of life goals most predictive of self-growth are examined; a summary table entitled "Self-Growth Behavior, Barriers, and Resources" provides a systematic outline featuring several dimensions of the self-growth process. A brief scenario focusing on a hypothetical student's experience suggests how personal, cultural, and contextual issues can be integrated into the self-growth process. Using this model and the tools associated with it will help mentors to become more skillful and also will increase their ability to enhance their own personal growth.

References

Bandura, A. (1997). *Self-efficacy: The exercise of control.* New York: W. H. Freeman and Company.

Baxter Magola, M. B. (Ed.). (2000). *Teaching to promote intellectual and personal maturity: Incorporating students' worldviews and identities into the learning process.* San Francisco: Jossey-Bass.

Csikszentmihalyi, M. (1997). *Creativity: Flow and the psychology of discovery and invention.* New York: Harper Collins.

La Fromboise, T., & Low, K. (1989). American Indian adolescents. In J. Gibbs & L. Hwang (Eds.), *Children of color.* San Francisco: Jossey-Bass.

Maslow, A. H. (1971). *The farther reaches of human nature.* New York: Viking Press.

Mettauer, J. (2002). *Life vision portfolio.* Lisle, IL: Pacific Crest.

Mussweiler, T. (2000). The "relative self": Informational and judgmental consequences of comparative self-evaluation. *Journal of Personality and Social Psychology, 79,* 23-38.

Prochaska, J. O., DiClemente, C. C., & Norcross, J. C. (1992). In search of how people change: Applications to addictive behaviors. *American Psychologist, 47,* 1102-1114.

Steele, C. (1997). A threat in the air: How stereotypes shape intellectual identity and performance. *American Psychologist, 52,* 613-629.

Personal Development Methodology

by Cy Leise, Bellevue University

Faculty Development Series

The Personal Development Methodology is a framework for people who are committed to growth. It allows them to address their limitations in practical ways, and it increases their ability to handle the challenges of reintegration as they move to higher levels of personal development. A logical pattern of actions related to meta-cognitive skills guides the self growth process in ways that can result in significant change, especially if an effective mentor provides guidance over an extended period of time. Individuals who learn to use this methodology can expect to gain a greater sense of self-confidence, increased self-esteem, and enhanced appreciation of themselves as persons with unique identities and talents. This module provides information about the processes and tools involved in the steps of the methodology. An example illustrates how the methodology might work for an individual with a particular area of focus.

Table 1   **Personal Development Methodology**

1.	**Recognize the need for change and growth.**	*Current limitations or constraints require some action or decision.*
2.	**Explore contextual issues.**	*Assess the current situation, resources, priorities, and barriers.*
3.	**Prioritize based on values.**	*Decide what is important for you.*
4.	**State clear outcomes.**	*Set goals with outcome criteria.*
5.	**Develop a plan.**	*Create an operational plan that includes defined activities and time allocation.*
6.	**Perform to the plan as set.**	*Execute the planned steps or actions.*
7.	**Assess performance.**	*Monitor progress towards the objectives.*
8.	**Adjust the plan.**	*Assess, during activities, on the basis of criteria, measuring progress, and making adjustments accordingly.*
9.	**Appreciate gains.**	*Acknowledge growth and progress.*
10.	**Reward achievement.**	*Motivate yourself for future successes; celebrate your successes with family and friends.*

Description of the Personal Development Methodology

The Personal Development Methodology is a systems framework or guide that offers a whole-person orientation, an emphasis on integration of skills with values, and a focus on achieving life goals. Sometimes these goals may be blocked by some barrier—whether internal or external

*(see **Becoming a Self-Grower** for more information on barriers).* Performance skills in the affective domain, especially commitment to self, are central to success with personal development goals. By contrast, affective skills are secondary in other methodologies (reading, teamwork, etc.) which have a focus on more discrete performance skills. In all methodologies, however, repeated looping among the steps and intense personal commitment to performance improvement are essential for successful results. The complexity of the personal development process and the many ways it can be derailed make it imperative to be aware of the significant processes involved in each step.

Selecting a Mentor

Individuals without experience with the first four steps in the methodology usually need to select a mentor before entering the methodology. The selection of a mentor (Johnson, 2002) is a highly significant personal decision that must be approached with discernment, including special focus on the ability of the prospective mentor to establish rapport and trust quickly. Kitchener (1992) explores the ethical dimensions of the mentoring role in the context of higher education, especially the issue of differences in power and status. Individuals offering to be mentors must have strong affective skills in the area of valuing others, and they must be able to facilitate self-management and emotional management skills in those mentored. Having clear ethical and policy guidelines is a wise preventive strategy for mentoring programs, and individual mentors should carefully discuss the nature and expectations of the relationship with those mentored.

Analysis of Steps in the Methodology

Each of the ten steps in the methodology involves a specific action. These action steps will be reviewed to identify the main intent, processes, tools, and outcomes for each.

Step 1 – Recognizing the need for change and growth.

It is difficult to accurately assess growth issues and to clearly state priorities for change. Often a mentor's most important contribution is helping a person become aware of a need for change and for commitment to growth (Prochaska, DiClemente, & Norcross, 1992). Individuals may initially seek assistance about a crisis or problem that is creating negative emotions and cognitive distortions (Piattelli-Palmarini, 1994) that disrupt their ability to cope. Because it usually takes repeated efforts before the direction of change in personal priorities becomes clear, the initial steps in the Personal Development Methodology may take some time. Individuals, however, often seek an immediate fix instead of engaging in a truly life-changing process that incorporates a longer-term, developmental approach. Cauce et al. (2002) found that many individuals, especially from ethnic minority groups, need help from counselors, family members, or mentors if they are to become aware of ways to pursue a positive mental health and personal development path despite negative influences from their life contexts.

Step 2 – Exploring contextual issues.

Exploration of the current situation, resources, and barriers is a task that complements the Step 1 process of recognizing need for change and growth. Step 2 puts emphasis on the environments, social situations, and contextual aspects of the person's life that are likely to create variations in successful self-growth. It is challenging, but essential, to accurately assess contextual issues such as family support, peer behaviors, experiences with authorities, and sufficiency of resources to support goals or overcome barriers. A strong way to address Steps 1 and 2 is to complete a life vision portfolio with guidance and assessment from a trusted mentor.

Step 3 – Prioritizing based on values.

Values are often difficult to bring fully to consciousness. Making them conscious, however, is necessary when individuals are in transition phases which force them to make life changes or to engage life in a more challenging way. Value statements express the essence of life's most meaningful aspects in a person, organization, or society. Academic disciplines are based upon values, organizations are anchored in a set of values, societies coalesce around collective values, and the quality of a person's life is based upon living consistently with positive values. The better the analysis and clarification of values, at any level or context, the better the probability of consistency between values and behavior. As noted, the life vision portfolio is a significant tool for analyzing and clarifying individual values.

Step 4 – Stating clear outcomes.

Outcomes must be carefully distinguished from the behaviors and processes used to meet or achieve intended outcomes. The performance criteria for the outcomes in a personal development plan must be clear, measurable, realistic, and relevant to the person's intent and priorities. In most cases a personal development plan will involve learning skills contained in the social and affective domains. The contexts in which a person plans to carry out the plan must be carefully considered to assure that the wording of expected outcomes is specific and concrete.

Step 5 – Developing a plan.

Achieving outcomes requires attention to deadlines, availability of resources, and opportunities. The Planner's Report form in the *Learning Assessment Journal* (Pacific Crest) is designed with teamwork in mind, but it can be adapted for describing the practical steps and logistics needed in personal development tasks. Chapter 10 of *Foundations of Learning* (Krumsieg & Baehr, 2000) provides general resources for personal development. A complete personal development plan should include behaviorally defined steps, record keeping requirements, definite timelines, identification of resources, specification of contexts for tasks, and assessment criteria for each outcome.

Step 6 – Performing to the plan as set.

Individuals vary in how well they monitor their achievement of the steps that lead toward outcomes in their personal development plans. Mentors must support growth and refuse to accommodate lack of responsibility or task avoidance on the part of the mentee. Procrastination is a common problem that can be addressed by shortening timelines and breaking processes into smaller steps. If an individual views a goal as essentially one large step, he or she will avoid approaching any aspect of the goal and, therefore, make no progress. Cook (2000) found that it is less important to identify why procrastination occurs than to directly address it as a behavior needing improvement. The most important safeguard is a carefully written, detailed, and mutually agreed upon personal development plan that includes clear methods of assessment.

Step 7 – Assessing performance.

Personal growth objectives must be assessed *(see Overview of Assessment)* at intervals established in the plan to determine how well the outcomes are being achieved. Mutually agreed upon assessment methods during the planning stage will facilitate resolution of difficulties that occur because of ambiguities or missing elements in the plan. The SII technique *(see **SII Method for Assessment Reporting**)* is the recommended assessment method because it is readily adjustable to the qualitative changes involved in the Personal Development Methodology.

Step 8 – Adjusting the plan.

Assessing performances related to the outcomes in the plan is likely to result in new insights related to (a) changes in challenges and opportunities impacting the person's life, (b) growth in values, and (c) increased self-regulation (e.g., Patrick & Middleton, 2002) indicated by independent use of the Personal Development Methodology. A mentor can apply the accelerator model *(see **Accelerator Model**)* to help a mentee continue to move past his or her comfort zone if it appears necessary to set new or different standards of performance.

Step 9 – Appreciating gains.

Mentors can help mentees recognize improvements in attitudes about learning, risk, and life vision that result from taking on increasing challenges. Even small life changes are highly significant because they predict an increased ability to actualize potential in the future. Reflection on growth experiences, e.g., by using the *Learning Assessment Journal*, involves ongoing exploration with the goal of capturing creative insights that will directly influence decisions. The module **Performance Levels for Self-Growers** provides a set of behavioral standards to guide assessment of progress toward personal development outcomes.

Step 10 – Rewarding achievements.

Important accomplishments need to be recognized and celebrated with family and friends. Making personal development goals public in this way helps individuals feel positive while also adding powerful social motivation for continuing to set challenging personal development goals. How achievements will be rewarded should be built into the personal development plan to help individuals stay motivated to achieve outcomes.

Application of the Personal Development Methodology

Kardash (2000) reported on an Undergraduate Research Experience (URE) that involved mentoring science students with the goal of improving their ability to "do science." The instructional theory included the assumption that this level of learning requires a cognitive apprenticeship in situated cognition (i.e., a specific type of learning environment in which learning occurs) so the students will

learn to think of the tasks in the same ways as do expert mentors. Despite careful guidance by URE faculty related to the central learning goals or priorities (e.g., students' ability to ask new scientific questions), these appeared to be less well achieved, based on the data, than secondary ones such as effective oral presentations.

A strong focus on the first three steps of the Personal Development Methodology (recognizing the need for change and growth, exploring contextual issues, and prioritizing based on values) is essential for helping students focus on central growth issues--such as improved ability of the URE students to ask questions like professional scientists. Students need conscious awareness not only of personal learning and growth potential, but also of their ability to overcome barriers within themselves. Without this awareness, learners will not be able to reach the new levels of growth that result from deepening reflection on attitudes, values, and skills related to a life goal.

In this simulated example, Amy, an imaginary high-achieving science student in a URE, uses the Personal Development Methodology with support from her faculty mentor in order to enhance the value of the experience.

Amy already knows that she intensely enjoys the laboratory procedures and detail involved in biology and chemistry courses, but she has spent little time consciously reflecting on how her personality and learning style will fit with her career aspirations. Initial discussions about her conceptualization of a science career lead her mentor to suggest that she focus on the bigger picture and learn more about the responsibilities and challenges that go with such a career by joining him in the upcoming URE.

Amy knows that she deeply admires the persistence and creativity of many scientists, especially those who have made historically significant contributions, but she begins to wonder how well her values will fit with those common in many science jobs outside the university. She reflects on questions like "Will it bother me if seeking truth turns out to be a smaller part of my career than grantsmanship? Can I generate enough original ideas?"

Amy can easily state clear outcomes for her science project but she struggles with how to state outcomes for her goals of clarifying the fit between her personal life priorities and a career in scientific research. She accepts her mentor's challenge that she demonstrate her increasing awareness of the practical nature of doing science by stating ten substantive insights about the fit between herself and a science career by the end of the URE. Standards for insight statements include the following characteristics: (a) they must be related to processes needed in science work (b) they must be at "level 3" quality *(see **Elevating**

Knowledge from Level 1 to Level 3), and (c) they must be elaborated in ten, one-page write-ups that differentiate the insights and include supporting observations and reasoning.

From her learning journal, Amy notices that she is starting to think of herself as an active and independent scientist and that it is becoming easier to write her insights at the generalized level modeled by her mentor during their discussions. Amy's mentor arranges for special URE awards for her and several of her peers who also have taken on the personal development challenge.

Concluding Thoughts

Learning how to stay on an accelerating path of personal growth is a high-priority for anyone with the desire to create a more meaningful life by overcoming barriers and increasing positive changes. This module provides an overview of the Personal Development Methodology, including supporting tools, resources, and research for its ten steps. The purpose of the methodology is to guide individuals seeking to learn the skills for achieving self-regulated personal growth, the basis for a well-lived life. Those who learn to flexibly use the methodology to guide planning, actions, and assessment will gain greater personal confidence, increase their ability to respond to mentoring, become more aware of the role of values, and seek continuous increases in self-growth in all life contexts.

References

Cauce, A. M., Domenech-Rodriguez, M., Paradise, M., Cochran, B. N., Munyi Shea, J., Srebnik, D. & Baydar, N. (2002). Cultural and contextual factors in mental health-help seeking: A focus on ethnic minority youth. *Journal of Consulting and Clinical Psychology, 70,* 44-55.

Cook, P. F. (2000). Effects of counselors' etiology on college students' procrastination. *Journal of Counseling Psychology, 47,* 352-361.

Johnson, W. B. (2002). The intentional mentor: Strategies and guidelines for the practice of mentoring. *Professional Psychology: Research and Practice, 33,* 88-96.

Kardash, C. M. (2000). Evaluation of an undergraduate research experience: Perceptions of undergraduate interns and their faculty mentors. *Journal of Educational Psychology, 92,* 191-201.

Kitchener, K. S. (1992). Psychologist as teacher and mentor affirming ethical values throughout the curriculum. *Professional Psychology: Research and Practice, 23,* 190-195.

Krumsieg, K., & Baehr, M. (2000). *Foundations of learning* (Chapter 10: Personal Development). Lisle, IL: Pacific Crest.

Patrick, H., & Middleton, M. J. (2002). Turning the kaleidoscope: What we see when self-regulated learning is viewed with a qualitative lens. *Educational Psychologist, 37,* 27-39.

Piattelli-Palmarini, M. (1994). *Inevitable illusions: How mistakes of reason rule our minds.* New York: John Wiley & Sons, Inc.

Prochaska, J. O., DiClemente, C. C., & Norcross, J. C. (1992). In search of how people change: Applications to addictive behaviors. *American Psychologist, 47,* 1102-1114.

The Accelerator Model

by Jim Morgan, Texas A&M University and Daniel Apple, Pacific Crest

The conventional wisdom is that teachers teach best by reducing the stress (of any kind) on students to make them comfortable during learning activities. This is often implemented by methods that have the effect of lowering expectations, even though nothing could be farther from the real needs of the students or the desires of their teachers. This module outlines a model which educators can use to reflect on the right level of challenge in different learning situations. The model considers the interaction of learner ability, level of academic challenge, and level of affective skills. It supports the idea that education needs to begin with ambitious learning outcomes and should be executed in a manner that supports students strengths, provides opportunities for practice with assessment feedback, and treats learner skills as abilities that can grow and change over time.

Role of Challenge and Support in Learning

Learning outcomes achieved in the classroom are a product of the level of learner challenge and the level of learner support maintained by the educator. The learning experience needs to be knowledge centered as well as student centered and should be mediated by ongoing assessment (Bransford et al, 2000). Typically, students seek a comfort zone in which the challenge they take does not exceed their perceived level of skill or competency. This is often the learning state outside the classroom or in passive learning environments, and educational researchers have concluded that limited learning is likely to occur under these circumstances (Ames & Archer, 1988).

Putting students in an active learning environment places more challenge and stress on students, and the literature demonstrates that this is highly effective in generating mastery and increasing student motivation for attempting tasks that exceed their current abilities (Bandura, 1997). A key element of cooperative learning is managing the stress (affect) of team members. If this stress is properly managed, the team will experience increased creativity and productivity. The increase in higher-level learning by individual members of the team often exceeds the expectations of team members who thought the standard was too high, and sometimes exceeds levels that faculty thought too high (Michaelsen, Knight, & Fink, 2004).

Many authors emphasize the critical role of affect in decision making and performance because of its influence on cognitive processes (Damasio, 1994; Goldman, 1995; Picard, 1997). Mikulincer (1988) found that learners who use an "internal" attribution perspective (an assumption that they are personally invested and that results depend on their efforts) are more strongly affected initially by frustrating feedback—or failure—but will persist if there is only one failure. External attribution learners may not take as much responsibility and, therefore, may be less frustrated. Gist, Schwoerer, and Rosen (1989) found that the students who believe they will be able to meet the challenge tend to be more comfortable with the task and do (as they predict) perform better. Their study and others combine to form a compelling case for a more active classroom environment in which affect, as well as the cognitive gains of the student, are closely monitored. It is easy to increase challenge in a lecture environment, but without the support system created by active feedback and/or a team environment, students will rapidly move beyond frustration to anger and disengagement.

Elements of the Model

The Accelerator Model shown in Figure 1 incorporates three variables that regulate the growth and development of students' cognitive and affective learning skills. These variables are the *cognitive skill set* of students, the *affective skill set* possessed by students, and the *degree of challenge* initiated by the instructor.

- The **x-axis** represents the challenge or degree of difficulty associated with a task or activity; typically, the instructor can control this factor (by varying the time allowed and/or varying the quality requirements of the performance/work product).

- The **y-axis** represents a person's current level of cognitive ability or the strength of his or her cognitive skills.

- A **45-degree line** called the *"equal match line"* represents situations where the degree of challenge matches a person's skill set. This line represents learning situations in which a person feels comfortable but is not challenged to grow his/her cognitive skill set.

- The **z-axis** represents the current strength of a person's "affective" skill set (e.g. risk-taking, persisting, handling failures, experiencing successes).

Figure 1   **The Accelerator Model—Axes**

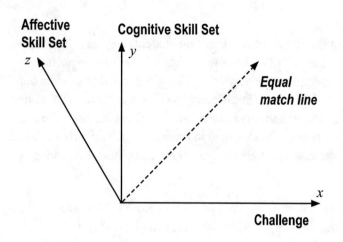

Setting the Level of Challenge

If a facilitator's main goal is to increase or maximize the learning of content, then the degree of challenge should be set above the equal match line at a maximum cognitive growth line. Figure 2 shows how increasing the learning challenge (x-axis) without a corresponding increase in the cognitive skill set (y-axis) leads to increasing levels of negative affect, which typically follow a pattern of anxiety followed by frustration, anger, and disengagement. The greatest potential for learning occurs at the lower edge of the "happy zone" where the degree of challenge exceeds a person's cognitive skill set but not enough to cause anxiety or frustration. One implication of Figure 2 is that, if a facilitator already has detailed knowledge of the affective and cognitive skill sets of a learner, it would be possible to predict the appropriate level of challenge. Effective use of the Accelerator Model therefore depends on regular and careful monitoring of the affect levels of learners in order to maintain the "best fit" level of challenge. The accelerator model provides justification for increasing or backing off the "accelerator" if the level of challenge moves slightly too far in either direction.

Maximizing Learner Growth

It is important to realize that personal growth in the affective domain occurs only when a learner is *below* his or her happy zone (see Figures 3 and 4). Therefore, a facilitator focusing on affective growth must set the degree of challenge so students experience some degree of uneasiness. A facilitator should be careful to guard against anger and disengagement, and control the amount of time spent in frustration. Ideally, a little time at the *anxiety* level can be motivating, but when learners move to *frustration* and beyond, significant disruption of the learning process

occurs. It is difficult to discern *anxiety*, and in a class of any size, some students will be anxious, while others may be bored. To add to the facilitator's assessment challenge, evidence presented in the research review above indicates that the attribution perspective (internal versus external) of a learner has a subtle but significant impact on the level of challenge that the learner will accept in a given context. Figures 3 and 4 represent how learners with low versus high affective skill sets react to the same learning challenge.

Figure 3 shows that for a given level of cognitive skills, a person with low affective skills (a) has a smaller happy zone and, therefore, can handle lesser degrees of challenge before encountering anxiety, and (b) takes less time to move through the stages from anxiety to frustration to anger and finally disengagement. Figure 4 shows that as a person's affective skill set increases, he or she is better able to handle increased levels of challenge because (a) the comfort zone itself becomes wider, and (b) the person is better able to perform outside his or her comfort zone, effectively managing anxiety and frustration when it occurs. In general, as the affective skill set improves, the comfort zone widens and the accelerator can be pushed down further before anxiety and frustration are reached. Increasing or decreasing expectations by varying the level of challenge is analogous to variations in pressure on an "accelerator." For example, the level of challenge (pushing down on the accelerator) can be achieved by decreasing the amount of time allocated and/or by increasing the criteria for performance.

Managing Frustration

Because the benefits from the Accelerator Model derive from occasionally and *intentionally* pushing students "over the line," special attention should be given to assessing and managing the level of student frustration. A number of proven techniques are suggested below.

Course Orientation

The beginning of a course is an ideal time to connect course learning outcomes with different skill sets (cognitive, social, and affective) required for successful performance in the modern workforce. In this discussion you may want to introduce rubrics and skill listings from the ***Classification of Learning Skills, Cognitive Domain,*** and ***Social Domain***. Finally, explain how the accelerator model supports a productive learning environment and inform students that you will remind them of its use throughout the course.

Figure 2

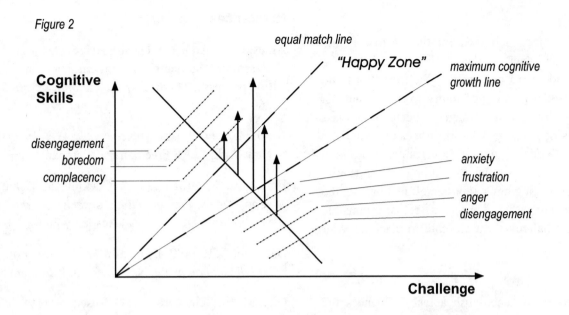

Figure 3

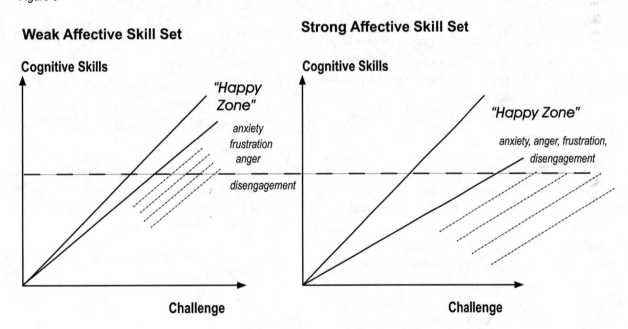

Diversity in Activities

Mix the types and levels of learning activities used throughout the course so that the strengths of each student are affirmed and challenged. Respect different learning styles when structuring learning activities so that all students have similar opportunities to become engaged in the course.

Reflective Writing Assignments

Use free writing as a means to help students express their emotions and become self-aware of their growth as well as their frustrations. Read what they write and provide observations of your own. The *Learning Assessment*

Journal by Pacific Crest offers a variety of structured reflections that can stimulate metacognition as well as teacher/student dialogue.

Monitor Classwide Affect

Show your students that you care about their personal and professional development as well as their ideas for teaching improvement by asking for feedback in midterm assessment exercises. Effective inquiry questions are suggested in *Midterm Assessment*. Take time to process what your students are learning and feeling, publicly report your findings, and adopt some of the corrective actions they suggest.

Don't Overreact

Faculty often project their own emotions into teaching situations and pull back on the accelerator prematurely. Allow your students to demonstrate their emotions and treat these episodes as an opportunity to relieve but not transfer stress. Visit with an angry student after class and affirm his or her anger, but do not take ownership for it. The key to dealing with most affective issues is to understand that the person who is feeling bad is usually responsible for making himself or herself feel bad. At the same time, recognize that your own affect is responsible for how much challenge you are able to place on your students.

Gear Shift

The time allowed to accomplish a task influences the degree of challenge and thus represents depressing of the accelerator. Learners benefit from opportunities to control the pacing or speed of their learning. Once your class is comfortable with your use of the accelerator model, you might consider giving individuals in your class control of the "gear shift". This allows them to define their resource needs and negotiate the time needed to meet the performance criteria of a learning activity.

Concluding Thoughts

Adding complexity or restricting time available for a learning activity will increase the load on the affective skills. One of the most important factors in the growth of your students is the development of their affective "skill set" for managing the anxiety, frustration, and even anger or disengagement that sometimes impedes their learning progress. Until students discover "the pleasure of finding things out" and become self-growers, teachers need to manage the affect of their students as well as help them strengthen skills in cognitive, social, and affective domains. To more effectively use the accelerator model you should periodically reflect on the following questions:

- Are my learning outcomes appropriate for the developmental level of my students?

- What are the top three reasons for frustration in my course?

- What situations appear to cause movement from anxiety to frustration, anger, and disengagement?

- What actions can be taken to reduce the current frustration without compromising key course outcomes?

References

Ames, C., & Archer, J. (1988). Achievement goals in the classroom: Students' learning strategies and motivation processes. *Journal of Educational Psychology, 80,* 260-267.

Bandura, A. (1997). *Self-efficacy: The exercise of control.* New York: W. H. Freeman and Company.

Bransford, J., Brown, A., & Cocking, R. (2000). *How people learn: brain, mind, experience, and school.* Washington, DC: National Academy Press.

Damasio, A. R. (1994). *Descartes error: Emotion, reason and the human brain.* New York: G. P. Putnam Sons.

Gist, M. E., Schwoerer, C., & Rosen, B. (1989). Effects of alternative training methods on self-efficacy and performance in computer software training. *Journal of Applied Psychology, 74,* 884-891.

Goldman, D. (1995). *Emotional Intelligence.* New York: Bantam Books.

Michaelsen, L. K., Knight, A. B., & Fink, L. D. (2004). *Team-based learning: A transformative use of small groups in college teaching.* Ridley Park, PA: Stylus Publishing.

Mikulincer, M. (1988). Reactance and helplessness following exposure to unsolvable problems: The effects of attributional style. *Journal of Personality & Social Psychology, 54,* 679-686.

Picard, R. W. (1997). *Affective computing.* Cambridge, MA: MIT Press.

Annotated Bibliography — Learning Theory

by Cy Leise, Bellevue University

Design of effective learning experiences requires consideration of learners' assumptions about knowledge, their level of learning (see ***Bloom's Taxonomy—Expanding its Meaning***), and their individual differences. Educators need to measure substantive outcomes and assess and evaluate processes. This annotated bibliography provides resources about learning theory to support educators in doing literature searches and in exploring journals, Internet sites, and professional associations. The references have been selected with emphasis on the ten principles of learning in the overview module for the Learning Theory Section.

Books

Anderson, L. W., & Krathwohl, D. L. (Eds.). (2001). *A taxonomy for learning, teaching, and assessing: A revision of Bloom's taxonomy of educational objectives.* (Abridged ed.). New York: Longman.

This volume provides some new conceptual and application material related to Bloom's cognitive domain. The addition of a more extensive list of learning assumptions and a new matrix for analyzing each level make this book an improvement over Bloom's seminal work, but also a challenge in terms of integration with process education. Bloom's work on levels of educational objectives has retained its power for guiding curriculum decisions despite being written in 1957.

Bandura, A. (1986). *Social foundations of thought and action.* Englewood Cliffs, NJ: Prentice-Hall.

Albert Bandura summarizes basic social learning research, a perspective that has transformed understanding of learning by integrating animal and human learning research related to important issues, such as aggression, phobias, imitation and modeling, self-efficacy, and cognitive-behavioral techniques. The basic tenets of the theory support contemporary emphasis on social, affective, and contextual aspects of all learning. Although Bandura emphasizes theory, he always relates it to practice by selecting experimental models that validate results. His formulation of basic learning theory provides a foundation for generalized processes and outcomes rather than mainly description or procedures. Bandura and his associates have continued to publish extensively on self-regulation of learning and other educationally relevant processes.

Berliner, D. C., & Calfee, R. C. (Eds.). (1995). *Handbook of educational psychology.* New York: Simon & Shuster Macmillan.

This thousand-page master reference has articles by major experts on a wide range of topics, such as motivation, individual differences in learning, problem solving, curriculum differences by discipline, instruction, and evaluation research. The Educational Psychology Division of the American Psychological Association produced this volume to update educational psychology. The volume is accessible for non-specialists and recognizes that the future challenge for education psychology is to support the effectiveness of teaching and learning.

Bransford, J. D., Brown, A. L., & Cocking, R. R. (Committee on Developments in the Science of Learning); Donovan, M. S., Bransford, J. D., & Pellegrino, J. W. (Committee on Learning Research and Educational Practice). (Eds.). (2000). *How people learn: Brain, mind, experience, and school* (Expanded edition). Washington, DC: National Academy Press. Available online at <www.nap.edu/catalog/9853.html>

Bransford and associates summarize research about learning from a cognitive perspective, with an emphasis on applications to improvement of schooling at all levels so that individuals can optimize their potential. They consider how experts differ from novices, provide insights related to brain physiology, identify how learning environments should be designed, and examine how learning occurs differently across disciplines. The clarity of the presentation and attention to practical and research issues, makes this an especially powerful resource.

Leonard, D. C. (2002). *Learning theories: A to Z.* Westport, CT: Greenwood Press.

Leonard provides a handy reference glossary for over 600 terms related to learning theories, models, and processes. The book is organized alphabetically but the author provides several ways to access related theories and concepts. An alphabetic list at the beginning and an extensive index at the end enable a reader to quickly find any term or name used. In an appendix, he organizes the terms under the dominant learning paradigms which include behaviorism, cognitivism, constructivism, humanism. He adds as related paradigms organizational learning and educational technology. Another valuable resource is an annotated bibliography of the major books and articles, both contemporary and classic, which provide the knowledge base for the volume. Readers of the *Faculty Guidebook* will find Leonard highly valuable as an introduction to almost any term in the Knowledge Table for Process Education module.

Pinker, S. (1997). *How the mind works.* New York: W. W. Norton & Company.

This popular and witty—but sophisticated—volume presents the mind as understood from a cognitive psychology/psycholinguistic perspective. Pinker is a well-known associate of Noam Chomsky, whose theory of language led to current thinking about the genetic and brain foundations of human ability to handle symbolic meaning through language. Although Pinker's concern is broader than education, his insights provide a strong sense of assumptions that appear to be built into the human brain and biology in general from evolution. Being sensitive to how the brain is designed, including some substantive limitations of logical capabilities, will improve curriculum design and facilitation.

Smith, M. C., & Pourchot, T. (Eds.). (1998). *Adult learning and development: Perspectives from educational psychology.* Mahwah, NJ: Lawrence Erlbaum Associates.

The editors' goal for this volume is to provide an integration of educational psychology with adult development and learning. Among the relevant issues addressed are how learning and development in adulthood are interrelated; how social and cultural contexts influence adult learning; patterns of adult moral development; how adults achieve meta-cognitive skills; and the role of adult beliefs about knowledge in school, work, and life. Granott reinterprets theories such as Piaget's to show that learning across domains requires ongoing cognitive development, not just learning. Schommer explains how variations in beliefs about the nature of knowledge create variations in its application that help explain learner attitudes.

Zimmerman, B. J., & Schunk, D. H. (Eds.). (2001). *Self-regulated learning and academic achievement: Theoretical perspectives.* Mahwah, NJ: Lawrence Erlbaum Associates.

This edited volume summarizes current knowledge from social cognitive research about the relationships between successful self-regulation of learning processes and levels of academic achievement. The participating authors examine this problem from a variety of viewpoints, such as reinforcement, information processing, developmental readiness, social learning, and phenomenology. A final chapter analyzes construction of integrated theories of self-regulation of learning.

Journals

British Journal on Educational Psychology. *(Peer reviewed journal of the British Psychological Society.)*

This journal "carries empirical and theoretical studies, case studies, action research, surveys, experimental studies, psychometric or methodological research."

Educational Psychologist. *(Peer-reviewed; published by Lawrence Erlbaum Associates for Division 15, Educational Psychology, of the American Psychological Association; by subscription to non-members.)*

This journal provides reviews of research and theories on teaching/learning processes. It is especially strong in relating conceptual and theoretical perspectives to practice by consistently featuring work related to influences on learning and cognition.

Journal of Educational Psychology. *(Peer reviewed, publication of APA.)*

This journal includes primary psychological research for K-12 as well as higher education.

Web Sites

Funderstanding—About Learning. <http://www.funderstanding.com/theories>

Twelve learning theories are explored with emphasis on the constructivist approach to learning.

Learning Theory & Instructional Strategies Matrix. <http://chd.gse.gmu.edu/immersion/knowledgebase>

This matrix chart provides a quick overview of how learning theories correlate with educational practices.

The Theory into Practice (TIP) Database: Explorations in Learning & Instruction. <http://tip.psychology.org>

This database of fifty learning theories contains brief descriptions of the main principles of each theory, with an adult-learner focus, as well as practice tips for learners and teachers.

Annotated Bibliography — Mentoring

by Victor Harms, Bellevue University

Mentoring and coaching require performance skills designed to facilitate change and growth in individuals by means of supportive, but focused relationships. Mentoring and "life coaching" are substantially similar in their focus, approach, orientation, and content. Strategies for improving learning, as opposed to growth, include "peer coaching" and "managerial coaching." The following reading list contains useful resources related to mentoring, as defined by the ten principles of mentoring *(see Overview of Mentoring)*. These references provide principles, models, and discussions of issues related to mentoring, and how to mentor in a variety of contexts.

Books

Ambrose, L. (1998). *A mentor's companion*. Chicago: Perrone-Ambrose.

A Mentor's Companion is a compendium of action and reflection about mentoring in business and service industries. Its seven brief chapters are designed to help individuals improve job performance in collaboration with colleagues, supervisors, senior executives and peers. Ambrose developed the book from application and thoughtful experimentation during two decades of local, national and international consulting. He draws on examples from the finance, health care, retail, publishing, manufacturing, and a host of service industries to provide valuable insights and strategies. Although the title specifies "mentoring," the author may be considered a practitioner of coaching in the sense of learning improvement rather than mainly growth-oriented mentoring, as it is usually defined in process education.

Daloz, L. A. (1999). *Mentor: Guiding the journey of adult learners*. San Francisco: Jossey-Bass.

Daloz approaches mentoring from an adult development perspective and bases his strategies and recommendations on extensive life experience as a mentor. He provides a personal sense of the promises, joys, problems, and contradictions endemic to mentoring. The book includes many practical vignettes that capture the nature of mentoring as a process as well as the social and emotional experiences that often occur during a mentoring relationship.

Spears, L. (Ed.). (1995). *Reflections on leadership: How Robert K. Greenleaf's theory of servant leadership influenced today's top management thinkers*. New York: Wiley.

Spears brings together a set of authors with varying perspectives on Greenleaf's 1977 book *Servant Leadership* (Mahwah, NJ: Paulist Press) in which he first articulated his vision of servant-leadership. The influence of Greenleaf, the "grandfather" of the modern empowerment movement in business leadership, has steadily increased. Greenleaf describes true leaders as those who lead by serving others and thus empowering others to reach their full potential. He sees the ideal leader as one who transforms and integrates an organization, a steward with a commitment to the growth of people and the building of community. Spears' volume is one of the more comprehensive sources dedicated to assessment of the servant leadership philosophy.

Stoddard, D. A., & Tamasy, R. (2003*). The heart of mentoring: Ten proven principles for developing people to their fullest potential*. Colorado Springs: NavPress.

Stoddard and Tamasy explore how, in mentoring relationships, giving often involves receiving—and receiving involves giving. The volume represents mentoring as a process that gets its power from the mentor's helping others to develop their own values and priorities by sharing aspects of his or her own life. There is no definite formula or agenda, but in the natural course of a well-focused and meaningful relationship, mentors provide life-changing facilitation to their mentees.

Stone, F. M. (1999). *Coaching, counseling & mentoring: How to choose & use the right tools to boost employee performance*. New York: AMACOM.

Stone addresses three crucial professional roles and associated sets of tools to help managers improve the learning, adjustment, and growth of employees. Coaching tools, such as ways to gather information, develop active listening, and improve awareness, can be used when individuals need assistance in engaging in new types of learning to improve their work or their lives. Counseling tools, aimed at helping to fix poor performance, become essential when people experience emotional, social, or other barriers that must be overcome to make progress in learning and/or growth. Mentoring tools, which enable top performers to excel, facilitate growth-oriented change that is independently desired by individuals. The focus of this resource is on helping readers to improve in skills related to use of each of these three roles to address change and growth in workplace performance.

Whitmore, J. (2002). *Coaching for performance: Growing people, performance and purpose*. (3rd ed.). Naperville, IL: Brealey.

This handbook helps with learning the skill and the art of good coaching to unlock people's potential to maximize their own performance. The author advises avoiding a "blame culture" and recommends fostering empowered performance. The book contains examples of effective questions for generating awareness and individual responsibility. New sections cover motivation and building self-esteem through coaching, feedback and feed-forward, and a specific chapter addresses learning and enjoyment. Whitmore provides strong tools and insights about enhancement of learning and improvement of performance.

Whitworth, L., House, H., Sandahl, P., & Kimsey-House, H. (1998). *Co-active coaching: New skills for coaching people toward success in work and life*. Palo Alto: Davies-Black.

For professional coaches, as well as those wanting to integrate coaching skills into their consulting practice, "co-active coaching" presents a collaborative approach for client and coach. The book offers a detailed look at the fundamental principles, skills, and practices critical to coaching success. Consulting Psychologists Press (CPP) is a large purveyor of tests, including the Myers-Briggs Type Indicator, and of supporting books that help practitioners interpret and apply test data. CPP offers a "Coaching Report for Leaders," which is based on a standardized and validated instrument that yields scores for skills in self-management, team-building, problem solving, and other areas in which individuals can benefit from coaching and mentoring.

Williams, P., & Davis, D. C. (2002). *Therapist as life coach: Transforming your practice*. New York: Norton.

Life coaching (or personal coaching) is the second biggest consulting industry after management consulting. Therapists are well positioned to move into this rapidly growing field since they are already experts at listening, encouraging, and facilitating change. Coaching allows therapists to use their current training with a wide population of clients who are not "suffering mental illness," but rather seeking to maximize their life potential. Becoming a coach usually requires only a little additional fine-tuning and specific skill building. This book is designed for the therapist wishing to enter the coaching field.

Zachary, L. J. (2000). *The mentor's guide: Facilitating effective learning relationships*. New York: Wiley.

Lois Zachary is a specialist in adult development and learning, and principal of a consulting firm. She presents mentoring as a learning journey, in which the mentor and mentee are companions. By using the worksheets and exercises in the book, managers, teachers, and leaders in any setting can successfully navigate the learning journey.

Zeus, P., & Skiffington, S. (2002). *The coaching at work toolkit: A complete guide to techniques and practices*. New York: McGraw-Hill.

This resource book is a toolkit of coaching tools and psychology-based techniques. It is also a guide to understanding the practice of coaching and applying the theories and language associated with it. Through the use of case studies, practical instructions, and application guidelines, the authors have provided models, principles and techniques that enable professional coaches to achieve what they describe as "breakthrough results." This book builds upon the authors' first general coaching reference, *The Complete Guide to Coaching at Work*.

Web Sites

International Coach Federation. <http://www.coachfederation.org>

This site identifies training organizations. It is useful for accessing current research and links to many coaching resources, and it also includes information on ethics and credentialing of coaches.

The Coaching Business: Create Your Own Magic. <http://www.coachvilleannualconference.com>

This site provides information about resources for locating a coach and about selecting training to become a coach. It provides links to the two major credentialing organizations. CoachVille is a "grassroots" organization that provides many networking and community link opportunities.

International Mentoring Association. <http://www.mentoring-association.org>

This site includes resources related to theory and professional issues of mentoring. Links to current research and a glossary of mentoring terms are useful resources of this site. The site is designed from a perspective of distinguishing mentoring processes from counseling and other associated processes.

Section Three
Facilitation in a Quality Learning Environment

Modules in this section:

Overview of Facilitation

by Peter Smith, St. Mary's College

Facilitation is an essential ingredient in teaching/learning, and all faculty members can benefit immensely from improving their skills in this performance area. Facilitation can be used with students to help them grow as learners, with graduate students to help them grow as researchers, with committee members to promote team problem solving, and with professional organizations to create effective mission statements and accomplish strategic objectives. Facilitation involves a mindset of helping others perform better by creating growth opportunities and by providing coaching that allows others to take on more ownership and control of their performance. A facilitated activity should have advance planning, thoughtful and efficient set-up, ongoing activity management with an appropriate level of intervention, and effective closure. This module shows that quality facilitation depends on understanding the facilitation methodology, attention to key principles, and cultivation of specific facilitation skills.

Need for Facilitation

As outlined in the module Overview of Process Education, economic and cultural changes in society have highlighted learning outcomes and institutionalization of effective processes in measuring academic performance (Huba & Freed, 2000). This has led to wide adoption of learner-centered teaching and responsibility-centered management (Boyer Commission, 1998). As such, many faculty members are now interested in how they can become less of a "sage on the stage" and more of a "guide on the side" (Barr & Tagg, 1995). This module introduces a framework for strengthening facilitation in a variety of higher education contexts. The first element is the Facilitation Methodology explored in detail in the module ***Facilitation Methodology***. The second element is a set of key principles for enhancing learning skills in addition to producing learning. These principles shown in Table 1 are intended to provide guidance in developing a number of high-level assessment, affect management, and interpersonal skills that are critical in facilitation.

Facilitation Principles

Effective facilitators are very disciplined in their role and fluent in their use of cooperative learning practices (Johnson et al., 1998). They are prepared to guide teaching/learning activities toward pre-determined learning outcomes, to monitor participant's emotions during the process and provide needed support without accommodation, and to interrupt performance by asking questions that are intended to improve participant performance. Effective facilitators:

1. **Do not make assumptions.**

   Whenever the facilitator is on a different page than the audience, the facilitator will quickly lose their attention and confidence. Therefore, ask questions frequently, do perception checks, pre-assess, and fill in missing gaps by assessing continuously. Inquire before intervening.

Table 1   ***Principles for Quality Facilitation***

1. Do not make assumptions.
2. Shift ownership of the process to the participants.
3. Establish shared expectations.
4. Develop a strong, flexible facilitation plan.
5. Perform continuous real-time assessment.
6. Intervene on *process*, not *content*.
7. Shift role to consultant when the participants use the facilitator as an expert.
8. Bring closure to each activity.
9. Perform a summative assessment of the facilitation process.
10. Connect with each and every participant.
11. Make sure that every key finding, consensus, and valuable insight is documented.
12. Make the process rewarding and growth-oriented for the participants.
13. Don't compromise the means for the sake of the ends.

2. **Shift ownership of the process to the participants.**

   The performance of a process and its outcomes must be valued by participants for optimal results. This requires full engagement and commitment of all parties involved, especially the facilitator.

3. **Establish shared expectations.**

   The outcomes of any facilitated process must be defined clearly, connected to its goals, and agreed upon by the participants and facilitator. These outcomes should be specific, measurable, achievable, results-oriented, and time-bound.

4. **Develop a strong, flexible facilitation plan.**

   Have an infrastructure and plan thought-through for each facilitation. This is enhanced by a set of resources/tools for making on-the-spot changes. Remember that improvisation is 90% preparation and practice—and only 10% inspiration.

5. **Perform continuous real-time assessment.**

Constantly determine and update individuals' needs. Determine which needs are being met and how to meet those that are not. Also, work to improve the dynamics governing interactions of the participants. *(See Overview of Assessment.)*

6. **Intervene on *process*, not *content*.**

Whenever an expert or outsider as a facilitator introduces his or her expertise on content, it implicitly says that the participants are discounted; they reduce their ownership of the content/outcomes, and become more passive, opening the door for the facilitator to do more. By focusing on the learning skills that underlie learning new content, facilitators affirm participant abilities and build greater capacity for future performance.

7. **Shift role to consultant when the participants use the facilitator as an expert.**

Whenever the participants need the facilitator's expertise as a resource, the facilitator can switch roles and answer questions freely. It is helpful to place restrictions on the number of questions or the time allocated to consulting. The key is to assume this role only when invited by the participants.

8. **Bring closure to each activity.**

At key milestones, and at the completion of the process, summarize what has been accomplished and what still needs to be done. Strive to do this through horizontal communication between and among participants, rather than through a lecture by the facilitator. It may be necessary to rephrase and synergize participant discoveries, but do this by acknowledging participant contributions to your message.

9. **Perform a summative assessment of the facilitation process.**

At the end of a process (e.g., class, meeting, research project, semester, etc.), collect and analyze evidence about the quality of the entire process to bring closure to it. Many facilitators find it effective to keep a notebook where they record strengths, areas for improvement, and insights gained from the activity. *(See SII Method for Assessment Reporting.)*

10. **Connect with each and every participant.**

During the facilitation, make each participant aware that he or she is valued. This can be done directly or indirectly, with spoken words or with body language.

11. **Make sure that every key finding, consensus, and valuable insight is documented.**

It is the recorder's job to do this documentation while the teams are engaged in the activity. It is vitally important that someone be appointed to perform the recorder's role during the closure period. No matter how deep the insights are when expressed verbally, if they are not written down, they will be lost. It is effective to edit these findings and play them back to participants at the start of a future activity.

12. **Make the process rewarding and growth-oriented for the participants.**

Learning should be enjoyable—even fun—and the facilitator is responsible for keeping the participants challenged, not angry or disengaged. Growth requires a well-maintained balance between support and challenge.

13. **Don't compromise the means for the sake of the ends.**

The results shouldn't be made more important than the people in the learning process. Don't be afraid to make adjustments if learning objectives are not possible with the participants' levels of preparation or personal development.

Facilitation Skills

While the principles outlined in the previous section explain the essence of quality facilitation and motivate the steps in the Facilitation Methodology, focusing on several of the following skills at a time is probably the best method for elevating facilitation capability.

Listening and rephrasing — the ability to understand from the perspective of others the meaning of what they are trying to say and being able to restate it in one's own words to make sure that shared understanding is there.

Setting criteria — the ability to identify areas of measure by which the quality of a product or performance can be assessed. A criterion often points to competency areas cited in program objectives, project plans, course syllabi, and accreditation documents.

Parallel processing — the ability to focus on more than one task at a time. An example of parallel processing is meta-cognition, where one monitors one's understanding of a process during its performance by conducting an internal conversation.

Identifying key issues — the ability to ask critical questions to identify important issues associated with a problem which should be considered during the problem-solving process.

Identifying assumptions — the ability to distinguish between the available information relevant to a problem and the assumptions needed in order to model and solve the problem. It is important to validate assumptions since altering them can lead to new and completely different solutions.

Making connections — the ability to make linkages, to provide structure to content, to reach conclusions that are not obvious, and to analyze and synthesize to find answers that are not directly available from sources.

Open to feedback — the readiness to learn from and accept assessment of one's performance from both peers and activity participants.

Being open-minded — the ability to approach situations creatively; being inventive; remaining aware of all possibilities.

Risk-taking — the self-confidence to put oneself into challenging environments that require an ever-increasing level of performance and possibility of failure.

Managing frustration — the ability to handle the emotional consequences that accrue to not performing up to one's expectations by trying to figure out how to improve the next performance.

Summarizing — the ability to present the substance of a proceeding in concise form without losing or changing its meaning.

Recognizing emotions — the ability to identify the correct emotion(s) being felt by oneself or another from verbal and non-verbal signals so that a growth-producing response can be made.

Examples of Facilitation

The following sections present examples of the many different situations in which facilitation is appropriate.

Classroom Facilitation

There are many facilitation opportunities available in education, ranging from one-on-one to large lecture classrooms. Traditionally, large classes utilize lecture exclusively, often accompanied by small discussion sections or labs once a week. Collaborative problem-solving activities using classroom communication technologies, such as Classtalk, can promote active learning in large lecture classes and, if used appropriately, highlight the reasoning processes that students use to solve problems (Bransford et al., 2000). Classtalk allows student groups to enter answers on palm-held input devices which then display histograms of class responses. The goal is to stimulate class discussions in which students justify the procedures they used to arrive at their answers and listen critically to the arguments of others. It is possible to facilitate small group activities in large classes using creative seating arrangements (leaving every third row empty) to allow the facilitator to move freely about the lecture hall, monitoring the small groups.

The opposite extreme of large group facilitation is the facilitation of a small group—often as small as a single individual. In mentoring, the professional works intensively with one person while focusing on affect management and skill development. The facilitation of one-on-one learning challenges him or her to achieve significant growth as a learner.

Facilitation is not restricted to a faculty-student model. Student peers can also serve in this role of facilitating learning. Note that this process is different from *collaboration* between peers, since the relationship involves an expert's trying to help a less experienced learner discover a significant concept, solve a problem, use a tool, etc.

A faculty member must not fall into the trap of thinking that facilitation is simply supervising or managing teams of students. As mentioned in the opening paragraph, quality facilitation produces a challenging learning environment, where performance is continually improved, learning skills are grown, and students work towards becoming self-growers. Facilitators must change their thinking so they do not revert to the old paradigm of teaching, based on the assumption of John Locke that the untrained student mind is like a blank sheet of paper—a "tabula rasa"—waiting for the instructor to write on it. Instead, they must adopt a new paradigm based on cooperative learning where faculty guide and mentor students as they actively construct their own knowledge (Johnson et al. 1998, p. 1-6).

Facilitating a Committee

The Facilitation Methodology is also helpful for facilitating committee meetings. To ensure a successful outcome, it is essential to do the following: identify what needs to be accomplished; choose a time and place; design an agenda; decide what strategies will be used to handle each agenda item; send preliminary information to the participants and check that they have read it; get participant buy-in for the meeting structure and agenda; introduce each agenda item; encourage focused discussion; intervene to bring discussion back on track and to a conclusion; summarize the points of agreement and disagreement at the end of the time period; remind each person of his responsibility for the action item assigned him; ask the participants to identify strengths and areas for improvement of the meeting process; and set a time and place for the next meeting, if necessary.

The above description is an example of the broad application of the facilitation methodology to handle many situations where people purposefully interact. The following facilitation issues (except grading) also have wide application.

Issues Affecting Facilitation

There are a great number of issues facing facilitators, but the following five are probably the most universal and the most significant.

Buy-in

It is essential that all students in the class commit themselves fully to the class and the groups to which they are assigned. To accomplish this "buy-in," the facilitator must continuously emphasize student learning as a primary goal, must create high expectations for the session, and must then uphold them through constructive interventions.

Maintain a quality learning environment

Build mutual trust, share commitment, avoid judgmental statements, promote risk taking, provide timely assessment, and document progress and growth.

Grading

Effective grading rewards and motivates students to devote themselves wholeheartedly to their learning growth. We all know that grades matter greatly to students. Grading affects how students study, what they focus on, how much time they spend, and how involved they become in the course. Thus, grading is a powerful part of the motivational structure of the course (Walvoord and Anderson, 1998).

Planning

Successful facilitation requires continuous planning of the course as a whole, including course assignments, class activities, and assessments. *(See **Facilitation Methodology**.)*

Assessment

Successful facilitation requires continuous assessment and feedback using learning journals, mid-course assessment instruments, and daily reflectors' reports. *(See **Assessment Methodology**.)*

Concluding Thoughts

This Overview of Facilitation module has introduced facilitation as a key process in Process Education. Effective use of this process in conjunction with a Process Education philosophy has motivated hundreds of classes of students to significantly improve their learning skills, perform quality assessment of their performance, and make progress towards attaining competencies expected by the modern workplace (SCANS, 1991).

These results need to be carefully documented and reported using pedagogy research methods. Faculty are challenged to constantly improve their facilitation processes.

References

Barr, R., & J. Tagg. (1995). From teaching to learning: A new paradigm for undergraduate education. *Change, 27*, 13-25.

Boyer Commission. (1998). *Reinventing undergraduate education: A blueprint for America's research universities*. Carnegie Foundation.

Bransford, J., Brown, A., & Cocking, R. (2000). *How people learn*. Washington, DC: National Academy Press.

Huba, M., & Freed, J. (2000). *Learner-centered assessment on college campuses*. Needam, MA: Allyn and Bacon.

Johnson, D. W., Johnson, R., & Smith, K. (1998). *Active Learning: Cooperation in the College Classroom*, Edina, MN: Interaction Book Company.

Secretary's Commission on Achieving Necessary Skills (SCANS). (1991). *What work requires of schools: A SCANS report for America 2000*. Washington, DC: Department of Labor.

Walvoord, B., & Johnson Anderson, V. (1998). *Effective grading*. San Francisco: Jossey-Bass.

Profile of a Quality Facilitator

by Peter Smith, Saint Mary's College

Quality facilitators improve their performance through behaviors that can be classified and quantified. By encoding these behaviors into a profile, by integrating them into a facilitation rubric, and by regularly assessing facilitation using these tools, participants and facilitators can develop a shared vision of facilitator performance criteria for many different contexts. In formulating these criteria, special attention was given to classroom teaching, committee meetings, and faculty development workshops.

Need for a Facilitator Profile

Many facilitators have little or no training for this important work. Often the facilitation they have experienced during both their educational and professional careers has been mediocre. Lacking good models, it is difficult for them to become quality facilitators. This module, together with others in this chapter, attempts to remedy this situation. Research and experience have shown that in order to improve performance, it is essential to have clear criteria to measure it against. Without these criteria, facilitators have no way to assess their progress *(see Overview of Assessment)*. An effective way to identify performance criteria is to list the behaviors one would expect to find in a quality performer. This collection of behaviors organized by activity components is known as a profile.

Organization of the Profile

Six key facilitation areas were used to construct a profile for a quality facilitator *(see Facilitation Methodology)*. These areas are preparation, needs assessment, setup, facilitating experience, closure, and follow-through. The profile was developed by isolating a few behaviors possessed by a quality facilitator in each area (see Table 1). To determine the most important behaviors in each area, it was necessary to review the essential elements of facilitation *(see Overview of Facilitation)*, the research on process educators over the last ten years, and the experience of observing quality facilitators in action. The profile provides a goal for facilitators to strive to attain, and a snapshot of performance at the highest level, but the rubric (see Table 2) described in the next section should be of greater help during their gradual improvement process.

Facilitation Rubric

Once the performance criteria have been encapsulated in the profile, it is important to prepare a tool to measure where a facilitator is currently positioned along the continuum leading to the goal identified by the profile. The rubric outlined in Table 2 provides a basis for ranking a facilitation performance based on its quality *(see Identifying Potential Measures)*. A rubric classifies different levels of performance, giving the participant behaviors commonly found at each level *(see Fundamentals of Rubrics)*. The five levels of facilitator performance are ranger, manager, director, coach, and change agent. A ranger does little preparation when pursuing the goal and attempts to meet crises as they arise. A manager prepares carefully to present information needed to attain the goal to the participants, but does little to assess whether or not the information is being well utilized. A director engages others to achieve the goal by setting up a sequence of milestones and making sure the participants meet these milestones. The focus is not on individual or team growth, but bringing the project to a successful conclusion through active participation. A coach focuses on the growth of each participant as the goal is attained, while a change agent (quality facilitator) melds the individuals into effective teams, changing the system on the way to the goal, and making sure that team members become interdependent (Johnson et al, 1998) and individually accountable for team success.

To use the rubric, a facilitator looks at the paragraph attached to each level and tries to find the set of behaviors that best define his or her approach. Even though facilitators will possess some of the qualities from higher levels, they should place themselves at the level whose description best describes their strengths. With the help of a mentor, facilitators should identify the specific steps needed to achieve the next level, modifying their behavior so that it conforms to the higher levels of the rubric as quickly as possible. Each level has behaviors pertaining to the six areas from the profile of a quality facilitator.

A professional growth plan provides a step-by-step model for improvement. There are several tools developed to assist faculty members identify their goals when constructing professional growth plans. One of the most helpful is the "Teaching Goals Inventory and Self-Scoreable Worksheet" (Angelo & Cross, 1993). It is also important to engage in regular self-assessment to ensure continued performance at each level—no backtracking. For example, many facilitators possess all the director qualities, but will allow teams to "remain at task beyond peak performance."

Table 1   **Profile of a Quality Facilitator**

Preparing	• Develops resources for multiple scripts/tasks. • Designs strong structures through a facilitation plan (road map). • Predicts the major issues that must be addressed including "what done looks like." • Prepares background conceptual knowledge. • Defines metrics for project success (cost, schedule, performance, quality).
Assessing audience needs	• Affirms what each brings to the table. • Discovers major issues people are confronting. • Seeks out the outcomes for each person. • Identifies collective outcomes. • Clearly predicts and verifies everyone's role in moving along the road map.
Setup	• Clarifies expectations. • Creates a framework for the process (Describes road map and major milestones). • Establishes teams. • Motivates individuals for the experience. • Performs risk assessment and predefines risk management.
Facilitating experience	• Constantly transfers ownership to participants. • Actively assesses progress of individuals and teams. • Constructively intervenes on process issues, not content. • Continuously raises the bar to challenge participants. • Monitors objective metrics and actively acts on data to ensure success.
Closure	• Cuts off activity at top of production curve. • Requests each team representative to summarize issues (good and bad). • Does a perception check for consensus within each team. • Makes sure that each issue has an owner and due date to ensure resolution. • Insists on assessment of learning processes.
Follow-up	• Makes sure team members achieve individual/collective outcomes. • Accepts constructive criticism and promises action toward improvement. • Ensures that all data is collected for participant reflection. • Reinforces negative and positive issues as equally important. • Clarifies the next step in the process.

Table 2   **Facilitation Rubric**

Change Agent: promotes team growth and mentors other facilitators

Researches the audience, prepares a varied set of resources, scouts the environment, identifies issues and challenges, and prepares personally to give all of self during the event. Quickly assesses the collective and individual needs of the participants in the form of outcomes and creates the learning or growth environment that has characteristics such as risk taking, mutual respect, challenge, and support. Provides constructive interventions on group process. Constantly challenges performance. Monitors project in real time and knows its day-to-day pulse by comparing each individual's performance to established metrics. Has the ability to embed assessment in a variety of activities, both formal and informal. Always assesses his or her facilitation plan after each event to improve performance.

Coach: empowers participants and promotes individual growth

Designs activities that promote growth. Adept at adapting facilitation plan to meet individual needs. Establishes a learning situation in which participants succeed, rather than fail. Communicates clear performance criteria. Is aware of individual strengths and areas for improvement. Encourages participants with positive messages (verbal and written). Delegates issues and ensures team members commit and deliver. Allows participants freedom to make decisions and knows the project's pulse through MBWA (Management by Walking Around) concepts and practices (Peters & Waterman, 1982). Provides direct support to those who need assistance. Helps participants question ideas and concepts. Can assess individual performance in real time. Helps team members identify and mitigate risks. Cares for and respects the learner. Has the ability to grow the assessment skills of participants. Encourages documentation of learning at the close of each event. Interacts with participants between events.

Director: Engenders success, organizing sequences of activities to meet an objective

Uses multiple facilitation techniques in varied situations. Works to obtain participant commitment and buy-in to the project. Makes sure people know where they are headed. Keeps teams conscious of time and on task. Allocates time for new learning when there is clear and immediate payback. Has strong affective skills and is able to handle frustration. Follows continuous quality improvement principles. Guides projects to successful conclusion. Works with participants between events to produce documentation to illustrate product quality.

Manager: Effectively manages time, following own agenda over participant needs

Has mastery of the supporting tools of the content. Has strong self-confidence. Is organized and prepared content-wise for the facilitation. Provides a clear outline. Uses models effectively. Resists wasting time using assessment processes – relies on evaluation to provide motivation. Maintains focus during the activity. Sticks to the facilitation plan without regard for affective issues. Reviews content at the end of the activity. Holds participants accountable for the content covered. Believes the statement, "If I said it clearly and they answer correctly, then they must have understood it" (Wiggins & McTigue, 1998).

Ranger: Avoids planning for goals of any type, reacting to problems when they occur

Always remains at the center and in control of the learning process. Does not share the performance criteria (if any) with the participants. Allows teams to flounder unproductively and remain at task beyond the peak of their performance. Intervenes only to avert disaster and blames participants for poor performance. Seldom brings closure to an activity, leaving participants frustrated. Has no time for follow-up with participants between events.

Efficacy of the Profile in Different Faculty Facilitator Contexts

Faculty are expected to be able to facilitate in a number of different contexts. The most common are classroom teaching, committee meeting, and faculty development activities. It is helpful to think about how to use the profile and its accompanying rubric to improve the quality of facilitation in each of these contexts.

Since the facilitation of student learning is the most important responsibility of a faculty member (Millis & Cottrell, 1998), it is important to examine the application of the profile to classroom teaching. The organization of the profile follows closely the essential steps in the facilitation of a classroom activity. The behaviors in the profile, if carefully followed, will ensure that faculty will help students enhance their learning before, during, and after the activity.

A faculty member also has certain service responsibilities that almost always include committee work. When given an opportunity to facilitate a committee meeting, he or she can build a good reputation as an effective leader by following the profile. Careful perusal of the profile confirms that its organization is just as appropriate for a committee meeting as for a classroom activity. Some of the behaviors need to be interpreted differently in this new context, however. The behaviors in the preparation, needs assessment, and follow-up sections are the same. The setup section recommends establishing teams. The committee as a whole could be one team, or, as the meeting progresses, the facilitator may break off subcommittees (teams) to be responsible for parts of the work. If the facilitator feels comfortable with assigning roles to the committee members, the active use of a reflector can alleviate the need for the facilitator to directly challenge participants or to intervene on process issues in both the facilitating experience and closure sections. In the context of a committee meeting, the behavior "cuts off activity at top of production curve" means sensing when enough discussion has occurred so the committee can act on the issue.

Finally, faculty often engage in professional development alone and in departmental or larger groups. At times, they will be called upon to facilitate these activities. At other times, they will be asked for feedback on the facilitation. In both cases, the profile is helpful, and the behaviors outlined therein are all pertinent, although it is much more challenging to facilitate faculty activities than those involving students. Faculty are more likely than students to resist behavioral change, so it is recommended that faculty strive to become quality facilitators of student activities before attempting the leadership of professional development processes.

Concluding Thoughts

The profile of a quality facilitator provides a tool for assessing facilitation skills and also a goal for improving them. Using this profile and its accompanying rubric productively will be a challenge, however. An inexperienced facilitator should find a mentor who is willing to serve as a peer coach and provide assessment feedback. Such a mentor can also help the faculty member develop and follow his or her professional development plan. A mentor should pick three to five key metrics for each level and help the facilitator move quickly through the lower three levels. Eighty percent of the mentoring effort should focus on the coach and change agent levels. Also, a research effort is needed to clearly specify what it means to achieve each level and to address the concepts of delegation, multitasking, and risk management in the rubric. Finally, every facilitator, no matter how skilled, will benefit from using the profile and rubric to measure his or her skills.

References

Angelo, T., & Cross, K. P. (1993). *Classroom assessment techniques.* San Francisco: Jossey-Bass.

Johnson, D., Johnson, R., & Smith, K. (1998). *Active learning: Cooperation in the college classroom.* Edina, MN: Interaction.

Millis, B., & Cottrell Jr., P. (1997). *Cooperative learning for higher education faculty.* Westport, CT: Oryx.

Peters, T. J., & Waterman, R.H. (1982). *In search of excellence.* New York: Harper & Row.

Wiggins, G., & McTigue, J. (1998). *Understanding by design.* Upper Saddle River, NJ: Prentice-Hall.

Pacific Crest

Faculty Development Series

Facilitation Methodology

by Peter Smith, St. Mary's College and Daniel Apple, Pacific Crest

The Facilitation Methodology is a tool to help a faculty member prepare for, facilitate, and assess a learning activity/process/learning experience. This methodology is helpful in all contexts where one needs to shift from a "sage on a stage to a guide on the side," including teaching, administering a grant project, chairing a department, running a faculty development event. Faculty members have found increased confidence as facilitators with improved learning outcomes by following the facilitation methodology. The vital role of assessment appears as a thread throughout the methodology and the importance of defining learning outcomes, setting up the activity, and providing closure is emphasized. Additional modules discuss facilitation issues and tools.

Facilitation Methodology

Table 1 presents the Facilitation Methodology—applicable when facilitating an activity, a process, or any learning experience.

Table 1   **Facilitation Methodology**

1. Define the key measurable outcomes.
2. Design and prepare for every activity.
3. Decide which strategies, processes, and tools are appropriate for each specific activity.
4. Pre-assess to determine participants' readiness.
5. Set up each specific activity.
6. Release individuals/teams to pursue the activity.
7. Assess team and individual performances.
8. Provide constructive interventions based on process, not content.
9. Bring all the individuals and/or teams back together at conclusion of the activity.
10. Provide closure with sharing of collective results.
11. Use various forms of assessment to provide feedback on how to improve everyone's performance.
12. Plan for follow-up activities.

Simple Example of the Methodology

The context for this example is a classroom activity taking place at the beginning of a semester or term. Students are put in teams where they introduce themselves and begin the process of building a new learning community.

1. **Outcomes**: (a) Help each group member begin to recognize the special qualities of each other community member; (b) Make the first team activity a confidence-building one; (c) Emphasize the fact that learning is fun and everyone is accountable for their own learning.

2. **Design and prepare for the activity**: Decide to have each pair of team members introduce themselves, sharing their goals and learning styles with their partner; and then each introduce their partner to the team. Preparation involves deciding the team composition and identifying interview questions.

3. **Choose activity type and team roles**: As described in step 2, use a pair-share interview style activity. Roles are not needed.

4. **Pre-assess**: Determine that all basic needs have been taken care of (i.e., registration, food, materials, etc.), so the participants can focus on the activity.

5. **Set-up**: Describe the purpose and expectations for the activity. If there are an odd number of people on any team, describe a round-robin interview style. Specify the time limits (e.g., 20 minutes)

6. **Release teams**: Start the team interview process.

7. **Assess team and individual performances**: Walk around and listen in on each team to make sure the pairs are engaged, asking relevant questions that focus on the interview process, and making sure that each pair is making sufficient progress.

8. **Provide constructive interventions**: If teams are falling behind, ask if they are going to finish on time. If teams finish early, suggest additional tasks, such as choosing a team name.

9. **Bring teams together**: Announce in your own style that we are ready to bring closure to the activity.

10. **Closure**: Have each person identify and share a goal and a characteristic of their interview partner.

11. **Provide feedback**: Conduct a three-minute discussion of how people feel about the community that has been created.

12. **Follow-up**: Collect interview sheets and prepare a group directory.

Discussion of the Methodology

Note that steps 1-3 should be done prior to the event, step 4 either before or at the start of the event, steps 5-11 during the event, and step 12 after the event.

Step 1 – Define the key measurable outcomes.

This step is absolutely essential and the one most often omitted. When defining these measurable outcomes (two or three are sufficient), assess what your students need most in order to improve their learning performance. Avoid "over-scoping" what can be accomplished in the given time frame. Outcome-based learning is a very popular concept in higher education today, because unless teaching can be assessed against a set of outcomes, its effectiveness cannot be measured, and therefore it cannot be improved (Astin, 1985).

Step 2 – Design and prepare for every activity.

At this stage one must choose an activity that will help achieve the learning outcomes from step 1. It is important to think carefully about what the designer of the activity was trying to accomplish. Be sure to plan for contingencies that may arise during the facilitation. What individual or team behaviors are expected? Determine which learning skills (two or three) will be focused on and assessed during the activity. Make sure the activity resources can be provided.

Step 3 – Decide which strategies, processes, and tools are appropriate for each specific activity, including the roles for participants. *(See Designing Teams and Assigning Roles.)*

In this step the facilitator must decide what activity format is best suited to engage the participants based on the activity content and meeting the outcomes of the activity. It is best to incorporate at least ten different activity formats during a semester to ensure student involvement, which research (Angelo & Cross, 1993) has shown to be critical to student growth. Note that student-faculty and student-peer involvement have positive correlations with every area of student intellectual and personal growth (Astin, 2001).

Step 4 – Pre-assess to determine participants' readiness.

To ensure that all participants are sufficiently prepared to perform well during the activity, it is important to determine their level of preparation and the extent of their prior knowledge about the activity content. This can be accomplished in a number of ways: a quiz, a short written assignment about what they know or learned from their preparation, a set of questions each has prepared from the pre-event reading, or the answers to assigned study questions.

Step 5 – Set up each specific activity.

This is another highly critical step during which the facilitator ensures that participants know why they are doing the activity as well as the learning objectives, performance criteria, resources, and general tasks for the activity. Performance criteria should be set in terms of both process and content. It is important that each participant know exactly what is expected, but the facilitator must be careful not to usurp responsibility for the learning by each participant. The extent of the set-up also depends on the activity type—from discovery learning (minimal content set up) to lecture (extensive content description), and also on the personality of the facilitator. If the use of team roles is required, this is the point that the facilitator ensures that each team member has a role to play.

Step 6 – Release individuals/teams to pursue the activity.

Here we give control to the participants to start working on the activity and strive to promote learner ownership. In other words, participants should feel in control of the quality of their performance and the outcomes they produce. The first order of business for the teams is to set up a plan if one is not already provided in the activity description. One of the resources should always be the amount of time reserved for the activity.

Step 7 – Assess team and individual performances. *(See Assessment Methodology.)*

This step involves gathering information by listening to and observing the dynamics between individuals, based on verbal interchanges and body language, and written documentation from the activity—the recorder's report gives clues as to how well the participants are learning the content. The goal is to foster independent learning. Therefore, it is important to plan in advance, identifying the top three to five issues affecting performance. Link these issues with specific learning skills that can be improved and the outcomes from step 1.

Step 8 – Provide constructive interventions based on process not content.

During this step, the facilitator uses the data collected during the last step to know when to intervene, but avoids doing things for participants that they could do themselves—even if it may be the easiest way to remedy the situation. By making it harder to get information from the facilitator and by replying with questions rather than direct answers, participants will use and develop their information processing and critical thinking skills. Be careful not to intervene unless a team asks for help, because unwanted interventions can disrupt the flow of the team and even cause resentment of the facilitator. When making an intervention, focus on helping participants address the skill or process that is lacking rather than focusing completely on the content. Examples of appropriate times for an intervention include: after an extended period of struggling or frustration, when participant's actions stray too far from meeting the performance criteria for the activity, or when there is a complete breakdown in performance (Apple et al., 2000).

Step 9 – Bring all the individuals and/or teams back together at conclusion of the activity.

This is not easy because teams work at different speeds. It may be necessary to assign enrichment exercises to some teams and stop others before they have fully completed the activity.

Step 10 – Provide closure with sharing of collective results.

This is a vitally important step and should not be skipped, even when time is short because participants need feedback. Have the teams share quality performances that others can benefit from as well as areas where performance needs improvement. Identify star performances and areas that need more discussion and discovery. Summarize what has happened and what has been learned, but don't spend time on what participants already know. Challenge them to articulate their discoveries at higher levels of knowledge beyond facts and information. *(See Elevating Knowledge from Level 1 to Level 3.)*

Step 11 – Use various assessments to provide feedback on how to improve everyone's performance.

Realize that participants want assessment feedback based on the activity performance criteria that will help them improve future performance. Make regular use of oral reflector's reports.

Step 12 – Plan for follow-up activities.

The written team products should be assessed and returned with comments to each team at the next class. If some points need clarification, a quiz or further discussion may be employed. The facilitator should assess his or her own performance, striving for continual improvement. If the performance was peer coached, the facilitator and peer coach should meet after the facilitation for a mentoring session.

Another Example of the Methodology

The context for this example is a faculty development activity where participants are to learn about using the Facilitation Methodology.

1. **Define the key measurable outcomes.**
   - Prepare participants so they can complete a facilitation plan.
   - Enable participants to create criteria for assessing the quality of a facilitation plan.
   - Produce a model for facilitation that others can learn from.

2. **Design and prepare for every activity.**

In the 1997 *Teaching Institute Handbook* (Apple & Krumsieg, 1997), Activity 4.3 was designed to help faculty understand the Facilitation Methodology, learn to assess the quality of a facilitation, and create a plan for becoming a better facilitator. Expect to spend an hour reviewing the activity and anticipating how it can help achieve the outcomes from step 1. Focus on the following learning process skills: divergent thinking, analyzing differences, and managing frustration. These were chosen because it is anticipated that the activity will produce wide-ranging ideas which must be worked into a coherent report—a frustrating endeavor.

3. **Decide which strategies, processes, and tools are appropriate for each specific activity.**

The facilitation activity mentioned in step 2 was designed as a guided-discovery activity. However, students often rebel against too many such activities, so convert to a 50-minute problem-based learning activity (Barrows, 1994). With this format, the participants are presented with a problem—in this case to identify the issues involved with preparing and assessing a high quality facilitation plan—and must establish their own learning objectives and performance criteria. Decide to provide them with this facilitation plan as a model. Use standard roles and make use of reflector and recorder's reports.

4. **Pre-assess to determine participants' readiness.**

It seems best to give the activity and background information to the participants to read beforehand. Assess how many have done the reading and their level of understanding by giving a two-minute quiz that asks which are the three most difficult steps in the methodology and why. This will be an individual self-assessment quiz to let the team know the level of preparation of its members.

5. **Set-up each specific activity.**

In two minutes, emphasize why facilitation plans are critical to successful facilitation and the role of assessment to ensure quality. Give the teams five minutes to review the activity and identify learning objectives and performance criteria, and answer questions for two minutes at the end of this period. Also, state the learning skills identified in step 2.

6. Release individuals/ teams to pursue the activity.

Teams will have twenty minutes (with a planned five minute extension) to assess the model facilitation plan and to identify the issues they anticipate in developing such a plan for activities in their own disciplines.

7. Assess team and individual performances.

Look to assess the three learning skills: divergent thinking, analyzing differences, and managing frustration. Also assess the product—the quality of the facilitation plan's assessment, and the level of issues identified for developing a facilitation plan. Potential problems to be ready for: (1) perceived complexity of the Facilitation Methodology, (2) teamwork issues related to time pressure and doing several concurrent tasks, especially the reflector collecting data during the activity and the recorder making high level discoveries before the end of the activity.

8. Provide constructive interventions based on process not content.

Typical interventions to anticipate: remind learners to perform their respective team role (especially the reflector), time management, challenging level and quality of issues, and the recorder's ability to synthesize the multitude of issues raised.

9. Bring all the individuals/teams back together at the conclusion of the activity.

Make sure that all teams have enough recorded to be able to engage in class discussion, including three learning outcomes, two performance criteria, the reflector's report, an SII assessment *(see SII Method for Assessment Reporting)* of the model facilitation plan, and five issues with developing their own facilitation plans. If some teams finish early, challenge them to improve the quality of their issues and/or assessment. Give other teams three minutes after the first team finishes.

10. Provide closure with sharing of collective results.

Inventory the top two issues raised by each team. The facilitator will model the process of raising the level of some of the issues presented. Allow ten minutes.

11. Use various assessments to provide feedback on how to improve everyone's performance.

Reflector's reports will be used to determine the quality of the team performance. Allow five minutes.

12. Plan for follow-up activities.

Provide fifteen minutes of consulting for each participant working on a facilitation plan for their own activity.

Concluding Thoughts

This module emphasizes the importance of following the methodology during each facilitation performance and highlights three steps as critically important: identifying outcomes, setting up the activity, and providing closure for the students. While it is true that once one gains experience with some methodologies, they are no longer needed, even the most experienced facilitator would do well to step through this methodology when preparing for each facilitation because it is very hard to break ingrained sloppy facilitation habits. When implementing this module it is helpful to also use the module *Creating a Facilitation Plan* since the latter contains a template which helps organize the facilitation before, during and after an activity. Taking the time to carefully apply this methodology for each facilitation is both a challenge and an opportunity for radical improvement.

References

Angelo, T. A., & Cross, K. P. (1993). *Classroom assessment techniques: A handbook for college teachers*. San Francisco: Jossey-Bass.

Apple, D., Duncan-Hewitt, W., Krumsieg, K., & Mount, D. (2000). *Handbook on cooperative learning*. Lisle, IL: Pacific Crest.

Apple, D., & Krumsieg, K. (1997). *Process education teaching institute handbook*. Lisle, IL: Pacific Crest.

Astin, A. (1985). *Achieving educational excellence*. San Francisco: Jossey-Bass.

Astin, A. (2001). *What matters in college? Four critical years revisited*. San Francisco: Jossey-Bass.

Barrows, H. (1994). *Practice based learning: Problem based learning applied to medical education*. Carbondale, IL: Southern Illinois University.

Feldman, K., & Paulson, M. (1998). *Teaching and learning in the college classroom*. Needham Heights, MA: Ginn Press.

Johnson, D. W., Johnson, R., & Smith, K. (1998). *Active learning: Cooperation in the college classroom*. Edina, MN: Interaction Book Company.

McKeachie, W., Pintrich, P., Yi-Guang, L., & Smith, D. (1986). *Teaching and learning in the college classroom: A review of the research literature*. Ann Arbor: The Regents of the University of Michigan.

Pritchard, K., & Sawyer, R. M. (1994). *Handbook of college teaching: Theory and applications*. Westport, CT: Greenwood Press.

Creating a Facilitation Plan

by Vicky Minderhout, Seattle University

Facilitated classroom activities make up the public face of teaching. When preparing to facilitate these activities, teachers should use a facilitation plan for reasons made evident in this module. Such a plan arises from applying the facilitation methodology *(see Facilitation Methodology)* in a step-by-step fashion. This facilitation plan module includes a plan template (found on the third and fourth pages of this module) and exemplifies how to fill it out. It emphasizes the importance of assessing facilitation performance after each classroom activity.

Need for a Plan

Careful planning lies at the heart of successful performance (Millis, 1998). The planning process recommended in this module will help the teacher attend to the facilitation principles *(see Overview of Facilitation)*, work through the facilitation methodology, and anticipate learner needs. Since these needs revolve around process issues that impact learning, most facilitators will find it beneficial to reflect on these issues and plan how to address them. In addition, the preparation of a written organizational framework before facilitating an activity not only serves as a prompt during facilitation but also forms a permanent record of what was attempted by the teacher during the activity and becomes the basis for assessing performance.

Elements of a Plan

A complete plan consists of three components. The first component encompasses planning prior to the facilitation (page one of the Facilitation Plan template). The second component involves recording data during the facilitation (page two of the template). And the third concludes the data collection and provides for reconciliation of the planning with the execution and assessment of the facilitation and the learning outcomes (also on page two of the template). Before reading the next section, it will be helpful to have the blank facilitation plan template available.

Prior to the activity

1. To prepare to facilitate a classroom activity, begin by reviewing relevant previous activities: e.g., the activity you most recently facilitated, this particular one done in a previous offering of the course, an activity of the desired type, and/or ones that emphasize the skills you intend to stress. Establish your outcomes for the activity (three are sufficient), and incorporate skills from more than one domain (cognitive, social, affective, and psychomotor domains). *(See Classification of Learning Skills.)* Early in the term, you might consider building teamwork and communication skills. It is useful to consider and note anticipated evidence for each outcome on page one of the template, along with the outcomes.

To illustrate this process, look at the first example in the Facilitation Methodology module. The example is an activity to introduce members of a new community to each other with the following desired outcomes: (a) help each group member begin to recognize the special qualities of each other community member; (b) make the first team activity a confidence-building one; (c) emphasize the fact that learning is fun and everyone is accountable for their own learning.

Note that the skills needed to accomplish these outcomes are empathizing and building self-esteem (affective domain), attending and rephrasing (social domain), and: making connections/convergent thinking (cognitive domain). Evidence that the outcomes are being accomplished would be (a) respectful language as the teams interview each other, (b) full participation of all team members in the activity, and (c) smiles but signs that no one is goofing around.

2. Once your outcomes are established, select an activity type to facilitate the outcomes. The outcomes or activity type you selected may require certain roles for group members.

3. Therefore, in the plan you should define the roles to support the outcomes and activity type. In the example above, the facilitator has decided to use a pair-share interview style activity. Roles were not needed.

4. For many activities students must complete an assignment prior to class in order to prepare themselves to participate. Some pre-assessment of the preparation should be planned to make sure that all students have completed the pre-class assignment. If the pre-assessment is a quiz, include an estimate of its time in the plan. In the example, the facilitator needs to ask the students if all their basic needs have been taken care of—i.e., registration, food, materials, etc—so the participants can focus on the activity. This will probably take only a minute or two.

5. Instructions to the students for the activity are outlined in the activity set-up. Focus on the purpose, expectations, roles, and the amount of time allocated, including the closure time. Also identify for the students the

learning skills they should focus on during the activity, usually one skill for each domain. In the example, the facilitator tells the students the purpose of the activity is to get everyone introduced and comfortable in their groups, that they are accountable for their interview information, that the format of the activity will be pair-share for 20 minutes, and that each student should focus on attending and rephrasing.

6. Anticipate what to expect when observing the group work. List the skills on which learners should focus (which were listed in the outcomes) and anticipate situations during the activity in which you might observe them performing the skill. This will help you make better real-time observations and improve the interventions on process. Since attending and rephrasing were given as skills in the outcomes, you expect to see some interchange between the two in the pair share, rather than just nodding of heads.

7. Very often, one or more teams complete the activity before the others, due either to superior organization and focus or to shallow performance. Plan challenges for these groups which raise the bar for their performance and motivate them to become more deeply engaged.

8. Plan for closure of the activity. What will be shared between the teams? Will the facilitator participate in sharing? Will the data be recorded on an overhead or computer or will sheets be collected from the groups? Will groups report on and/or turn in reflector and recorder reports? For the example in the facilitation methodology, each student might be asked to introduce his or her interviewee and share a goal and something unique about the interviewee with the class. For activities that involve more cognitive outcomes, sharing discoveries about the material can enhance growth.

During the Activity

9-10.   At the beginning of the activity, note the effectiveness of the assessment of participant preparation and of the activity setup, particularly how much time was spent.

11. During the activity, monitor the teams for real-time data on the interactions in the groups. Collect data by focusing on the identified skills, but being open to other observations. Things to consider would be evidence of outcomes being met, questions asked by team captains, and your responses. Record any interventions you make and the result.

12. During the closure period, document the oral reports that cannot be captured from written reports or inventorying discoveries. The better your notes are during the classroom session, the more real-time data you will have to improve your own performance as a facilitator.

After the activity

13. You have collected notes during the activity and the teams have supplied recorder reports, reflector reports, and closure notes. From this wealth of data comes the reconciliation of what was planned for the activity and what actually occurred. Review the outcomes. Were they met? If the activity went well, it is useful to identify the key issues that came together to make it a success. If the activity did not help the student meet the outcomes, then a review of the components of the activity is necessary. Were the outcomes too broad? Was the activity type appropriate to achieve the outcomes? If the students were not prepared, what could be done about that? Did closure result in significant learning growth?

Assessing facilitator performance using the plan

14. A facilitation plan is also useful for improving the facilitator's performance. If the activity outcomes are not met, it is necessary to decide if something is wrong with the activity and how to fix that, but, more importantly, what to do at the next class session to improve the facilitation. For best results, this assessment should give strengths, areas for improvement and insights about the facilitator's performance (*see SII Method for Assessment Reporting*).

Concluding Thoughts

The facilitation template provides an organized format to promote the use of a plan. It will take strong discipline to complete the template for each class, especially the *during* and *after* activity portions. Faculty who do complete facilitation plans are often motivated by the opportunity to use a portfolio of these plans as research for publication and/or to enhance their tenure applications.

References

Johnson, D. W., & Johnson, F. P. (2003). *Joining together: Group theory and group skills.* Boston: Allyn and Bacon.

Millis, B. J., & Cottell, P. G. (1998). *Cooperative learning for higher education faculty.* Phoenix: Oryx Press.

Facilitation Plan *(prior to class)*

1. **Outcomes** *(List 2-3 outcomes and underlying skills from different domains and describe anticipated evidence that each has occurred.)*

    •

    •

    •

2. **Activity Type** _____

3. **Roles** *(See **Designing Teams and Assigning Roles**)*

    _____   _____

    _____   _____

    _____   _____

4. **Preparation Assessment Plan**   time allotted_____

5. **Activity Set-up Plan**   time allotted_____

6. **Group Work**   time allotted_____

    Identify issues that may affect performance, link them to learning skills, and describe your anticipated response.

	Situation	Skill	Intervention
Cognitive:			
Social:			
Affective:			

7. **Challenge Ideas for Deep Divers**

8. **Closure**   time allotted_____

Facilitation Plan *(during/after class)*

9. **Preparation Assessment Notes**   time spent_____

10. **Activity Set-up Notes**   time spent_____

11. **Group Work Notes**   time spent_____

Situation	Skill	Intervention	Result

12. **Closure Notes**   time spent_____

13. **Reconciliation**

    What evidence demonstrates outcomes were met? Use data from group work to document.

14. **SII of class period**

Overview of Creating a Quality Learning Environment

by Peter Smith, St. Mary's College and Daniel Apple, Pacific Crest

Faculty Development Series

For more than ten years, a team of innovative educators has investigated and experimented with ways in which the learning environment motivates, sustains, and enriches the learning process. Creating and growing an educational setting helps faculty engage meaningfully with students. It is important, however, to distinguish the effort of establishing a learning environment from that required for facilitation, assessment, and curriculum design. The process of setting up a quality learning situation can be simplified by employing a clear methodology, using a set of well-defined principles and key skills. Such an environment is intricate and must be sustained through the use of assessment procedures and methodologies designed to enhance learning. This module shows how social processes, physical space, and learning tools must be combined using the "glue" of assessment to create a quality learning environment.

Need for a Quality Learning Environment

Most educators are aware that a collaborative, stimulating, and challenging learning environment can significantly enhance performance and growth for every individual, whether it be an infant learning to speak, a worker on the job, or a student in the classroom. It has always been important to structure temporal space, improve collaborative processes, and employ appropriate tools in order to help learners achieve desired learning outcomes. Every teacher is looking for those magical moments when "the lights go on" and transformational change occurs. A learning environment conducive to such breakthroughs definitely increases the likelihood that those satisfying events will occur.

Faculty and administrators are continuing to work at all levels of undergraduate education to find ways to improve the learning environment. Within community colleges, the Learning College movement has illustrated the range of learning environments that are possible. Liberal arts colleges have consistently pioneered new and more effective learning environments to increase collaboration between students and faculty, using such approaches as cohort models, residential colleges, and paired courses (Gabelnick et al, 1990).

The Boyer report recommends that universities transform their learning environments to support inquiry-based learning—a collaborative effort among research faculty, graduate students, and undergraduates to address the following: "Many students graduate having accumulated whatever number of courses is required, but are still lacking a coherent body of knowledge or any inkling as to how one sort of information might relate to others. And all too often they graduate without knowing how to think logically, write clearly, or speak coherently" (Boyer, 1998).

To achieve a quality learning environment in which the greatest growth is possible for all students, faculty need to follow a few key principles, as listed in Table 1.

Table 1　　**Principles for Establishing a Quality Learning Environment (QLE)**

1. Establish a high degree of trust and respect.
2. Make sure both learner and mentor are committed to the learner's success.
3. Get student buy-in very early in the process.
4. Challenge students.
5. Set clear and high expectations.
6. Encourage risk taking.
7. Seek student feedback regularly by using assessment on a consistent and timely basis.
8. Measure and document progress and growth.
9. Create a collaborative learning space.
10. Create a balance between structure and flexibility.

1. **Establish a high degree of trust and respect between students and teacher.** Mutual trust and respect enable learning to take place. A successful learning environment must be learner-centered, knowledge-centered, assessment-centered and community-centered (Bransford et al, 2000).

2. **Make sure both learner and mentor are committed to the learner's success.** The learner needs to believe that the mentor is committed to his or her success in order to persist in the face of failure. Conversely, a teacher is reluctant to invest in students who show no interest in learning. Thus, a signed commitment is often required at the beginning of the learning process.

3. **Get student buy-in very early in the process.** We know that students commit themselves to improving their performance through a number of different strategies *(see Getting Student Buy-In)*. A successful learning environment requires this commitment from each student before any content learning can take place.

4. **Challenge Students.** As illustrated in the *Accelerator Model*, transformational learning requires a balance of support and challenge. There is a temptation for faculty to enable dependent behavior in students by overemphasis on support. The goal is to provide an environment that will encourage and challenge students to live up to their potential and become self-growers.

5. **Set clear and high expectations.** Students' productivity is highly correlated to the expectations set at the beginning of the educational process in which they are engaged. In general, they perform to the level of these expectations, so it is important that they be challenged to achieve at the highest possible level (Wingspread 1993)—and that those expectations be clearly articulated for them.

6. **Encourage risk taking.** In an environment governed by high expectations, there is always the potential for students to experience failure on the road to success. When a less than desirable outcome does occur, it is important for mentors not to react adversely. When all parties involved in the learning process feel supported, they will be ready to take the risks involved in achieving genuine learning together.

7. **Seek student feedback regularly by using assessment on a consistent and timely basis.** At the initial buy-in session, after three or four weeks, after midterm, and whenever problems spring up, it is helpful to ask students for assessment feedback. This gives students ownership of the learning environment. It is just as important in a quality learning environment for faculty to regularly mentor and assess each student as it is for the students to provide feedback about the environment. *(See Overview of Mentoring.)* Self-assessment is necessary for students to improve their performance.

8. **Measure and document progress and growth of both faculty and students.** The learning environment must include records documenting growth and tracking the progress that has been made. Students need to see evidence that demonstrates their performance is improving or sloughing off. Otherwise, they will lose their motivation to work hard and put forth a quality effort.

9. **Create a collaborative learning space.** While the learning space in which we teach is often not under our control, faculty should communicate to administrators plans for their ideal classroom whenever possible. This is especially important when renovations are being planned. For instance, would round tables, rolling chairs, functional workstations, and state-of-the-art projection equipment enhance the environment? Even traditional classrooms can be transformed into collaborative learning spaces simply by rearranging chairs and tables or leaving empty rows for the facilitator to move among teams.

10. **Create a balance between structure and flexibility.** The ideal learning environment is one that is well organized and conceived, yet flexible and responsive to the need for change. The objective is to support and encourage a free-flowing give-and-take between and among the students, instructors, and other people involved in the learning process, allowing for dynamic interaction. *(See Introduction to Learning Communities.)*

These principles are helpful when addressing the following commonly mentioned learning environment issues. The first seven issues are explained, and the remaining ones are listed in a table with links to other modules.

Issues Regarding A Quality Learning Environment

1. **Shifting ownership of learning to the students.** While faculty would like students to be more independent, self-directed learners, many students come into their courses as passive, non-aggressive learners wanting the faculty to direct their learning. The quality learning environment is based upon learners' focusing on peak performance, setting their own learning objectives, and reflecting on their own learning performance to maximize both their learning and learning growth.

2. **Motivating students.** Many faculty are concerned that some students do not care about their learning; this attitude can demoralize their peers, as well as the instructor, thus degrading and depressing the learning environment

3. **Diversity of learners.** Students today "vary considerably by age, gender, ethnic background, home country or region of the country. . . . 'Traditional' students are becoming hard to find" (Davis, 1993). A major goal of the learning environment is to set up a culture based on high expectations, challenges, and risk-taking which can support the learning growth of these diverse students.

4. **Administrative attitude towards valuing learning improvement.** Creating a quality learning environment often requires resources and encouragement that only administrators can supply. Lack of this administrative support can erode faculty motivation.

5. **Having students prepare for class.** Even the best learning environment will be rendered ineffective if students do not prepare for class. It is important to build into the environment a way to check preparation. Techniques include providing quizzes, integrating short in-class writing assignments into the course structure, and checking homework assignments at the door. Conversely, productivity is decreased by lecturing on previously assigned reading material, allowing students to use class time for preparation, ignoring work students have completed for class, and making assignments that are vague and unclear in purpose, presentation, or due date.

6. **Creating an assessment culture in your environment.** Recall that a learning environment maintains a balance between support and challenge. Assessment is often used to assist students as they struggle to learn course materials; it helps them to monitor their progress. Evaluation, on the other hand, is typically employed to challenge both students and faculty to higher levels of achievement. Ideally, the two processes are woven into the fabric of the course, used alternately to goad and encourage participants to greater growth.

7. **Who should teach which courses.** The conventional wisdom operating at many colleges is that the most qualified faculty teach the higher level and more content-heavy courses. Yet, research has shown the need to re-evaluate that thinking; assigning experienced faculty (as opposed to adjuncts and graduate assistants) to entry-level courses can help increase the retention of students, create a fully functioning society, and improve student success (Astin, 2001).

Other Issues and Supporting Modules

- Setting clear expectations. See *Methodology for Creating a Quality Learning Environment*.
- Time periods for course. See *Introduction to Learning Communities*.
- Connecting effectively with students/building rapport.

Quality Learning Environment Skills

The principles stated above set the stage for a quality-learning environment. Yet, participants in this process need to develop the following skills to monitor the effectiveness of that environment and continuously work to improve it.

Risk-taking. The self-confidence to put oneself into challenging environments that require an ever-increasing level of performance and possibility of failure.

Following convictions. Consistently acting according to one's beliefs. This behavior builds trust, an essential component of a learning environment.

Respecting. Feeling and showing honor or esteem for others in the learning environment; showing consideration for the different qualities they bring to it. Without mutual respect, creativity is limited, people avoid risks, and the likelihood of inducing quality collaboration lessens.

Committing to others. Pledging oneself to work for the well-being and success not only of oneself but of others in the learning environment. This is often done formally with all parties completing and signing a pledge or contract outlining the details of their commitment, listing the actions they will take.

Valuing process. Esteeming the methods used to do something, as opposed to valuing the accomplishment itself. In other words, unless students actually see the value of the methodologies used—such as sharing, collaborating, and assessing their own and others' work—and openly engage in using them, it will be difficult for authentic learning to occur.

Quality Learning Environment Contexts

Although all student learning requires a supportive environment, the following contexts have proved especially important: first-year courses, entire programs (e.g., economics), academic skill centers, and faculty.

Students in a first-year course need special attention when creating a quality learning environment. Generally, they lack self-confidence, good study habits, and the ability to work together effectively. Each step in the Methodology for Creating a Quality Learning Environment must be implemented for every class period of a first-year course, but especially during the first two weeks. Until students feel supported, respected, and ready to take risks, it makes little sense to expect them to learn in-depth content. A worthwhile goal for a first-year course is the significant improvement of learning skills and experience with all phases of assessment.

Once the learning environment has been well established during the first course of a program, it is much easier to recreate it in subsequent courses. Thus, it behooves program directors to help faculty value and actively contribute to this environment. Teachers of some courses, such as statistics for economics majors, find it particularly difficult to motivate students to buy into the material. It is best to treat such courses as first-year courses, and not expect that the program's quality learning environment will automatically overcome the lack of student motivation.

The learning environment in an academic skills center is different from that in a class—in that the former depends primarily on one-on-one interactions. Thus, it is necessary to establish a positive learning environment with each student from the start. It is important to work through the QLE methodology with each student, rather than hastily jumping in to address the immediate problem the student presents. Most students who seek the center need help not just with course content but with specific learning skills. Unless the center personnel focus on assessing and teaching students those skills, they are treating only the symptom and not the underlying problem.

Perhaps the greatest challenge to creating a quality learning environment in an institution can be found in dealing with the faculty. In some programs, the leadership has emphasized student-oriented teaching within their professional development programs, urging faculty to work as teams to build quality learning environments. In other programs, innovative faculty guided by the principles enumerated above are considered to be troublemakers—largely because they raise student expectations regarding the quality of their learning experiences. It takes great courage on the part of faculty (especially those who are non-tenured) to persevere in these circumstances.

Concluding Thoughts

Pressured by the demands inherent in designing courses and preparing classes, many faculty can end up neglecting or even totally ignoring the quality of the learning environment itself. Time spent incorporating the principles, considering the issues, and mastering the skills contained in this module will help streamline the teaching process and stimulate student learning growth. When attempting to implement the methodology for creating a quality learning environment, the reader should proceed slowly, making use of supporting modules at each step. Much research has highlighted the importance of the learning environment, but we do not yet fully understand to what extent and in what ways this multi-dimensional factor affects student learning. By keeping that question in mind as we design, teach, assess, and evaluate our courses, we can report our experiences and expand the research base.

References

Astin, A. (2001). *What matters in college? Four critical years revisited.* San Francisco: Jossey-Bass.

Boyer, E. (1990). *Scholarship reconsidered: Priorities of the professorate.* San Francisco: Jossey-Bass.

Boyer Commission (1998). *Reinventing undergraduate education: A blueprint for America's research universities.* Stony Brook, NY: SUNY Stony Brook.

Bransford, J., Brown, A., & Cocking, R. (2000). *How people learn: Brain, mind, experience, and school.* Washington, DC: National Academy Press.

Davis, J. R. (1993) *Better teaching, more learning: Strategies for success in postsecondary settings.* Phoenix, AZ: Oryx Press.

Fink, D. (2003*). Creating significant learning experience: An integrated approach to designing college courses.* San Francisco: Jossey-Bass.

Gabelnick, F., Macgregor, J., Matthews, R.S., & Smith, B. L. (1990). Learning communities: Creating connections among students, faculty, and disciplines. *New directions in teaching and learning, 41.* San Francisco: Jossey-Bass.

Johnson, D. W., Johnson, R., & Smith, K. (1998). *Active learning: Cooperation in the college classroom.* Edina, MN: Interaction Book Company.

McTighe, J., & Wiggins, G. (1998). *Understanding by design.* Upper Saddle River, NJ.: Prentice Hall.

Secretary's Commission on Achieving Necessary Skills (1991). *What work requires of schools: A SCANS report for America 2000.* Washington, DC: U.S. Department of Labor.

Wingspread Group (1993). *An American imperative: Higher expectations for higher education.* Report of the Wingspread Group on Higher Education, Racine, WI: Johnson Foundation, Inc.

Methodology for Creating a Quality Learning Environment

by Daniel Apple, Pacific Crest and Peter Smith, St. Mary's College

An effective learning environment has a strong impact upon a person's growth, development, and performance. In order to improve student learning performance, faculty must create an environment which allows for greater student ownership, responsibility, and control of the learning process. It is important to create this environment early in the course so that mutual trust and respect can develop. Against this background, judgment is minimized and quality assessment of performance is more likely to occur, ultimately leading to student success. This module describes a step-by-step process for creating a quality learning environment. It is presented first through a scenario depicting a summer orientation program and then followed by a step-by-step explanation. Other modules in this section provide techniques for implementing each of the various steps.

Table 1   ***Methodology for Creating a Quality Learning Environment***

1. Establish initial respect.
2. Start with no prejudging.
3. Obtain shared commitment.
4. Foster and support risk-taking.
5. Permit the learner to fail.
6. Set high expectations.
7. Establish clear performance criteria.
8. Implement a quality assessment system.
9. Document performance.
10. Continuously challenge performance.

Example of Using the Methodology

The context for the example is preparing a summer orientation session for new students to acclimate them to a learner-centered environment, as advocated by Bransford et al. (2000).

1. Establish initial respect.

It is important to arrange the group space where learning is to take place so that each student can readily contribute to the discussion or activity—i.e., use circular tables or arrange chairs in circles. Another way to show respect is to set up name signs at each place that can be read by other participants. It is essential that no one thinks he or she is in an assembly process.

2. Start with no prejudging.

When arranging activities, make sure all students are treated equally. For example, students from influential families, honor students, or athletes should not be singled out for special treatment; those eligible for significant financial aid should not be segregated.

3. Obtain shared commitment.

Students commit to a strong performance on the obligatory placement and assessment exams provided as part of summer orientation. In exchange, program facilitators commit to completely answering students' questions and issues.

4. Foster and support risk-taking.

Since students are averse to risk-taking, it is important to have them take initial risks within a small group. Use small group discussions with high performance criteria, but insert an experienced student as a mentor in each group.

5. Permit the learner to fail.

Incorporate tasks that are challenging yet allow students to fail (e.g., a scavenger hunt around the campus). It is important that the failure is turned into a learning and growth experience.

6. Set high expectations.

Clearly state that you expect students to connect to the college, to carefully process the information and experience, and to come in the fall ready for success.

7. Establish clear performance criteria.

Students will know they have met the orientation expectations if they complete the full registration process, give a strong performance on the placement exam(s), and complete a financial aid plan and package, if appropriate.

8. Implement a quality assessment system.

Some components of this system include: real-time monitoring as students work on the placement exam; pre-assessment of their readiness to complete the financial aid package; a process to assess issues that will cause problems in the fall; an instrument to survey each student's interests and suggest to them opportunities to investigate campus programs related to these interests.

9. **Document performance.**

The results of the placement exam should be communicated to students—ideally, before they leave the orientation event, or as soon thereafter as possible. Students may be given a written exercise to plan their first few weeks of school. They should also be required to do a written self-assessment which includes the most important things learned and areas to focus on to improve readiness for college.

10. **Continuously challenge performance.**

Most students could learn much more during orientation. Find ways to intervene so that students are challenged to perform the tasks more productively.

Discussion of the Methodology

Note that the Methodology to Create a Quality Learning Environment can be applied within the context of a single course, a cohort group in a program, a department, or within the culture of a college.

Step 1 — Establish initial respect.

From the faculty perspective, it is important that each and every learner be recognized as an individual—for who he or she is, for what he or she can contribute, and, most importantly, respected for his or her potential to perform. Note that the focus here is on faculty respect for student *potential* to perform, as compared to respect earned through *actual* performance.

The more one facilitates student growth and sees individual successes, the greater one's belief that every student can be a star. As this belief is communicated to students through faculty actions and attitudes, they gain confidence in themselves.

When faculty are well organized, maintain a demeanor free of judgmental language and statements, accept each student as an individual with unique value, take on the student's perspective, understand his or her personality and learning preferences, and connect with his or her cultural values, they establish an interpersonal relationship with students and earn their respect (Roscoe & Peterson, 1982).

Step 2 — Start with no prejudging.

Nobody likes to be prejudged. People like to start with a "clean slate" that has no history or baggage that could negatively influence the building of a new relationship. This does not mean ignoring information faculty might

know about a student but rather not letting this information create a prejudicial attitude toward him or her. Do some form of pre-assessment to determine a person's knowledge and skill level before starting to work with him or her. Avoiding assumptions allows an instructor to approach the student with a clear and open mind.

In the case of a classroom learning community, the absence of prejudging helps relationships among learners, as well as between the learners and the instructor/facilitator. Defuse prejudgments, the more students are judged, the more they withdraw.

Also, realize that students are coming into the class with information they have gathered about the instructor—and judgments they have made about him or her. Students who are not prejudged are less likely to prejudge their instructors.

Step 3 — Obtain shared commitment.

Best results will occur in a course when both faculty and students are "on the same page" with respect to their commitment to work together to achieve the course outcomes. A faculty member wants students to be committed to learning, to their community, and to hard work. Students want to know that he or she is determined to help them achieve the course outcomes. This agreement should be made public so that there is no misunderstanding.

A quality educator must go beyond his or her devotion to his or her discipline and a strict emphasis on content to include a genuine desire to help students grow and develop as learners. He or she must get them to believe that he or she is committed to their growth, their success in the course and beyond, and that the faculty member has students' best interests at heart. *(See **Getting Student Buy-In**.)* This is the beginning of creating an environment of trust—one that promotes growth without judgment.

Step 4 — Foster and support risk-taking.

Most students are not risk-takers in the classroom. Past educational experiences have discouraged them from taking risks because of the negative reinforcement that often follows. In order to change this perception, it is important that faculty be supportive of risk-taking students from an affective or emotional perspective, immediately after an unsuccessful event occurs. For example, when a bad outcome occurs, an effective instructor congratulates a student for taking the risk and then provides constructive feedback to address the problem.

Faculty who care make clear that risk-taking will be supported and not penalized in the course. They encourage students to "experiment and try it," not always doing what they think the instructor wants. Students need to know their demands for affirmation, validation, and answers to every question will not necessarily be met. Working in a risk-taking environment also means challenging students to think critically, to affirm and validate on their own, and to generate possible answers to their own questions.

Share with students that entrepreneurial environments, such as high-tech firms, often encourage risk-taking in their cultures (SCANS, 1991).

Step 5 — Permit the learner to fail.

Most faculty find it difficult to watch students struggle in a learning situation. Their natural tendency is to jump in and remedy the situation—typically, with a content-related intervention. This serves to temporarily end the struggle and provide momentary success. However, be careful to avoid enabling behavior which does not allow for failure, and, in the long run, is not in a student's best interest.

It is emotionally difficult to watch someone failing in a particular situation. Yet the key question to ask in these situations is, what action will produce the best long-term result for the person who is struggling? Sometimes not taking action is best.

It is important that faculty not view a student's short-term failures as a reflection of the instructor's performance. Realize that when a student experiences these moments, it builds emotional resilience and increases his or her ability to cope and respond. Allowing failure to happen in small steps actually empowers a student. The "good learner experiments, discovers and is secure in his or her emotions, so he or she can take risks and accept failure as a frequent and productive event on the road to success at a new task" (Krumsieg & Baehr, 2000).

Step 6 — Set high expectations.

Student productivity within a learning environment is highly correlated to the expectations that faculty set up for their students. *(See Introduction to Learning Communities.)* In general, students will typically perform to the level of faculty expectations. Students will raise their level of performance accordingly—a principle advocated by industry representatives examining the preparedness of graduates for the workplace (Wingspread Group, 1993).

As faculty observe students achieving at higher levels, expectations for their future performance increase, lead-

ing to setting higher standards. However, not allowing for failure often results in lowering standards to accommodate lower levels of performance.

Step 7 — Establish clear performance criteria.

People in challenging situations which require high quality performance want and need explicit and clear (performance) criteria. Students want explicit criteria so they know what an instructor expects; implicit criteria are of little use to students. Faculty need to avoid hidden or implicit objectives or criteria; lack of specificity erodes the trust built with students.

When expectations for student performance are high, it is critical to have clear performance criteria. Without them, students do not know what they need to do to be successful and are likely to rebel, stray off target, or disengage. Students want feedback relative to the criteria so they know how to succeed.

Step 8 — Implement a quality assessment system.

Acting upon assessment feedback is the key to students' future performance. *(See Overview of Assessment.)* Especially when performance does not meet the established standards, students want specific feedback to know how to improve. This information will have greatest impact and benefit when given promptly. Over time this feedback can be replaced by self-assessment which then leads to greater student autonomy.

Assessment feedback should be given in a positive tone or manner and be limited to the most important points. An assessor should be consistent, complete, direct, and honest with his or her assessment. As an educator, be a "straight shooter" with your students; be genuine, not manipulative.

Step 9 — Document performance.

A process-oriented course requires more effort on the part of students (and faculty) than does a traditional, lecture-based one. Faculty often think students are excited by the prospect of learning new subject matter. But, in reality, students are far more motivated by experiencing and becoming aware of their own growth and skill improvement.

Students need to see evidence that they are making progress; otherwise, they will lose their motivation to work hard and put forth a quality effort. They also need to see tangible proof of their progress. Therefore, it is extremely important to document performance (both failures and successes) over time. By charting the trajectory of their learning, faculty can help students visualize their successes and learn to value the growth associated with these gains.

Step 10 — Continuously challenge performance.

The implicit goal behind this methodology is to create learning environments that can facilitate quality outcomes. It is presumed that course outcomes include skill development, in addition to content mastery (Fink, 2003).

Growth occurs not when we are "coasting," but, rather, when we are challenged. For this reason, do not let students get complacent. Continuously challenge performance. Keep students motivated by raising performance criteria and by challenging work that is mediocre or not up to that student's level of capability. Realize that, by challenging the student to a higher level of performance, a faculty member shows respect and a sense of caring. Letting that person "slide by" with work that does not do justice to his or her potential is an insult to him or her.

Nobody can be at peak performance at all times. While it is important to challenge students, they cannot always be in high-performance situations. There needs to be some "down time" scheduled into the design of a course which can be used to celebrate individual and class accomplishments. Note, however, that providing such respites is different from lowering performance standards.

Concluding Thoughts

The learning environment created in most classrooms is often less than ideal; typically, it does not provide students with the optimal environment to support and nurture their growth and development. In courses that do, it may take the entire semester or term to achieve this result. Herein lies the problem: research shows that the key learning characteristics outlined in the QLE Methodology have a dramatic impact on student learning and growth. So, if faculty do not create an environment that incorporates those characteristics—and do so as early as possible within the course—they are missing out on an opportunity to reach and teach their students.

By researching questions such as those that follow, faculty can build knowledge about how to create and sustain a quality learning environment in their courses. This section provides a guide for translating this knowledge into classroom practice. It is recommended that practitioners focus on one question at a time.

1. Why is it important that we let students fail in order to set high expectations?

2. What differentiates challenging students from badgering them?

3. What type of commitment is the student expecting from the faculty member?

4. Why do students need and want clear performance expectations?

5. Why do students need to see documentation of their growth and development?

References

Bransford, J., Brown, A., & Cocking, R. (2000). *How people learn: Brain, mind, experience, and school*. Washington, D.C. National Academy Press.

Fink, D. (2003). *Creating significant learning experiences: An integrated approach to designing college courses*. San Francisco: Jossey-Bass.

Krumsieg, K. & Baehr, M. (2000). *Foundations of learning* (3rd ed.). Lisle, IL: Pacific Crest.

Roscoe, B., & Peterson, K. L. (1982). Teacher and situational characteristics which enhance learning and development. *College Student Journal, 16*, 389-394.

Secretary's Commission on Achieving Necessary Skills (SCANS). (1991). *What work requires of schools: A SCANS report for America 2000*. Washington, DC: Department of Labor.

Wingspread Group. (1993). *An American imperative: Higher expectations for higher education*. Report of the Wingspread Group on Higher Education, Racine, WI: Johnson Foundation, Inc.

Pacific Crest

Faculty Development Series

Introduction to Learning Communities

by Suzanne Ashe, Cerritos College and Virginia Romero, Cerritos College

Learning communities are effective and innovative structures colleges are using to enhance student involvement, learning, growth, and academic success. They were first developed early in the 20th century and have evolved in different ways among U.S. colleges and universities. They come in a variety of shapes, as documented by the National Learning Communities Project. Learning communities provide multiple benefits, including curricular alignment, faculty rejuvenation, and the overall enhancement of students' educational experience. A blending of the academic and non-academic aspects of student life also unlocks opportunities for attaining a broader spectrum of learning outcomes. The most distinctive feature of vibrant learning communities is effective use of mentoring that has major impacts on the mentor as well as the mentee.

What is a Learning Community?

The term "learning community" has taken on many meanings since this instructional approach was instigated, back in the 1920's. For some, it means the "intentional restructuring of curriculum" around a cohort of courses. For others, it signifies a cooperative approach to instruction in which students engage in cooperative learning activities. Still others may define this approach in social or affective terms, stressing the emotional/psychological benefits. A variety of approaches has emerged, including those inventoried in Table 1 (Gabelnick et al., 1990).

By comparing the models in Table 1, a learning community is seen as a cohesive group of students taking two or more courses together that are taught by faculty who are committed to a collaborative, student-centered enterprise that supports achievement of shared learning outcomes. This definition is proposed to create a deeper connection to the course content as well as a deeper connection with the learning styles of peers and colleagues. Curricular integration is reflected in a coordinated syllabi, learning activities, assignments, and evaluations. Organizational innovation is often required to support interdisciplinary experiences that feature active learning (MacGregor, 1999).

Historical Development

From the beginning, learning communities have been revolutionary in nature. In 1927 the University of Wisconsin implemented a radical approach to education by establishing the Experimental College that emphasized student engagement through a "living-learning community" (Meiklejohn, 1932). This effort put theories of John Dewey, Malcolm Knowles, and Bloom into practice.

Though it faded from the educational scene for several decades, the learning community model reemerged in the form of "federated learning communities," "integrating seminars," and other formats in institutions such as UC Berkeley, SUNY Stony Brook, and LaGuardia Community College in the 1970's. In the 1980's Evergreen State College in Olympia, Washington, took the lead in

Table 1 **Common Learning Community Models**

- **Team-taught Paired or Linked Model:** A cohort of students enroll in two different classes. The classes are linked by thematic connections between the disciplines or courses. However, instruction is done separately by each instructor.

- **Team-taught Triads:** This is typically a year-long program involving three courses each semester taught in a similar manner as the linked model.

- **Team-taught Learning Community:** A cohort of students interact with a group of 2-4 faculty who collaborate in teaching an integrated program, resulting in the blurring of boundaries between disciplines or courses in favor of a larger whole.

- **Learning Clusters:** Three or more courses with syllabi coordinated around a common theme and linked assignments.

- **Federated Learning Communities:** A cohort of students register for three "federated" courses that are linked by a common theme. The students also participate in a seminar that unites the three courses. The seminar leader serves as "Master Learner", taking all courses with students and integrating ideas from them in seminar activities.

- **Freshman Interest Groups (F.I.G.'s):** These are triads of courses offered around an area of interest, an interdisciplinary topic, or courses related to a specific major. These are typically peer-led and feature discussion groups as well as study groups around common courses. F.I.G.'s often serve to introduce students to campus resources and organize social gatherings.

reactivating and implementing the learning communities concept. This has been formalized in the National Learning Communities Project. <learningcommons.evergreen.edu>

Benefits of Learning Communities

Research shows that students involved in a learning community are "significantly more likely than their less involved peers to show growth in intellectual interest and values, and apparently more likely to get more out of their college education" (Cross, 1998). Significant gains in student retention, achievement, rates of degree completion, and intellectual development have also been reported (Gabelnick et al, 1990). By participating in learning communities, faculty can explore a wider repertoire of teaching approaches and new, more effective, ways of relating to students and colleagues. Institutional effectiveness is also positively impacted through adoption of learning communities as large groups of students and faculty become better aligned with institutional vision, mission, and culture.

Essential Elements

Learning communities are characterized by the following elements: absence of threat, mastery learning, immediate feedback, collaboration, meaningful content, freedom to make choices, and adequate time on task (Geri et al, 1999). They require the creation of a positive learning environment in which students find support, engage authentically in learning tasks, and relate course content to life experience. Ideally, the classroom also becomes an interactive place in which fear is minimized, and students become more responsive and willing to take risks. Table 2 describes a number of key features of learning communities.

Concluding Thoughts

Effective learning communities demand commitment from both learners and educators. They require a balance between structure and flexibility, a free-flowing give-and-take between student and professor. They also require the incorporation of new ideas and insights, strong leadership, and continued assessment of performance for all participants (including faculty). It is not enough to simply rewrite curriculum and include a few "enriching" activities, such as guest speakers, field trips, and visits to the campus library or labs. Launching learning communities requires a fair amount of courage, as well as a sense of adventure. It requires a spirit of "collective inquiry" in which the unique talents, abilities, and perspectives of all participants are honored and brought to fruition by a skilled mentor (Palmer, 1998). If your institution supports learning communities, get involved; if it does not, seek out other like-minded faculty and start the process to introduce them.

Table 2   *Central Features of Learning Communities*

- A **culture of exploration**, meaning that the course design and implementation, though grounded in solid principles, are constantly evolving in response to students' learning needs;

- **Active, student-centered learning**, using structured learning activities to construct and reconstruct knowledge at all levels in Bloom's Taxonomy;

- A set of common, **shared experiences** (inside and outside of the classroom), serving to draw students out of isolation and bond them with faculty in the pursuit of meaningful learning;

- A commitment to **instructional innovation** grounded in a willingness to challenge paradigms and investigate alternative methodologies that align better with program objectives and workplace requirements;

- The use of **collaboration** to reach deeper meaning and, at times, consensus or synthesis of ideas;

- Dependence on a **mentoring model** in which individuals frequently switch between roles of learner and teacher;

- Facilitating the **growth and development** of each student by regularly assessing progress and addressing skill development in the cognitive, social, affective, and psychomotor domains;

- Responding to students' diverse **learning styles** to insure that educational and career opportunities remain open to all participants.

References

Cross, P. K. (1998). "Why learning communities? Why now?" *About Campus*. July-August, 1-11.

Gabelnick, F., MacGregor, J., Matthews, R. S., & Smith, B. L. (1990). Learning communities: creating connections among students, Faculty, and disciplines. *New Directions for Teaching and Learning, 41.*

Geri, L., Kuehn, D., with MacGregor, J. (1999). "From innovation to reform: Reflections on case studies of 19 learning community initiatives." *Strengthening learning communities*. The Evergreen State College. Olympia, Washington. May 1999, 195-203.

Meiklejohn, A. (1932). *The experimental college.* New York: Harper & Row.

Palmer, P. J. (1998). *The courage to teach.* San Francisco: Jossey-Bass.

Pacific Crest

Faculty Development Series

Getting Student Buy-In

by Kathleen Burke, SUNY Cortland

Students can commit themselves to improving their performance through a number of different strategies. This module examines why this commitment, the "buy-in" process, is essential for successful facilitation of student growth. Complete student buy-in is a process that must be pursued throughout the course, although the greatest emphasis should be early in the term. This module examines the conditions necessary for buy-in to occur, the attributes of a bought-in student, and the behaviors that may hinder student buy-in. Then it discusses some strategies that instructors can use to achieve buy-in.

The Importance of Student Buy-In

Without student buy-in, creating a quality learning environment is nearly impossible *(see **Overview of Creating a Quality Learning Environment**)*. When students buy in, there is a commitment to excellence (on both the students' and instructor's parts), a motivation to learn and grow (again, on both the students' and instructor's parts), and an intellectual atmosphere in the classroom. Student buy-in allows for a much richer course for both the students and the instructor. When student buy-in occurs, students begin to ask probing questions, take risks, work with others, participate fully in class, accept increasing challenges, welcome new situations, and assess performance willingly. Thus, student buy-in enables the instructor and the students to delve deeper into the material.

Student buy-in is a process. To improve students' motivation, attendance, expectations, class preparation, and critical thinking, instructors should plan to expend significant time and effort at the start of the course to obtain buy-in. For some students, buy-in seems automatic; for others, it may require more time and effort to achieve. But for everyone, certain conditions facilitate buy-in.

Conditions Necessary for Buy-In

Instructors can facilitate student buy-in by establishing a conducive class atmosphere.

Trust is one of the most critical components to achieving student buy-in because trust is crucial to promoting risk-taking behaviors. For example, trust allows students to feel comfortable asking questions. The instructor can build trust by using non-evaluative language and showing respect for students' questions and answers.

Another component for achieving buy-in is accommodating different learning styles by approaching the same material from many different angles. Students are more apt to buy-in if they trust the instructor's teaching abilities.

Moreover, students will be better prepared to buy-in if they can see the big picture. A key component for this task is to demonstrate and maintain the material's relevance (Small and Lankes, 1996). Some students will not buy-in unless they see the relevance of the subject matter. One effective approach to gaining student interest is to incorporate real-life examples to which the students can relate.

Another important precondition to obtaining student buy-in is to set clear, attainable objectives for the course and for each class session. Furthermore, students should know and understand these objectives. In some cases, the instructor may want to facilitate the development of some of the objectives by the class.

Student ownership is a vital condition for student buy-in. If students can take ownership of their own learning, then they must buy-in, at least to some extent. Student ownership can occur in many different ways. For example, setting high (yet attainable) expectations for the class as well as for individual performance and holding students to these expectations will permit students to take ownership of their own performance.

A final key condition for student ownership is engagement with the material. It is difficult for students to be engaged and excited about learning if the instructor shows no enthusiasm for it. Therefore, an essential part of getting students excited about the material is that the instructor models the appropriate behavior. Furthermore, instructors must walk a fine line while keeping everyone involved and interested because some students will understand the material more quickly and easily than others. Maintaining a balance between the material's challenge and students' cognitive skills promotes engagement in the learning process.

The course assessment and evaluation systems function most effectively when students buy-in to the processes, when objectives are clearly understood, and when the level of challenge is appropriate. Buy-in is promoted through student involvement with assessment of their own performance, as well as that of their peers and the instructor. A fair, objective-based evaluation process also contributes to student buy-in. Grades should be readily accessible to students soon after an evaluation is made.

Table 1

Top Ten Conditions that Promote Student Buy-In

1. Developing trust with students that allows risk-taking behavior.

2. Accommodating different learning styles.

3. Using material that is relevant to real life.

4. Presenting and sharing clear objectives.

5. Students taking ownership of the learning process.

6. Setting high but attainable expectations for performance.

7. Engaging with the material by instructor and students.

8. Setting the appropriate level of challenge.

9. Implementing an effective assessment process.

10. Using a fair evaluation process.

Characteristics of a Bought-In Student

When buy-in has occurred, students will exhibit certain attributes. They are willing to trust the faculty member and the classroom learning process. They are willing to take risks. Students show that they understand the course framework and want to take ownership of their learning. They are ready for high performance and welcome challenges. Students are engaged with the material and excited about learning. They see a strong relevance between the material and their needs. Finally, students seek access to the available resources for help, i.e., office hours, supplemental instruction, workshops, etc. *(see Overview of Effective Learning Tools)*.

Resistance to Student Buy-In

Although many things can be done to promote student buy-in, it is also important to understand what may cause students not to buy in. Resistance to student buy-in can be explained by the attitudes and behaviors of the student, the teacher, or the institution (see Astin, 1993, for a detailed discussion). There are many possible behaviors in each category, but only three of the most important are listed.

Student Attitudes and Behaviors that Hinder Buy-In

- Students may lack confidence in their abilities, not believe that they can grow, and/or have low self-esteem.

- Students may have low expectations for their own performance, which may cause them to willingly accept merely a passing grade.

- A student's failure to attend class makes it impossible for a student to buy in; however, this problem can sometimes be altered with an attendance policy.

Faculty Behaviors that Hinder Buy-In

- Faculty may not hold students accountable for their individual and/or group performance.

- Faculty may violate students' trust by making assumptions, being judgmental, and/or using evaluative language.

- Faculty may not communicate performance criteria clearly and consistently.

Institutional Behaviors that Hinder Buy-In

- An institution may establish classes with very high enrollment. In large classes, it is sometimes hard to know all students and hold them accountable for their learning on a daily basis. Students feel that they can hide. It is important that the instructor does not allow this to happen by making sure all students feel that they are an important part of what is occurring in the classroom.

- An institution may take control of the class composition away from the instructor. Students are affected by their peers. When there is a group of students who actively resist buy-in, it can be very challenging to achieve it. For example, having a class with many students who have low expectations for their performance makes it difficult (but not impossible) to obtain buy-in. It is difficult to get students excited and motivated if their only goal is just to pass. In this situation, it is important for the instructor to manage his or her own frustration.

- Assigning classes to rooms that are not conducive to quality instruction. For example, the chairs may be bolted down in rows, making group work awkward. However, it is possible for the instructor to work around most of these difficulties *(see Overview of Creating a Quality Learning Environment)*.

Strategies for Obtaining Student Buy-In

It is important to remember that not all classes are alike. The strategies that are used to achieve buy-in with one class may not necessarily work well with another. However, it is essential to create an atmosphere where students do buy in and to do it early (within the first three weeks), in order to create a quality learning environment.

Obtaining student buy-in is especially difficult in required courses. The difficulty usually arises from the same **key issues**:

1. Students have no choice about taking the course.

2. Students may be passive towards the material.

3. Students view the course as a barrier towards graduation that they must suffer through.

4. Students may be apprehensive about not having the skill set that is required for the course.

Strategies to overcome these issues have been developed. The following three **key strategies** provide double coverage of the key issues faced by students:

A) Shift the ownership to the student immediately. *(Addresses issues 1, 2, and 4.)*

B) Provide a strong justification on why the course is important within the discipline. *(Addresses issues 2 and 3.)*

C) Reinforce how the extra benefits of having this course (both process and content) will be beneficial after the course is completed. *(Addresses issues 1, 3 and 4.)*

Just as classes vary, the mechanisms, tools and techniques to implement the preceding strategies into a course also vary. To provide an example of the possible mechanisms, tools and techniques, a statistics course will be used, since this is commonly a required course in many disciplines.

Strategy A: Shifting ownership

1. Use project-oriented learning. For example, students create their own survey, input their data, and analyze their results using the tools and techniques used in class. This strategy will force students to engage with the material. Moreover, if they choose the topic of personal interest for their projects, they will better internalize the material.

2. Students learn and apply a new statistical technique (possibly in teams). This strategy allows students to become "experts" with a particular technique. Letting the student(s) teach the technique to the rest of the class further reinforces the student's ownership and understanding. Nothing else forces a student to completely understand something better than having to explain it to others.

3. The class determines the weights for the components of the course evaluation system. If the instructor feels uncomfortable, he or she can put a range around each component weight's midpoint. By the way, students will almost always weight a component very close to the instructor's desired weight. The added benefit of this buy-in strategy is that students cannot complain about their grades if they set the criteria upon which their performance is to be evaluated!

Strategy B: Providing justification

1. Describe your own personal use of the content in your professional life. Furthermore, have a practitioner visit your class and discuss how the material is used in the field.

2. Discuss how statistical concepts and applications are imbedded within other courses they will take. Furthermore, discuss how statistics affects their lives outside the discipline. For example, when discussing descriptive statistics, such as bar or pie charts, have your students use a chart taken from a newspaper article.

Strategy C: Reinforcing benefits

1. Let students know that they will learn a quantitative analysis tool, such as Excel, Minitab, SPSS, etc. The instructor can tell students that they will be using this tool to develop their quantitative analysis skills all term, and by the end of the term, their skills will be proficient enough so that they could include this tool on their resumes.

2. Display how the development of specific data analysis skills will be applicable to their professional (or even personal) lives. The ability to understand simple descriptive statistics, such as tables, charts, or even means and standard deviations, will enable students to think critically about analytical issues, as well as discuss issues quantitatively.

Concluding Thoughts

Achieving student buy-in is essential to developing the intellectual climate that will foster student learning and growth, but it is a very difficult endeavor. The first few times achieving buy-in is attempted, the instructor may feel awkward and frequently question his or her competence in this endeavor, as well as the appropriateness of focusing on learning skills in a college classroom.

If it is possible, observe an experienced facilitator conduct a buy-in session and ask him or her to observe and assess your effort. The benefits of teaching a course with students who have bought in far outweigh any awkwardness at the beginning of the process.

References

Astin, A. (1993). *What matters in college? Four critical years revisited.* San Francisco: Jossey-Bass.

Felder, R. I., & Brent, R. (1996). Navigating the bumpy road to student-centered instruction. *College Teaching, 44 (2),* 43-47.

Millis, B. J., & Cottel, P. G. (1997). *Cooperative Learning for higher education.* Phoenix: American Council on Education/Oryx Press Series on Higher Education.

Small, R. V., & Lankes, R. D. (1996). Motivating students. In L. M. Lambert, S. L. Tice & P. H. Featherstone (Eds.), *University teaching: A guide for graduate students* (p. 95-106). Syracuse: Syracuse University Press.

Weimer, M. (2002). *Learner-centered teaching.* San Francisco: Jossey-Bass.

Annotated Bibliography — Facilitation

by Peter Smith, St. Mary's College

Facilitation involves a structured interconnection among students, teachers, colleagues, and other professionals wherein knowledge is created and communicated, and process skills are improved. This annotated bibliography includes some of the most important theoretical and practical works that serve as the underpinning for understanding and dealing with the facilitation issues faced by quality educators. Each of the texts contributes its own slant to the facilitation of learning.

Books

Astin, A. W. (1985). *Achieving educational excellence.* San Francisco: Jossey-Bass.

This book examines and rejects four traditional views of academic excellence: reputation of the institution, resources (both financial and personnel), measurable outcomes (e.g., retention rates, lifetime earnings of graduates, exit surveys), and content of the curriculum. The author claims that facilitating the maximum growth of student and faculty talent is a much better measure of excellence and is the best means to meet the three criteria of educational excellence: consistency with the institution's primary purpose, enhancing the overall quality of the educational system in the U.S., and increasing equity—equal opportunities for all in higher education. The book advocates a theory of student involvement, which refers to the quantity and quality of the physical and psychological energy the student invests in the college experience (i.e., absorption in academic work, participation in extra-curricular activities, and interaction with faculty members and student development professionals). Because this data is from the late 1960s and 1970s, the trends the author observes may not be as applicable to today's students, but the recommendations for achieving educational excellence are certainly still valid.

Astin, A. W. (2001). *What matters in college: Four critical years revisited.* San Francisco: Jossey-Bass.

The purpose of this book is to answer questions about the effects of a college education that have been raised by students, parents, public officials, and educators. The Cooperative Institutional Research Program (CIRP), initiated at the American Council on Education in 1966, is the largest ongoing study of the American higher educational system with longitudinal data covering 500,000 full-time, traditional-aged students in 1,300 four-year institutions. The results of this study highlight the need for structured interconnection between students and faculty. The author attempts to isolate the changes in students over four years, 1985-89, which would not have occurred if the students were not in college. The narrative is mostly descriptive, although the analysis underpinning the book relies on significant statistical work. The most interesting results appear in the last three chapters where the author describes outcomes associated with particular environmental or student involvement variables. The major findings of interest to effective educators are that the level of student-centeredness by faculty produces more substantial direct positive effects on student outcomes than any other variable.

Johnson, D. W., Johnson, R. T., & Smith, K. A. (1998). *Active learning: Cooperation in the college classroom.* Edina, MN: Interaction Book Company.

Johnson, Johnson, and Smith have been pioneers for over 35 years in building and presenting both theory and applications of cooperative learning in the classroom. The philosophy behind this book is to create a more productive and effective learning experience. This book contains a conceptual framework and a set of practical strategies for structuring cooperative learning, which have been gleaned from observation of faculty members from all over the world. The authors discuss the shift from passive to active learning, including the pros and cons of lecturing. They also make the case for cooperative learning throughout the institution, using both formal and informal strategies, and describe in detail how to create, organize, and work with cooperative groups to enhance learning. The book contains many examples illustrating both lesson planning and sample student activities.

Millis, B. J., & Cottell, P. G. (1998). *Cooperative learning for higher education faculty.* Phoenix: Oryx Press.

While the authors summarize the research establishing the efficacy of cooperative learning, the real strength of the text is the inclusion of many concrete suggestions for introducing, managing, and assessing cooperative learning in the classroom. These techniques help create a structure for improving student process skills in the classroom. The authors discuss dozens of "structures" which quality educators call activity types or formats, such as brainstorming and think-pair-share. These structures are content-free building blocks to which instructors add their own content-specific information to create classroom activities. The book's in-depth coverage of team formation and the importance of team roles to advance individual accountability and positive interdependence is very helpful. One drawback is the implication that faculty should begin using cooperative learning techniques without necessarily committing themselves to the philosophy that their primary task is helping students grow as learners.

Walvoord, B. E., & Anderson, V. J. (1998). *Effective grading.* San Francisco: Jossey-Bass.

The authors present the case that grading can be used to organize a course to maximize student learning by identifying the primary learning outcomes for the course, aligning the grading system to measure these outcomes through several large projects and/or tests, and constructing the curriculum to ensure that students are well prepared to succeed with these projects. The essence is to use motivation as an important aspect of the learning environment. The authors also challenge the assumption that "you can't use grades for assessment," by outlining a rich assessment system using grades to motivate student learning. The importance of setting clear criteria and standards for grading and of communicating these to students is emphasized. The book suggests ways to make grading time-efficient, how to use grading to improve student learning, and how grading can be part of assessment that meets regional accreditation standards.

Journals

Active Learning in Higher Education. *(From the UK offices of Sage Publications Online; published for the Institute for Learning and Teaching in Higher Education; available by subscription.)*

This journal publishes analyses and research by educators interested in improving learning facilitation and assessment practices. The articles often take a "systems" approach in that learning results are viewed in terms of how all parts of the educational system must be integrated.

Journal on Excellence in College Teaching. <www.ject.lib.muohio.edu>

This peer-reviewed journal from Miami University available by subscription—print or online. The editors offer this publication as "an answer to Boyer's call for a forum to present the scholarship of teaching and learning."

Web Sites

Deliberations on Learning and Teaching in Higher Education. <http://www.lgu.ac.uk/deliberations/home.html>

This international website on issues of learning and teaching for the higher education community is designed to be a resource and interactive forum. Content includes extracts of published articles, case studies, articles contributed by readers, comments and discussion between participants, and relevant links.

Educational Technology. <http://www.aace.org/pubs/etr/issue3/index.cfm>

An online publication of the American Association of Computing in Education, Educational Technology Review features articles about practical applications of technology in education at all levels.

Penn State University's Center for Excellence in Learning and Teaching (CELT). <http://www.psu.edu/dept/celt>

Some parts of this site are accessible only to Penn State faculty, but resources on a wide range of teaching issues are available to the public.

Professional and Organizational Development Network. <http://www.podnetwork.org>

This network of 1200 members sponsors conferences and an active listerv. Its peer-reviewed journal is *To Improve the Academy.*

Annotated Bibliography — Quality Learning Environment

by Peter Smith, Saint Mary's College

The learning environment, which involves social processes, physical space, and learning tools, is an important support structure for facilitation of learning. This annotated bibliography establishes the importance of creating and maintaining a quality learning environment and illustrates the range of ideas and practices for implementation.

Books

Boyer Commission. (1998). *Reinventing undergraduate education: A blueprint for America's research universities.* Stony Brook: SUNY Stony Brook Press.

This report was inspired by the thinking of Ernest Boyer, who died while the commission was doing its work. It identifies key deficiencies in undergraduate education in research universities and provides creative and detailed suggestions for improvement. Interspersed in the report are suggestions for radical changes in the traditional learning environment in these universities—large lectures given by mediocre teachers. The commission argues persuasively for a learning environment that is an "intellectual ecosystem … [where] inquiry, investigation, and discovery are the heart of the enterprise," and undergraduates are integrated meaningfully with faculty and graduate students in research projects. Two highlights of the paper are a Bill of Rights for Undergraduates and a set of ten well-supported and detailed recommendations for improving education in research universities.

Bransford, J., Brown, A., and Cocking, R. (2000). *How people learn: Brain, mind, experience, and school.* Washington: National Academy Press.

How People Learn is a joint report by two committees of the National Research Council—the Committee on Developments in the Science of Learning and the Committee on Learning Research and Educational Practice. It is based on a two-year study of the science of learning linking research to classroom experience. Its premise is that the classroom environment must be centered on four aspects: learner, knowledge, assessment, and community. These four aspects are closely related to the steps in the module *Methodology for Creating a Quality Learning Environment*. Some strengths of the report are the plethora of helpful diagrams and practical examples of classroom interactions that illustrate the learning theory being presented and a set of 33 well-defined research topics for future exploration. This book also contains highly readable descriptions of recent research in the physiology and psychology of learning.

Fink, L. (2003). *Creating significant learning experience: An integrated approach to designing college courses.* San Francisco: Jossey-Bass.

The author is an experienced teacher and instructional consultant with more than 20 years experience. He is the 2004-2007 president of the POD network (see Organizations). In this text, he covers three main concepts: significant learning, integrated course design, and organizational support. The book is also applicable to several other guidebook sections: Instructional Design, Program Design, Course Design, and Effective Teaching Practices. Its relevance to the Quality Learning Environment section is that it presents creative ideas about the underlying structure for dynamic, student-centered learning. The author's central message is that faculty can and should design creative curricula to make student learning significant to their lives. When defining significant learning, the author introduces a replacement for Bloom's Taxonomy. The components of Fink's taxonomy—foundational knowledge, application, integration, human dimension, caring, learning how to learn—are "interactive and relational." One confusing point in the discussion of an assessment system is the reversal of the terms assessment and evaluation from the Guidebook definitions.

Gabelnick, F., Macgregor, J., Matthews, R., & Smith, B. (1990*). Learning communities: Creating connections among students, faculty, and disciplines.* New directions in teaching and learning, 41. San Francisco: Jossey-Bass.

The authors have much experience with learning communities and give an excellent history of their development. The text examines the impact of curriculum, faculty, and students on the learning environment. It also discusses five models of a learning community: linked courses (2 courses with the same cohort of students), clusters (2, 3, or 4 courses linked by a common theme), freshman interest groups (small cohorts in 3 large courses with peer advisor), federated learning communities (master learner and cohort of students enroll in 3 regular courses and engage in "content-synthesizing seminar"), and coordinated studies (cohort of students and multidisciplinary team of faculty engage in block of courses with central theme). The authors include the results of many quantitative and qualitative studies to show how learning communities significantly improve student retention, GPA, intellectual development, and faculty job satisfaction. The book describes how to design and implement a learning community and discusses the problems in doing so. Because learning communities integrate most of the facets of a quality learning environment, this monograph is an excellent resource for all of the modules in this section of the guidebook.

McTighe, J., & Wiggins, G. (1998). *Understanding by design*. Upper Saddle River: Prentice Hall.

McTighe and Wiggins have played central roles in performance assessment development for many years. This work clarifies the need to implement a quality assessment system in a successful learning environment. It separates assessment into three levels: quiz and test questions, open-ended critical thinking questions, and performance tasks and projects. The central tenet of the book is the need for backward design: first identify desired results; then determine acceptable evidence that the results have been achieved; and finally plan the learning experiences. The text also provides a number of classroom examples that apply the backward design process. The authors present many lists, figures, and tables that help the reader understand and apply their design concepts. Especially helpful are a series of misconception boxes and a detailed rubric outlining various stages contained in the six facets of understanding: explanation, interpretation, application, perspective, empathy, and self-knowledge.

Wingspread Group. (1993). *An American perspective: Higher expectations for higher education*. Racine, WI: Johnson Foundation, Inc.

This report attempts to explain why so many students are unable to finish college and why many who do graduate are not prepared to "function in a knowledge-based economy." The book's emphasis on the need for higher education to inspire life-long learning supports the recommendations found in the module *Overview of a Quality Learning Environment*. The Wingspread group was a collection of 16 influential members of the higher education community brought together by four foundations at the Wingspread facilities of the Johnson foundation to study the question, "What Does Society Need from Higher Education?" The group discussed and developed detailed questions on the following topics: taking values seriously, putting student learning first, and creating a nation of learners. After answering these questions, they hope that colleges and universities will improve their goals and procedures. The study also includes 32 essays dealing with the societal need question, but these add very little to the theory and practice of improving the learning environment.

Organizations

Professional and Organizational Development Network. <http://www.podnetwork.org>

This network of 1200 members sponsors conferences and an active listerv. Its peer-reviewed journal is *To Improve the Academy*.

The National Learning Communities Project. <http://learningcommons.evergreen.edu>

The National Learning Communities Project, housed at Evergreen College, is a Pew Charitable Trust-funded effort to foster learning communities. Resources on this site include a variety of articles and video clips on theory and practice with learning communities. Site visitors can post information related to their own experiences with learning communities.

National Center for the First Year Experience and Students in Transition. <http://www.sc.edu/fye/research/index.html>

This center at the University of South Carolina conducts research and publishes in multiple formats on the first year experience. In 1999 the Center conducted the first national survey of senior capstone courses. Most of the publications are for sale on this site as monographs and journal articles. The amount of information directly available and free is rather limited.

Journals

American Association of Higher Education (AAHE) Bulletin. <http://www.aahebulletin.com>

This monthly newsletter of AAHE is available by subscription only to AAHE members. It offers news, interviews, and how-to articles on the wide range of AAHE activities.

Educational Technology Review. <http://www.aahebulletin.com>

This publication of the Association for the Advancement of Computing in Education became an online journal in 2001. Its focus is the use of technology, and it contains articles related to quality learning environments for distance learning and hybrid class models.

Section Four
Effective Teaching Practices and Learning Tools

Modules in this section:

Overview of Effective Teaching Practices

by Kathleen Burke, SUNY Cortland

Faculty Development Series

Effective teaching is the key to strong student learning. For students to learn and to become self-growers, the most effective and contextually appropriate teaching techniques should be used. Implementing the proper techniques can assist in engaging the students not only with the material, but also with their own growth and success. Understanding the basic principles behind effective teaching practices makes it easier to choose, adjust, and improve implementation of teaching practices. Implementing the proper teaching practices takes planning prior to the term. Furthermore, a faculty member needs to assess his or her performance after each class and to make needed adjustments. The instructor must not be afraid to try new techniques, understanding that they may not always be as effective as he or she had planned. However, adjusting and modifying techniques by applying classroom assessment and educational research can make them work for individual instructors.

Role of Effective Teaching Practices

Effective teaching practices incorporate curriculum design, assessment, learning practices, facilitation, and learning environment. These are entwined to address the learning outcomes. Teachers can be viewed as designers (Wiggins and McTighe 1998, p. 7). Selecting and utilizing the proper teaching practice at the appropriate time is a skill as well as an art. The instructor must identify the learning outcomes to be achieved. The course design and day-to-day teaching must address these selected learning outcomes (see section titled "Instructional Design"). Furthermore, assessment *(see Overview of Assessment)* must constantly be performed to determine if the selected teaching tools have effectively achieved the desired outcome(s).

Principles of Effective Teaching Practices

1. **Effective teaching must be outcome-centered.**

   Teaching is only effective if the desired learning outcome is achieved. The instructor must ensure that the teaching practices employed address the appropriate outcomes effectively.

2. **Effective teaching should be student-centered.**

   Students should be the number one priority for a teacher. An effective teacher recognizes that different students learn differently. Incorporating different tools and techniques into teaching to accommodate these differences will enable a teacher to become more effective (McKeachie, 1994). Furthermore, the instructor should be open to student concerns and be available to the students *(see Effective Use of Office Hours)*.

Table 1   **Principles of Effective Teaching Practices**

1. Effective teaching must be outcome-centered.

2. Effective teaching must be student-centered.

3. Effective teaching is informed by continuous assessment.

4. Teaching must be appropriate for the level of student knowledge and learning skills.

5. Teaching must be adapted to the discipline.

6. Effective teaching practices require long-term and short-term planning.

7. Teaching practices should enhance student learning skills.

8. Teaching practices can be enhanced by a learning culture in a department and a college.

9. Teaching practices can be customized to individual teaching styles.

10. Taking the risks of trying new things is essential for continuous improvement of teaching practices.

3. **Effective teaching is informed by continuous assessment.**

   To determine if the teaching practices are effective, continuous assessments of both the students and the instructor must be implemented *(see Assessment Methodology)*. After each class, the instructor should assess his or her performance and modify the next class appropriately. Furthermore, the instructor should have the students assess their own performance and understanding as well as the instructor's performance.

4. **Teaching must be appropriate for the level of student knowledge and learning skills.**

Instructors must gauge their students' abilities and modify their teaching techniques appropriately. It is the instructor's responsibility to maintain the balance between the material's challenge and the students' cognitive skills (see *Accelerator Model*).

5. **Teaching must be adapted to the discipline.**

Certain teaching techniques are more appropriate for certain disciplines than other. For example, labs may be more appropriate in the natural sciences than in the humanities. However, any teaching tool or technique can be utilized in any discipline with the appropriate modifications. For instance, a writing lab could be instituted in an English class.

6. **Effective teaching practices require long and short-term planning.**

Teaching practices are selected during the course design and syllabus production. However, as a term progresses, modification of teaching practices based on student assessment and self-assessment will probably be needed.

7. **Teaching practices should enhance student learning skills.**

Beginning with common skills that students already possess will reinforce their abilities with those skills and provide a good base for growing their skill sets. The students will develop confidence in their performance and validate their belief in themselves. This affect will enable the instructor to further develop the students' skill sets and to introduce additional learning skills.

8. **Teaching practices can be enhanced by a learning culture in a department and a college.**

As McKeachie (1994) notes, students have developed expectations of the learning processes throughout their college career. If the culture of the department (or college) sets a tone for utilizing innovative teaching techniques and setting high expectations for student performance, then experimenting and employing new techniques will be more easily accepted by students and colleagues. Moreover, the department or college will see the value in what innovative faculty are trying to do. Implementing more effective teaching practices in a place where this type of learning culture is not present is not impossible; however, it will take more time and effort to implement and the value may not be as apparent to the students and colleagues.

9. **Teaching practices can be customized to individual teaching styles.**

Teaching style is an individual trait, and so what works for one instructor may not be a good fit for another instructor. An effective teacher will be able to adapt and modify particular techniques to fit his or her personality. Moreover, an effective teacher will be able to restructure tools to meet the needs of his or her students to insure the greatest probability of achieving the desired outcomes.

10. **Taking the risks of trying new things is essential for continuous improvement of teaching practices.**

Changing or implementing a new teaching technique can be scary. However, as faculty encourage students to take risks, they need to take risks as well, by trying new ways to convey an understanding of the information. Things may go terribly the first time a new technique is implemented. But, after assessing the strengths and weaknesses of the technique, instructors can modify it and try it again. Hindsight is 20/20; the second time will often be better.

Issues in Implementing Effective Teaching Practices

Many issues affect teaching practices at many different levels (personal, institutional, or higher education in general). Below are some of the most common issues that contribute to difficulties in implementing certain teaching practices.

1. **Prior student experience with tool**

It takes time to develop and personalize a particular teaching technique. Instructors and students need to become comfortable with a technique before they perform optimally. If students have experience with a particular technique, implementing it into a class will be easier than if the technique is unfamiliar. Desired outcomes can be achieved more quickly when students are experienced with the teaching technique being used.

2. **Training required for effective use**

Implementing a new technique involves costs. The instructor has to take time to learn a tool and determine how to implement the tool to produce the desired learning outcome. Given the multiple demands on faculty, the price of learning a new teaching technique can be quite high. However, after some experience with implementing a technique, the time involved in planning to achieve desired outcomes will diminish.

3. **Lack of supporting resources**

Some institutions lack material or collegial support for innovative teaching techniques. The lack of physical resources, such as lab equipment, computer labs, etc., is difficult to overcome without monetary support from some funding source. Lack of collegial support to investing time in improving teaching skills is a different issue. In some institutions, teaching is regarded as a task that should be done well, but the primary focus is on research. Faculty have to balance becoming effective teachers with conducting quality research.

4. **Attitude of instructor**

A key factor in student success is the attitude of the instructor. An instructor's enthusiasm can motivate students. Moreover, nonverbal communication can also send signals to students. As McKeachie (1994) notes, the instructor's facial expressions, energy, and intonation are as important as what the instructor says. Student excitement and motivation begin with the instructor.

5. **Real world application of teaching techniques**

Students will realize the effectiveness (or appropriateness) of the instructor's teaching when they can see the implications for real world usage. For instance, employing the use of case studies enables the students to see exactly how the information is used in a real world situation. Research has shown that students' ability to apply concepts improves overall knowledge and understanding when case studies are used. (See McKeachie, 1994, for details.)

Implementation and Planning

"For teachers, courses do not start on the first day of classes. Rather, a course begins well before they meet their students." (McKeachie, 1994)

An effective teacher plans and strategizes the layout of his or her course well before the beginning of the semester. During this development time, as an instructor prepares the syllabus and creates a course outline, he or she should begin to think about specific techniques to enhance teaching certain topics. Furthermore, teachers may want to visit other classes to determine what techniques their colleagues employ and to modify those techniques to meet the needs of their students.

Once the term begins, student and teacher performance should be assessed day by day *(see **Assessment Methodology**)*. Assessment information may reveal a need to modify the course outline. Flexibility is necessary. Developing student understanding is more important than covering a certain number of chapters. In some cases, slowing down at the beginning of a term allows picking up the pace later in the term when students have a better foundation to draw upon and will grasp the material more quickly. Flexibility and day-to-day adjustments make teachers more effective.

While an effective teacher puts students' needs first, balancing the time to learn new teaching techniques with the need to fulfill research and service obligations can be challenging. Fortunately, the time cost for utilizing a new technique diminishes. After first implementing a technique, the time needed for class preparation for subsequent implementations decreases dramatically. However, constant interruptions from students can take attention away from research, preparing for class, or any of the many other tasks that faculty must complete during the day. Therefore, getting the students to value your time is important *(see **Effective Use of Office Hours**)*.

Concluding Thoughts

Becoming an effective teacher combines many skills. An effective teacher keeps his or her students in mind when making all decisions regarding the classroom. What works well one semester in a course may not be as effective with a different class composition. A teacher must always be flexible and open to student ideas. Most of all, a teacher should be true to himself or herself to realize the great rewards that the profession has to offer.

References

McKeachie, W. (1994). *Teaching tips: Strategies, research and theory for college and university teachers.* Lexington, MA: D.C. Heath.

Wiggins, G., & McTighe, J. (1998). *Understanding by design.* Alexandria, VA: Association for Supervision and Curriculum Development.

Mid-term Assessment

by Richard Armstrong, Madison Area Technical College

Mid-term course assessment is a process and a tool to help faculty members and students improve current and future learning. The process is best implemented at least twice during a term, using a few important questions. This module describes the value of mid-term assessment and describes the process of implementing it. Furthermore, the module provides an adaptable tool and sample student responses.

When to Use Mid-term Assessment

Ideally, mid-term course assessment occurs two or three times a term, scheduled within the first third of the course, at about the 60% point, and a week before finals. The intent of mid-term assessment is to assess performance at different stages of the semester, not to evaluate performance. Mid-term assessment gathers quality information to produce improvements for faculty, courses, and students (Angelo & Cross, 1993).

Important Purposes

Mid-term assessment records student feedback at a specific point of a course and emphasizes understanding what is working well and why. It provides clear direction for immediate and long-term improvements in course structure and the learning process. It provides enough data to reduce over-reaction to outliers and to help faculty focus on what is best for all. Mid-term assessment can provide important research data on student learning needs and improve the performance of the reflective practitioner. The impact of a mid-term course assessment truly supports a continuous quality improvement model (Apple, 2002).

Benefits

Mid-term assessment builds trust in the learning community of the class and shifts ownership for learning toward students. It also provides opportunities for instructors, learners, and teams to improve their performances. Mid-term assessment models the assessment process, expands the culture of assessment, and helps students modify their goals and refresh their commitment to the learning process. Overall, mid-term assessment is one of the more important best practices of quality educators.

Key Principles

The key principles In Table 1 help to make the mid-term assessment successful. Although these principles may initially seem complex, the principles become common sense in practice.

Table 1 **Key Principles of a Mid-term Assessment**

1. The faculty member shows no defensiveness.
2. Feedback is followed by a discussion session.
3. Specific analysis of the feedback is shared with students.
4. After discussion and class approval, some identified areas of improvement should be implemented.
5. The faculty member's mindset should focus on improving the course and learning versus concerns about how good the course has been.
6. Mid-term assessment should not be about affirmation.
7. When repeated, the process increases in effectiveness.
8. The feedback discussion should occur during the next class meeting after the assessment.
9. Mid-term assessment should not take place right before or after a major exam or project.
10. The instructor must ignore student affect within the student assessments in order to identify the real significant discoveries.

Implementation Process

Mid-term course assessments may be completed in class or as homework. The instructor then analyzes the feedback to look for important information. What is working well for the students? What are two to three areas where improvements could be made in the course? During the following class period, the assessments should be discussed with the class to decide together on any changes to be made.

Sample Mid-term Course Assessment and Student Responses

Table 2 on the next page is an example of a mid-term course assessment form that follows the SII format of assessment. *(See **SII Method for Assessment Reporting**.)*

The following are actual student responses from the mid-term assessment. The students are from College Chemistry II, the second semester of a sequence of freshman chemistry.

Table 2   ***Mid-term Course Assessment***

Name _____   Date _____

I. What are the three greatest strengths of this course and its instructor so far and why?

II. During the remaining time of this term, what are three improvements that the **instructor** could make in **this class/his teaching** to help you learn better? Suggest how these improvements could be made.

III. What personal action plans can **you** put in place **to help yourself** learn the content better this semester?

IV. What are the three most important things you have learned about **learning** (not course content) in this course so far?

V. What insights do you have about learning, teamwork, and helping others learn and grow?

Strengths:

- Flexibility. The course and the instructor have changed a great deal since last semester, due, in large part, to feedback from students.

- High level of challenge. This is a challenging class that requires a commitment on the part of the student. This is a strength in that it raises the level of seriousness toward the subject with most of the students, which I find motivating.

- The course has forced me to learn actively all of the time that I am in class and working at home. The plethora of drills and in class exercises keeps me from coasting through class, with the thought that I'll just take it all in and integrate my knowledge later. I seem to work better when I am actively involved.

Areas for Improvement:

- More group activities and models would be a very helpful tool for increasing our understanding of the concepts being taught.

- Utilize the method of short lecture, short critical thinking activity that has recently been introduced. This technique seems to get ideas across easily and capture student's attention.

- When we don't finish an activity, it would be nice to go over it briefly during the next class. I find that, while they really help me learn, I remain unclear on some of the reasoning behind the finer points.

- I would like you to be able to teach more in class, rather than outside of class. I have had my best learning moments outside of class when I have come to the office or over the phone.

The three most important things you have learned about learning in this course, so far:

- That steady, gradual learning sticks longer than the last minute cram.

- Learning doesn't just happen. I have to work at it, and to work at it I have to be motivated by the value of learning.

- Learning is more dependent on how hard you work than on how intelligent you are.

Things learned about learning, teamwork and helping others:

- I have learned that most often, I am my worst critic. I have to evaluate fairly and objectively what I am doing within a group. Sometimes I contribute better than other times and I have to step back and ask, "What have I done well?"

- When I work as a team, it helps me to learn, not only from my teammate's insights, but also by having to explain concepts to them. It also reinforces to myself that I do know the material and helps build confidence in my abilities.

- I've learned that the people in this particular class are really interested in doing well and understanding the material. This makes it so easy to get work done. What I love the most about the people in this class is that because we all want to do well, everyone contributes significantly and one person's weakness is often another person's strength.

Concluding Thoughts

The process of mid-term course assessment allows the instructor to do real-time classroom research and to be in the learning mode, rather than in the teaching mode. The mid-term course assessments help students investigate their preferred learning style(s) and provide tools they can carry over into other courses. The students feel empowered by their new role in the teaching and learning process, and the process of mid-term course assessment builds stronger trust and rapport between students and instructor. Therefore, using mid-term assessment in every course is highly recommended.

References

Angelo, T. K., & Cross, K. P. (1994). *Classroom assessment techniques: A handbook for college teachers*. San Francisco: Jossey-Bass.

Apple, D. (2002). *Assessment institute handbook*. Lisle, IL: Pacific Crest.

Classroom assessment techniques. Southern Illinois University-Edwardsville. <www.siue.edu/~deder/assess/catmain.html>

Effective Use of Office Hours

by Kathleen Burke, SUNY Cortland

Faculty Development Series

For faculty members, time is precious. Interruptions from students can take attention away from research, class preparation, and other tasks. Getting students to value instructors' time is important. By recognizing why students are attending office hours, faculty can effectively minimize time demands and maximize benefits for students.

Why Students Attend Office Hours

The main reasons that students come to office hours are confusion about assignments or policies; requests for special privileges; and help in solving specific problems (Wankat and Oreovicz, 1999). Clarifying assignments or policies is usually not very time-consuming. Faculty need to draw a fine line for students at the beginning of the term to uphold guidelines for the course, yet remain approachable to students. If guidelines are in place, then requests for special privileges can take little time. For example, when a student misses an assignment and asks to turn it in late, if the syllabus specifies that no late assignments are accepted, then it is easy to refuse to accept the assignment.

Most of the time in office hours is spent with students seeking help with specific problems. There are some time-saving ways of dealing with certain problems. For example, some students believe that they can miss class and then see the instructor to obtain the work/notes on the material that was discussed. Re-teaching the course in office hours is not an instructor's job. Students who miss class (excused or not excused) should obtain the notes before seeking the instructor's assistance. Again, this procedure can be indicated in the syllabus.

Furthermore, students may come to office hours to discuss the course without bringing relevant course materials. Any discussion can begin with determining whether the student has brought the required materials.

Most students like to work together. To avoid having multiple students come in separately to ask the same question, students should be encouraged to come to office hours as a group. In some cases, sending a group representative who will report back to the group also works.

Another time-saving method is to use time right after class sessions to answer individual questions and handle minor problems, such as grade changes, picking up materials, inquiries about grades, and so forth. These issues can usually be handled relatively quickly.

Regardless of why a student is coming to office hours, the door should remain open. Leaving the door open helps to avoid accusations of impropriety.

Proper Mentoring During Office Hours

It is important for faculty members to establish why a student is attending office hours to determine how to handle his or her situation. While it may sound harsh to "classify" students, doing so provides an easy way to quickly determine how best to help them. Each person should be dealt with in a patient, sympathetic and supportive manner, regardless of why he or she came to office hours. Below are some of the different types of student visitors, along with suggestions about how to handle each situation.

"Petrified to speak"
Although this student is having problems, he or she rarely attends office hours. The instructor should reach out during class and suggest meeting if necessary. Online office hours may be the best resource for this type of student.

"The drop-in or pest"
This student is frequently at the door, but not always for a particular reason. Some students feel comfortable with certain instructors and just drop in to say hello or just "hang out." If an assessment of the visit reveals no significant reason for a student to be there, the faculty member may need to explain, in a kind way, that the student should not visit at this time.

"I don't understand"
Since re-teaching an entire lecture during office hour is impractical, instructors should encourage this type of student to come with specific questions and to ask questions during class when he or she does not understand what is being covered.

"The procrastinator"
This student is a version of the "I don't understand" student. However, this student will come to the office just before an exam claiming that he or she does not understand any of the material and expecting the faculty member to teach it on the spot (and expect to comprehend it as well). Instructors should be clear that students with problems and questions should seek help earlier and not expect the instructor to re-teach all of the material just prior to an exam. On the other hand, specific questions (on certain aspects of the material) that students might have should be welcomed.

"The no show"

This student does not come to class, then comes to the office and expects to be taught the material individually during office hours. The instructor may ask this student if he or she has the notes from the class missed (most of the time, he or she will not). Then the instructor can explain that he or she may come back and ask any questions that remain after he or she obtains and reviews the notes.

"I don't know if I am doing this right!"

This student usually lacks the self-confidence to validate his or her own knowledge or problem- solving skills. This type of student usually requires a lot of time at the beginning, but helping the student begin to self-validate will enable the student to need less and less support.

"The advice seeker"

This student may seek advice with respect to academic issues, such as whether to withdraw from a course, what courses to take, and so on. These situations usually require a time to gather information and assess before responding. While faculty members may assist in the decision-making process, ultimately each student must make his or her own decision.

Additionally, a student may seek advice on personal issues. Instructors must restrict giving advice to areas in which they are knowledgeable. Otherwise, they can recommend or assist with finding the proper person or office to further assist the student. Furthermore, it is very important to follow all institutional policies regarding sensitive issues.

"The engaged student"

This student wants to discuss the class. Although speaking with an engaged student is intellectually exciting, instructors need to be conscious of time and task priorities. If the discussion is relevant to others, this student could be asked to bring the topic up again during class.

Using Email and Online Discussions to Supplement Office Hours

Using email is an effective way of controlling office hours because of its asynchronous nature. Email is particularly effective for non-traditional students, who may not be on campus during regular office hours. Students who use email should clearly present their questions or issues. Email offers the advantages to instructors of answering students at convenient times and avoiding interruptions.

Online discussions and synchronous chats also extend student-instructor and student-student communication. Benefits of discussion forums include: (1) being more accessible to students; (2) facilitating collaborative learning; (3) ensuring student-to-student interaction; and (4) allowing an outlet for students who would not normally voice their opinions in class (McKeage, 2001). However, as McKeage (2001) warns, instructor facilitation of online discussions is imperative.

Table 1   **Top Ten Tips for Successful Office Hours**

1. Determine the reason for the visit immediately.
2. Enforce announced guidelines.
3. Ensure that absentees get and review class notes before the visit.
4. Encourage use of email for questions.
5. Announce and post changes to office hours.
6. Encourage group visits.
7. Be supportive, sympathetic, and patient.
8. Set hours when students are able to attend.
9. Ensure that students are prepared and have needed materials.
10. Encourage attendance during office hours using class announcements and inviting individuals who need help.

Concluding Thoughts

Office hour time can and should be managed to increase student learning without overburdening busy faculty members. Students have to be taught what to expect from an office visit and how to prepare for a visit.

References

Lardy, L. J. & Porter, M. K. (1996). *Office hours and tutoring.* In Lambert, L. M., Tice, S. L., & Featherstone, P. H. (eds.), *University Teaching: A Guide for Graduate Students.* Syracuse, NY: Syracuse University Press.

McKeage, K. (2001). Office hours as you like them. *College Teaching* 49 (1), 32-38.

Wankat, P. C., & Oreovicz, F. S. (1999). Office hours Rx. *ASEE Prism* 8 (5), 15.

Overview of Effective Learning Tools

by Carol Nancarrow, Sinclair Community College

Central to the philosophy of process learning is the importance of growing learning skills to enable students to become self-growers. By using appropriate learning tools, students can improve key learning skills in the affective, cognitive, social, and psychomotor domains. Learning tools are primarily used by the learners, rather than by the facilitator, although the facilitator may certainly need to train the students in the use of the tools and monitor their use. Learning tools can reinforce desirable learning behaviors, such as class preparation, and/or provide a structure for thinking about content or self-assessment. Learning tools should also be integral to the assessment and evaluation of learning in a course. The modules in this section describe some important learning tools and their use to improve learning.

Defining Learning Tools

A learning tool is an instrument designed to be used by learners to provide a structure for growing learning skills and behaviors and/or systematically collecting and thinking about key information. While teaching tools are primarily used by faculty, learning tools are primarily used by students. Faculty provide appropriate tools and the necessary instruction in how to use the tools, but students use learning tools on their own. Learning tools may involve technology, such as computers and calculators, but they can also be pencil and paper tools, such as the Persistence Log *(see **Persistence Log**)*.

Table 1   ***Principles of Effective Learning Tools***

1. Effective learning tools must be learner-centered.

2. Learning outcomes and productivity can be increased through using learning tools.

3. Learning tools must be appropriate for the level of the learner.

4. A learning tool should be engaging.

5. Learning tools enhance the development of learning skills.

6. The learning curve for using a learning tool should be appropriate for the learning benefits derived.

7. Diverse learners and situations can be accommodated by adaptation of learning tools.

8. Learning tools can provide a framework for meta-cognitive thinking and learning.

9. Learning tools align with and support assessment and grading systems.

10. Learning tools should be designed for independent use by students and transfer to new applications.

Principles of Effective Learning Tools

1. **Effective learning tools must be learner-centered.**

   While an instructor may design a tool, model its use, assess the process of using the tool, and possibly evaluate the results of using the tool, most of the time and effort involved with the tool's use should be the student's. Therefore, it is essential that the results of using the tools will be sufficient to motivate the students to use the tool and to carry the tool into future learning activities. Otherwise, a tool may be perceived as just busywork. The learner must get value for his investment of time and effort in using the tool.

2. **Learning outcomes and productivity can be increased through using learning tools.**

   The Persistence Log *(see **Persistence Log**)* is an example of a tool that increases learning outcomes by improving students' learning skills. The Reading Log increases productivity by enabling students to get maximum benefit from reading assignments. The tool is a means to an end, not an end itself.

3. **Learning tools must be appropriate for the level of the learner.**

   Since learning tools are primarily used independently by students, the structure, vocabulary, and process associated with using a tool should be within the current skill set of the learner, or be learned with a reasonable investment of effort.

4. **A learning tool should be engaging.**

   A tool that students perceive as fun and challenging will get a lot more use than one that seems like boring busywork. Of course, including the use of the tool in the assessment and evaluation systems can provide some motivation within a course, but if a tool is to become part of a student's repertoire of learning tools across courses and learning tasks, then it needs to be rewarding to use.

5. **Learning tools enhance the development of learning skills.**

These learning skills may rely on future use of the tool, but tools also enhance development of such learning skills as class preparation, attendance, and participation *(see Persistence Log);* as well as affective skills, such as self-assessment and goal setting. A tool can be chosen or designed to meeting an assessed need for improvement of learning skills.

6. **The learning curve for using a learning tool should be appropriate for the learning benefits derived.**

A complex tool may take considerable time to learn and use, but yield commensurate rewards. If the tool is more trouble than it is worth, it will not be valued by anyone.

7. **Diverse learners and situations can be accommodated by adaptation of learning tools.**

A quality learning tool can easily be used in a wide variety of contexts and for various levels of learners. For example, the idea of tracking and rewarding desirable learning behaviors, as shown in the Persistence Log, could be used for any observable, defined set of desirable learning behaviors to enhance the way of being for many disciplines.

8. **Learning tools should provide a framework for meta-cognitive thinking and learning.**

Current research into learning and the brain establishes strongly that learning has to become part of an individual's cognitive network to be retained and applied to new situations *(see Learning Theory section)*. By providing a structure for thinking and recording thoughts, learning tools such as the Learning Assessment Journal and the Life Vision Portfolio encourage such meta-cognition and reflection.

9. **Learning tools align with and support assessment and grading systems.**

By embedding the use of learning tools in the course assessment and grading systems, the instructor sends the message that using the learning tools is valued by the instructor. Grading is a strong motivator for quality use of a learning tool such as the Reading Log. By enabling the instructor a written representation of a student's thinking process and self-concept, a learning tool can make assessment much richer and more individualized.

10. **Learning tools should be designed for independent use.**

When a new learning tool is introduced, students may need considerable training in the use of the tool. Therefore, tools should be designed so that trained students can use the tools by themselves, and, even more significantly, recognize when the tool would be appropriate and helpful for their own learning process in diverse situations.

Issues in Developing and Using Learning Tools

1. **Resources required for development of learning tools**

Designing a learning tool can be a fairly complex process, especially since the tool should be tested, assessed, and revised to ensure its efficacy. However, some of that investment in time can be compensated by students being able to do more on their own, and by re-use in other circumstances and courses. In addition, many learning tools have already been developed and can be used or adapted and used without a large investment in development time. This section of the *Faculty Guidebook* offers a good selection of cross-curricular learning tools that can be used with little development time and significant return in increased learning. An instructor should be sure to use a tool to accomplish a task before introducing students to the tool.

2. **Motivating students to use tools**

At first some learning tools may be perceived by students as busywork. The first obstacle may be getting students to use the tools effectively. One way to overcome that initial barrier is to include the use of the tool in the class evaluation system. That sends an immediate message that the instructor considers the use of the tool to be an important part of success in the course.

Once the student has experience with a well-designed tool, the advantages of using the tool should become apparent. For example, the first time students are required to use a self-assessment form for a writing project, many students see it as just something to do to satisfy the instructor. Over the course of the term, though, as they see how thinking about their work process has enabled them to make positive changes, they begin to see other areas in their lives that could benefit from using self-assessment.

In some cases, students can begin a task without a tool and see for themselves that they need some systematic way to approach the task. Then a learning tool can be introduced and it will be valued immediately. The reading log may be used in this way when students are having trouble getting value from assigned readings.

3. **Additional resources for finding learning tools:**
   - the *Learning Assessment Journal*
   - the *Faculty Guidebook*
   - learning objects repositories, such as Merlot.org
   - textbooks and teacher's guides
   - networking and mentors
   - professional journals
   - students

4. **Assessing the quality of a tool**

   Since a learning tool should be chosen to meet some learning need, it should be assessed by how well it meets that need. The time and effort in using the tool, including both faculty effort and student effort, should show real rewards in learning outcomes. In addition, the tool should show dividends in the students' way of being as learners and as practitioners of their discipline and profession. The section on characteristics of a quality tool in this module is a helpful starting place for assessing a tool.

5. **Cost of the tool**

   Some technology-based tools, such as calculators, laptops, and instruments, can involve considerable monetary cost. Tools also have a cost in terms of time and effort, both in learning and in using the tools. The instructor will have to do some cost/benefit analysis to ensure that the value of the tool justifies its expense. An important consideration in this area will be whether the tool transfers into other coursework and into the professional lives of the students.

6. **Faculty belief in the value of the tool**

   If the faculty member has used the tool for his or her own learning and found it valuable, the level of commitment to the tool will be apparent to students. So, it is a good idea for faculty members to try tools in an appropriate learning situation themselves before introducing students to the tools. For example, reading logs, learning journals, and self-assessment forms are easily and profitably test-driven by faculty. Such use before introducing a tool to students will also help the faculty member anticipate student issues with use of a particular tool. If the faculty member is ambivalent about the value of a tool, that attitude is likely to be communicated to students and to sabotage their success with the tool.

7. **Alignment of tool with student needs**

   Students are much more receptive to the effort involved in learning and using a tool if the tool has the potential to make their work more effective and efficient. Sometimes a period of struggling along without

a tool will engender appreciation of a new tool when it is introduced. The value of the tool to students needs to be apparent rather quickly in order for students to commit to learning and using a new tool. Tools should promote defined and desired learning outcomes.

8. **Complexity of tool**

   In general, tools should be as simple as possible. With the current push to employ technology, there is some risk of creating a tool that uses technology just for the sake of using technology, when a simple paper and pencil tool would do the same thing more easily. As tools become more complex, the investment of time and money to learn and use the tool also goes up. Since tools are a means to an end, and not an end in themselves, simplicity is a virtue.

9. **Establishing a tool set for learning**

   Successful students are often resourceful in inventing their own tools for learning situations, such as making vocabulary flashcards. Sharing of such tools is a quick way to build a tool set for a course or discipline. A repertoire of learning tools forms a foundation for lifelong learning. Students with a good set of learning tools can readily adapt tools to meet future needs and to use their own learning styles. Students should be prepared to enter into their professional lives with proficiency in the regularly used tools of the practice.

10. **Inhibiting creativity and originality**

    There is some danger in using tools that take away the student's need to think through problems and find creative approaches. For example, students often enter college so used to using the five-paragraph theme paradigm that they limit their writing unnecessarily. Part of learning to use a tool is recognizing the limitations of the tool and knowing when to deviate from it. Tool design and choice should be made with cognizance of the needs of the learners, and tools may need to evolve as students' skills develop.

Learning Tools and Technology

The huge growth in use of technology in education has lead to an explosion of computer-based learning tools. Online courses and course enhancements provide a convenient way to access and work with learning tools. Repositories for sharing learning objects *(see **Glossary**)* are growing rapidly. Many learning objects include learning tools that can be used in the context of the complete learning object or extracted and adapted for other uses, including paper and pencil formats. No matter whether a learning object is delivered with technology or not, the same indicators of quality still apply.

Characteristics of a Quality Learning Tool

Table 2 presents characteristics that can be used for assessment and evaluation of learning tools. These factors should be considered by faculty when a tool is chosen. Once students have gained some facility with a tool, they can provide valuable insights into whether the tool has these desirable characteristics.

Table 2   **Characteristics of a Quality Learning Tool**

A quality learning tool is:	
Growth-oriented	The tool leads to significant growth toward a desired learning outcome or learning skill. This characteristic is crucial.
Transferable	The tool is flexible so that it has applications to other courses and to professional life.
Time-efficient	Student and instructor time using the tool will be highly productive.
Results-oriented	Using the tool produces significant results. Learning the tool is not an end in itself, but a means to an end.
Essential	The tool meets a real need of students.
Feasible	Start-up and use costs, in time and money, are reasonable and in proportion to learning value of the tool for faculty and students.
Engaging	Using the tool is fun and rewarding for students, not a boring chore.
Functional	Tool is elegant in design, so that results are readily achieved.

Concluding Thoughts

Success in using learning tools is highly dependent upon the faculty member's belief in the efficacy of the tools. Faculty members tend to work best with tools that they have used and found valuable in their own learning process. If a tool is provided without sufficient training in the use of the tool, it may just add noise and frustration to the learning environment. Therefore, faculty should choose a few tools that they can fully implement, rather than overwhelming students with tools that are not fully integrated into the course. Often the full value of a tool is not apparent until it has been used over time in multiple applications. It is possible for faculty and students to give up on a valuable tool because they have not used it enough to develop facility with it and thus appreciate its value. Well-chosen and well-implemented learning tools provide significant dividends in increasing student learning and ability to apply skills in future contexts.

References

Apple, D. (2000). *Learning assessment journal* (4th ed.). Lisle, IL: Pacific Crest.

Bean, J. (2001). *Engaging ideas: The professor's guide to integrating writing, critical thinking, and active learning in the classroom.* San Francisco: Jossey-Bass.

Fink, D. (2003). *Creating significant learning experiences: An integrated approach to designing college courses.* San Francisco: Jossey-Bass.

Krumsieg, K., & Baehr, M. (2000). *Foundations of learning* (3rd ed.). Lisle, IL: Pacific Crest.

Wiggins, G., & McTighe, J. (1998). *Understanding by design.* Alexandria, VA: Association for Supervision and Curriculum Development.

Designing Teams and Assigning Roles

by Peter Smith, St. Mary's College

Faculty Development Series

For many faculty members, the issues surrounding team construction and management are significant. This module explores methods for implementing the use of roles in the classroom, including assigning students to teams and requiring team members to perform in roles. Learning to work well in teams is important because the workplace has become much more team-oriented over the past two decades (Scans, 1991), and students who participate in team environments are much better prepared than those without teaming experience to succeed on the job. Although it is not yet common for business or industry to employ formal process-oriented roles for team members, graduates who have used roles frequently in under-graduate courses realize that the use of roles would dramatically improve team performance.

Why Roles are Important

Using roles helps team members to become interdependent (Johnson, 1998) and to be individually accountable for team success, to increase their learning skills (Duncan-Hewitt, 1995), and to speed up the four stages of team development—forming (goal setting), storming (conflict resolution), norming (problem-solving), and performing (Tuckman, 1965). Roles should be rotated frequently so that each student has the opportunity to practice each role and to realize that effective learning requires that teams use all of the roles simultaneously. Rotating roles discourages dominance by one person and gives all students opportunities to practice social, communication, and leadership skills (Millis and Cottell, 1998). The roles introduced in this module are effective for enhancing team performance because each team member is empowered by his or her role to make a unique and significant contribution to the learning process.

Cooperative versus Collaborative Learning

The use of roles in learning activities is at the heart of the controversy between cooperative and collaborative learning. Although both approaches use small-group learning and encourage cooperative behavior, positive interdependence, and individual accountability, collaborative learning advocates hold that interdependence will occur naturally and no attempt should be made to structure it. Therefore, the facilitator should not assign teams or roles, assess learning skills and performance, or structure their development (Davidson 1994). Cooperative learning is much more structured. The facilitator strives to ensure that the teams have diverse membership, and he or she is constantly assessing the skill level and performance of each student and planning activities that will allow the students to improve. When fulfilling the responsibilities of team roles, students must use many learning skills, so the facilitator has opportunities to intervene to help the individual student while ostensibly helping the team improve its performance *(see **Facilitation Methodology**)*.

Table 1 **Various Team Roles and When to Use Them**

E = Essential   O = Optional   NA = Not Applicable

Learning Situation	Captain	Recorder	Reflector	Spokes-person	Technology Specialist	Planner	Time Keeper	Skeptic	Optimist	Spy
Cooperative Learning	E	E	E	O	O	O	O	O	O	O
Laboratory	E	E	E	NA	E	O	O	O	O	O
Project	E	E	E	O	O	E	O	O	O	O
Problem Solving	E	E	E	O	O	E	O	O	O	NA
Student Presentation	E	O	E	E	O	O	E	O	O	O
Student Teaching	E	O	E	E	O	O	E	O	O	O
Committee Work	E	E	E	E	O	E	O	O	O	NA
Department Business	E	E	O	NA	E	E	O	O	O	NA
Grant Writing	E	E	E	O	O	E	O	O	O	NA
Peer Assessment	O	E	E	E	NA	NA	O	O	O	NA

Performance Criteria for Team Roles

Captain

1. Facilitate the team process, keeping it enjoyable and rewarding for all team members.
2. Make sure each member has a role and is performing within that role.
3. Ensure that all team members can articulate and apply what has been learned.
4. Manage time, stress, and conflict.
5. Accept accountability for the overall performance of the team.
6. Contribute to the group as an active learner.

Recorder

1. Record group roles and instructions at the beginning of a task or activity.
2. During an activity, record and collect important information and data, integrating and synthesizing different points of view.
3. Document group decisions and discoveries legibly and accurately.
4. Accept accountability for the overall quality of the "recorder's report."
5. Control information flow and articulate concepts in alternative forms if necessary.
6. Contribute to the group as an active learner.

Reflector

1. Assess performance, interactions, and the dynamics among team members, recording strengths, improvements, and insights (see *SII Method for Assessment Reporting*).
2. Be a good listener and observer.
3. Accept accountability for the overall quality of the "reflector's journal."
4. Present an oral reflector's report positively and constructively if asked to do so.
5. Intervene with suggestions and strategies for improving the team's processes.
6. Contribute to the group as an active learner.

Spokesperson

1. Speak for the team when called upon to do so.
2. Ask questions or request clarification for the team.
3. Make oral presentations to the class for the team.
4. Use the recorder's journal to share the team's discoveries and insights.
5. Collaborate periodically with the recorder.
6. Contribute to the group as an active learner.

Technology Specialist

1. Use the available technological tools for the team activity.
2. Listen, converse, and collaborate with team members; synthesize inputs, try suggestions and/or follow directions for the technology.
3. Retrieve information from various sources; manage the available resources and information.
4. Help team members understand the technology and its use.
5. Be willing to experiment, take risks, and try things.
6. Contribute to the group as an active learner.

Planner

1. Review the activity, develop a plan of action, and revise the plan to ensure task completion.
2. Monitor the team's performance against the plan and report deviations.
3. Contribute to the group as an active learner.

Timekeeper

1. Observe the time resource for the activity and/or record the time allocation announced by the facilitator.
2. Keep track of the elapsed time for various tasks and notify the captain when the agreed-upon time has expired.
3. Contribute to the group as an active learner.

Optimist

1. Focus on why things will work.
2. Keep the team in a positive frame of mind.
3. Look for ways in which team discoveries can be applied or used to the team's advantage.
4. Contribute to the group as an active learner.

Skeptic

1. Question and check the assumptions that are being made.
2. Determine the issues or reasons why quality is not being met at the expected level.
3. Be constructive in helping the team improve performance.
4. Contribute to the group as an active learner.

Spy

1. Eavesdrop on other teams during an activity to gather information and seek clarification of direction.
2. Relay information that can help the team perform better.
3. Contribute to the group as an active learner.
[Myrvaagnes et al, 1996]

Issues Surrounding Team Design

1. Although teams can contain any number of participants, most college and university level practitioners prefer groups of four for cooperative learning activities (Millis and Cottell, 1998). Quads are small enough to engage each student, but large enough to provide a rich mix of ideas. Four person teams can also be easily split into pairs for "think, pair, share" activities. Cooperative learning advocates David and Roger Johnson recommend three-person teams, and up to three of these may be necessary if the number of participants is not divisible by four. If absenteeism is a serious problem, five-person teams may be optimal, although regular attendance is vital because each student has a responsibility to contribute to the team's efforts. Sporadic attendance is a severe handicap to success with cooperative learning.

2. Project, problem-solving, committee-work, and grant-writing teams can be, and probably should be, larger than four, depending on the task to be accomplished and the number of available participants. It is best to assign permanent roles in these teams based on the strengths of the individual members because consistently high performance is more important than learning growth in these circumstances. The captain should be extremely well organized, self-confident, and able to inspire the team to excel; the recorder should be skilled at synthesizing the essential meaning from team discussion and keeping very organized records; the reflector should excel at multiprocessing and be confident enough to bring up suggestions for improvement, even if they may imply substandard performance by one or more team members; the planner should be very creative and persistent, but flexible enough to accept changes in the plan as the project evolves.

3. Peer assessment and student teaching teams may well be smaller than four, perhaps as small as two, since they have sharply focused goals. All required role activities have to be accomplished, but perhaps no formal role assignments need be made. The work in these teams is usually divided fairly between the members.

4. Cooperative learning teams may be formed in a number of ways, such as random selection by counting off or drawing cards from a deck, student or participant selection, teacher or supervisor selection, or a combination of the last two. The goal is always to provide the greatest diversity within each team. Random teams often provide this diversity, but there is no way to ensure it. Research shows that participant-selected teams are not diverse and are unlikely to be successful (Fiechtner and Davis, 1985). Participants can suggest several people they would like to work with, and the facilitator can take these requests into account when assigning teams—the aim being to preserve diversity in gender, ethnic background, academic preparation and ability, and discipline or major. In order to gather the information needed to assign teams, many facilitators delay forming permanent teams until they can collect data sheets from students and observe them in learning situations.

5. Teams should be designed to accomplish the task for which they are formed. They can be short-term (e.g. formed to complete a five-minute in-class exercise), work together for several weeks to complete a project, or stay together for a whole semester or longer to provide long-term emotional and academic support (Duncan-Hewitt, 1995). Forming new groups midway through the semester gives students the chance to work with new individuals, thus providing a more realistic simulation of on-the-job teamwork. When deciding if and when to restructure the teams, it is important to carefully consider the learning needs of the participants and how well the current teams are functioning. Younger or more inexperienced students are more likely to need the support that long-term groups provide. Those close to graduation may profit from more frequent team membership changes.

6. One of the first team activities should encourage the team members to introduce themselves and learn about each others' learning styles. At this time, the team should agree to expectations or ground rules for all members.

Suggested ground rules for team activities [Silberman, 1998]:

- Start on time with everyone present.
- Get to know members who are "different" from oneself.
- Let others finish speaking without interrupting them.
- Be brief and to the point.
- Be gender/race/ethnicity sensitive.
- Be prepared.
- Give everyone a chance to speak.
- Share the workload.
- Rotate group roles.
- Reach decisions by consensus.
- Assess team functioning periodically.

Guidelines for Implementing Team Roles

1. The facilitator must check that students have assumed and rotated roles, intervene to improve role performance, and give credit via learning journal reports or otherwise for conscientious role fulfillment *(see Assessment Methodology)*.

2. To ensure that reflectors improve their performance, the facilitator should take time for reflectors to share oral reports with the class, frequently in the beginning of the term and at regular intervals thereafter.

3. Students with roles other than captain, recorder, and reflector often fail to appreciate the importance of their roles. The facilitator should intervene to recognize team members who do well in these other roles or to ask the team if they would like to be informed of specific instances when using these roles would enhance performance.

4. Reflectors may withdraw from active participation in the group in order to observe and write down their assessments. The facilitator should encourage them to observe while fully participating and to take a minute at 15-20 minute intervals to jot down their assessment.

5. Recorders may complain that they are so busy writing that they have no time to think or to process what the team is doing. They need to be encouraged not to write everything down, but to synthesize the discussion in a few well-constructed sentences.

6. When the captain is very shy, introverted, or not confident, another team member is likely to take over that role. To fix this situation, the facilitator should address all team intervention questions to the captain, refer to the team using the name of the captain (unless the team has chosen another name), hold the captain responsible for time management, and attempt to make eye contact with the captain when giving positive nonverbal feedback to the team.

7. The nature of the team roles and the responsibilities of those fulfilling the different roles may well change as the team moves through stages of development. More permanent roles may be appropriate in the latter stages of team development.

Concluding Thoughts

The effort needed to establish team roles and train students in their use pays big dividends in increasing learning. Roles also help ensure fair participation in the group process by all the learners. Students who value and experience defined roles in the group process will be prepared to assume a variety of roles in the workplace and in community and extracurricular activities as well.

References

Apple, D., Duncan-Hewitt, W., Krumsieg, K., & Mount, D. (2000). *Handbook on cooperative learning*. Lisle, IL: Pacific Crest.

Davidson, N. (1994). Cooperative and collaborative learning: An integrative perspective. In Thousand, J., Villa, R., & Nevin, A. (Eds.). *Creativity and collaborative learning: A practical guide to empowering students and teachers*. Baltimore, MD: Paul H. Brooks.

Fiechtner, S.B., & Davis, E.A. (1985). Why groups fail: A survey of student experiences with learning groups. *The organizational behavior teaching review, 9*(4), 58-73.

Johnson, D., Johnson, R., & Smith, K. (1998). *Active learning: Cooperation in the college classroom*. Edina, MN: Interaction Book.

Millis, B., & Cottell Jr., P. (1998). *Cooperative learning for higher education faculty*. Westport, CT: Oryx.

Myrvaagnes, E., et al. (1996). *Foundations of problem solving*. Lisle, IL. Pacific Crest.

Secretary's Commission on Achieving Necessary Skills (SCANS). (1991). *What work requires of schools: A SCANS report for America 2000*. Washington, DC: Department of Labor.

Silberman, M. (1998). Building cooperative learning teams. *Cooperative learning and college teaching*, 8(3), 16-17. Stillwater, OK: New Forums Press.

Tuckman, B. W. (1965). Developmental sequence in small groups. *Psychological Bulletin, 63(6)*, 384-399.

Persistence Log

by Carol Atnip, Developmental Mathematics Consultant

Three obstacles to student success often cited by post-secondary faculty are attendance, punctuality, and class participation. Most students who do not consistently attend class either under-perform or fail the course. Non-punctual students disrupt class, are not ready to perform, and often disrespect other established rules. These behaviors are particularly common for "at-risk" students who do not recognize the importance of establishing successful habits and attitudes. The Persistence Log described in this module is a tool that helps create a classroom culture that values personal engagement in learning and rewards habits associated with academic success.

The Persistence Log

The Persistence Log is a tool that tracks student preparation, participation, and application of skills in an efficient, visual chart. The Persistence Log maps student progress in establishing a successful pattern in three critical stages of learning: pre-class preparation, in-class participation, and post-class activity (homework). The Persistence Log can be easily integrated in the course assessment and evaluation systems. In an assessment context, students use the Persistence Log to record data on course effort that can serve as the basis for student-instructor dialogue. In an evaluation context, the Persistence Log allows students to improve their course grade by rewarding the effort of establishing successful student habits.

Classroom Implementation

The Persistence Log is a record of the history of student effort. Students earn a check for coming to class prepared, participating in class activities, and doing homework. One bonus point is typically awarded after a student gets five checks in a row. Earning this bonus requires a student to come to class prepared, participate, do homework, and then come to class prepared and participate again, thus establishing a positive pattern and a better foundation for academic success. If a student misses an assignment or class, he or she must begin again to earn five checks in a row to receive a bonus point. Table 1 contains a partially completed Persistence Log and illustrates both of these scoring principles.

Each student is responsible for his or her own log. The instructor initials each time a student earns a point to ensure integrity of the form. After several weeks, the student and facilitator have a concrete, visual map of the student's persistence. If there are many "holes" in the log, both student and facilitator can pinpoint the problem and design an action plan to remedy the situation. The Persistence Log can be adapted to fit many types of classes.

Table 1   *Partially Completed Persistence Log*

Date	Preparation	Participation	Skills	Bonus	Sign
1/14		X	X	0	
1/16	X	X	X	1	CA
1/23	O	X	X	0	
1/28	X	X	X	1	CA

Carrye Wilkins, Jefferson Community College, Louisville, KY: *"The first time I implemented the Persistence Log into three pre-algebra classes my completion rate averaged 72% with the highest class reaching 85%. The students who persisted passed the course. I continue to have good success with the log."*

Implementation Tips

Being in class on time is the first step in preparing for class. The Persistence Log can reflect a student's basic preparation by being on time and ready to go, as well as more sophisticated preparedness, such as having done the required outside readings. The suggestions listed below can be used to gauge preparation, participation, or application of skills, thus earning a student a check in a particular category and rewarding him or her for good performance. *Note: most of the suggestions were compiled from experienced facilitators at a Pacific Crest Developmental Math Institute at the University of Louisville in August, 1998.*

Suggestions for enhancing preparation:

1. **Provocative daily question**. The facilitator posts a question on the board before a class. The question should be relevant to that class or the previous class. As the class begins, the question is erased. The facilitator then returns to the question at the end of the class period. Grading or assigning points is optional, but suggested for lower level courses.

2. **Warm-ups**. The facilitator begins each class with a two-minute oral drill of questions from the assigned reading(s) or material from the previous class. The questions should be short answer or yes/no in order to maximize the number of questions in the time allowed. Students should know that the questions are important enough to be on the next exam.

3. **Group work**. Points are awarded to the first group with all members present and ready to begin to work. Group members will quickly see the value of being prompt and ready, thus putting added pressure on students to get to class on time.

4. **Pre-class study groups**. The facilitator arranges a location for pre-class study groups to meet just prior to a class. The facilitator occasionally supplies pertinent class information to the groups present, such as announcement of a quiz. Students will quickly see the value of getting information from attendees before class starts. Transfer of information to non-group attendees can be made only before class begins.

Suggestions for enhancing participation:

1. **Quizzes, one-minute papers, and attendance sheets**. These are all good ways to hold students accountable for each day's work. Daily participation and attendance are especially important for students who have not learned the relationship between attendance and class performance. The facilitator should emphasize the importance of attendance and let students know that attendance will be checked. In-class work can be used as documentation of attendance.

2. **Web support**. Announcements and updates can be posted on the facilitator's web page before class or made ready for distribution on a handout. Updates can be referred to during class without taking away great amounts of class time. Alternatively, the facilitator can consider asking questions about information that can only be found on the course web site.

3. **Vary classroom routines**. Facilitators should not allow their classes to become routine. For example, the beginning of class should vary. Also, students' papers can be returned as discretely as possible, preferably while students are involved in other tasks.

4. **Student-involved questioning**. Groups can be assigned three minutes to come with one question from the homework. Groups can trade or revise to reach consensus on questions. At the end of three minutes, the facilitator answers the allotted number of questions and then moves on with the class.

Suggestions for enhancing skills:

1. **Homework quiz**. Use two questions from recent class material (or homework) as a quiz during the first five minutes of class.

2. **Collect a question**. At the beginning of a class period, students are given one minute to write down a question from a reading or assignment. The facilitator then collects the questions. Thus students who are late will not have the opportunity to ask a question. During the last 2-5 minutes of class, the facilitator answers some of the collected questions, choosing questions randomly, selecting the most important, or answering (rapid-fire) as many as time allows.

3. **Self-assessment**. Students need to learn to be accountable for the skills they are developing. Self-checking and comparing answers, analyzing mistakes, and discussing procedural difficulties with team members give students a chance to compare their work to others without depending on the facilitator. A periodic self-assessment is a good documentation tool for keeping track of growth. *(See SII Method for Assessment Reporting.)*

4. **Instructional technology**. Computer tools should be incorporated, when appropriate, to challenge and elevate the skills development of students. Software can assist with recording time on task and the number of attempts, checking the accuracy of spelling and grammar and the appropriateness of answers, as well as providing other forms of instant feedback to students. Lower-division courses may find such skill development especially beneficial.

Concluding Thoughts

Holding students accountable for their attendance and class preparation yields great rewards in increased learning success. The Persistence Log is a simple and effective learning tool for accomplishing that purpose.

References

Angelo, T., & Cross, K. (1993). *Classroom assessment techniques: A handbook for college teachers* (2nd ed.). San Francisco: Jossey-Bass Publishers.

Cohen, D. (Ed.). (1995). *Crossroads in mathematics: Standards for introductory college mathematics before calculus*. Task Force and Writing Team of the Standards for Introductory College Mathematics Project.

Ellis, D. (1994). *The master student* (7th ed.). Boston: Houghton-Mifflin.

Sembera, A., & Hovis, M. (1990). *MATH, A four letter word: The math anxiety handbook*. (2nd ed.). Wimberly, TX: The Wimberly Press.

Annotated Bibliography — Effective Teaching Practices

by Kathleen Burke, SUNY Cortland

The following references are a selection of works that can be used to enhance teaching practices. By no means should this bibliography be considered a comprehensive resource of effective teaching references.

Books

Bonwell, C., & Eison, J. (1991). *Active learning: Creating excitement in the classroom.* ASHE-ERIC Higher Education Reports No. 1. Washington, DC: The George Washington University, School of Education and Human Development.

The authors present a comprehensive guide to active learning. They discuss what active learning is, why it is important, and how active learning can be incorporated into the classroom. Finally, the authors discuss some of the barriers to employing active learning at the college level, incorporating the concerns faced by faculty. A nice feature of this text is that it discusses the risks involved with employing specific active learning strategies on both the instructor's and the student's parts.

Delisle, R. (1997). *How to use problem-based learning in the classroom.* Alexandria, VA: The Association for Supervision and Curriculum Development.

This reference is an excellent resource for exploring problem-based learning (PBL) in the classroom. The author discusses the theory behind problem-based learning and why it is effective. Moreover, he discusses the elements of a problem-based learning problem, including: simplicity, clarity, consistency, and communication. He then provides a structure for developing problems for students to explore. The author finishes with case studies/applications in five different subjects. While these examples are all within the context of elementary/secondary school, one can easily adapt them to the college setting.

Harmin, M. (1994). *Inspiring active learning: A handbook for teachers.* Alexandria, VA: Association for Supervision and Curriculum Development.

The main goal of this text is to provide a set of strategies for instructors. It includes a set of activities that would promote active learning in the classroom. Furthermore, it discusses strategies that would motivate student performance. A nice feature of this text is that the author provides many examples of how to employ different strategies in various disciplines.

Marzano, R., Pickering, D. J., & Pollock, J. (2001). *Classroom instruction that works: Research-based strategies for increasing student achievement.* Alexandria, VA: Association for Supervision and Curriculum Development.

This text compiles research on teaching effectiveness and lists key teaching strategies from research findings. It includes the references and the extent of the effect of each strategy. These strategies include identifying similarities and differences, summarizing and note taking, reinforcing effort and providing recognition, homework and practice, nonlinguistic representations, cooperative learning, setting objectives and providing feedback, generating and testing hypotheses, cues, questions and advance organizers. The examples in the text are for a non-collegiate audience. However, the strategies that are discussed can be employed in a classroom at any level.

McKeachie, W. (1994). *Teaching tips: Strategies, research and theory for college and university teachers.* Lexington, MA: Heath.

This text is an excellent resource. It covers all aspects of teaching in higher education. The text discusses issues, such as how to prepare for a course, how to balance research and effective teaching, and how to grade students. It includes a section on teaching techniques, tools, and methods. This text should be read by all new faculty in higher education and anyone who would like a different perspective on teaching in higher education.

Tileston, D. W. (2000). *Ten best teaching practices: How brain research, learning styles and standards define teaching competencies.* Thousand Oaks, CA: Corwin.

While most of the examples in the text are at the elementary school level, and the assessment tool that is relied on the most is a teacher's lesson plans, the author provides interesting insight into how students think. One interesting aspect of the text is the information provided on a student's transfer skills. The author indicates that there are four factors that contribute to a student's ability to transfer skills: association, similarity, critical attributes and context, and degree of original learning. The author also discusses the importance of employing different learning techniques in order for all students to succeed. She introduces an interesting concept of a J-curve. While most people see their class as falling into a bell- shaped curve in terms of student performance, the author suggests that instead we should strive for a J-shaped curve where most of the class is at the upper end.

Wiggins, G., & McTighe, J. (1998). *Understanding by design.* Alexandria, VA: Association for Supervision and Curriculum Development.

This text concerns itself with a student's understanding of material and how proper curriculum and assessment can ensure student understanding. In particular, the authors discuss the idea of a "backward design process" whereby the instructor identifies the desired results, determines acceptable evidence that a student has achieved these results, and lastly, plans instruction that will attain these results. They further discuss the facets of understanding. A student understands when he or she (1) can explain, (2) can apply, (3) can empathize, (4) can interpret, (5) has perspective, (6) has self-knowledge. Finally, the authors discuss how these six facets should be incorporated to make an instructor's teaching more effective.

Web Sites and Journals

Faculty Development Teaching Techniques Index.
<http://honolulu.hawaii.edu/intranet/committees/FacDevCom/guidebk/teachtip/teachtip.htm>

This website provided by Honolulu Community College provides insights into and resources for many aspects of teaching. These include sections on teaching techniques, motivating students, and preparing a syllabus.

The Cooperative Learning Center. <http://www.co-operation.org>

This website is run through the University of Minnesota and provides general information on cooperative learning, various essays on all aspects of cooperative learning, and, most interestingly, a Q&A section where teachers can ask questions about implementing cooperative learning and receive a response from the website's authors.

Professional and Organizational Development Network in Higher Education. <http://www.podnetwork.org>

According to their statement, the three purposes of POD are to (1) provide support and services for its members through publications, conferences, consulting, and networking; (2) offer services and resources to others interested in faculty development; and (3) fulfill an advocacy role, nationally, seeking to inform and persuade educational leaders of the value of faculty, instructional, and organizational development in institutions of higher education.

The Journal on Excellence in College Teaching. <http://ject.lib.muohio.edu/>

This peer-reviewed journal is published at Miami University of Ohio. Its audience is faculty in higher education. The goal of the journal is to "increase student learning through effective teaching, interest in and enthusiasm for the profession of teaching, and communication among faculty about their classroom experiences." This journal is an outlet for faculty to discuss all issues regarding teaching, including pedagogy, teaching innovations, and student learning.

Modules in this section:

Overview of Assessment

by Marie Baehr, Elmhurst College and Steven Beyerlein, University of Idaho

Simply put, assessment is a process used for improving quality. Assessment is critical for growing life-long learning skills and elevating performance in diverse contexts (SCANS, 1991). However, the value of assessment is not always apparent nor is the process always understood. Because there has not always been agreement on a specific definition, there has been some confusion on how to approach assessment so the feedback is valuable. The overview outlines a purpose and use of assessment that is consistent throughout the entire *Faculty Guidebook*. Elements of quality assessment feedback are identified and discussed. Methods for implementing assessment in a variety of teaching/learning contexts are detailed in companion modules.

Nature of Assessment

Assessment leads to improvement. Both the assessor (person giving feedback) and assessee (performer) must have trust in the process. Although the assessor gives the feedback to the assessee, the assessee is always in control. The feedback given by the assessor to the assessee may be used by the assessee for improvement. Although a well-designed assessment process yields high quality improvements in a timely manner, any assessment process can lead to some improvement. Assessment is an area in which assessors can start simple and increase the complexity as the process is better implemented *(see Assessment Methodology)*.

One can use assessment to improve a performance or an outcome. For example, a composition instructor could assess a student's writing by looking at a completed assignment draft (outcome) and finding strengths and areas to improve in the writing. The instructor could also observe the student as he or she writes the paper to assess strengths and areas to improve in using the writing process (to develop the written sample).

Principles of Quality Assessment

Table 1 outlines ten principles for undertaking assessment in any teaching/learning situation. These principles address the mindset under which assessment is conducted, the circumstances surrounding assessment activities, and the nature of the dialogue between the assessor and assessee. A brief discussion of each principle follows.

1. **Assessment focuses on improvement, not judgment.**

   It is important that both the assessee and assessor understand that assessment's use is to add to the quality, not to judge the level of quality or not to give interesting feedback that will not be used.

Table 1   **Principles of Quality Assessment**

1. Assessment focuses on improvement, not judgment.

2. Assessment focuses on performance, not performer.

3. Assessment is a process that can improve any level of performance.

4. Assessment feedback depends on who both the assessor and the assessee are.

5. Improvement based on assessment feedback is more effective when the assessee seeks assessment.

6. Assessment requires agreed-upon criteria.

7. Assessment requires analyses of the observations.

8. Assessment feedback is accepted only when there is mutual trust and respect.

9. Assessment should be used only where there is a strong opportunity for improvement.

10. Assessment is effective only when the assessee uses the feedback.

2. **Assessment focuses on performance, not performer.**

   Assessment is only about improving a performance. It is not judging the quality of the performance nor is it in any way judging the qualities of the performer. Assessment may be used to give feedback on how a performer's skills could be improved to improve a performance. It should never be used to point out weaknesses in the performer, because doing so would undermine both the building of trust needed for effective assessment and the purpose of assessment.

3. Assessment is a process that can improve any level of performance.

Regardless of the level of quality of performance, there are always areas to improve, and there are always areas that made the performance as good as it was. So, assessment can always be used to give feedback that can be used for improvement of a performance.

4. Assessment feedback depends on who both the assessor and assessee are.

Assessment, although focusing on the performance alone, is much more effective when both the assessor and assessee understand their own as well as the other's abilities. This understanding helps in creating realistic performance criteria and feedback that can be used effectively (see *Performance Levels for Assessors*).

5. Improvement based on assessment feedback is more effective when the assessee seeks assessment.

As in most things in life, feedback is useful only when it is valued. One of the components of valuing assessment feedback is the assessee's desire to obtain it. When the assessee seeks assessment, it is clear that he or she sees the need for improvement and has plans to act on the given feedback.

6. Assessment requires agreed-upon criteria.

Both the assessor and assessee must have a common understanding of what will be assessed. In any performance, the purpose lends itself to numerous areas in which to look for strengths and areas to improve. The involved parties should decide in advance on the criteria that will be used in the assessment. These criteria can focus on the performance itself (performance criteria) and/or the final outcome (outcome criteria). Both types of criteria can be used in assessing a performance or in assessing a product. The chosen criteria should focus on areas both the assessee and assessor believe are important; they must be appropriate to the performance; and they must be appropriate for the assessment abilities of the assessor (Astin et. al, 1992).

7. Assessment requires analyses of the observations.

Once performance criteria are set, the assessor must collect information germane to the set criteria by observing the performance. While or after the information is collected, the assessor must identify the strengths of the performance and why the strengths contribute to the quality of the performance. In addition, the assessor must identify the areas where improvement could occur and how the improvements could be made (see *Fundamentals of Rubrics*).

8. Assessment feedback is accepted only when there is mutual trust and respect.

The assessee must trust in the assessment process and in the assessor's abilities. The assessor must trust in the assessee's willingness to accept and use feedback. Often this trust takes time to build, but it builds quickly once the assessee sees improvement. To help build the trust, an assessor should make sure to follow these guidelines in the feedback report:

- Use only positive language (for example, *area to improve*, instead of *weakness*).
- Include no judgmental statements (see *Distinctions between Assessment and Evaluation*).
- Focus only on agreed upon criteria.
- Describe real strengths and why they are strengths.
- Provide substantial supporting evidence for both strengths and areas to improve.
- Offer specific suggestions about how to improve.
- Provide interesting and relevant insights.
- Convey support and encouragement for change.

9. Assessment should be used only where there is a strong opportunity for improvement.

It makes sense to carry through an assessment process only if there is the opportunity for improvement. If assessment feedback is given during the performance (formative assessment), the performer has the opportunity to use the feedback to improve the current performance. If the feedback is given at the end of the performance (summative assessment), the feedback can be used to improve future performance. If there are no plans for future performances, summative assessment should not be used.

10. Assessment is effective only when the assessee uses the feedback.

The assessee must have the opportunity and desire to improve in order for the feedback to be used. Not only must there be an opportunity to improve, but also there must be a willingness to implement the suggested improvements. Even if the assessment process could help in identifying needed improvements, there is little point in taking the time to assess if there will be no effort to improve.

Issues that Affect Assessment Quality

A variety of factors influence the quality of an assessment process. These include skills of the parties involved as well as resources available for conducting the assessment.

Factors Related to the Skills of the Parties Involved

Content expertise of the assessor

An assessment performed by a content expert in a field specific to the performance or outcome will typically give more useful feedback than an assessment done by a novice in the content area, assuming assessment skills are equivalent in the two people. Understanding how knowledge is constructed within a discipline can be important for understanding the evidence to collect and how to analyze it. Understanding the content helps in collection of the evidence as well. This advantage does not mean, however, that an assessor must be a content expert in order to provide any useful assessment feedback. For example, it would be helpful for a novice in a content area to assess a performance if one of the criteria is "the use of technical jargon."

Assessment skills of the assessor

The knowledge and skill level of an assessor with assessment is as important as expert knowledge about what is being assessed. Experts in the field are not automatically strong assessors. Highly effective assessors:

* display respect for the assessee.
* work closely with the assessee to set appropriate criteria for the assessment.
* assess only with respect to the agreed upon criteria.
* apply keen observation skills that put findings in context.
* employ strong recording skills.
* collect relevant and high quality evidence.
* analyze results to extract important patterns and gain understanding.
* generalize findings so they can be transferred to new situations.
* offer timely and constructive feedback.
* enjoy reflecting/introspecting.
* have a comfort level in their role, which is solely focused on improvement of the assessee's performance.

Usefulness of the assessment report

Once the assessment process is completed, the assessee is left with the report of the findings. Since the purpose of the assessment is for improvement, it is important that the report outlines in a concise way what was well done and why it was well done (strengths) and areas that could be improved, along with some strategies for improvement *(see SII Method for Assessment Reporting)*. A quality assessment report:

* includes only non-judgmental statements.
* follows a concise, well-organized format.
* focuses on agreed upon criteria.
* describes real strengths and why they are strengths.
* provides substantial supporting evidence for both strengths and areas to improve.
* offers specific suggestions about how to improve.

Factors Related to Available Resources

Quality of the tools used

An assessment can be completed by using elaborate tools or by relying on the memory of the assessor. As a general rule, the more structured the tool, the wider the audience of potential assessors and the more specificity likely in the assessment report. Many of the assessment instruments in the *Faculty Guidebook* have been implemented in dozens of faculty development workshops and in hundreds of college classrooms. However, there is no need to wait to assess something until the tools are in place to assess everything.

Development and implementation costs

The cost of assessment can vary from very little to quite a lot. Elaborate expense can only be justified for educational research questions that have programmatic implications. Many suggestions for assessment instruments in the *Faculty Guidebook* offer a point of departure that will minimize the cost of developing effective, special-purpose instruments for courses, projects, and institutions.

Time required to conduct an assessment

An assessment may have a complex design or be carried out with little or no preparation. Instructors and administrators need to balance assessment activities with planning and facilitation activities. Often spending 5% of in-class and out-of-class time on assessment is adequate to determine strengths and areas to improve.

Examples of Assessment

Peer Coaching

A second set of eyes in the classroom provides a great way to get feedback on facilitation skills. An instructor can meet with a trusted colleague before class and outline two or three focus areas to be assessed in the class. The peer coach should avoid becoming a second instructor and instead keep relevant notes that are reported back to the instructor after the class. This method is beneficial to both the assessor and assessee, for the assessee gets valuable feedback, while the assessor can observe teaching strategies that he or she might find valuable. Assuming peer coaching is an ongoing process between the two parties, this would be an example of formative assessment of a performance.

Course outcome review

At the end of a course, an instructor can have students review the desired course outcomes listed in the syllabus and estimate how well they completed each outcome (outcome criteria). When students identify outcomes that have and have not been met fully and explain alternative actions that could be taken in future semesters to insure achievements of each outcome, the instructor can use the information to assess the course instruction and curriculum. This is an example of summative assessment of an outcome.

Assessment of student learning

Students can be tested early in a course to determine how well they have learned and retained the skills and concepts they need to carry over from a previous course. The information can be used to revise the content, focus, and teaching of the previous course. This is an example of indirect assessment in which one group is evaluated in order to improve something that affects the quality of the evaluated group's performance.

Concluding Thoughts

Learning to use assessment widely and frequently is likely to produce a positive, trusting learning environment. The creation of "magical or teachable moments" will stimulate student engagement in the teaching/learning process and promote productive risk-taking. Long-term use of classroom assessment techniques provides opportunities for "raising the bar" for learner performance and shifting responsibility for learning to students (Cross and Angelo, 1993). When instructors model assessment in their daily classroom and professional activities, both instructors and students can improve significantly over the term.

References

Research

Applebaum, E., Bailey, T., Berg, P., & Kalleberg, A. (2000). *Manufacturing advantage: Why high performance work systems pay off*. Ithaca, NY: Cornell University Press.

Astin, A. W., Banta, T. W., Cross, K. P., El-Khawas, E., Ewell, P. T., Hutchings, P. et al. (1992). *Nine principles of good practice for assessing student learning*. Washington, DC: AAHE.

Bransford, J., Brown, A., & Cocking, R. (2000). *How people learn, brain, mind, experience, and school*. Washington, DC: National Academy Press.

Glaser, R., Linn, R., & Bohrnstedt, G. (1997). *Assessment in transition: Monitoring the nation's educational progress*. New York: National Academy of Education.

Scriven, M. (1991). *Evaluation thesaurus* (4th ed). Newbury Park, CA: Sage Press.

Application

Cross, P., & Angelo, T. (1993). *Classroom assessment techniques*. San Francisco: Jossey-Bass.

Pellegrino, J., Chudowsky, N., & Glaser, R. (2001). *Knowing what students know: The science and design of educational assessment*. Washington, DC: National Academy Press.

Secretary's Commission on Achieving Necessary Skills (SCANS). (1991). *What work requires of schools: A SCANS report for America 2000*. Washington, DC: Department of Labor.

Stiggins, R. J. (1997). *Student-centered classroom assessment*. Old Tappan, NJ: Prentice Hall.

Assessment Methodology

by Daniel Apple, Pacific Crest and Marie Baehr, Elmhurst College

Faculty Development Series

The Assessment Methodology is a tool for understanding the steps needed to do a quality assessment. By following this process, faculty members can learn what they need to know and change what they need to change in order to improve a performance or a product. The discussion and examples of the use of this methodology are geared toward assessment of student learning. Much of the terminology used in this methodology is taken from the module *Overview of Assessment*.

Assessment Methodology

The Assessment Methodology consists of four main steps with a set of sub-steps. The methodology is as follows:

1. Develop guidelines for the assessor to follow when assessing a performance or a product.

Before the performance, both the assessee and the assessor should:

a) Define the purpose of the performance or the product.

b) Define the purpose of the assessment.

c) Determine what is appropriate to assess.

d) Agree on what should be reported and how it should be reported in the assessment report.

2. Design the approach to be used for the assessment.

Both the assessee and assessor should:

a) Inventory a list of possible criteria to be used as part of the assessment.

b) Choose the criteria from the list in step 2a that best meet the previously established guidelines (Step 1). If appropriate, determine the attributes that indicate quality for each criterion.

c) For each attribute (or simple criterion), determine the evidence needed to perform the assessment.

d) Agree on the scale and range to be used in looking at each piece of evidence.

e) Agree on the method of collection that will be used to collect evidence.

f) Determine the specific instruments that will be used to collect evidence.

g) Set up a plan to collect the evidence in a timely manner.

3. Collect and analyze the evidence.

The assessor should:

a) Collect the evidence agreed upon in Step 2.

b) Use the collected evidence to determine and document the strengths and areas to improve.

c) Offer feedback during the performance, if appropriate and agreed upon beforehand with the assessee.

4. Report the findings to the assessee.

The assessor should:

a) Create the assessment report for the assessee, using the results from Step 1d as a guide.

b) Analyze various contributions when evidence of attributes suggests a poor performance or product. Determine what part is due to the evidence collected, the criteria chosen, the use of the product (if appropriate), and/or the performance or product itself.

Discussion of the Assessment Methodology

Develop guidelines for the assessor to follow when assessing a performance or a product.

The first step in setting up an assessment is to define the purpose for the performance or product and the purpose for the assessment. With this information, the person whose performance is being assessed or the group who have developed a product (assessee) can better determine what is important to assess, and the person who is observing the performance or collecting information about the product (assessor) is equipped to give accurate and appropriate feedback.

After determining these two purposes, the two parties should collaborate to determine what is appropriate to assess. This depends on the nature of the activity being performed or the purpose of the product, the skill of the person performing that particular activity or the background of the people who developed the product, the level of assessment skill on the part of the person assessing, and the assessor's knowledge of what he or she is assessing. Finally, the assessee and assessor must decide on the form and content of the assessment report, what the report should include and how it should be reported.

Design the approach to be used for the assessment.

In designing an approach for assessment, both parties should collaborate to generate a list of possible criteria that could be used by the assessor to give feedback to the assessee. From this list, both should agree and select the most important criteria that best fit within the guidelines from the first step in the methodology. In most cases, this list should contain no more than four criteria.

For each chosen criterion, both parties determine appropriate attributes to look for during the performance or in the product. In some cases where the assessment is narrowly focused, the criterion may be manageable enough without defining attributes. It is important for both the assessor and the assessee to discuss how evidence will be collected, the expected range the assessor might find when collecting evidence, and the scale the assessor will use when collecting the evidence. Typically the range will be set by the assessee's abilities, while the scale will be set by the assessor's abilities. Finally, the assessor and the assessee should agree on a plan to collect the needed information as well as the specific instruments that will be used to collect the desired evidence.

One of the keys to learning how to assess is to start simple. Often the evidence collected for analyzing quality can be measured on a basic scale. For example, to assess an oral presentation, one of the attributes could be "eye contact." A veteran assessor might collect evidence by determining the eye contact on a scale of 1 to 10. However, a novice assessor could use a scale of *none*, *some*, and *lots*. Both scales elicit information to create constructive feedback.

It is important for the assessor and assessee to agree on the method of collection. This method could be in the form of observing, looking at test results, filling out checklists, or collecting questionnaires. The method of collection is more general than the particular instrument chosen. The assessee needs to be a part of the discussion of choosing the method, but the assessor alone chooses the particular instrument to use, i.e. the particular method, once the general method is mutually satisfactory to both parties.

Both the assessor and assessee should also determine HOW the evidence can be collected in a timely manner.

Collect and analyze the evidence.

Once the design is in place, it is up to the assessor to collect the agreed-upon evidence. Once the evidence is collected, the assessor must make sense of it by looking at what it says about the attributes and criteria. This information can then be used to document strengths and areas to improve. The process itself can help the assessor with insights (*see* **SII Method for Assessment Reporting**).

When the assessment plan includes the collection of evidence during the performance, rather than waiting for the final assessment report, the assessee may ask the assessor for feedback during the performance, called "real-time" feedback or authentic assessment. If appropriate to the situation and agreed upon prior to the start of the performance, the assessor may offer feedback (to the assessee) during the performance. For example, a basketball coach may give feedback to a player during a game, but it is more difficult for an orchestra conductor to give feedback to musicians during a concert.

Report findings to the assessee.

The final step of the methodology is for the assessor to provide the report to the assessee. The assessment report documents the evidence collected and provides a discussion on how it relates to each attribute and/or criterion. An assessment report also includes feedback about how the assessee can improve future performance.

When a performance has not gone well from the perspective of the assessor, it can typically be attributed to the poor quality of one or a combination of the following:
- the performance or product itself,
- the evidence collected,
- the choice of criteria or attributes, or
- a person's use of a product being assessed.

Finally, the assessee may offer feedback about the assessor's performance so that the assessor can improve his or her assessment techniques in the future.

Examples of Assessing

Scenario #1

The members of the physics department at the local university have worked during the past year to develop student learning goals and alter the required curriculum to support the newly formulated goals. They would like to have someone outside the department check to see how the designed curriculum supports the stated goals. They ask a member of the physics department at a neighboring college, Professor Baker, to take a look at the stated goals and course descriptions.

Product: curriculum
Assessee: members of the physics department responsible for curriculum design
Assessor: Professor Baker

Develop guidelines

1a) Purpose of the product:

The product is to be used so that students completing the curriculum will fulfill the goals.

1b) Purpose of the assessment:

The assessment will help to keep the links strong and show how to improve the links between the curriculum and the stated learning goals.

1c) Determine what is appropriate to be assessed:

The department has five goals and developed thirteen major courses. Because Professor Baker has a background in physics and has been active in curricular design, those involved feel that all links should be investigated.

1d) Agree on what should be reported:

The links seen between the goals and the courses will be reported as well as the areas of strengths and the areas to improve.

Design the approach

2a) Inventory possible criteria:
1. the number of links each course has to goals,
2. parallel building of goals, and
3. the length of time a student spends in class fulfilling each goal.

2b) Choose criteria:

The department determines that collecting data for criterion #1 and criterion #2 makes the most sense.

2c) Determine attributes:

For criterion #1, the number of links is sufficient, and no further attributes are necessary. For criterion #2, the goals touched upon within a term, and the sequence of terms each goal is touched upon are attributes.

2d) Agree on the scale and range:

For criterion #1, the number of links ranging from 0 to 5 are the scale and range.

For criterion #2, attribute #1, the number of goals touched upon each term from 0 to 5 are the scale and the range; for attribute #2, the scale will be the number of years a goal is touched upon, and the range will be from 0 to 4.

2e) Method of collection:

The method of collection will be tabulation of information by Professor Baker.

2f) Instruments used:

The instrument that will be used is a grid of courses versus goals that Professor Baker will fill in using abbreviations for none, introduce goal, develop goal, and test goal fulfillment.

2g) Set up a plan:

Professor Baker plans to take the stated goals and the course descriptions to fill in the grid.

Collect and analyze evidence

3a) Collect the agreed upon evidence.

3b) Use the collected evidence to determine and document strengths and areas to improve.

3c) Offer feedback during the performance.

Report the findings

4a) Create the assessment report:

Professor Baker's report consisted of the grid he created along with a summary of his findings, including a list of goals that seem to be developed most strongly and the goals that seem to be developed less strongly, along with suggestions of places some of the goals could be developed more strongly.

4b) Analyze contributions:

The department and Professor Baker sat down after the department had a chance to read the report. Many of the points Professor Baker made were quite helpful to the department in modifying its program. However, in a few cases, the goals were being fulfilled in certain spots, but the course descriptions did not indicate that this was so. So, rather than modifying the curriculum, the department modified the description of the courses.

Scenario #2

The program developed for Economics majors at City College includes a first-year course in economics. Professor Kramer, a second year faculty member, is teaching this course for the first time. He has asked Professor Chandler, chair of the Economics Department and one of the developers of the new program, to assess the learning of the students in his class this year.

Performance:	teaching
Type of assessment:	summative
Assessor:	Professor Chandler
Assessee:	Professor Kramer

Develop guidelines

1a) The purpose of the performance is for students in the class to learn first-year economics.

1b) The purpose of the assessment is to find out what the students are learning well and what they should be learning better.

1c) Because Professor Kramer's teaching style is similar for most of what he teaches, both Professors Kramer and Chandler agree that the learning of one or two key concepts should be assessed. In looking through the material in the course, they both decide to focus on the concept of supply and demand.

1d) Dr. Kramer does not want Dr. Chandler to spend much time on reporting back. Dr. Kramer requests that Dr. Chandler report what the students seemed to learn well with a rationale for this determination. In addition, he would like to know what the students seem to be missing and what might be changed in order for it to be learned better.

Design the approach

2a) Criteria include 1) understanding the principle of supply and demand, and 2) applying the principle of supply and demand.

2b) Both professors determine that collecting data for #1 makes the most sense.

2c & 2d) Dr. Chandler will look at two attributes: 1) the ability to state the principle of supply and demand, with a scale of expectations that range from below expectations to above expectations; and 2) the ability to draw a supply and demand curve, with a grading scale from A to F.

2e) The method of collection will be answers to test questions and graded lab reports.

2f) The instruments will be: 1) a lab report where the students graph real data and answer questions about supply and demand and 2) a final exam question that requires the student to state the principle and give an example of its use.

2g) The assessor will collect the data before the assignments are handed back.

Collect and analyze evidence

3a) The assignments are analyzed. It was found that almost all students could state the principle of supply and demand, and two thirds of the students had examples that supported the understanding of the principle. For the lab assignment, several students misread the graphs and came up with conclusions that were inaccurate, but correct based on their wrong readings.

3b) Dr. Chandler determined that a strength was the ability to apply the principle, and an area to improve was the ability of the students to read graphs accurately.

3c) Not appropriate for this scenario.

Report the findings

4a) Dr. Chandler's report included an evaluation of the students' work, some examples of work that he felt was above and below expectation for each attribute, and a summary of the strengths, areas to improve, and insights regarding Dr. Kramer's teaching of the curriculum.

4b) In discussing the report with Dr. Kramer, it was discovered that Dr. Kramer assumed that the students had learned how to read supply and demand graphs in the math course that was a prerequisite for the economics course. After receiving the assessment report, Dr. Kramer found out from the mathematics professor that this concept was not taught in the required mathematics course, but was taught in a different mathematics course. Based on this information, the prerequisite for the course was changed, and Dr. Kramer vowed to find out early in the term whether or not the students could analyze graphs sufficiently.

Concluding Thoughts

As shown by the examples above, a well-designed and conducted assessment, based on collaborative planning between assessee and assessor, can provide significant information to lead to improvement of a process and product. An assessment gives information about strengths, so that what is working well can be continued, and about areas of improvement, so that specific ways to improve can be determined. A quality assessment process may also include assessment of the assessment process itself. An assessment report documents the quality of a process or product and leads to positive steps for improvement.

References

Angelo, T. K., & Cross, P. (1994). *Classroom assessment techniques: A handbook for college teachers*. San Francisco: Jossey-Bass.

Marzano, R. J., Pickering, D., & McTighe, J. (1993). *Assessing student outcomes: Performance assessment using the dimensions of learning model*. Alexandria, VA: Association For Supervision and Curriculum Development.

Wiggins, G. (1998). *Educative assessment: Designing assessments to inform and improve student performance*. San Francisco: Jossey-Bass.

Wiggins, G., & McTighe, J. (1998). *Understanding by design*. Alexandria, VA: Association For Supervision and Curriculum Development.

Overview of Evaluation

by Marie Baehr, Elmhurst College

Evaluation is a process for determining the quality of a performance or a product. When accountability is an issue, an evaluation process should include ways to collect and accurately interpret artifacts regarding the quality displayed over a specific period of time. This overview discusses appropriate uses of evaluation and points out factors that can affect the quality of an evaluation. For details on the evaluation process, see the module *Evaluation Methodology*.

Principles of Evaluation

1. Evaluation focuses on the level of quality based on set standards.

2. The client must determine how decisions will be made prior to the evaluation.

3. Evaluation determines the quality of a performance, focusing only on the performance criteria.

4. Evaluation results are valid only when the evaluatee is aware of the performance criteria.

5. Evaluation results are valid when the decisions are based only on the performance criteria known to the evaluatee.

6. Evaluation should take place only after there has been sufficient opportunity for the evaluatee to achieve excellence.

7. Evaluation techniques must be fair and trusted for sound, accepted judgments to occur.

8. The evaluator must be able to use or develop an evaluation tool that can measure at what level the performance criteria are met.

9. Evaluation results must be based on credible, understandable evidence.

10. Evaluation systems should be assessed after each use.

Discussion of the Principles of Evaluation

1. Evaluation focuses on the level of quality based on set standards.

The purpose of evaluation is to determine the level of quality of a performance, regardless of the skills used or needed for the performance. The knowledge of the level can be used in making judgments or decisions or to track progress. In most cases, the level of quality will be judged against set standards.

2. The client must determine how decisions will be made prior to the evaluation.

For the evaluation process to be fair and unbiased, the person making the decisions or judgments based on the evaluation outcomes (the client), must determine what decisions will be made *before* the evaluation results are known.

3. Evaluation determines the quality of a performance, focusing only on the performance criteria.

The client and the person setting up the evaluative methods (evaluator) must agree on what qualities of a performance will be observed to judge quality. Defining the performance criteria precisely can be a time-consuming task, but it makes the results reliable and perceptually valid.

4. Evaluation results are valid only when the evaluatee is aware of the performance criteria.

Because the evaluatee is rarely involved in designing the evaluation process, the client or evaluator should communicate the purpose of the evaluation, the decisions that will be made based on the findings, and the performance criteria on which the evaluation is based to the evaluatee. In this case, the evaluatee will know the basis for the decisions to be made and can control how he or she wants to perform based on the criteria.

5. Evaluation results are valid when the decisions are based only on the performance criteria known to the evaluatee.

Although it is sometimes tempting to deviate from the original performance criteria, once the performance criteria are set and communicated to the evaluatee, all decisions should be based on these criteria. At the end of the process, the evaluation system should be assessed so improvements can be made when the system is used again. If the criteria set clearly do not link sufficiently to the decisions that must be made, the client is better off to start over rather than to evaluate on un-communicated criteria.

6. **Evaluation should take place only after there has been sufficient opportunity for the evaluatee to achieve excellence.**

It makes little sense to spend time and money on evaluating someone in an area unless the person has had an opportunity to acquire the skills needed to perform well.

7. **Evaluation techniques must be fair and trusted for sound, accepted judgments to occur.**

Because decisions are being made that often have long-term effects, it is critical for both the client and evaluatee that the decisions be based on valid information. The evaluatee may not be happy if a negative decision is made, but he or she will be more likely to accept the decision if it is based on fair, unbiased evidence.

8. **The evaluator must be able to use or develop an evaluation tool that can measure at what level the performance criteria are met.**

After setting criteria and standards, often a client leaves the evaluator with the responsibility of developing an evaluation tool that will measure the level at which the criteria are met. Some flexibility in the wording of the performance criteria allows the evaluator to align the evaluation tool appropriately.

9. **Evaluation results must be based on credible, understandable evidence.**

Although the client uses the evaluation results to make decisions, the evaluatee and other parties need to be able to review the process, outcome, and decisions to determine the fairness and accuracy of the process.

10. **Evaluation systems should be assessed after each use.**

No matter how carefully one sets up an evaluation process, there is always room for improvement. After each use of the process, the client and evaluator should assess the strengths and areas to be improved based on performance criteria, such as "quality of decision-making process."

Issues

1. **Evaluation of one performance can be used to evaluate or assess another performance.**

While there are many different reasons to evaluate, there are two main types of evaluation, direct evaluation and indirect evaluation.

Direct evaluation

With direct evaluation, artifacts collected directly from the evaluatee's performance are used to determine quality. Some examples of direct evaluations include job performance evaluations, Olympic competitions, and grades earned in a course. Direct evaluation can be used to collect evidence of the quality of a performance or product. Almost always, the determination of the level of quality in an evaluation has consequences. In a job evaluation, the person might get a raise or be fired; in evaluation of student performance in a class, a student can earn an "A" or fail the course; in a tenure decision, a candidate may receive or be denied tenure. If no consequences are attached to the outcome of an evaluation, it usually makes little sense to evaluate.

Indirect evaluation

Indirect evaluation occurs when the performance of one group (Group A) can only be determined by studying the performance of another group (Group B). In this case, Group B's performance must be evaluated to determine the quality of Group A's performance. An indirect evaluation does not affect the evaluatees in the decision-making process.

For example, a coach's performance is determined by the performance of the team he or she coaches. The team's performance is evaluated, and this evaluation of others is used to evaluate the performance of the coach (who is expected to get his or her team to play well).

Another example can be found in the assessment of student learning. In this case, students are evaluated to determine their fulfillment of stated learning outcomes. This evaluative information is used to provide assessment feedback to instructors so that they may improve the students' learning for the next batch of students. In this case, figuring out the strengths and areas to improve in teaching requires knowledge of the level of performance of the already-taught students.

2. **The evaluator must take into account the context of the performance when deciding on the evaluative methods.**

An evaluative tool may be applicable only in specific circumstances. For example, there are several different IQ tests, given to people of different ages. An IQ test written for an adult could not be used to accurately determine the IQ of a child. If the evaluator does not take the context into consideration, the set standard can be skewed either too high or too low.

3. **Standards can be based on either set criteria or norms.**

For evaluation to be valuable, it is important that the correct tools are used, the expected criteria are in place, and levels of success and/or failure are defined clearly. Reasonable benchmarks must be set for a reward system to work. Generally the benchmarks can be set in two distinct ways.

Criterion-based standards

With criterion-based standards, the benchmarks marking quality are set independent of the sample being evaluated. That is, quality is defined ahead of time, before the evaluation takes place. For example, many colleges and universities set a minimum score students must achieve on the ACT or SAT in order to be accepted. In the case of a six-month performance review for a new job, typically a minimal quality of performance is needed. This level is independent of the people who are being evaluated.

Norm-referenced standards

With norm-referenced standards, the benchmarks marking quality are affected by the samples being evaluated. For example, when determining the best athletic team in a league, regardless of how good (or bad) the teams are, the one who wins the most games is considered the best. From one year to another, the "best" quality can vary widely. Grades determined on a curve are norm-referenced. The definition of "excellent" when grades are given on a curve is defined by the quality of work of the students in the class, not by a predetermined standard.

Once the benchmarks have been set, artifacts must be collected on the level of quality for the criteria being evaluated. This evidence must be compared to what has been predefined as success or failure. This information must then be fed back to the client to do with as he or she sees fit.

4. **Evaluation must distinguish between effort and performance.**

Evaluation methods and criteria must take into account how much of the judgment will be based on effort and how much on performance. For instance, in a first-year piano recital, often rewards are given for "showing up." At a conservatory recital, only students with strong skills would be invited to participate.

5. **Problems can arise when the evaluator and client are the same person.**

Because the results of the collected data are used to make decisions, sometimes difficult decisions, a person acting as both the evaluator and client can inadvertently bias the information collected as evaluator in order to make the job as client less difficult.

6. **Problems can arise when the evaluator is not committed to the evaluation system in place.**

The evaluator must be able and willing to collect the needed information for evaluation. If not, the information collected can be incomplete, poor, and/or misleading. For example, often in a General Education program, an instructor must collect information of the level of student learning to indirectly assess the curriculum and instruction. Unless the instructor sees a value in knowing whether or not objectives have been met, the evaluations could be carried out haphazardly and therefore have unreliable results.

7. **Consistent follow-through is an important component to an unbiased, trusted evaluation system.**

If an evaluation system is put in place in which all persons involved know what decisions will be made based on the known criteria, it is important that the decisions be made, even if they are painful. There are occasions when first using an evaluation system when the information is unreliable enough to be questionable. But when the information is accurate, follow-through is important. Otherwise, it is difficult to get people to buy into the evaluation process, and some people might see the process as inconsistently used.

8. **The client must set high, realistic targets that signify success.**

This issue, often overlooked, is critical for collecting information that can be used beneficially. Setting the bar too low for defining success can diminish effectiveness in the future. Setting the bar too high can limit inclusion of capable people or valuable performances. For example, it is important to set realistic standards before creating a job description and interviewing applicants. If the standards are set too high, no applicant will be deemed qualified for the job. If they are set too low, a person lacking necessary skills might be hired.

9. **Bias and distortion of information must be eliminated or taken into account.**

When decisions are being made based on the evaluation, the information from the evaluation must be accurate. For direct evaluations, there must be enough reliable information collected, ideally over a period of time, to know the level of performance. For example, when evaluating a secretary's performance, it would make more sense to evaluate his or her word-processing skills by looking at documents he or she has produced (and deemed complete), rather than to ask him or her to create one document in a test setting.

For indirect evaluations, several performances must be used in the evaluation. A coach should not be evaluated regarding his ability based on the outcome of one game. An instructor should not judge his or her ability to teach by evaluating the level of learning of one student. A sample of performances must be evaluated, and the sample should be random. If all sports games or all students cannot be evaluated, there must be some unbiased sampling mechanism in place to choose the groups that will be evaluated.

For both direct and indirect evaluation, bias and distortion can cause the evaluation to be unknowingly inaccurate. Bias or distortion can lead to decisions that may adversely affect future performances. This issue is particularly important when the evaluator and client are the same person, or if the results of the evaluation will be used to evaluate the client. For example, there could be radically different feedback about the quantitative skills of a math professor's students if the students evaluated were all art majors or all math majors.

10. **The time and cost required to conduct an evaluation must be considered.**

The amount of time and the set timeline are constraints that often cannot be changed. When planning an evaluation process, it is important to consider the time frame. Also, in most cases, costs are set or limited. A quick cost-benefit analysis allows those involved to figure out if the decisions that will be made are worth the expected costs.

Examples of Evaluation

Evaluating student learning

Evaluation of student learning is used both as a direct (grading) and indirect (feedback on curriculum and/or instruction) process. Expected outcomes are set in place, and evidence is collected to see to what level each student or a sample of students have met the outcomes.

Tenure

This is an example of high stakes, mostly criterion-based, direct evaluation with a clear reward and punishment system in place. One criterion is always the quality (as defined by the institution) of the performance of the person up for tenure, although other issues can influence the standards set each year for quality.

Evaluating a job applicant

Typically as a group, those hiring (usually requestor or evaluator) determine the desired qualities and abilities of the successful candidate in order to write the advertisement. Job applicants are evaluated first from the information sent in response to the advertisement. When people are invited to interview, often the process becomes a normed evaluation by which the "best" candidate is offered the job. However, there are usually minimal, criterion-based standards in place. Therefore, if the "best" candidate has not met these standards, more people are interviewed, or the advertisement is altered to convey the needs of the job.

Benefits of Regularly Using Evaluation

- Developing good evaluation processes can aid in decisions being made based on unbiased information. Documenting and identifying how information is obtained helps the client in dealing with disputes, such as disagreement about the consequences (either positive or negative) of performance quality.

- Practicing good evaluation processes can save time and money. Hiring the "right" person, accepting the "right" students, and setting and communicating appropriate expectations help in creating situations in which there is high retention, minimal retraining, fewer job searches, and less repetition in explanations.

- Implementing good evaluation processes makes reporting to external agencies easier. The processes can be explained and the results tabulated in an unbiased, easy-to-understand way.

- Regular evaluation sets explicit expectations and allows evaluatees to self-assess based on the evaluations they receive.

Concluding Thoughts

Evaluation, when done well, can be a very powerful tool to determine quality and compare it to a desired level of quality. The results of a strong evaluation process can inform the decision-making process and help to make people accountable for their performances. A good evaluation process ensures that tough decisions are made fairly and consistently.

References

Jacobs, L. C., & Chase, C. I. (1992). *Developing and using tests effectively: A guide for faculty (how to create evaluative tools effectively)*. San Francisco: Jossey-Bass.

Joint Committee on Standards for Educational Evaluation. (1994). *The program evaluation standards*. Thousand Oaks, CA: Sage.

Shepard, L. A. (1976). A checklist for evaluating large-scale assessment programs. *Occasional Paper Series, 9*. Kalamazoo, MI: The Evaluation Center, Western Michigan University.

Evaluation Methodology

by Marie Baehr, Elmhurst College

Faculty Development Series

The Evaluation Methodology is a tool to help one better understand the steps needed to do a quality evaluation. By following this process, a faculty member can learn what he or she needs to know to determine the level of quality of a performance, product, or skill. The discussion and examples of the use of this methodology are geared toward evaluation of student learning. Much of the terminology used in this methodology is taken from the module *Overview of Evaluation*.

Evaluation Methodology

The Evaluation Methodology consists of four main steps along with a set of sub-steps. The methodology is as follows:

1. **Define the parameters of the evaluation.**

   The client:

   a. determines the need for the evaluation.

   b. determines the use for the results of the evaluation.

   c. determines what should be reported to the evaluatee and by whom.

   d. determines what the evaluator needs to report to the client.

   e. chooses guidelines to follow to implement the evaluation.

2. **Design the methods used for the evaluation.**
   (This step is skipped if an already existing evaluation tool is used.)
   The evaluator alone (or the evaluator with the client):

   a. chooses criteria to use for the evaluation based on the guidelines in Step 1e.

   b. determines the evidence that will be collected for each chosen criterion.

   c. determines the sample that will be used, if appropriate.

   d. determines ways to collect the evidence.

   e. sets up a plan to collect the evidence.

3. **Set standards and collect evidence.**

   a. The evaluator informs the client of the scales that will be used to determine quality.

   b. The client develops the decision-making process to use based on the evaluated performance quality.

   c. The client sets the standards that will be used in decision-making.

   After the client has set the standards, the evaluator:

   d. collects the evidence.

   e. documents the findings.

4. **Report and make decisions.**

   a. The evaluator reports the information in Step 1d to the client.

   b. The client checks the quality against the standards set in Step 3c.

   c. The client makes and implements decisions based on the findings.

   d. The client and/or evaluator documents the results appropriately.

   e. Either the evaluator or client reports the findings to the evaluatee, if appropriate.

Discussion of the Evaluation Methodology

1. **Define the parameters of the evaluation.**

   a. The first step in setting up an evaluation is to determine the need for the evaluation. If there is no need to collect evidence and no decisions will be made based on the evidence, there is little point in an evaluation. Having the purpose in place gives a framework for the design process.

   b. Before designing an evaluation process, the client must decide how the results will be used and what decisions need to be made. Knowing these requirements in advance facilitates finding reliable criteria and determining the evidence needed.

   c. Using the rationale for the evaluation, the client can determine what results, if any, need to be reported to the evaluatee. Often during indirect evaluations, in which the level of one group's performance is used to evaluate or assess another groups' performance, no feedback is given to the evaluatees *(see **Overview of Evaluation**)*. On the other hand, when decisions are being made that affect the evaluatee directly, a plan should be in place before the outcome is known for reporting the information to the evaluatee.

   d. The client will make decisions based on the evaluation, so the client must know what evidence he or she needs to make a decision. This evidence might be an average (such as an ACT score), an individual score, or an annotated report. This information must be provided to the client by the evaluator.

e. Before planning the methods of evaluation, it is important to sketch out the time for completion, checks for reliability, and lists of needed and not acceptable quality criteria. Developing these guidelines ahead of time ensures that the evaluation will align with the client's needs.

2. Design the methods used for the evaluation.

a. The parameters set in Step 1 should be used to help determine the criteria used in the evaluation process.

b. Once the criteria are set, the evaluator determines what evidence should be collected. The time for collection, the cost, and the usefulness of the evidence must be considered in deciding what evidence to collect.

c. Particularly in indirect evaluation, a sample of performance is often used to determine quality. This sample must be unbiased and large enough for the results to be useful. *(See **Overview of Evaluation**)*.

d. Determining how to collect the data includes deciding what form of evidence (such as test questions, observation of behavior, performance) will be used and how it will be collected.

e. The evidence collection plan includes how, when, and where the information will be collected.

3. Set standards and collect evidence from a performance or outcome.

a. Once it is determined what evidence will be collected, a scale must be set to describe how the quality is judged. This scale could be a number scale, a rubric, or a description.

b. For the process to be unbiased, the client must decide before receiving the information from the evaluation what consequences will occur based on the outcome of the evaluation. This could be a simple process, such as for high quality, there will be positive consequences; for low quality, there will be negative consequences; and between the two, other evaluative methods will be used to determine the consequences.

c. Once the scale and the decisions to be made are known, the client can set standards for decisions. These standards define "quality" based on what will be reported by the evaluator.

d. Following the plan in Step 2, the evaluator collects the needed information and analyzes it.

e. The evaluator documents what has been found in the form of individual scores, level of performance, averages, or narratives. Results should be documented in a way that helps the evaluator write the requested report to the client, using the scales that informed the setting of standards.

4. Report and make decisions.

a. For criteria-based standards, after the client has set the standards, the evaluator can give the report to the client, and the standards will not be biased by the evaluative outcome. For norm-based standards, the evaluator must include in the report summaries of outcomes of all evaluations.

b. Once the client has set the standards and has received the evaluator's report, the client can check the evaluative outcomes against the standards that have been set.

c. Based on Step 4a and evaluative outcomes, the client makes the decision and develops plans to implement it.

d. Anything that needs to be documented for future use should be done at this point.

e. The contents of a report to the evaluatee, if appropriate, should be guided by the results of Step 1e.

Examples of Evaluating

Scenario #1
Winfield College uses ACT scores as part of its decisions in accepting students for admission and granting non-need based scholarships.

Client:	Director of Admissions Office
Evaluator:	ACT's administrator
Evaluatee:	student applicant

1. Define the parameters of the evaluation.

a. The purpose of the evaluation is to find the level of knowledge skills of a college applicant.

b. The results of the evaluation will be used to deny admission to students with weak knowledge skills and to offer scholarships to students with knowledge skills above expectations.

c. Acceptance and/or scholarship decisions, based on decisions made by client, and the level of quality of knowledge-based skills by the evaluator should be reported to the evaluatee.

d. The evaluator needs to report the overall score and subscores for each applicant to the client.

e. Guidelines to follow are: the level of quality of a student must be known the spring before fall matriculation; the cost must fall on the applicant, not the college; and there must be a way to compare two students.

2. **Design the methods used for the evaluation.**

   In this case, the client decides to use the ACT test to test the students' knowledge skills needed for college. Since this test already exists, this step is complete.

3. **Set standards and collect evidence.**

   a. ACT (evaluator) informs the client of the scales. In this case, the ACT uses a norm-based scale on which 36 is perfect and 20 is "average." The scores that are one standard deviation above or below the mean are set at 16 and 26 respectively.

   b. The client develops the decision-making process to use based on the evaluated performance quality: a student with weak skills will not be considered for admission; a student with very strong skills will be considered for a non-need based scholarship; a student with average skills will have his or her acceptance based on other criteria.

   c. Standards used include: a student with a composite ACT score below 16 will not be considered for admission; a student with a composite ACT score above 26 will be accepted to the college unless other acceptance criteria are all of very poor quality; a student with a composite ACT score above 28 will be considered for a non-need based scholarship; other evaluative tools will be used for admission for a student with a composite score between 16 and 26.

   d. The evaluator collects the evidence as a result of the applicant completing the ACT test.

   e. ACT scores the test and documents the results.

4. **Report and make decisions.**

   a. Applicant scores a 21 ACT composite score, which is sent to Winfield College by ACT (at the evaluatee's request).

   b. This score eliminates the possibility of a non-need based scholarship, but opens the door to admission, assuming other evaluative findings support the decision.

   c. The client informs the financial aid office that the student will not be receiving a non-need-based scholarship. He then looks at the student's high school record, which will be used to determine whether or not the student is accepted.

   d. The client puts a note in the applicant's file that the applicant is ineligible for scholarship, but that ACT scores do not prohibit admission. Either the evaluator or client sends a report of the findings to the evaluatee, if appropriate. ACT has already informed the student of the scores. The client will contact the student once an admission decision has been made. Because non-need-based scholarships are awarded, not denied, the client will say nothing to the student.

Scenario #2

The program developed for economics majors at State College includes a first-year course in economics. Professor Backer, a second year faculty member, is teaching this course for the second time. Professor Chadler, chair of the Economics Department and one of the developers of the new program, wants to evaluate the learning of the students in Professor Chadler's course this year, particularly since students have complained often about his teaching in the last year. The results will be used to help Professor Chadler either draft a letter to the tenure board that supports Professor Backer's quest for tenure or draft a letter to Human Resources justifying the termination of Professor Backer.

Performance:	teaching
Type of evaluation:	indirect
Evaluator:	Professor Chadler
Evaluatee:	students (directly)
	Professor Backer (indirectly)
Client:	Professor Chadler

1. **Define the parameters of the evaluation.**

   a. The purpose of the evaluation is to determine the quality of teaching (indirectly) and students' learning of concepts (directly).

   b. The results can provide job security for Professor Backer.

   c. The students (direct evaluatees) will get a grade for an assignment used to evaluate their learning. The students will get a report indicating how well they learned the introductory concepts. Dr. Backer (indirect evaluatee) will get a report indicating how well his students learned the introductory concepts as well as a summary of how well all students learned the introductory concepts. Dr. Backer will receive a report from the client to explain any decisions made based on the evaluation.

   d. Professor Chadler will receive information for each individual student indicating which instructor the student had in the introductory course and how well he or she understands the introductory concepts.

   e. All students should understand the concept of supply and demand after finishing an introductory economics course. The information on quality must be received before October 15th in view of termination and tenure date deadlines. The cost must be minimal.

2. **Design the methods used for the evaluation.**

   a. The criteria (based on the guidelines) are the ability to explain and exemplify the concept of supply and demand.

b. There will be a pretest given in the second economics course. The pretest establishes the extent to which each student has met each criteria. Questions to ask:

1. *State the principle of supply and demand.*
2. *Give an example of supply and demand.*
3. *Given a change in demand, what would be the change in the cost?*

c. All students who take the second term of economics will be evaluated. This could cause a certain bias, since the most likely candidates to stop after one term are those who did badly the first term and who might not have learned the concepts. Dr. Chadler is willing to have this bias since he believes it will be the same for all faculty teaching introductory students. However, he will look at the dropout rate for each faculty member to find out if his assumption is true.

d. Collect the data and other evidence using pretest questions in a subsequent course.

e. Collect data on the first day of the next term.

3. **Set standards and collect evidence.**

a. The scales used to determine quality are:

i.	Stating the principle.	
	ALL POINTS STATED:	A
	BASICS IN PLACE WITH SOME POINTS MISSING:	C
	NO EVIDENCE OF KNOWLEDGE:	F
ii.	Giving an example of the principle.	
	EXAMPLE SUPPORTS THE PRINCIPLE:	A
	EXAMPLE SUPPORTS ONLY PART OF THE PRINCIPLE:	C
	EXAMPLE HAS NO RELATIONSHIP TO THE PRINCIPLE:	F
iii.	Give examples of changes in supply, stating the effect on cost.	
	COMPLETELY CORRECT ANSWER:	A
	SOME MINOR ERRORS, BUT BASIC UNDERSTANDING PRESENT:	C
	NO EVIDENCE OF UNDERSTANDING:	F

b. If Dr. Backer's students' average grade falls below the set standard, Dr. Chadler will request his termination. If the average grade is above the set standard, Dr. Chadler will use this evaluation as evidence for Dr. Backer's tenure request.

c. If Dr. Backer's students' average grade is more than one letter grade below the other faculty members' grades, Dr. Chadler will request his termination. If it is one letter grade above the other faculty members' grades, he will use this evaluation as evidence for his request for tenure.

d. Dr. Chadler collects the answers to the exam questions and grades them.

e. He finds that Dr. Backer's students' average grade on the questions was a "D." The average grade of the other professors was "A."

4. **Report and make decisions.**

a. Students who had Professor Backer had a grade average of D on the questions. The average for all faculty was a "B."

b. Dr. Backer's students do not appear to have learned the concept of supply and demand nearly as well as the average of all instructors' students. This result falls below the standard set for continuing employment.

c. Dr. Chadler decides to terminate Dr. Backer's contract.

d. Dr. Chadler puts the evaluation report in Dr. Backer's employment file. He also contacts all the people on campus who need to know that Dr. Backer will not be rehired.

e. Dr. Chadler notifies Dr. Backer that his contract will not be renewed.

Concluding Thoughts

As shown in these examples, decisions that have serious ramifications can be made with confidence and documentation when a systematic, well-planned evaluation process is used. The planning process reduces the occurrence of bias from evaluations and justifies decisions, even difficult decisions. The quality of confidence in results from a quality evaluation process clearly justifies the effort to perform the process systematically.

References

Angelo, T. K., & Cross, P. (1994). *Classroom assessment techniques: A handbook for college teachers*. San Francisco: Jossey-Bass.

Marzano, R., Pickering, D., & McTighe, J. (1993). *Evaluating student outcomes: Performance evaluation using the dimensions of learning model*. Alexandria, VA: Association for Supervision and Curriculum Development.

Wiggins, G. (1998). *Educative evaluation: Designing evaluations to inform and improve student performance*. San Francisco: Jossey-Bass.

Wiggins, G., & McTighe, J. (1998). *Understanding by design*. Alexandria, VA: Association for Supervision and Curriculum Development.

Distinctions between Assessment and Evaluation

by Marie Baehr, Elmhurst College

Educators use two distinct processes—assessment and evaluation—to help students build lifelong learning skills. Assessment provides feedback on knowledge, skills, attitudes, and work products for the purpose of elevating future performances and learning outcomes. Evaluation determines the level of quality of a performance or outcome and enables decision-making based on the level of quality demonstrated. These two processes are complementary and necessary in education. This module draws important distinctions between assessment and evaluation, underscoring the need for both processes to occur at separate places and times, and ideally through different roles *(see Assessment Methodology and Evaluation Methodology)*.

Inconsistent Use of the Terms

In the last fifteen years, much has been written about assessment and evaluation, but the terms have not always had distinct meanings. As accrediting agencies have become increasingly interested in improvement, it has become imperative to have a word that describes feedback for improvement distinct from a word that describes the determination of quality. To add another layer of confusion from the literature, typically *formative* (used as an adjective with assessment or evaluation) has been used to describe an improvement process, while *summative* has been used to describe a decision-making process (Brown, Race, & Smith, 1996). However, the words *formative* and *summative* mean "as it is being created" and "addition of all things," respectively. Since both a process for improvement and a process to determine quality can be accomplished as a performance is being created or after it is completed, other words should be used to distinguish the two processes.

In looking through the literature for the last several years, assessment has usually been used with at least some hint that improvement is expected in the assessment process (Bordon & Owens, 2001; Palomba and Banta, 1999). As well, evaluation is usually used to indicate that some sort of judgment of quality will be made. This guidebook is consistent in its delineation of these two processes of improvement and judgment. Assessment is the term used to look at how the level of quality of a performance or outcome could be improved in the future, which includes strengths that should be sustained as well as high priority areas for improvement. The assessment process has no focus on level of quality, only in how to improve the level of quality. Evaluation is the term used to describe the determination of the level of quality. The evaluation process focuses only in the actual level of quality with no interest in why that level was attained.

Assessment and evaluation both have their purposes, and, when used correctly, both can add significant value to teaching/learning. However, there can be detrimental effects when the people involved have not agreed on whether the process is evaluation or assessment or when the assessment methodology gets confused with the evaluation methodology.

Key Attributes

Although assessment and evaluation are used for different reasons, they do have some similar steps. Both involve specifying criteria to observe in a performance or outcome. Both require the collection of data and other evidence by observing the performance by looking at the outcome or product. Both require a performer as well as a person collecting information about the performance. As well both processes conclude with a report of the findings With all the similarities, there are at least as many differences. The relationship of the people involved is different in assessment and evaluation processes. In both cases a person (either evaluator or assessor) observes or collects evidence about a performance or outcome. Another person (either assessee or evaluatee) performs or develops an outcome. In both cases a person (either the assessee or client) requests the process (either evaluation or assessment). The locus of control rests with the performer in assessment and with the observer in evaluation. The report to the performer (assessee or evaluatee) is also vastly different. For the assessment process, the report includes information on why the performance was as strong as it was as well as what could be done to improve future performances. In assessment there is no mention of the actual quality of the performance, only on how to make the next performance stronger. There is no language indicating the level of quality (such as good, terrible, terrific, horrible). Conversely, in the evaluative report, only information regarding the actual quality of the performance is given. This might be in the form of a grade or a score or an evaluative comment, such as "good work." The purpose of the evaluative report is to report the level of quality and possibly any consequences based on the determined level of quality. It is not used to suggest improvements in future performances. Table I clarifies the similarities and differences in the two processes. The modules *Overview of Assessment, Overview of Evaluation, Assessment Methodology*, and *Evaluation Methodology* give supporting explanations.

Table 1   **Differences Between Processes of Assessment and Evaluation**

	Assessment	**Evaluation**
What is the purpose?	to improve quality of future performances	to determine quality of present performance
Who requests?	assessee	client
Who performs?	assessee	evaluatee
Who observes performance?	assessor	evaluator
Who sets criteria?	assessee and assessor	client (with possible consultation with evaluator)
Who uses the information?	assessee (in future performances)	client (to make decisions)
When can feed-back occur?	during or after a performance	during or after a performance
On what is feed-back based?	observations; and strongest and weakest points	level of quality based on a set standard
What is included in the report?	what made the quality of the performance strong; and how to improve future performances	the quality of the performance, often compared to set standards
Who receives the report?	assessee	client
For what is the report used?	to improve performance	to make judgments

Case Studies

Examples of the use of the assessment process or evaluation process can be found in *Overview of Assessment* or *Overview of Evaluation* respectively. This section addresses ways that evaluation and assessment can become confused.

Case 1: The person observing a performance believes he or she is assessing, but the performer perceives the feedback as evaluative because the performer has not worked with the observer to set up criteria and valuable feedback.

Dysfunctional partners

One of the first steps in the Assessment Methodology is for the assessor and assessee to determine the performance or outcome criteria for which the assessee would like to gain feedback. If this step is skipped, no matter how well-meaning the person is giving feedback, the feedback is likely to be considered judgmental by the assessee. Feedback will be used for improvement only if the person receiving the feedback wants to use feedback from the assessor in that area, since the control in assessment rests with the assessee.

Parent-child relations

All parents want their children to improve. However, parents also want their children's levels of performance to be at an acceptable quality. When a parent gives feedback for improvement using evaluative language to a child in an area where the child has no desire to improve, the child will perceive this feedback as judgmental. For instance, there is a big difference in the message sent between saying, "Your room is a mess. Clean it up now or you will be punished." And "If you put your books away and make your bed, your room would look much nicer."

In-class assessment exercises

Students are more used to feeling that they are evaluated by instructors, rather than assessed. Part of the reason for this perception is that instructors do evaluate students by giving grades. Part is that the students are not often included in determining what should be fed back to them. In order for assessment of student learning to work effectively, the students must be a part of the process in determining the criteria that will be used for the feedback. For example, after giving an assignment that requires a draft, you could ask students to tell you in what areas they would like feedback for improvement. In this way they would have to determine the areas where they feel improvement would make a difference, and it would help clarify that the purpose of the draft is not for a "free" grading cycle.

Figure 1

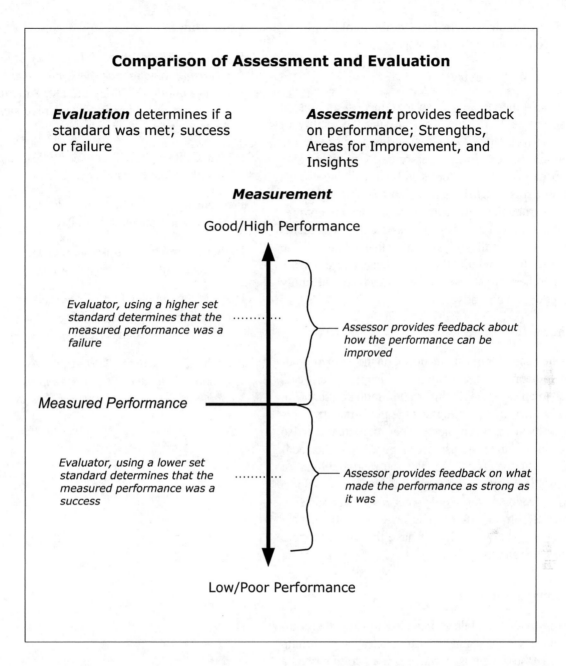

Comparison of Assessment and Evaluation

Evaluation determines if a standard was met; success or failure

Assessment provides feedback on performance; Strengths, Areas for Improvement, and Insights

Measurement

Good/High Performance

Evaluator, using a higher set standard determines that the measured performance was a failure

Assessor provides feedback about how the performance can be improved

Measured Performance

Evaluator, using a lower set standard determines that the measured performance was a success

Assessor provides feedback on what made the performance as strong as it was

Low/Poor Performance

Case 2: A person, observing a performance and using the same criteria, gives assessment feedback as well as evaluative judgments.

Interim feedback on work products

Students are often dismayed when they make all suggested improvements on a paper that was turned in for comment as a rough draft and do not receive an A on the final product. In this case, the instructor has given feedback for improvement without determining the quality of the paper. The student perceives that if he or she improves in the areas noted, he or she would have an excellent paper. One way to avoid this problem while strengthening the assessment process is to ask the students to request feedback on the draft based on set criteria.

Supervisor as mentor

Often chairs of departments are expected to mentor their nontenured faculty in their department at the same time they are expected to make decisions on continuing employment. Although the individuals might agree on criteria to use, it becomes difficult for the assessee to feel in control of using or not using the feedback as he or she sees fit, since, at some point, the assessor will become the evaluator. Although this is sometimes unavoidable, the problem can be reduced by choosing the criteria differently in the two cases. In the mentoring situations, the non-tenured faculty member should choose the criteria for focus, while in the evaluative situations, the chair should. In both cases the criteria need to be known by both parties.

Case 3: A person who is more comfortable with the evaluator role is put in the role of assessor.

Expert assessing a novice

Sometimes, someone who is so ingrained in an area of expertise is unable to stop from judging the quality of a novice performance. Though all criteria and scale are agreed upon, the expert as assessor can sometimes give the feedback in evaluative terms without realizing it. This sometimes happens when faculty start teaching right after they have earned their graduate degree. They are not prepared for the limited understanding and skills the students have who are taking their class. Rather than mentoring the students to help them build their knowledge and skills, the faculty members are sometimes apt to evaluate the study body as poor and unmotivated.

First-time assessor

Often, when used for giving feedback on the level of quality only, someone can feel uncomfortable giving "critical" feedback to an assessee, feeling that pointing out areas to improve is the same as criticizing the performance. This can cause even more problems when the situation also includes the issue of the assessee's perceiving the feedback as evaluative (Case 1). Practice and building of trust help this situation the most, but it can also help to think what feedback you would want if you had been the performer. It is important for the assessee to send the message that he or she would like to have the feedback from someone he or she trusts.

Concluding Thoughts

Discussion in this module is intended to strengthen outcomes from assessment and evaluation in teaching/learning situations. Assessment is a process used to improve a performance or outcome. Evaluation is a process used to determine the quality of a performance or outcome and make decisions based on the quality. Both processes can be formative (undertaken while an educational process is ongoing) or summative (taken at the conclusions of an educational process). Before starting either assessment or evaluation it is essential for instructors to clarify the purpose of the process. It is then critical to communicate this purpose to everyone involved and to establish whether this will be conducted as assessment or evaluation. Finally, one should be cautious whenever an assessor will ultimately be an evaluator or when assessment is initiated without buy-in of the assessee.

References

Borden, V., & Zak Owens, J. L. (2001). *Measuring quality: Choosing among surveys and other assessment of college quality.* Washington, DC: American Council on Education and Florida State University—Association for Institutional Research.

Brown, S., Race, P., & Smith, B. (1996). *500 tips on assessment.* London: Kogan Page.

Freeman, R., & Lewis, R. (1999). *Planning and implementing assessment.* London: Kogan Page.

Higher Learning Commission. (2001). <www.ncahigherlearningcommission.org>

Huba, M., & Freed, J. (2000). *Learner-centered assessment on college campuses: Shifting the focus from teaching to learning.* Needham Heights, MA: Allyn and Bacon.

Palomba, C. A., & Banta, T. W. (1999). *Assessment essentials: Planning, implementing, and improving assessment in higher education.* San Francisco: Jossey-Bass.

Performance Levels for Assesors

by Sharon Jensen, Seattle University

A major role of an assessor is to describe and analyze data accurately and then share conclusions without judgement so that it is easy for the assessee to use the information for growth. The *Assessment Methodology* gives guidelines for conducting the assessment process. The *SII Method for Assessment Reporting* gives guidelines for structuring an assessment report. The purpose of this module is to identify and describe five important behaviors of an assessor, ranging from novice to expert. By examining the quality of one's assessment efforts against this rubric, assessors can become more aware of their current level of performance and can formulate improvements needed for higher level performance.

Performance Areas

There are five core aspects of assessor performance: values, criteria, evidence, interpretation, and reporting. Values relate to the extent to which the assessor appreciates the potential of the assessment process in personal and inter-personal development. Criteria describe the assessor's ability to set specific, but complete, performance criteria so that both the assessor and assessee are clear about what is being assessed. Evidence describes the assessor's ability to gather accurate data and analyze it in a systematic manner. Interpretation refers to the assessor's ability to create meaning from observations, analysis, and understanding of context. Reporting describes the assessor's ability to communicate assessment findings and their implications in a compelling manner to an assessee.

The rubric presented in Table 1 defines five levels of performance in each of these core areas. The lowest level is that of a rookie who is unaware of the role of assessment in personal development and has little commitment to its practice. The next level is that of a learner who can see the benefits of assessment, but is in the beginning stages of implementation so that important data are often missed or disorganized. The middle level is that of a guide. At this level, an assessor feels comfortable performing assessment activities and is working on giving higher quality feedback that facilitates growth. The fourth level is that of a mentor who possesses strong skills in collecting and extracting meaning from assessment data, including nonjudgmental insights that are valuable for growth. The highest level is that of a veteran who uses assessment continuously and effectively with individuals and groups across contexts.

Elevating Assessor Skills

As explained in the *Overview of Assessment* and in *Distinctions between Assessment and Evaluation*, feedback that can be used for future growth is much more meaningful than evaluative feedback. Part of valuing the assessment process is respecting the assessee's intentions and abilities. This begins in conferring with the assessee to define the criteria that will be examined during the performance. During the performance use all of your senses, paying particular attention to non-verbal behavior. Write down observations frequently, referring to the performance criteria as an outline. After the performance, review your notes and take a moment to reflect upon the data gaps, omissions, and incongruencies (Anderson & McFarlane, 2000). Analyze whether the data accurately reflect the performance. If not, add to the data to make them more complete. Remove judgmental or inaccurate information. Make sure to consider only criteria that were negotiated with the assessee. As new issues outside the performance criteria emerge, they should be identified and negotiated separately with the assessee.

Avoid making premature conclusions. Carefully consider the performance and data for each criterion. Ideally, a pattern of performance is identified; rarely is one piece of data enough to warrant an intervention. Be honest if you have incomplete data. Collaborate with the assessee on making the observations richer and more complete; rarely can one assessor gather all pertinent data on all students at one time. Validate your data with the assessee; he or she may have a different perspective about the data and its meaning. Listen carefully to the assessee as you share your assessments.

Assessment activities will have greatest impact if they are combined with constructive interventions that are multi-dimensional and integrated (AAHE, 2003). Appropriate interventions help assessees and assessors shift priorities, connect with new resources, and change performances that have suffered for a period of time. It is highly important to listen, provide support, and be honest. Remember that plans for improvement are most successful if they are accompanied with positive strategies that focus on specifics.

Concluding Thoughts

Interaction with an assessee provides fertile ground for obtaining feedback on five core aspects of assessment. By examining your performance as an assessor against the rubric provided in this module, you will become more aware of the behaviors that allow you to make successful interventions on student learning as well as peer collaborations. You will also have a better idea about which behaviors are most limiting and how you might work on these to move to the next level of assessor.

References

Astin, A. W., Banta, T. W., Cross, K. P., El-Khawas, E., Ewell, P. T., Hutchings, P., et al. (2003). Nine principles of good practice for assessing student learning. *American Association for Higher Education*. Retrieved May 25, 2004 from <www.aahe.org/principl.htm>

Anderson, E. T., & McFarlane, J. (2000). Community analysis and nursing diagnosis. In *Community as partner* (3rd ed.). Philadelphia: Lippincott.

Table 1   **Performance Levels for Assessors**

Veteran

Values:	Continuously seeks assessment in varied contexts while respecting assessee needs.
Criteria:	Clearly articulates a comprehensive set of measurable criteria accepted by assessees.
Evidence:	Collects data that is complete, well-documented, and supportive of assessment criteria.
Interpretation:	Insightfully connects key performance areas with relevant assessee actions.
Reporting:	Supplies integrated and robust plans of action in positive, assessee-centered, language.

Mentor

Values:	When asked, uses real time assessment to improve performance of self and others.
Criteria:	Accurately proposes criteria for individuals and groups in a variety of contexts.
Evidence:	Able to observe, record, and recall key aspects of a performance as they relate to criteria.
Interpretation:	Accurately identifies strengths, improvements, and insights in familiar and some unfamiliar contexts.
Reporting:	Regularly creates non-judgmental reports that are relevant and valuable to assessees.

Guide

Values:	Feels comfortable scoping out an assessment plan with an assessee.
Criteria:	Selects key performance criteria for a specific context with help of an assessee.
Evidence:	Collects and organizes data from a performance related to major criteria.
Interpretation:	Accurately identifies strengths, improvements, and insights in familiar contexts.
Reporting:	Occasionally provides helpful feedback to assessees on key performance issues.

Learner

Values:	Believes in the value of assessment, but not always convinced that it is worth the effort.
Criteria:	Within familiar contexts, is able to set some performance criteria of interest to assessee.
Evidence:	Able to collect data that support criteria, but limited in ability to analyze these data.
Interpretation:	Able to see strengths in key areas, but has difficulty giving guidance on how to improve.
Reporting:	Provides superficial, often evaluative, feedback on items that may not be related to criteria.

Rookie

Values:	Understands concept of assessment but not interested in engaging in supportive activities.
Criteria:	Proposes some relevant and some invalid criteria without asking for assessee input.
Evidence:	Gathers data that do not align with criteria while missing important data that do.
Interpretation:	Frequently misinterprets performance data and unable to support conclusions with data.
Reporting:	Comments only on obvious performance issues, often injecting personal bias in feedback.

Mindset for Assessment

by Sharon Jensen, Seattle University

Faculty Development Series

The appropriate mindset for assessment is an important component of an effective assessment process. The assessor must respect the values and ideas of the assessee. The assessee must desire feedback to use for improvement and must remember that the assessor's sole role is to give feedback for improvement. Both need to remember that the locus of control of the assessment process is always with the assessee and that the assessment process is useful only if it is positive, individualized, meaningful, and important to the assessee. Effective assessment in the classroom enhances student engagement in the teaching /learning process. Effective assessment motivates both assessors and assessees to strive to elevate the level of performance. It focuses on individual improvement, not on judgment.

Mindset of Assessment from the Assessor's Perspective

The purpose of assessment is to facilitate improvement, and the process is multidimensional and integrated (American Association for Higher Education, 2003). For long-term improvement, the assessment process should be ongoing, tracking patterns and progress over time. For the assessor to give meaningful feedback that will be accepted by the assessee, the assessor has to be cognizant of the following mindsets.

An assessor:

- values the ideas of the assessee,
- respects the assessee for seeking feedback for improvement,
- gives feedback without giving explicit or implied judgment of level of quality,
- focuses only on feedback that can help the assessee improve performance, and
- focuses on characteristics of the performance, not the performer.

Example

An instructor is developing the mindset of an assessor. To give the students more ownership within the context of a course, the instructor could change the question from, "What will I teach?" to "What do they want to learn?" The instructor could ask students to write down their goals for the course. If the student goals encompass the course design, they could become some of the goals for the course. The criteria would be developed collaboratively between the students and instructor. The instructor might give feedback on the goals and assignments set by the students at specified times during the course. The student and the instructor could communicate on improvements and progress at the end of the term as well as discuss ways to improve further and directions for future growth.

Mindset of Assessment from the Assessee's Perspective

It is equally important that an assessee is open to feedback and intends to improve performance.

An assessee:

- desires to improve performance,
- respects the assessor for giving honest feedback that can lead to improvement,
- considers assessment feedback as non-judgmental,
- does not desire or ask for evaluation feedback from an assessor,
- works with the assessor to set criteria, negotiate feedback, and moderate pace,
- requests from the assessor what the assessee would find useful,
- looks at the assessor as a mentor, and
- understands that assessment is not about getting it right; it is about getting it better.

Example

A student can change his or her focus from "What do I have to learn?" to "What do I want to learn?" if the instructor asks the students what they would like to learn in a course. This may be the first time that the students have ever encountered an instructor who is willing to consider student learning goals. The students have to think about what they really want to get out of the class. If the course goals are developed in collaboration with the students, the students can be more active and invested in the course. The students will have to consider what is important. The instructor checks in periodically to assess the students' fulfillment of goals. When students can ask questions without the threat of "not getting it right," they ask better questions. Meeting goals of value to the students motivates students and establishes a positive student-instructor relationship. A summative assessment shows students how they have grown over time.

Figure 1   **Venn Diagram of Comparing Assessment and Evaluation**

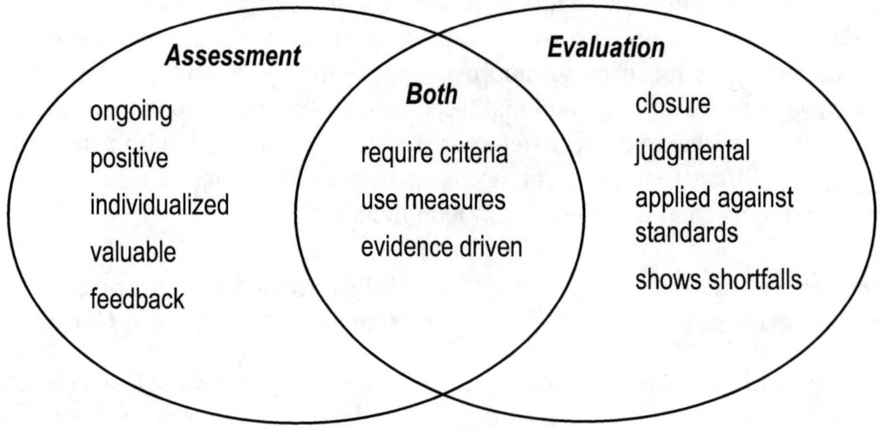

Similarities and Differences between Assessment and Evaluation

Some areas of assessment and evaluation overlap. (See Figure 1.) Both processes:

- require setting and using criteria,
- use measures to identify the level of performance,
- are driven by evidence,
- need accurate and holistic data for an accurate summary,
- provide motivation, and
- require reporting to the performer.

Because of the similarities in assessment and evaluation processes, it is easy to jump from one to the other without realizing it. Keeping the appropriate mindset helps in appropriately assessing or evaluating. Table 1 summarizes some of the differences in the two processes.

The remainder of this module focuses on faculty assessment of student learning within the classroom and how this process is affected by mindset.

Quality Factors Affected by Mindset for Assessment

Placing value on assessment

Assessment is a complex process. It does take thought and commitment on the part of the faculty member to incorporate it in the classroom. As improvements in curriculum and teaching are made based on assessment feedback, most faculty will begin to see even more value of assessment through increased student learning. However, a faculty member must first believe in the ability of the process to improve student learning.

Table 1

Differences between Assessment and Evaluation

Assessment	Evaluation
Focuses on desired outcomes of assessee	Focuses on desired outcomes of evaluator
Is requested by the assessee	Is requested by the evaluator
Focuses on growth	Focuses on quality
Has no consequences	Often has consequences
Never compares quality	Often compares quality
Has standards for quality developed by the assessee in collaboration with the assessor	Has standards for quality developed by the evaluator

Setting aside time

Assessment and evaluation are both necessary within the academic setting. Many activities focus on the evaluation side of the balance since almost all faculty must assign grades. Commonly, assessment gets neglected in the day-to-day tasks of busy lives. Once an instructor begins to value the process of assessment in student learning, he or she will be willing to find time to incorporate assessment strategies into courses.

Setting criteria

The criteria for assessment should address the things that are really important, not necessarily the easiest to assess. Assessment begins and ends with the assessee's vision for the future. Setting criteria pushes both assessor and assessee toward clarity about where to aim and what standards apply (American Association for Higher Education, 2003). At the beginning, the students (assessees) can identify which criteria are most important for them to work on during the next time frame; these criteria can then be used during the assessment process by the instructor. Collaborating to set criteria for assessment builds respect for diverse interests and ways of learning (Cross & Steadman, 1996). In an environment focused on the assessee, more time will be spent developing the criteria and assessing work at various stages of the process (Huba & Freed, 2000).

Focusing on what is important

The focus is on a process that is ongoing, positive, individualized, meaningful, and important to the assessee (American Association for Higher Education, 2003). It makes a difference when assessment begins with issues of individual growth and illuminates questions that people really care about.

Giving feedback

When an instructor gives feedback to a student, the instructor models the assessment process and helps the student improve. It is important that the feedback:

* focuses on the set criteria,

* gives suggestions or strategies for improvement,

* uses only non-judgmental words, and

* remembers that the assessee is the audience.

Instructors can observe how their feedback is received as a cue about how well it is delivered. They will have evidence for the importance of trust, and they can observe how the feedback can be geared based on the comfort level of the student. They will be able to look for and see the effects of evaluative words on the assessee (Mahara, 1998).

The timing of feedback is an important consideration. At times, feedback can be given to the group, while at other times feedback should be shared one-on-one. Office hours, time during and after class, and additional study or meeting times open the door for a mutual exchange. Assessment leads to more public sharing (e.g., peer reviews) to discuss work and its strength and improve-

ments. Peers have valuable insights, and the assessment format can moderate the affect of students who have the mindset of evaluation. An assessor should always ask for permission to share assessment findings with people other than the assessee. The assessee has the right to be involved in identifying a time and place where assessments can be shared.

Building trust in the system and in the environment

Once the instructor has found value in the assessment process and determined how to incorporate effective assessment strategies into a course, the improvement of student learning will depend in part on the trust the students have in the process. This trust can be developed as students begin to see their improvements due to assessment. Part of developing the trust includes assessment strategies that:

* guide improvement,

* align with goals of the course,

* include timely feedback,

* give feedback to individuals confidentially,

* include individual feedback based on desires of the individuals, and

* include students as equal partners (American Association for Higher Education, 2003).

By creating a trusting environment, assessment produces opportunities for "magical or teachable" moments, enhances learner ownership, and shifts responsibility for learning to students. The more an assessor's feedback enables a student to learn independently, the more a student will desire to work with the assessor and respond to his or her assessments. In future situations, the assessor becomes better at self-assessment. Thus an assessor's current level of performance builds power for the assessor in future assessment situations. It motivates both assessors and assessees to strive to elevate the level of performance. A trusting environment is respectful, supportive, and open. Engagement is encouraged and dialogue is regarded as a process. Students are encouraged to question and challenge the teacher, and the process generates growth (Mahara, 1998).

At the beginning of the assessment process, students may want to mask their skills that need improvement because they feel they will earn lower grades if the instructor knows where their weaknesses are. This commonly occurs when the assessor and evaluator are the same person. In the ideal world, these would be separate processes and people. In the real world, the best case might be explicitly separating feedback for assessment and evaluation into separate time periods. Also, assignments can be designed that give credit to honesty, accurate identification of personal learning needs, and a high quality action plan to improve. As trust in assessment and in the instructor builds, students begin to appreciate how much the instructor cares for student learning and how much the instructor can facilitate growth.

The assessee may need repetition and time before this assessment process is trusted. It is important to be patient and to reinforce the idea that the reason for giving feedback is that it enhances student learning.

Getting buy-in

Issues may surface related to either the buy-in of the assessor or assessee. When the assessee looks for "what you want" rather than "what I need," the assessee may have the mindset to please others, rather than deriving the desire to learn internally. On the other hand, the assessor may be looking for "what's wrong" rather than for "what can be improved." When the assessee is hesitant to let the assessor see the weaker areas, his or her history might indicate that disclosure is not rewarded. Assessors should be alert to cues that may indicate some hesitation to participate in the assessment process and address them explicitly as they occur. Buy-in happens in the beginning stages, but can re-surface as the current situation brings up unresolved issues from the past.

Concluding Thoughts

Effective assessment enhances student engagement in the teaching/learning process, motivating both assessors and assessees to strive to elevate the level of performance. Wider improvement is fostered when people from across the educational community are involved. The mindset of both the assessor and assessee during the assessment process is fundamentally different from the mindset during evaluation because the locus of control moves from the observer (in evaluation) to the performer (in assessment).

Assessment makes a bigger difference when it addresses questions that assessees really care about (American Association for Higher Education, 2003) and when the assessor keeps improvement as the focus. Although some improvement comes out of almost any assessment process, the mindset makes a huge difference in both the quality of the feedback and the receptiveness to the feedback. Being conscious of the mindset and working to align the mindset with assessment can enhance the assessment process and accelerate improvements.

References

American Association for Higher Education. (2003). AAHE assessment forum definitions of assessment. Retrieved June 30, 2003, from <http://wwwaahe.org/assessment/principl.htm>

Cross, P. K., & Steadman, M. H. (1996). *Classroom research: Implementing the scholarship of teaching.* San Francisco: Jossey-Bass.

Huba, M. E., & Freed, J. E. (2000). *Learner-centered assessment on college campuses: Shifting the focus from teaching to learning.* Boston: Allyn and Bacon.

Mahara, J. S. (1998). A perspective on clinical evaluation in nursing education. *Journal of Advanced Nursing, 28 (6)*, 1339-1346.

McMillan, J. H. (2001). *Classroom assessment: Principles and practice for effective instruction* (2nd ed.). Boston: Allyn and Bacon.

National Research Council (2001). *Knowing what students know.* Washington D.C: National Academy Press.

Parker, P. E., Fleming, P. D., Beyerlein, S., Apple, D., & Krumsieg, K. (2001). *Differentiating assessment from evaluation as continuous improvement tools* [Abstract]. 31st ASEE/IEE Frontiers in Education Conference, 1462.

SII Method for Assessment Reporting

by Jack Wasserman, University of Tennessee at Knoxville and Steven Beyerlein, University of Idaho

Assessment results are most likely to be put into action by an assessee when they are concisely stated, supported by evidence, and delivered in a positive manner. This module outlines a format for informal assessment reports that meets these needs. Known as the SII method, it includes a thoughtful description of assessee **S**trengths, areas for **I**mprovement, and **I**nsights that can be transferred to other contexts. The SII method is assessee-centered in its language, specific in its use of data from a specific learning context, and enlightening in its recommendations for future action.

Role of Self-Assessment

Psychological studies of highly successful people across all domains of intelligence—linguistic, musical, mathematical, scientific, interpersonal, kinesthetic, intrapersonal, and spiritual—reveal that these extraordinary individuals share three behaviors that are the source of sustained personal growth (Gardner, 1998).

- These individuals stand out in the extent to which they reflect—often explicitly—on the events of their lives.

- These individuals stand out less by their impressive "raw powers" than by their ability to identify and then exploit their strengths.

- These individuals fail often and sometimes dramatically, but they stand out in the extent to which they learn from their setbacks and convert defeats into opportunities.

Extraordinary individuals, therefore, possess a strong internal process of thinking about their circumstances, their performance capabilities, and their opportunities for effecting change. The SII method strives to make these attributes explicit in the dialogue between assessor and assessee. It embodies several characteristics known to improve critical thinking, including positiveness, process-orientation, recognition of contextual details, and role of emotion as well as reason in human behavior (Brookfield, 1987).

SII Report Organization

While the assessee is performing, the assessor must collect information consistent with the chosen criteria (see *Methodology for Assessment*). It is important for the assessor to note: (1) the strong points of the assessee's performance (things done well) and why they were considered strong, (2) the areas in which the assessee's performance can improve, along with how the improvement could be made, and (3) any insights that might help the assessee in other contexts. The SII format provides a succinct way to communicate these findings in a cooperative learning environment.

Strengths identify the ways in which a performance was of high quality and commendable. Each strength statement should address what was valuable in the performance, why this attribute is important, and how to reproduce this aspect of the performance.

Areas for Improvement identify the changes that can be made in the future (between this assessment and the next assessment) that are likely to improve performance. Improvements should recognize the issues that caused any problems and mention how changes could be implemented to resolve these difficulties.

Insights identify new and significant discoveries/ understandings that were gained concerning the performance area; i.e., what did the assessor learn that others might benefit from hearing or knowing. Insights include why a discovery/new understanding is important or significant and how it can be applied to other situations.

These statements should be delivered in the order given above to first affirm the assessee and then to apprise them of opportunities for additional growth. Care should be taken to cast these statements in a succinct manner and avoid using judgmental language. As a matter of convenience in written SII reports, each statement can be identified with the appropriate letter (S or I).

Rubric for Elevating SII Reports

The following rubric has been developed to help students visualize different levels of assessment quality and to rate the sophistication of their SII reports. As assessments move up the scale, there is a discernible shift from assessing effort to meaningfully assessing performance.

Level 1 — Observation

Strengths and areas for improvement are presented as simple statements. The following statements are typical of this level.

- (S)　The presenter was energetic.

- (I)　The introduction was too long.

- (I)　The score was not the only goal.

Level II — Comprehension of Key Issues

Strengths and improvements are clearly stated and the reasons for the strength and suggestions for improvement are given. Insights tend to be related to the specific context of the assessment. The following statements are typical of this level.

(S)   The enthusiasm of the presenter inspired the audience to ask many questions.

(I)   Much of the material in the introduction was secondary to the purpose of the talk.

(I)   The team kept the problem statement in mind, not just the score.

Level III — Application in a Related Context

This feedback builds on comprehension of key issues and gives specific ideas for improving performance in a related context. The following statements are typical of this level.

(S)   Taking time to practice your presentation can help you deliver your message in a confident and convincing tone.

(I)   The introduction should highlight a single hypothesis and explain why it is justified.

(I)   The team's focus on the goal of good technical communication as opposed to just the score reminded everyone about the educational objective of the project.

Level IV — Transfer to a New Context

This feedback illustrates generalized understanding and is instructive in applying this understanding across a broad range of contexts. The following statements are typical of this level.

(S)   Researching the background of your audience can help stimulate interest and attention to your message.

(I)   Section divisions appear to be seamless in a carefully planned and practiced presentation.

(I)   Communicating your interpretation of the underlying purpose of an activity helps everyone assess whether they could have learned more from the activity.

Implementing SII Reports

SII reports represent a powerful formative assessment tool that can be used with a great deal of flexibility in the classroom. The following techniques have proven successful in elevating and adding variety to SII reports.

Prioritize findings: Students share only the greatest strength, the greatest area for improvement, and the best insight. This encourages participants to rank the significance of their observations and to defend their thinking.

Limit response time: This is especially valuable for sharing oral assessment reports from multiple teams. Challenge participants to limit SII reports (all three parts) to less than 30 seconds.

Build common understanding: Participants are asked to rephrase what they hear in other's SII reports. This process can help clarify muddy ideas as well as emphasize important discoveries.

Focus attention: The instruction directs attention to a narrow set of learning skills or performance criteria. Focusing the assessment helps to minimize motherhood and apple pie statements in favor of commentary connects with specific behaviors.

Rate performance on a scale: As a reference for writing SII statements, the instructor provides several scales or rubrics for ranking performance in key areas. Assigning numerical scores can trigger recollection of supporting evidence that adds more specificity to a written SII report.

Collective feedback: The instructor may use the SII format at the end of a reporting session (oral or written) to comment on the entire spectrum of reports. This serves to reiterate key findings and to establish performance expectations for future reporting sessions.

Concluding Thoughts

One of the driving forces for change in higher education is the need to develop students who are life-long learners so they can adapt to the ever, and rapidly, changing world around us (Brookfield, 1987). Quality self-assessment provides a solid foundation for such self-growth (Gardner, 1998). By giving and receiving SII reports, learners at any level in the curriculum gain the practice and experience they need to become quality self-assessors and self-growers. SII reports support an assessment culture where students are motivated to perform better and proactively seek to improve their own performance.

References

Brookfield, S. (1987). *Developing critical thinkers: Challenging adults to explore alternative ways of thinking and acting.* San Francisco: Jossey-Bass.

Gardner, H. (1998). *Extraordinary minds.* New York: Basic Books.

Fundamentals of Rubrics

by Sandy Bargainnier, The Pennsylvania State University

High quality assessment and evaluation of any performance depends on accurate and reliable measurement of key performance factors. Low-level understanding is conveniently investigated with the help of simple, quantitative tools, such as multiple-choice tests, true-false quizzes, and vocabulary definitions. On the other hand, systems thinking, procedural knowledge, and attitude formation require more sophisticated measurement schemes. By explicitly stating significant performance criteria, rubrics classify and organize performance observations with respect to different skill levels, behaviors, and/or product quality. This module outlines attributes of a quality rubric and contrasts the purposes of holistic rubrics and analytic rubrics in performance measurement.

Purpose and Use of Rubrics

Measuring a performance, a work product, or a learning skill can prove to be challenging without the appropriate measurement tool. Rubrics are tools that can help multiple instructors come to similar conclusions about construction of higher-level conceptual knowledge, performance skills, and attitudes. Basic facts and concepts, also referred to as "declarative knowledge" (Angelo, T. 2002; Bloom, 1956, Anderson and Krathwohl, 2001), can be measured with selected-response methods. However, higher order thinking, procedural knowledge, and enduring understanding require more open-ended, complex and authentic types of assessment and evaluation (Wiggins and McTighe, 1998, Angelo, 2002). Assessments and evaluations that require students to "construct" knowledge (called constructed-response) cannot be scored easily with an answer key.

Rubrics are designed to help instructors measure ability to use and apply factual, conceptual, procedural, and metacognitive knowledge (Angelo, 2002, Anderson and Krathwohl, 2001, Bloom, 1956). For example, if an instructor wants to measure the ability to use a math formula to solve a biomechanics problem, the quality of a dance performance, or an attitude as reflected in journal writing, a rubric can help make the measurement more objective and meaningful.

Types of Rubrics

There are several types of rubrics. A generic rubric is used to assess or evaluate a process (i.e., problem solving) across disciplines, whereas a task-specific rubric is applicable only for a specific, defined task (see Table 1).

After selecting either a generic or a task-specific rubric, the facilitator needs to decide between holistic and analytic rubrics, depending on what he or she wants to assess or evaluate. Analytic rubrics work better when students self-assess a complex performance, product, process, or learning skill. Analytic rubrics help both learner and measurer identify strengths and areas for improvement. However, scoring and use may take longer with an analytic rubric than with a holistic rubric (see Table 1).

Table 1 **Dribbling Rubric (Task-specific, Analytic)**

Point Level	Description of Dribbling Ability
0 points	Cannot perform the skill.
1 point	Can control a ball through four cones three feet apart in more than ten seconds.
2 points	Can control a ball through four cones three feet apart in ten seconds.
3 points	Can control a ball through four cones three feet apart in seven seconds.
4 points	Can control a ball through four cones three feet apart in five seconds

From Physical Education Rubrics. Available on-line at
<http://www.cwu.edu/~gossge/curriculum/rubric/rubrics>

A holistic rubric (See Table 2) requires the measurer to score the overall process or product as a whole, without judging the component parts separately (Nitko, 2001). Performance expectations and criteria that are holistic in nature (i.e., problem-solving) are best measured and evaluated using a holistic rubric. Holistic rubrics are quick to use and provide the measurer with a snapshot of the performance at hand. One limitation of use includes the inability to provide detailed and specific feedback of the performance.

The Role of Rubrics in Instruction

Cognitive learning theory and its constructivist approach to knowledge suggests looking not for what students can repeat or mimic, but for what they can generate, demonstrate, and exhibit (Brooks and Brooks, 1999). Active learning suggests that students demonstrate what they know and are able to do. Rather than measuring discrete, isolated knowledge, authentic assessment emphasizes the application and use of knowledge. Authentic assessment includes the holistic performance of meaningful, complex tasks in challenging environments that involve contextualized problems (Montgomery, 2002).

Rubrics are the tools that provide the criteria and levels of performance to assess student work that is not traditional (i.e., performances, portfolios, papers, teamwork, etc.). When used for assessment, rubrics help both student and instructor identify strengths and areas for improvement in the learning process. A rubric should accompany all non-traditional assignments from the beginning.

The sample rubric is used in a variety of undergraduate courses that use oral presentations as a method of evaluation. The rubric is distributed with the assignment. Discussion about rubric use occurs from the beginning of the assignment. Students use the rubric for self-assessment. Peers use the same rubric to provide specific feedback on strengths and areas for improvement.

Analytic rubrics, which include specific and detailed criteria, can help the learner, peers, and instructors assess the learner's progress in a performance, work product, or learning skill. When students know the performance criteria, the mystery of "what is most important" to learn is removed and quality learning can begin.

The Role of Rubrics for Evaluation

When analytic rubrics are used for evaluation purposes (i.e., a grade, pass or fail for certification), the criteria are clear, and the scoring process publicly reflects the expectations of a high quality performance. Students know the expectations and do not question scores as much when the performance criteria are clear and outlined at the beginning of an assignment. The process of converting rubric scores to grades varies as much as rubrics.

Holistic rubrics are best suited for a summative evaluation of a performance, product, or process, so that the student receives an overall score based on overall performance. A holistic rubric provides a quick snapshot of a performance or achievement. The holistic rubric does not inform students where strengths and weaknesses lie, and therefore may not be as useful to them as an analytic rubric (see Table 2 on the next page).

Attributes of a Quality Rubric

The plethora of types and styles of rubrics can be daunting for a novice user (Coxon, 2003). The following attributes of a quality rubric can help novices and experts alike to assess the quality of a rubric (Arter and McTighe; 2001; Wiggins, 1998).

1. Clear criteria

The rubric must have clear criteria. Wiggins (1998) states that we must be careful to ensure that the criteria are necessary and, as a set, sufficient for meeting the targeted achievement. The criteria should define a comprehensive set of behaviors that make up the performance. The criteria defining each level of performance must be significant and should be mapped to the same scale.

Before deciding on the performance criteria, it is important to clearly define what will be measured. After this, it is important to research the best criteria (or best practices) in the areas to be measured before developing the criteria. For example, the measurer has to determine what the "problem solving" experts would identify as high performing and low performing criteria about this skill. The same holds true for any performance, work product, or learning skill.

It is important that the rubric covers the features that indicate quality performance because the relationship between performance criteria and rubrics is key to improved student learning (Arter and McTighe, 2001; Huba and Freed, 2000). For example, to assess the student's ability to write a persuasive paragraph, the rubric should not predominately be designed around the number of grammar, spelling, and typographical errors.

2. Rich, descriptive language

The rubric must include rich and descriptive language. Students and multiple instructors need to understand the definitions, indicators, and samples of work (Arter and McTighe, 2001) so they can use the rubric to improve learning and assessment. The descriptors that differentiate quality should be user-friendly to students. A rubric should always describe the different levels of performance in tangible, qualitative terms in each descriptor. Therefore, when using comparative language to differentiate quality, the rubric must compare a relative quality, not an arbitrary quantity (Wiggins, 1998).

The organization of a rubric should be effectively sequenced to flow with the natural steps in the performance. Related aspects should be clustered. Descriptive labels for levels of performance enhance the creation and application of rubrics.

Table 2

Problem Solving Rubric (Generic, Holistic)

Level 1 — Totally Dependent Individuals

1. Hardly ever see anything besides surface factors of a problem, and their understanding of the problem always stays unclear.
2. Miss most key issues and important assumptions.
3. Are disorganized, without priorities, and accept quick solutions without testing and validating.
4. Use information without assessment and take foolish risks, or become immobilized.
5. Use other peoples' solutions and never learn from past efforts.

Level 2 — Individuals who rely on others

1. Identify problems from how they feel and clarify them through expressing emotions.
2. State issues concerning personal needs and identify assumptions others make about them.
3. Are emotional and reactive to daily issues and test to see if solutions make them comfortable.
4. Use information provided and will do what others ask.
5. Modify other peoples' solutions and occasionally see patterns in how they use them.

Level 3 — Self-reliant Individuals

1. Can identify and clarify their key problems, so they can focus on the most important.
2. Identify several of the key issues and some of the important assumptions.
3. Are semi-organized with some priorities and make sure they are satisfied with the solution.
4. Make use of available information and take needed risks to get what they really want.
5. Produce acceptable solutions and sometimes reuse the most obvious solutions.

Level 4 — Professional Consultants

1. Can help others see problems they overlooked and clarify them to others' satisfaction.
2. Identify most key issues concerning context, constraints and needs, and most important assumptions.
3. Are more systematic and have priorities and criteria, which they use to test and validate solutions.
4. Access extensive information so they can take the risks others won't.
5. Are strong at modeling problems and at times generalize solutions for future reuse.

Level 5 — Premier Problem Solvers

1. Can see hidden problems others overlook and clarify them so others can see their importance.
2. Identify all key issues concerning context, constraints and needs, and important assumptions.
3. Are systematic, and apply clear priorities and quality criteria to test and validate both the process and solution.
4. Access all critical information so they can take the risks required at minimal cost.
5. Are excellent at modeling problems, taking time to generalize for future use and appropriate reuse.

3. Focus on positive attainment

The rubric should focus on positive attainment of the desired performance. Another key consideration when assessing rubrics is the use of positive language when describing the levels of performance. The narrative should clearly describe positive attainment, rather than lack of attainment. For example, stating that the learner "needs to project voice loudly so all in the audience can hear" provides positive guidance to improve performance as compared to "inaudible." The description for each level should help both the learner and measurer to clearly distinguish the differences in levels of performance.

4. Differentiation of performance, product, and effort

The rubric should clearly measure the desired performance (i.e., problem-solving, dribbling, oral communication) and not just effort. This requires very clear and specific performance criteria and observable descriptors at each level of performance. One should not confuse effort or product with actual performance. For example, in physical education, it is common to see rubrics that make shooting three out of four foul shots an exemplary performance. This rubric example is describing the product—the student made the foul shot.

What the above description does not capture is the quality of the performance. A description that helps the measurer distinguish between levels of performance might include proper technique, hand placement, location on the court, etc. Based on a "quantity versus quality" description, the student could have kicked the ball into the hoop with his or her feet to complete three out of four foul shots. Rubrics should clearly state the evidence that will be used to measure the performance. This evidence should distinguish between "just doing it" (a yes /no checklist type performance) and being able to differentiate quality levels of performance.

5. Universal validity and reliability

A rubric should be easy to interpret for instructors and students alike. Both should be able to use the rubric for instruction, assessment, and evaluation. Rubrics should be valid and reliable. A valid rubric measures key aspects central to quality of performance. A reliable rubric yields consistent results for different users. Reliability is increased by using rich, descriptive language. A rubric should also be fair to all students in regards to reading level, language, and examples.

Concluding Thoughts

Consistent use of well-designed rubrics significantly improves the facilitation of learning by providing both students and instructors with clarity and commonality of purpose. Students can better validate their own progress, and instructors can fairly and consistently document the students' skills and growth. Using rubrics across programs and/or course sequences can also insure consistent measurement of quality of performance by students who have different instructors. Rubrics can provide a well-founded measurement system for improving teacher performance and collecting data for research projects. Creating and using quality rubrics is well worth the considerable time and effort involved.

References

Anderson, L., & Krathwohl, D. (2001). *A taxonomy for learning, teaching, and assessing: A revision of Bloom's taxonomy of educational objectives.* New York: Longman.

Angelo, T. (2002). *Fostering critical thinking in our courses: Practical, research-based strategies to improve learning.* The Pennsylvania State University Teaching and Learning Colloquy VIII, May 8, 2002.

Arter, J., & McTighe, J. (2001). *Scoring rubrics in the classroom: Using performance criteria for assessing and improving student performance.* Thousand Oaks, CA: Corwin Press.

Bloom, B. (1956). *Taxonomy of educational objectives: The classification of educational goals. Handbook I: cognitive domain.* New York: David McKay.

Brooks, J., & Brooks, M. (1999). *In search of understanding: The case for constructivist classrooms.* Alexandria, VA: Association for Supervision and Curriculum Development.

Coxon, E. (2004). Rubrics. *The Staff Room for Ontario's Teachers.* Retrieved June 1, 2004 from <www.quadro.net/~ecoxon/Reporting/rubrics.htm>

Huba, M., & Freed, J. (2000). *Learner-centered assessment on college campuses: Shifting the focus from teaching to learning.* Needham Heights, MA: Allyn and Bacon.

Montgomery, K. (2002). *Authentic tasks and rubrics: Going beyond traditional assessments in college teaching.* College Teaching. Heldref Publication.

Nitko, A. J. (2001). *Educational assessment of students* (3rd ed.). Upper Saddle River, NJ: Merrill.

Wiggins, G. (1998). *Educative assessment designing assessments to inform and improve student performance.* San Francisco: Jossey Bass.

Wiggins, G., & McTighe, J. (1998). *Understanding by design.* Alexandria, VA: Association for Supervision and Curriculum Development.

Annotated Bibliography — Assessment

by Marie Baehr, Elmhurst College

This module summarizes a variety of references that distinguish between the process for improvement and the process for judgment. When these processes are called something other than assessment and evaluation, there is a notation given in the annotation.

Books

Palomba, C., & Banta, T. (1999). *Assessment essentials: Planning, implementing, and improving assessment in higher education.* San Francisco: Jossey-Bass.

This book guides the reader through the most current practices for developing assessment programs for higher education. It includes information on the general process as well as many examples. Some chapters are "The Essentials of Successful Assessment," "Developing Definitions, Goals, and Plans," "Listening to Students' Voices," and "Assessing General Education." It offers information on how to develop plans and goals that fit the needs of individual campuses, how to encourage involvement from all constituencies, how to select appropriate methods, and how to analyze, report and use assessment results. This book would be particularly useful for those relatively new to the assessment process, for it does not assume a working knowledge of the topic. However, it is also valuable for those who have been working in the assessment area for a while because it is a good reference on developments in the field.

Assessment Essentials is also useful in understanding the confusion caused in using the word *assessment* to describe both a process to improve and a means to know the level of quality. In this book, to assess is defined as "to examine carefully," which DOES NOT necessarily imply feedback. The focus in the book is to look to see if a process is doing what it is supposed to do, continuing to improve the process (without indication of how to know how to improve), and stopping once a predetermined level of success is achieved.

Freeman, R., & Lewis, R. (1998*). Planning and implementing assessment.* London: Kogan Page.

This book is a good reference for those who wish to design, implement or critique an assessment process. It is divided into six parts, including principles of assessment, methods toolbox, sources of assessment, using assessment methods, recording and reporting, and assessment issues. It is particularly strong in describing the use of criteria for both assessment and evaluation and in discussing how to move students to the point where they learn proactively.

It is important to note that some translation in terms will be needed, however. The author uses "judgmental assessment" or "summative assessment" for the *Faculty Guidebook*'s definition of evaluation and "developmental assessment" or "formative assessment" for the *Faculty Guidebook*'s definition of assessment. The term "final assessment" is used to describe assessment at the end of a process and "continuous assessment" as assessment during the performance.

Banta, T. (1999). *Assessment update: The first ten years.* San Francisco: Jossey-Bass.

This book is a compilation of articles written about assessment from 1990 to 2000. Trudy Banta is director of the National Center for Higher Education Management Systems in Boulder, CO. In reading it cover to cover, one gets the sense that the word *assessment* has slowly been redefined over the years. This book is particularly useful for getting a sense of the history of assessment in higher education.

Mager, R. (1997). *Preparing instructional objectives: A critical tool in the development of effective instruction.* (3rd ed.). Atlanta: Center for Effective Performance.

In an extremely straightforward way, this book explains the characteristics of well-defined objectives and the process for writing objectives that match the learning expected of the students. This book shows how quality objectives can focus instruction. Along the way, questions are asked of the reader to make sure the terms are understood. If the questions are answered incorrectly, the reader is requested to re-read some of the material until the differences in terms begin to make sense. Many of the examples of poorly written objectives will ring true for any present or former student. By reading both good and poor examples, the reader can begin to understand the qualities needed for good objectives. This is one of the most useful books in print for understanding how to write criteria and set measures.

Huba, M., & Freed, J. (2000). *Learner-centered assessment on college campuses: Shifting the focus from teaching to learning.* Boston: Allyn and Bacon.

This book combines research with practice to help readers understand the connections between assessment of student learning and improvement of student learning. It gives examples of how to shift to learner-centered paradigms from teacher-centered paradigms. It also gives some strategies that can be used in the assessment process. The book is written in three sections. The first section deals with the development of a learner-centered perspective, including chapters on the role of assessment in facilitating the shift, describing the hallmarks of learner-centered teaching, and discussing principles that work supported by research studies. The second section in the book is devoted to practical techniques that both strengthen teaching processes and enhance assessment strategies. The techniques in this section can be used in assessment at the course level, academic program level, and institution level. The final section focuses on the individual and institutional implications of shifting to a learner-centered paradigm.

Web Sites

American Association for Higher Education Initiatives—online assessment resources
<http://www.aahe.org/assessment/assess_links.htm>

There are many on-line resources, but this website seems to be linked to almost all of them. It is organized into three areas:

1. Readings—This area gives the user online access to AAHE's literature on assessment, including these two frequently referenced articles: "Nine Principles of Good Practice for Assessing Student Learning," and "Doing Assessment as If Learning Matters Most" by Thomas A. Angelo (May 1999 AAHE Bulletin).

2. Assessment Electronic Discussion Lists—This area of the website lists several listserves devoted to the area of assessment or evaluation of student learning. For each listserv, the website describes the basic topics of discussion and how to subscribe.

3. Assessment websites—This area has links to numerous other websites. It organizes the websites around twenty-four themes, including general readings and journals on assessment, assessment bibliographies, planning an assessment program, learning outcomes, goals and objectives, rubrics, and institutional assessment sites.

Internet Resources for Higher Education Outcomes Assessment, North Carolina State University
<http://www2.acs.ncsu.edu/UPA/assmt/resource.htm>

This on-line resource has many of the same links as the AAHE website and some the AAHE website does not have. Its main focus is on outcomes assessment, and some of the links refer to what this Guidebook defines as evaluation. It is organized into six areas.

1. General resources that link to other general websites, including but not limited to AAHE, forums, journal articles, grant results, instruments used in outcomes assessment, rubrics, classroom assessment techniques, conference lists, glossary websites, National Survey of Student Engagement results, discussion lists, and available tracking software.

2. Assessment handbooks that link to college and university assessment information.

3. Assessment of specific skills or content that links to specific programs' assessment plans and results.

4. Individual institutions' assessment-related pages for over 100 colleges and universities in alphabetical order.

5. Links to all the higher education accrediting bodies, including the Council for Higher Education Accrediting, the regional accrediting bodies, and specialized/professional associations.

6. Student assessment of courses and faculty links, including strategies and forms to use to get student feedback for improving teaching.

Annotated Bibliography — Evaluation

by Marie Baehr, Elmhurst College

This annotated bibliography includes references that support evaluation (defined as a process to determine the level of quality). There is a mix of philosophies, uses, and descriptions within the bibliography. This annotated bibliography is not intended to be comprehensive, but it does include several different views of evaluation.

Books

Herman, J. L. (Ed.). (1987). *Program evaluation kit*. Thousand Oaks, CA: Sage Publications.

The *Program Evaluation Kit*, a series of nine independently written books, provides a practical guide to planning, conducting, and interpreting evaluations. It was written as a learning tool for novice evaluators and as a reference for experienced evaluators. Each book is written to be used independently, so each is described separately below.

1. Herman, J. L., Morris, L. L., & Fitzgibbon, C.T. (1987). *Evaluator's handbook*. Thousand Oaks, CA: Sage.
   This book, the first in the series, includes an overview of planning, designing, and managing evaluations.

2. Stecher, B., & Davis, W. A. (1987). *How to focus an evaluation*. Thousand Oaks, CA: Sage.
   This second volume in the series focuses on how to use the knowledge background of the evaluator and client as well as the nature of the program and its constraints to decide what will be evaluated.

3. Fitzgibbon, C. T., & Morris, L. L. (1987). *How to design a program evaluation*. Thousand Oaks, CA: Sage.
   This book uses examples from a wide variety of fields to illustrate how design options can be implemented in the evaluation process. It also includes a section on what to do when things do not progress as expected.

4. Patton, M. Q. (1987). *How to use qualitative methods in evaluation*. Thousand Oaks, CA: Sage.
   This book focuses on how to develop an evaluation strategy using qualitative methods. It illustrates the differences between approaches when using qualitative and quantitative methods and provides a step-by-step guide for planning qualitative evaluations.

5. King, J. A., Morris, L. L., & Fitzgibbon, C. T. (1987). *How to assess program implementation*. Thousand Oaks, CA: Sage.
   This book, which also fits in the assessment bibliography, discusses how assessment strategies can be built into evaluation programs. It focuses on the evaluator's role in observing how a program is implemented as part of the evaluation process.

6. Henerson, M. E., Morris, L. L., & Fitzgibbon, C. T. (1987). *How to measure attitudes*. Thousand Oaks, CA: Sage.
   This book outlines how to determine whether the affective and attitude objectives of a program have been met. Some of the commonly used measures are described, and a list of available measuring instruments is provided. It also offers instructions for constructing evaluation tools to measure these types of objectives.

7. Morris, L. L., Fitzgibbon, C. T., & Lindheim, E. (1987). *How to measure performance and use tests*. Thousand Oaks, CA: Sage.
   This book, written for the evaluator, describes ways to select, create, and analyze collected results. It includes reviews of performance measures and explains how to determine which tools are appropriate for various evaluations, using examples from many different fields.

8. Fitzgibbon, C. T., & Morris, L. L. (1987). *How to analyze data*. Thousand Oaks, CA: Sage.
   This book, written for the evaluator, describes statistical techniques for data analysis. Examples are given to support each technique, and worksheets are provided with each technique. It also describes how to determine which technique is best for a constructed evaluation.

9. Morris, L. L., Fitzgibbon, C. T., & Freeman, M. E. (1987). *How to communicate evaluation findings*. Thousand Oaks, CA: Sage.
   This book describes what must be reported to clients and other stakeholders throughout the evaluation process. It includes worksheets for help preparing a report and practical tips on communicating effectively.

Miller, A. H., Imrie, B. W., & Cox, K. (1998). *Student assessment in higher education: A handbook for assessing performance*. London: Kogan Page.

This book, which uses the terms assessment and evaluation interchangeably to denote a process of judgment, is quite useful for its discussion of how evaluation can be used to determine the learning of the students. The book is organized into three parts: why evaluation systems are needed in higher education, the uses and challenges of evaluative tools, and how evaluative findings can be checked for validity and objectivity.

Sanders, J.R. (1994). *Program evaluation standards: How to assess evaluations of educational programs*. (2nd ed.). Thousand Oaks, CA: Sage.

This book, compiled by the Joint Committee on Standards for Educational Evaluation, provides guidance for evaluating educational and training programs, projects, and other materials. The Joint Committee on Standards for Educational Evaluation developed a list of thirty standards to use in program evaluation. These standards are organized into four groups—utility, feasibility, propriety, and accuracy. For each standard, the book provides an overview of intent, guidelines for application, common errors, and examples of use in educational settings. The book also contains a table of standards for various types of program evaluation. Although the focus of this book is on program evaluation, it is quite thorough in its examples in describing how to set up an evaluative process and how to collect unbiased, reliable information.

Scriven, M. (1991). *Evaluation thesaurus*. (4th ed.). Thousand Oaks, CA: Sage.

Despite the implications drawn from the name of the book, this book is a series of essays describing the place for and uses of evaluation in the academic world. This is the first overview across all academic disciplines of evaluation. It helps those new to the evaluation process with the major concepts, acronyms, processes, and techniques in various fields. It goes into great detail about some of the issues of reliable evaluation, such as subjectivity and multiple measures.

Stufflebeam, D. L. (2001). *Evaluation models: New directions for evaluation, no. 89*. San Francisco: Jossey-Bass.

Through examples, this book identifies, analyzes, and judges 22 evaluation approaches that could be used for almost all program evaluation efforts. The descriptions of each approach, including purpose and methods, are very useful. Like Sanders above, this book rates evaluation methods on utility, feasibility, propriety, and accuracy.

Walvoord, B. E., Angelo, T. A., & Anderson, V. J. (1998*). Effective grading: A tool for learning and assessment*. San Francisco: Jossey-Bass.

This book looks specifically at grading as a way to evaluate student learning effectively. It discusses how to link grades with course objectives that focus on student learning. Along with general information, it also includes specific information on how evaluation of students can be linked to assessment of curriculum and teaching. It focuses on aligning what is graded to what is stated as important through the learning objectives.

Worthen, B. R., Sanders, J. R., & Fitzpatrick, J. L. (1996). *Program evaluation: Alternative approaches and practical guidelines*. (2nd ed.). New York: Addison-Wesley.

This book illustrates a wide variety of approaches to evaluation while supporting the need to set criteria, be unbiased, and get reliable information. It stresses planning and informing the evaluatee of an evaluation before implementing it. It also discusses conducing evaluations ethically and professionally.

Web Site

The Evaluation Center, Western Michigan University. <http://www.wmich.edu/evalctr/>

This site has a wealth of information and links to many other useful sites. There is information on what evaluation is, when it should be used, how it can be used, and how to design methods to use evaluation.

The site is organized around five areas: the history and the mission of the Evaluation Center; Evaluation Center Projects; Evaluation Support Services, which includes templates and glossaries for evaluation processes as well as links; Publications, which includes extensive bibliographies and books for sale; and Affiliations, which has links to consortia and committees devoted to evaluation issues.

Section Six
Instructional Design

Modules in this section:

Instructional Systems Design Model, History and Application

by Temba C. Bassoppo-Moyo, Illinois State University

Faculty Development Series

Instructional Systems Design (ISD) is a systematic process of translating general principles of learning and instruction into plans for instructional materials and leadership of learning activities. The process involves creating detailed specifications for the development, implementation, evaluation, and maintenance of resources that facilitate learning. The process is intended to be iterative, initially culminating in developmental testing and/or expert review and frequently concluding with field testing and marketing of finished products. This module traces the evolution of ISD as a discipline and highlights best practices for program, course, and learning activity design.

The Historical Perspective of ISD

Instructional Systems Design dates back to classical philosophers such as Aristotle, Socrates and Plato. Early thinkers and classical philosophers contributed to our knowledge of learning theory through their development, implementation, and refinement of instructional strategies. Principles of questioning, argumentation, modeling, repeated practice, and timely feedback are still central to modern instruction.

One can trace the development of ISD in the past century through several different movements (Anglin 1971). In the early 1900's the behavioral approach to educational psychology dominated the field. Hull and Thorndike provided guidelines for using stimulus-response exercises as the basis for instructional materials. The advent of the Second World War witnessed the emergence of instructional techniques that were geared toward the rapid training of thousands of military and civilian personnel. These needs created a variety of teaching machines and mediated training modules. The 1950's witnessed the emergence of models for measuring behavioral outcomes inspired by Bloom's taxonomy. In the 1960's, Robert Gagne sought to differentiate instructional approaches used to promote psychomotor skills, verbal skills, reasoning skills, and attitudinal dispositions. While numerous other instructional design models were introduced in the 1970's and 1980's in conjunction with innovations in instructional technology, their proliferation confirms the notion that ISD consists of the five distinct iterative processes shown in Figure 1.

Needs Analysis

Generally the needs analysis component of the system design process serves to accomplish a number of goals. It establishes key long-term ingredients for the participants in the whole design process. It also sets a preamble to how the instructional environment will be established and establishes the requirements, measurable goals, timelines, and even potential roadblocks of what learners should expect in the whole instructional process. During this phase, the designer will analyze instructional goals, the instruction itself, and the context in which learning will take place.

Figure 1   **The Generic Instructional Design Model**

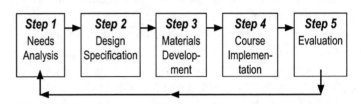

Goal Analysis: This initial step in the needs analysis phase is analogous to determining one's destination if given a map and the task of going to some specific destination. At this stage, one defines what the instructor wants his or her learners to know, and what students should be able to do when they have completed the instruction. Dick, Carey & Carey (2001) suggest that instructional goal statements may be derived from a combination of the following:

- list of goals
- description of long-term behaviors
- needs assessment and strategic plan
- practical experience in the subject matter
- someone who has delivered similar instruction

After identifying the instructional goal, it is imperative not only for the designer to determine who the learners are in terms of their characteristics, but what they will be able to do when they demonstrate knowledge, skills, abilities or attitudes that relate to the instructional goal. This should be translated into performance indicators that will serve as proof that the desired learning destination has been reached.

Instructional Analysis: Once the instructor/designer has a clear conception of what he or she wants the target audience to know and be able to do, they need to identify the specific skills, knowledge, abilities and attitudes necessary to achieve the learning goals. Again, using the road map analogy: "How will we get from our initial destination to the intermediate locations before we get to the final destination? What are the logistics involved in the whole trip." The results of this analysis will prescribe the subordinate skills and knowledge that must be created to insure that the desired learner performance is achieved.

Learner and Context Analysis: Typically in educational settings, teachers often assume they "know" all the characteristics that make up the profile of their student population at least well enough to design instruction without verifying whether their hunches are valid and reliable (Hirumi, 1998). In a traditional instructor-led, teacher-centered course, this may be the case, but for teachers attempting to apply more student-centered techniques, it is often necessary to gather data about each individual student to address individual student needs and interests. In business and industry, the instructional designer often does not know much about the target audience. Therefore, learner and context analysis is critical for defining entry-level and pre-requisite skills and knowledge, for identifying learning styles, for discerning learning motivation, and for revealing physical/social aspects of the site where learning will take place. Insights from learner and context analysis are valuable in selecting and customizing instructional strategies as well as assessment methods.

Design Specifications

Traditionally in instructional design, the design specifications phase spells out at least three very important ingredients of the whole process. These include the relationship between the final product and the target learners; the performance criteria by which successful learners will be assessed, and how that assessment will take place.

Performance Objectives: There is compelling evidence in the education literature that suggests students perform better if they have a clear understanding of what they are expected to learn (Bassoppo-Moyo, 1998). Taking the road map analogy one step further, fuzzy directions to the final destination will increase the probability of one getting lost. In instructional design, performance objectives take the place of a clearly labeled set of directions that point towards some predefined destination.

Writing performance objectives is therefore both an art and a science, and invariably it is the process that determines whether the goals or vision of the activity have been met. Since the 1960's, thousands of educators have been trained in the writing of what was termed "behavioral" objectives. However, as noted by Dick, Carey & Carey (2001), two major difficulties emerged from this approach.

First, without an overall systematic design process, instructors found it difficult to define objectives. With little or no training on analysis techniques (e.g., instructional, content, and task analyses), instructors often reverted to textbooks to identify topics for which to write objectives. As a result, most designers and instructors tended to focus on performance objectives that were more drill-and-practice oriented. Second, without an overall

systematic design process, instructors did not know what to do with the objectives once they were written. Instructors often listed objectives as a part of instruction, but did little else to align instruction or assessment with the objectives. Furthermore, educators have raised some objections to the use of behavioral objectives as the standard measures of performance. There now exists the argument that behavioral objectives: (a) reduce instruction to such small discrete components that learners loose the "trees from the forest"; (b) limit class discussions and student learning; and (c) can not be written for some areas such as humanities or even complex skills (Hirumi, 2002).

Performance Indicators: Performance indicators are the guideposts or milestones of what needs to be achieved. They are an important component of our road map to our instruction and in principle they should be easy to distinguish among indicators for inputs, outputs, intermediate outcomes, and end outcomes. In practice, these four concepts represent a continuum for which indicators can blend into one another and form a continuum or activities that are interlocking (Zook, 2002). A simplified description of the process of training nurses at community level illustrates the point. Community college nurses represent a final output from junior college and an input to colleges and universities (as well as an input to employers who hire them directly).

Materials Development

The materials development phase is an important link between the designer/instructor and the learners. It is at this stage that a designer is judged as to whether he or she is able to connect with the target audience. Through a creative approach, interesting and relevant materials, the instructional designer must articulate the instruction to the learner. The designer should be able to determine the course level (basic, intermediate or advanced) and determine the learning styles and characteristics of her target audience.

It is equally important that the instructor/designer create measurement instruments that are valid and reliable in order to gauge or assess the learning outcome(s). The instruments should reflect what the learners should be able to accomplish, through a performance driven criteria.

Hirumi (2002) and Oosterhof (2002) suggest that criterion-referenced (a.k.a. outcome-referenced) assessments be designed to measure an explicit set of learning outcomes. Traditionally, these tests have included multiple choice, true/false, fill-in-the-blank and short answer test items. These tests have become pervasive because they can be mass-produced, administered and scored with a certain degree of expediency. They also can provide a relatively precise outcome-based method for determining if learners have achieved specific learning goals. However, over the past decade, there has been a movement in education toward the use of performance, or portfolio assessments.

The method of portfolio assessment differs from traditional paper and pencil exams in two key respects. First, unlike traditional measures which tend to evaluate students' possession of knowledge, portfolio assessments judge students ability to apply knowledge in real life circumstances. Second, portfolio assessments are used as an integral part of learning. Such assessments tell students and their instructors how well they are developing their skills and knowledge in an incremental fashion. Thus, portfolio assessments serve as a diagnostic tool that provides students with profiles of their emerging skills to help them become increasingly independent learners. It is important to note that performance assessment techniques are not advocated as more appropriate than traditional, criterion-referenced assessments, but offered as an alternative to assessing student learning and performance. Generally, research suggests a multi-faceted approach to the assessment of learning outcomes in order to increase reliability and validity of the overall learner evaluation process. It is critical that the stated objectives correspond with the evaluation plan or strategies.

Course Implementation

Typically the implementation process seeks to determine the degree of success to which the goals of the instruction can be established. It is also at this stage that developmental testing and expert review often takes place during which the merit and worth of the instruction can be established. A wide range of strategies are generally employed during which the instruction is determined as to whether it is performing to its standards. Some of the questions answered here would relate to the final goals of the instruction. These would include establishing what is working now at this stage of the process, what could be improved, obstacles or challenges that exist, and what improvements can be made using a number of different perspectives? These would include applying different instructional strategies.

Instructional Strategy: Instruction is defined as a "deliberate arrangement of events to facilitate a learner's acquisition of some outcome-based performance objective" (Driscoll, 1994, p. 21). Research on training and instruction indicates that students who actively participate in the learning process are likely to perform better and remember more than students who remain passive (Hirumi, 2001). Based on a review of over 50 years of educational research, Angelo (1995) determined that being actively engaged in academic work is one of the

most highly correlated factors to student learning and achievement. The problem is that many current forms of instruction are based solely on prior experience, trial-and-error, opinions, fads and/or political agendas. They often fail to take into account what we know about learning and instruction. It is argued that instruction should be designed based on a combination of prior experience, learning theory and research Gagne's (1983). Events of instruction play a major role in developing instructional strategies by advocating a systematic approach to creating the learning environment.

Media Selection: Selecting media and materials is crucial in the whole instructional design process. There is an increasing variety of different media available to support the delivery of instruction. They include, but are not limited to a live instructor, print, audio-visual media, computer-based interactive systems, Internet and World Wide Web resources.

In selecting media, the question is not which is best technology, rather what combination of media are most appropriate considering learner and instructor characteristics, the instructional goals, environment, instructional strategy, and the availability of resources (Hirumi, 2001)? In addition, it is important not to use media simply because of its availability but rather each medium should serve a specific purpose.

Evaluation

Generally, evaluation links the lesson objectives to the actual outcomes. It is a way of determining the extent to which the instructional design process has been a success, and this phase can be accomplished in a number of ways.

Formative Evaluation: It is often the case that teachers and trainers frequently produce, distribute and implement the initial draft of their instruction. In such instances, many problems often occur and either the instructor is blamed for poor teaching or learners are blamed for insufficient studying when, in fact, the instructional materials were not well developed. In the 1960's, the problem of untested instructional materials was accentuated with the advent of large curriculum projects (Hirumi, 2001). At that time, "evaluation" was defined as the determination of instructional effectiveness as compared to other products and studies revealed relatively low student achievement with the new curriculum materials. Cronback and Scriven (as cited by Dick, Carey & Carey, 2001) concluded that designers must expand their concept of evaluation and thereby proposed that instructional developers conduct what is now known as formative evaluations or the collection of data during the development of instruction to improve its effectiveness.

Evaluation Plan & Instrument: Dick, Carey & Carey (2001), suggest that a summative evaluation be in place which has to be conducted in two phases namely: expert review and field trials. Expert judgments or reviews are designed to determine whether currently used instruction or other instructional programs or materials meet content, structure and organizational needs. Field evaluations should also be conducted to document the effectiveness of instruction with the target populations in its intended setting. Field trials can also consist of two components: outcome analysis and management analysis (Dick, Carey & Carey 2001).

Outcome analysis is conducted to determine the impact of instruction on learners, on the job (transfer), and on the organization (need resolution). Management analysis is conducted to determine instructor and supervisor attitudes related to learner performance, implementation feasibility and costs. An alternative view of summative evaluation, proposed by Kirkpatrick (1959a, 1959b, 1960a, 1960b cited in Dick, Carey and Carey, 2001), posits four levels of training evaluation: reactions, learning, behavior and impact. "Reactions" refer to learner attitudes toward instruction and "Learning" measures students' acquisition of specified skills and knowledge. These two levels combined are equivalent to what Dick & Carey refer to as, "impact on learners." "Behaviors" examine the extent to which skills and knowledge learned during training are applied in the performance context which is equivalent to what Dick, Carey & Carey 2001 refers to as, "impact on job." And "Impact" refers to the effect the behaviors have on the organization, which is equivalent to what Dick, Carey & Carey 2001 call, "impact on organization."

Peer Review: Hirumi (2001) observes that there exists significant differences between a novice and an expert in that an expert can analyze his or her own work, or the work of others, and accurately judge its quality while a novice cannot. Peer evaluation is designed to help the learners develop their expertise, as well as to expose them to alternative examples of how others apply the systematic design process. It also helps target learners improve their own work as well as create a good working rapport when working with others.

Concluding Thoughts

There are a number of historical assumptions underlying the process of instructional design. They all, however, illustrate that for those involved in developing instruction, there are distinct and added advantages in using the instructional design process. Generally these advantages include focusing on the learning outcomes or performance behaviors, and ensuring that instruction is efficient and effective. The ISD process also facilitates congruence among performance objectives, instructional activities, and assessment of learning outcomes.

References

Anglin, G. (Ed.). (1991). *Instructional technology: Past, present and future.* Englewood, CO: Libraries Unlimited.

Bassoppo-Moyo, T. C. (1998). The effects of preinstructional activities in enhancing learner recall and conceptual learning of prose materials for preservice teachers in Zimbabwe. *International Journal of Instructional Media, 24* (3), 1-14.

Dick, W., Carey, L. M., & Carey, J. O. (2001). *The systematic design of instruction* (5th ed.). Chapter 4—Identifying Subordinate Skills and Entry Behaviors. p. 52-85. New York: Addison Wesley.

Hirumi, A. (2002). The design and sequencing of e-learning: A grounded approach. *International Journal on Elearning, 1* (1), 19-27.

Kevin, Z. (2002). *Instructional design for classroom teaching and learning.* Boston: Houghton-Mifflin.

Gagné, R. M., & Dick, W. (1983). Instructional psychology. *Annual Review of Psychology, 34,* 261-295.

Krathwohl, D. R. (1998). *Methods of educational and social science research: An integrated approach* (2nd ed.). New York: Longman.

Oosterhof, A. (2002). *Classroom applications of educational measurement* (3rd ed.). Upper Saddle River, N.J: Prentice Hall.

Reigeluth, C. M., (1999). What is instructional-design theory, and how is it changing? In C. M. Reigeluth (ed.), *Instructional-design theories and models: A new paradigm of instructional theory, volume ii,* 425-459. Hillsdale, NJ: Lawrence Erlbaum Associates.

Reiser, R. A. (1987). Instructional technology: A history. In R. M. Gagné (ed.), *Instructional technology: foundations* (p. 11 - 40). Hillsdale, NJ: Lawrence Erlbaum Associates.

Seels, B., & Glasgow, Z. (1998). *Making instructional design decisions.* Columbus, OH: Merrill Publishing.

Learning Outcomes

by Steven Beyerlein, University of Idaho; Denny Davis, Washington State University; and Daniel Apple, Pacific Crest

Learner performance is more likely to improve if one is able to precisely define what one wants to achieve along with how this performance can be documented at the end of a learning activity. This module contrasts five different types of learning outcomes that are common in higher education—competencies, movement, accomplishments, experiences, and integrated performance. Each of these outcomes addresses a different aspect of social learning, is best suited to different educational methods, and requires collection of different evidence to demonstrate that the outcome has been achieved. A competency is a collection of knowledge, skills, and attitudes needed to perform a specific task effectively and efficiently. Movement is self-awareness of growth in a set of competencies over time. Accomplishments are significant work products or performances that transcend normal class requirements. Experiences are interactions, responsibilities, and shared memories that clarify one's position in relation to a community or discipline. Integrated performance is the synthesis of prior knowledge, skills, processes, and attitudes with current learning needs to address a difficult challenge within a strict time frame.

Need for Learning Outcomes

Adoption of a learner-centered approach to teaching requires a supportive environment and focused attention to what students should be able to do at the end of a learning experience (Fink, 2003). Good instruction begins with a statement of intentions or objectives. However, instructional success can only be measured by the level of behaviors that are elicited in response to well-defined situations at the conclusion of an instructional period (Mager, 1997). These can be formalized in measurable learning outcomes that can inform formative assessments, guide instructional methods, serve as the basis for course evaluation, and generate data needed for program accreditation.

The modern workplace demands a variety of cognitive, social, and affective behaviors that need to become more and more sophisticated over time (SCANS, 1991). Over the last decade, accreditation organizations have responded by defining a much more comprehensive set of student learning outcomes that must be rigorously demonstrated for program accreditation (ABET, 2004). These learning outcomes are subjective as well as objective in nature and individual as well as collective in participation. Skill listings in the *Cognitive Domain* and *Social Domain*, levels of knowledge outlined in *Bloom's Taxonomy—Expanding its Meaning*, and knowledge types described in *Forms of Knowledge and Knowledge Tables* provide a rich set of data for constructing a broad spectrum of learning outcomes. By recognizing different types of learning outcomes, educators are better equipped to select instructional methods and to align assessment systems (Wiggins and McTighe, 1999). This module presents a framework for mapping different aspects of social learning to five different types of learning outcomes.

Types of Learning Outcomes

Aspects of social learning can be mapped on two axes (Wenger, 1998). One axis is defined by what is learned (object) versus who is involved in the learning (subject); the other axis is defined by whether the learning has more of an individual or a collective orientation. When these axes are intersected, as shown in Figure 1, four different regions emerge that suggest distinctive educational activities and outcomes as follows.

Competency Outcomes focus on mastery of specific skills and knowledge under well-defined conditions. These are content-laden but depend on knowledge construction and deconstruction by individuals. Hence, competency development must be sensitive to needs associated with different learning styles. Movement Outcomes focus on awareness of issues involved in transferring knowledge to different situations over a period of time. These involve self-assessment about the learning process as well as awareness of personal development. Experience Outcomes are often shared among groups of people and they frequently serve to clarify goals, roles, and responsibilities within an organization. These outcomes involve considerable group processing and help build professional as well as personal connections within a community. Accomplishment Outcomes are significant additions to the knowledge base and capability of a wider audience. These can be innovations in knowledge, practice, or creative work, but they must have value beyond the classroom. Integrated Performance Outcomes stress how well expertise can be drawn together from all quadrants in response to a complex challenge. Integrated performance can be studied at the beginning of a course as a preassessment activity or at the end of a course as a summative evaluation.

All learning outcomes for a course share some common characteristics that are relevant to the discipline. They must be stated concisely to facilitate understanding and

Figure 1   **Types of Learning Outcomes
Mapped to Axes of Social Learning**

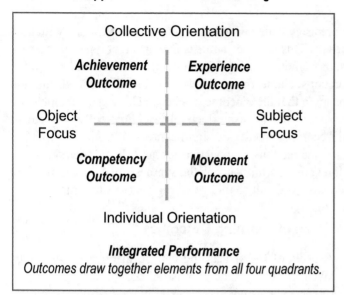

Identify Piaget's stages of childhood development and give an example of several behaviors that are typical for each stage. (Psychology)

Find all real positive roots of a second-order polynomial using the quadratic formula. (College Algebra)

Use a decision matrix to defend a design decision within the context of multiple alternatives, customer requirements, and resource limitations. (Capstone Project Course)

Within five minutes, produce a written assessment using the SII model format with meaningful analysis. (Faculty Development Workshop)

Movement Outcomes

Movement Outcomes focus on personal and professional development. They prescribe a desired direction and magnitude of growth that extend well beyond the present capabilities of all learners. Movement Outcomes require multiple samplings over time to document whether real growth has occurred. Several examples of Movement Outcomes are given below.

Describe and explain changes in the word choice, sentence structure, paragraph organization, and formatting of book reviews compiled over a semester. (English Composition)

Use the language of psychology to explain interactions between characters in a short story. (Psychology)

Increase speed and accuracy in converting simple word problems into symbolic equations. (College Algebra)

Manage project knowledge, resources, and the work environment leading toward timely and within-budget completion of a quality design product. (Capstone Project Course)

Strengthen use of the assessment process by elevating SII reports at least one level in the holistic rubric for Assessor Performance. (Faculty Development Workshop)

Experience Outcomes

Experience Outcomes capture changes in attitude and behavior as the result of a life-changing experience. They should reveal awareness and critical analysis of the causes and impacts of personal changes in the learner. Processing of the experience should produce new understanding that can be shared with others through purposeful reflection and self-assessment. Examples of experience outcomes are given below.

Enjoy accepting and giving feedback from peers as a means for improving writing assignments. (English Composition)

must capture major performance expectations associated with a learning experience. They must be specific enough to support measurement and be achievable within the time frame available considering the developmental level of the learners. They should be aligned with long-term behaviors expected within a program and be motivating to learners so that they take responsibility for specific actions that are required. Finally, learning outcomes are most compelling if they are defined within a specific application or context.

Each of the five learning outcomes can be distinguished by (a) the type of performance involved, (b) the conditions under which these performances are interpreted, and (c) the challenges associated with measurement of the performance. Table 1 contrasts the five types of learning outcomes with respect to these three areas. More detailed discussion about unique attributes of each type of learning outcome appears in subsequent sections of this module.

Competency Outcomes

Competency Outcomes are tasks that learners must perform at a prescribed level. These performance levels are often referenced to disciplinary standards and/or accreditation criteria. Competency Outcomes are snapshots of what learners can do at a specific point in time and hence they are relatively easy to measure. In writing these outcomes special attention should be given to exactly what levels of knowledge is expected so that these outcomes reach to the appropriate level in Bloom's Taxonomy. Examples of competency outcomes are given below.

Rewrite a paragraph using active rather than passive voice. (English Composition)

Table 1

Comparison of Outcome Types

	Competency	Movement	Experience	Accomplishment	Integrated Performance
Targeted Performance	disciplinary knowledge and methods	transferable skills and processes	attitudes, values and meaningful context	work product that can be placed on a resume	knowledge, skills, and processes used expertly in a very meaningful context
Situational Issues	disciplinary standard	unbounded continuum	critical analysis; meaningful; life changing	archival contribution	real-world application
Measurement Issues	snapshot of performance	trend sampling	reflective thinking	third party evaluation of product quality	focused challenge

Outline strategies you intend to follow to perform more effectively in cooperative learning activities. (Psychology)

Serve as a tutor once a week throughout the semester at math laboratory within local high school. (College Algebra)

Gain appreciation of professional practice through interactions with clients, mentors, team members, and support staff in a yearlong product development project, documenting issues and discoveries in a reflective journal that illustrates formation of a personal design philosophy. (Capstone Project Course)

Value the assessment mindset as a tool for challenging and supporting student achievement. (Faculty Development Workshop)

Accomplishment Outcomes

Accomplishment Outcomes are exemplified by a major work product or creative performance that is significant within a field. They usually represent a clear endpoint and can often be archived for future reference or study. Outside affirmation by other faculty, alumni, or practitioners in a field can be used to eliminate instructor bias in measuring Accomplishment Outcomes. Often these outcomes can be evaluated and celebrated at the same time in a public display. Examples of Accomplishment Outcomes are given below.

Write a poem that can be published in the campus literary magazine. (English Composition)

Create and present a poster describing benefits of a campus support group to which you belong for use in Freshman Orientation. (Psychology)

Place in the top 10% at a Student Math League competition. (College Algebra)

Produce a design product that impresses a client, your peers, and the general public at a year-end design show (winning a competition) while meeting key functional performance specifications, and it is used by your client. (Capstone Project Course)

Outline an assessment system for a course that eliminates three evaluation exercises and replaces them with assessment practices that promote desired student learning outcomes and that can be used as part of accreditation. (Faculty Development Workshop)

Integrated Performance Outcomes

Integrated Performance Outcomes draw on previous types of learning from multiple sources. They require extension and transfer of knowledge, skills, and perspectives in a professional environment. This type of outcome must be accompanied by a challenging and compelling situation that ensures peak performance on the part of the learner in a relatively short period of time. Integrated Performance Outcomes are especially efficient and effective in answering questions connected with program assessment. Examples of Integrated Performance Outcomes are given below.

Write a 500-word persuasive essay about a recent news item that you felt was shallow or one-sided. (English Composition)

For an assigned topic in the syllabus give a two-minute presentation of your knowledge about this to the entire class. (Psychology)

Use mathematical skills developed in this course to formulate, analyze, and report quantitative results related to a common work assignment. (College Algebra)

Table 2   **Research Questions, Learning Activities, and Assessment Tools for Learning Outcomes**

	Competency	Movement	Experience	Accomplishment	Integrated Performance
Classroom research question	What can the learner do at what level in a specific situation?	What does increased performance look like?	How has this shared experience changed the learner?	How well does student work compare with work products of practitioners in the field?	How prepared are students to respond to a real-world challenge?
Common learning activity	guided-discovery; active learning	study of processes; use of tools	team building; contests	project work	role playing; problem solving
Common assessment tool	exams with scoresheets	self-growth papers	personal interviews; focus groups	judging work products	panel of mentors or colleagues

Display professionalism in forming client relationships, assuming team responsibilities, achieving consensus, fulfilling commitments, applying prior knowledge, and conducting self-directed learning. (Capstone Project Course)

Plan and facilitate a team-based exercise that will generate insights about information processing, critical thinking, problem solving, communication, teamwork, assessment, and personal development from the perspective of facilitators, participants, and peer coaches. (Faculty Development Workshop)

Using Learning Outcomes

Learning Outcomes for a course should be small in number but consistent with the long-term behaviors supported by the course. Outcome types should be selected based on the behavior, situation, and performance level desired as suggested by Table 1. Regardless of type, learning outcomes should be relevant, concise, measurable, achievable, motivating, aligned with long-term objectives, and framed in a meaningful context. Each type of outcome answers different classroom research questions, is supported by different types of learning activities, and is aligned with different assessment tools as shown in Table 2.

Concluding Thoughts

Strong performers take a keen interest in increasing the quality of their outcomes and desire feedback on how to improve in the areas that they feel are important. Reminding yourself and your students about the major areas for content mastery and personal growth in your course is a great way to start a semester and to monitor progress toward this goal as the semester unfolds. By matching the most appropriate type of learning outcome to the desired area for performance improvement, both learners and teachers will better visualize performance expectations in the immediate course and future courses. If most of your course outcomes are of one type, tend to fall under the same level of knowledge, and are disconnected from follow-on courses, you might strive to expand their diversity and depth to better meet the program expectations for your course.

References

Dick, W., Carey, L., & Carey, J. (2000). *The systematic design of instruction* (5th ed.). Boston: Pearson Allyn and Bacon.

Engineering Accreditation Commission. (2004). *Engineering Criteria*. Baltimore, MD: Accreditation Board for Engineering and Technology.

Fink, L. D. (2003). *Creating significant learning experiences in college classrooms*. San Francisco: Jossey-Bass.

Mager, R. (1997). *Preparing instructional objectives: A critical tool in the development of effective instruction* (3rd ed.). Atlanta, GA: Center for Effective Performance.

Secretary's Commission on Achieving Necessary Skills (SCANS). (1991). *What work requires of schools: A SCANS report for America 2000*. Washington, DC: Department of Labor.

Wenger, E. (1998). *Communities of practice: Learning, meaning, and identity*. Cambridge, UK: Cambridge University Press.

Wiggins, G., & McTighe, J. (1999). *Understanding by design*. Englewood Cliffs, NJ: Prentice-Hall.

Pacific Crest

Faculty Development Series

Methodology for Program Design

by Chris Davis, Baker College

This module introduces a method for instructional design at the program level, the highest level of instructional design that in turn provides the framework for course and activity design. Program instructional design begins with the identification of program outcomes derived from the professional behaviors related to the program and the intentions of the program. These program outcomes drive the design, development, and sequencing of both courses and extracurricular learning experiences that provide the basis for the overall learning experience. The program outcomes also provide the basis for the development of program assessment and evaluation systems that insure continuous improvement of the program and its components.

Systematic Design of Instruction and Instructional Design for Process Education

Virtually all models of instructional design follow the ADDIE model (analysis, design, development, improvement, and evaluation) (Kruse and Keil, 2000 and Reiser, 2001).

Consistent with the instructional design model, the Methodology for Program Design (see Table 1) presents the steps taken for an effective program design process. A discussion of the sections and subsequent steps of the methodology follows.

Analysis: Learning-outcome driven instructional design

The analysis stage of instructional design addresses what the learner is to learn. The results of analysis should drive the rest of the instructional design. All content, methodologies, activities, sequencing, and assessment of the learning experience should be traceable to the results of the analysis. Analysis must be performed within the context of what the learner should be expected to already know and what the learner will need to know in the future. For programs, this means that the analysis must address what is covered in previous courses and what will be addressed in future courses to avoid either duplication or gaps in knowledge or practice. In addition, analysis needs to address what program prerequisite knowledge and abilities are required prior to starting the program. Analysis for a program must also examine how it fits within the context of the larger institution. Thus, the behaviors, objectives, and learning outcomes of the program should align with the behaviors, objectives, and learning outcomes of the institution and its discipline. Steps in the analysis stage include:

Step 1 — Identify professional behaviors.

The professional behaviors of a program are the behaviors that a graduate should practice throughout their life and professional career and includes working knowledge, performance skills, and attitudes. The professional behaviors of the program will be reflected in the long-term behaviors of the courses and other experiences of the program. The performance expectations of stakeholders for the program graduates are an important source of the required professional behaviors.

Table 1   ***Methodology for Program Design***

Analysis: Learning-outcome driven instructional design

Step 1 — Identify professional behaviors.

Step 2 — Identify program intentions.

Step 3 — Construct measurable learning outcomes.

Step 4 — Construct a meta-knowledge table.

Design: Activities and knowledge to support learning outcomes

Step 5 — Choose themes.

Step 6 — Create the appropriate methodologies.

Step 7 — Identify a set of experiences.

Step 8 — Identify a set of specific learning skills for the program.

Development: Construction and selection

Step 9 — Identify experience preference types.

Step 10 — Match the experience types with the chosen experiences.

Step 11 — Choose the formal course and extracurricular experiences.

Step 12 — Allocate time across the themes.

Step 13 — Sequence the experiences across the program.

Step 14 — Create individual experience from a priority list.

Step 15 — Enhance experiences by using technology.

Step 16 — Have the experiences you create peer reviewed.

Step 17 — Produce key performance criteria.

Step 18 — Locate or build key performance measures.

Step 19 — Design a program assessment system.

Step 20 — Design a program evaluation system.

Step 21 — Design a program description and schedule.

Implementation: Facilitating learning

Evaluation & assessment: Instruction that learns from itself

Step 2 — Identify program intentions.

Program intentions describe the intended results of the program. These can take the form of key learning objectives that identify the essential content of the program, including significant performance skills and attitudes. Other examples of program intentions include behaviors such as increased graduation rates and job placement that are not directly learning objectives for the learners.

Step 3 — Construct measurable program outcomes.

Program learning outcomes connect program intentions and professional behaviors. The program outcomes describe what knowledge and working expertise the student should have at the conclusion of the program. Measurable program learning outcomes are critical for the development of assessment and evaluation systems. These are the indicators that professional behaviors are being developed since the observation of long-term behaviors will generally be beyond the scope of a program of study. Program learning outcomes can be determined with both direct measures of student performance (i.e., student portfolios and capstone projects) and indirect measures (i.e., job placement data and alumni surveys).

Step 4 — Construct a meta-knowledge table.

Based on the program outcomes, a meta-knowledge table should be created for the program. The meta-knowledge table describes the most important concepts, processes, tools, contexts, and "ways of being" that the student must know to achieve the program learning outcomes. The meta-knowledge table should also show the sequential dependency between these different components.

Design: Activities and knowledge to support learning outcomes

The design process takes the learning outcomes determined in analysis and develops a plan for how the learner will achieve these learning outcomes. The design stage emphasizes creativity and generative processes for what the instruction will look like in contrast to the decisions embedded in the development stage that follows. Steps in design stage of instructional design include:

Step 5 — Choose themes.

The themes of a program focus on specific processes, tools, or ways of being to support the development of professional behaviors. The themes provide a continuous infrastructure through the program connecting multiple courses and course learning outcomes to help improve performance in these areas. A program will typically include 10-15 themes.

Step 6 — Create the appropriate methodologies.

Each key process that is to be included in a program must have a methodology identified or developed. Key processes are beyond the scope of a single course or sequence of courses. A methodology is an explicit model of how an expert practices that process that is essential for a novice student to learn how to practice the process. Key processes are introduced in a foundation course and integrated throughout the entire program both in formal courses and extracurricular activities.

Step 7 — Identify a set of experiences.

Experiences include both what happens formally in classes and what the student does informally outside of class through extracurricular activities. Each of the items in the meta-knowledge table must be supported by a learning experience appropriate for the type and level of knowledge of that item. At this step, the goal is to generate as many potential experiences as possible without fully developing the specifics of those experiences.

Step 8 — Identify a set of specific learning skills for the program.

In addition to the domain content of the program, the program should also incorporate key learning skills to focus on during the program. Learning skills come from four domains: cognitive, social, affective, and psychomotor. These skills support the learning outcomes of the program but are also transferable to other disciplines and environments. Program design should include the top 50 skills for graduates in the discipline. These might include skills such as risk taking, articulating an idea, and making connections.

Development: Construction and selection

The design and development phases are tightly intertwined, highly iterative, and often indistinguishable. At a certain stage in an instructional design project, the activities of the designers will shift away from brainstorming and generating possibilities to making selections and constructing materials and activities. Steps in development stage include:

Step 9 — Identify experience preference types.

Both student and instructor preferences for different types of experiences should be reviewed to assist in selecting what experiences should be incorporated into the program design. Types of learning experiences include the structure of courses (lecture, lab, seminar), integrated off-campus experiences such as study-abroad and internships, and extracurricular experiences.

Step 10 — Match the experience types with the chosen experiences.

The possible experiences identified earlier should be organized by the type of experience. No single type of experience should account for more than 25 percent of the total time in the program.

Step 11 — Choose the formal course and extracurricular experiences.

Items on the meta-knowledge table need to be mapped to either experiences that take place as part of a formal course or through a supporting extracurricular experience. In general, experiences that are the most critical and challenging for the student should be the focus of course work. Flexibility should be provided when possible and appropriate through electives and other opportunities for the student to tailor the program to his or her specific needs and interests.

Step 12 — Allocate time across the themes.

The time for each theme needs to be allocated to both formal courses and extracurricular experiences. The percentage of total student learning time should be allocated for each theme.

Step 13 — Sequence the experiences across the program.

The sequence of experiences should provide a progression across the program learning outcomes and the prerequisite knowledge needed to achieve those learning outcomes. In addition, the sequencing needs to provide a variety of experiences for the students.

Step 14 — Create individual experiences from a priority list.

The experiences that have been selected need to be developed and documented. At a minimum, the experience must include the "why" for the inclusion of the experience in the program as well as the components of the meta-knowledge table and themes that it addresses. The actual design of a program should follow the steps of the instructional design process for classes.

Step 15 — Enhance experiences by using technology.

The first role of technology is to insure that students develop the technical and information literacy skills required by the program. All disciplines require different skills with computers and other information processing tools. These skills need to be integrated into the experiences of the program.

The second role of technology in program design is in the area of distance and other forms of flexible delivery. Distance delivery can take many forms and can make a program accessible to a population of students that otherwise would not be able to participate due to schedule and/or geographic constraints. For maximum effectiveness, the implementation of technology should be approached systematically as part of the program design rather than on a piece meal, course-by-course basis.

Step 16 — Have the experiences you create peer reviewed.

Peer review of experiences increases the quality of the instructional design. Student review is also an opportunity for feedback.

Step 17 — Produce key performance criteria.

For the set of learning objectives and outcomes, performance criteria should be established that are comprehensive and integrative. The performance criteria describe the expectations for student performance at the end of the program and are used in the design of assessment and evaluation systems.

Step 18 — Locate or build key performance measures.

For each of the key performance criteria, identify or create instrument(s) to measure different levels of performance for each performance criterion (for assessment and evaluation). The performance measures should also be used to assess student performance of the learning skills.

Step 19 — Design a program assessment system.

The program assessment system provides a mechanism for both the student and faculty member to track student performance in the course and identify opportunities for performance improvement. The assessment system should relate to the performance measures, and address how students can improve their performance. This step focuses on the design of the student assessment embedded within the program rather than the assessment/evaluation of the program itself which is a separate stage of instructional design. Portfolios and capstone experiences are tools for supporting program assessment.

Step 20 — Design a program evaluation system.

The program evaluation uses the performance measures and criteria, but unlike the program assessment system, the output of the evaluation system is a grade based on the student's performance relative to standard benchmarks. This step focuses on the design of the student evaluation embedded within the program rather than the assessment or evaluation of the program itself which is a separate stage of instructional design. Common forms of program evaluation include portfolios, dissertations, theses, comprehensive exams, certification/licensure exams, capstone courses, and student portfolios.

Step 21 — Design a program description and schedule.

The program description and schedule should capture the results of the other steps of the design process. It should include a description of the program and its outcomes, a listing of courses and other experiences, and a sample schedule to provide students with a road map to completion.

Implementation: Facilitating learning

Implementation takes the materials and experiences created during the design and development stages and puts them into practice with learners. Implementation can be considered the delivery versus the design of the instruction. Implementation is the end-result of the instructional design combined with the teaching and facilitation practices of the instructor. The Teaching and Facilitation Sections of the Guidebook contain information related to the implementation stage.

Evaluation and assessment: Instruction that learns from itself

Traditionally in instructional design, the evaluation piece involves a summative evaluation that reviews whether the instruction achieved the goals determined during analysis (Reiser, 2001). A more effective way to approach this phase is to shift from an evaluation model to an assessment model that reviews what aspects of the instruction did not work and how the instruction can be better the next time. Ultimately, effective assessment leads to instruction that learns, improves, and adjusts from itself. The assessment piece provides a feedback loop back into the previous stages of the process to improve the analysis, design, development, and implementation for continuous improvement of the instructional design. Additional information on program assessment can be found in Section Five.

Evaluation and assessment activities at this stage of instructional design are not the same as the assessment or evaluation of learner performance within the class. Evaluation and assessment of the program should examine whether or not learners achieved the established learning outcomes, but it should also look at other aspects of the entire program for opportunities to increase the effectiveness and quality of the learning experience. This stage should provide feedback into any and all of the previous steps with guidance on how to continuously improve the instructional design.

Concluding Thoughts

Program design provides the overall structure that guides lower levels of instructional design. The design of an entire program includes the identification of program outcomes that define the required course outcomes. The program design also specifies what formal, curricular, and informal extracurricular experiences will be included in the total learning experience. Finally, the program evaluation and assessment systems provide feedback on the effectiveness and quality of the entire program at achieving the program outcomes. The results from this assessment process can have an important impact on the ongoing design and implementation of courses and other

components of the program. In a similar fashion, courses include multiple learning activities (or learning objects) to address the specific set of learning outcomes for that course. Learning activities are the smallest unit of instructional design and target singular learning outcomes.

The instructional design process uses a structured approach that begins with an analysis that determines the program learning outcomes followed by a process of design and development of learning experiences to enable students to achieve those learning outcomes. Each of those learning experiences will have an associated set of course outcomes that support the larger program outcomes. The learning experiences include a variety of learning activities to support each outcome in the experience. This structured approach of instructional design fosters learning on purpose rather than learning by accident or chance. Without a clear road map for how learning is to occur, the learning event can not be repeated nor can it be reviewed and assessed for continuous improvement. Program design in particular is essential to create a holistic and integrated learning program that insures the student achieves the program outcomes in a systematic rather than haphazard or piecemeal fashion that can lead to knowledge gaps or confusion.

References

Bloom, B. S., Engelhart, M., Furst, E. J., Hill, W. H., & Krathwohl, D. R. (1956). *Taxonomy of educational objectives: The classification of educational goals. Handbook 1: Cognitive domain.* New York: David McKay.

Dick, W., Carey, L., & Carey, J. (2000). *The systematic design of instruction* (3rd ed.). Glenview, IL: Addison Wesley Publishing.

Gagne, R., Briggs, L., & Wager, W. (1992). *Principles of instructional design* (4th ed.). New York: Holt, Rinehart, and Winston.

Kruse, K., & Keil, J. (2000). *Technology-based training.* San Francisco: Jossey-Bass/Pfeiffer.

Mager, R. (1997). *Preparing instructional objectives: A critical tool in the development of effective instruction* (3rd ed.). Atlanta, GA: Center for Effective Performance.

Merrill, D. M. (1997). Instructional strategies that teach. *CBT Solutions*, November/December, 1-11.

Reiser, R. (2001). A history of instructional design and technology: Part II: A history of instructional design. *Educational Technology Research and Development, 49*(2), 57-67.

Methodology for Course Design

by Chris Davis, Baker College

This module addresses the broad perspective of the sequential steps of quality course design, the middle level of instructional design between the broad perspective of program design and the specific implementation of learning activity design. Program design includes the identification of long-term behaviors that are reflected in learning outcomes in the course design. The course learning outcomes in turn determine the content, methodologies, activities of the course and are assessed with measures that can be compared to performance criteria. While the design of specific learning activities is addressed in activity design, the sequencing of the learning activities within the course to support student learning and enable a course assessment and evaluation structure is a critical step in course design.

Systematic Design of Instruction and Instructional Design for Process Education

Virtually all models of instructional design follow the ADDIE Model (analysis, design, development, improvement, and evaluation) (Kruse and Keil, 2000 and Reiser, 2001).

Consistent with the instructional design model, the Methodology for Course Design (see Table 1) presents the steps taken for an effective course design process. A discussion of the sections and subsequent steps of the methodology follows.

Analysis: Learning-outcome driven instructional design

The analysis stage of instructional design address what the learner is to learn. The results of analysis should drive the rest of the instructional design. All content, methodologies, activities, sequencing, and assessment of the learning experience should be traceable to the results of the analysis. Analysis must be performed within the context of what the learner should be expected to already know and what the learner will need to know and be able to perform in the future. For courses, this means that the analysis must address what is covered in previous courses and what will be addressed in future courses to avoid either duplication or gaps in knowledge or application. Analysis for a course must also examine how it fits within the context of the larger program. The behaviors, objectives, and learning outcomes of the course should mesh with the behaviors, objectives, and learning outcomes of the program. Steps in the analysis stage include:

Step 1 — Construct long-term behaviors.

The long-term behaviors of a program are the behaviors that a graduate should practice throughout their life and professional career and includes working knowledge, performance skills, and attitudes. The long-term behaviors of a course should reflect selected long-term behaviors of the program.

Table 1   *Methodology for Course Design*

Analysis: Learning-outcome driven instructional design

Step 1 — Construct long-term behaviors.

Step 2 — Identify course intentions.

Step 3 — Construct measurable learning outcomes.

Step 4 — Construct a knowledge table.

Design: Activities and knowledge to support learning outcomes

Step 5 — Choose themes.

Step 6 — Create the appropriate methodologies.

Step 7 — Identify a set of activities.

Step 8 — Identify a set of specific learning skills for the course.

Development: Construction and selection

Step 9 — Identify activity preference types.

Step 10 — Match the activity types with the chosen activities.

Step 11 — Choose the in-class and out-of-class activities.

Step 12 — Allocate time across the themes.

Step 13 — Sequence the activities across the term.

Step 14 — Create individual activities from a priority list.

Step 15 — Enhance activities by using technology.

Step 16 — Have the activities you create peer reviewed.

Step 17 — Produce key performance criteria.

Step 18 — Locate or build key performance measures.

Step 19 — Design a course assessment system.

Step 20 — Design a course evaluation system.

Step 21 — Design a course syllabus.

Implementation: Facilitating learning

Evaluation & assessment: Instruction that learns from itself

Step 2 — Identify course intentions.

Course intentions describe the intended results of the class. These can take the form of key learning objectives that identify the essential content of the course, including significant learning processes and skills. Other examples of course intentions include goals or objectives such as increased student retention and success that are not directly learning objectives for the learners.

Step 3 — Construct measurable learning outcomes.

Learning outcomes connect course intentions and long-term behaviors. The learning outcomes describe what knowledge the student should have at the conclusion of the program or course. Measurable learning outcomes are critical for the development of assessment and evaluation systems and should address the application of the knowledge as well as retention of the knowledge itself. These are the indicators that long-term behaviors are being developed since the observation of long-term behaviors will generally be beyond the scope of a class.

Step 4 — Construct a knowledge table.

Based on the course learning outcomes, a knowledge table should be created for the course. The knowledge table describes the concepts, processes, tools, contexts, and "ways of being" that the student must know to achieve the course learning outcomes. *(See Forms of Knowledge and Knowledge Tables.)*

Design: Activities and knowledge to support learning outcomes

The design process takes the learning outcomes determined in analysis and develops a plan for how the learner will achieve these learning outcomes. The design stage emphasizes creativity and generative processes for what the instruction will look like in contrast to the decisions embedded in the development stage that follows. Steps in the design stage include:

Step 5 — Choose themes.

The themes for a course should focus on specific processes, tools, or ways of being to support the development of the long-term behaviors. The themes provide a continuous infrastructure through the course connecting multiple course activities and course learning outcomes to help improve performance in these areas.

Step 6 — Create the appropriate methodologies.

Each key process that is to be included in a course should have a methodology identified or developed. A methodology is an explicit model of how an expert practices a process. It is essential for a novice student to learn how to practice the process.

Step 7 — Identify a set of activities.

Activities include both what happens in the classroom and what the student does outside of class. Each of the items in the knowledge table must be supported by a learning activity appropriate for the type and level of knowledge of that item. At this step, the goal is to generate as many potential activities as possible without fully developing the specifics of those activities.

Step 8 — Identify a set of specific learning skills for the course.

In addition to the content of the course, the course should also incorporate learning skills to focus on during the course. Learning skills come from four domains: cognitive, social, affective, and psychomotor. While these skills support the learning outcomes of the course, they are also transferable to other courses and environments.

Development: Construction and selection

The design and development phases are tightly intertwined, highly iterative, and often indistinguishable. At a certain stage in an instructional design project, the activities of the designers will shift away from brainstorming and generating possibilities to making selections and constructing materials and activities. Steps in the instructional design stage include:

Step 9 — Identify activity preference types.

Both student and instructor preferences for different types of activity should be reviewed to assist in selecting what activity type should be incorporated into the course design.

Step 10 — Match the activity types with the chosen activities.

The possible activities identified earlier should be organized by the type of activity. No single type of activity should be used more than 25 percent of the activities in an individual course, with the goal of using at least ten different activity types.

Step 11 — Choose the in-class and out-of-class activities.

Items on the knowledge table that students have had success with in the past can be addressed outside of class. In-class activities should emphasize both activities that are the most critical and challenging for the student and also the steps in the learning process that students have the hardest time learning. Flexibility should be included into the time allocations of the course to allow for adjustments as the course is being delivered.

Step 12 — Allocate time across the themes.

The time for each theme needs to be allocated both inside and outside of class activities. The percentage of total student learning time should be allocated for each theme.

Step 13 — Sequence the activities across the term.

The sequence of activities should provide a progression across the course learning outcomes and the prerequisite knowledge needed to achieve those learning outcomes. In addition, the sequencing needs to provide activity variety for the students.

Step 14 — Create individual activities from a priority list.

The activities that have been selected need to be developed and documented. At a minimum, the activity must include the "why" for the inclusion of the activity in the course as well as the components of the knowledge map and themes that it addresses.

Step 15 — Enhance activities by using technology.

Activities should be reviewed for opportunities to enhance them with instructional technologies.

Step 16 — Have the activities you create peer reviewed.

Peer review of activities increases the quality of the activity design. Student review is also an opportunity for feedback on the activity.

Step 17 — Produce key performance criteria.

For the set of learning objectives and outcomes, performance criteria should be established that are comprehensive and integrative. The performance criteria describe the expectations for student performance at the end of the course and are used in the design of assessment and evaluation systems.

Step 18 — Locate or build key performance measures.

For each of the key performance criteria, identify or create instrument(s) to measure different levels of performance for each performance criterion for assessment and evaluation. The performance measures should also be used to assess student performance of the learning skills.

Step 19 — Design a course assessment system.

The course assessment system provides a mechanism for both the student and faculty member to track student performance in the course and identify opportunities for performance improvement. The assessment system should relate to the performance measures, and address how students can improve their performance. This step focuses on the design of the student assessment embedded within the class rather than the assessment/evaluation of the class itself which is a separate stage of instructional design.

Step 20 — Design a course evaluation system.

The course evaluation uses the performance measures and criteria, but unlike the course assessment system, the output of the evaluation system is a grade based on the student's performance relative to standard benchmarks. This step focuses on the design of the student evaluation embedded within the class rather than the assessment/evaluation of the class itself which is a later stage of instructional design.

Step 21 — Design a course syllabus.

The course syllabus should capture the results of the other steps of the design process and make a clear presentation to the student of the course design and expectations.

Implementation: Facilitating learning

Implementation takes the materials and activities created during the design and development stages and puts them into practice with learners. Implementation can be considered the delivery versus the design of the instruction. Implementation is the end-result of the instructional design combined with the teaching and facilitation practices of the instructor. The Teaching and Facilitation Sections of the Guidebook contain information related to this stage.

Evaluation and assessment: Instruction that learns from itself

Traditionally in instructional design, the evaluation piece involves a summative evaluation that reviews whether the instruction achieved the goals determined during analysis (Reiser, 2001). A more effective way to approach this phase is to shift from an evaluation model to an assessment model that reviews what aspects of the instruction worked, what aspects did not work, and how the instruction can be better the next time. Ultimately, effective assessment leads to instruction that learns, improves, and adjusts from itself. The assessment piece provides a feedback loop back into the previous stages of the process to improve the analysis, design, development, and implementation for continuous improvement of the instructional design. Additional information on course assessment and program assessment can be found in Section Five and Section Seven.

Assessment or evaluation of learner performance and activities at this stage of instructional design are not the same as the assessment or evaluation of learner performance within the class. Evaluation and assessment of the class should examine whether or not learners achieved the established learning outcomes. In addition, other aspects (of the entire class) should be looked at for opportunities to increase the effectiveness and quality of the learning experience. This stage should provide feedback into any and all of the previous steps with guidance on how to continuously improve the instructional design.

Concluding Thoughts

Instructional design process has significant differences at three levels: program design, course design, and activity design. At the heart of all three are learning outcomes and the means to assist students to achieve these outcomes, assessment of processes, and evaluation of achievement. Courses include multiple activities to address a set of learning outcomes derived from the long-term behaviors determined in the program design process. Learning activities (or learning objects) are the smallest unit of instructional design and target singular learning outcomes.

The instructional design process uses a structured approach that begins with an analysis to determine the course learning outcomes. This is followed by a process of design and development of instructional activities to enable students achieve those learning outcomes. The output of instructional design is learning on purpose rather than learning by accident or chance. Without a clear road map for how learning is to occur, the learning event can not be repeated nor can it be reviewed and assessed for continuous improvement.

References

Apple, D., & Krumsieg, K. (2001). *Curriculum design handbook*. Lisle, IL: Pacific Crest.

Bloom, B. S., Engelhart, M. D., Furst, E. J., Hill, W. H., & Krathwohl, D. R. (1956). *Taxonomy of educational objectives: The classification of educational goals. Handbook 1: Cognitive domain.* New York: David McKay.

Dick, W., Carey, L., & Carey, J. (2000). *The systematic design of instruction* (3rd ed.). Glenview, IL: Addison Wesley Publishing.

Gagne, R., Briggs, L., & Wager, W. (1992). *Principles of instructional design* (4th ed.). New York: Holt, Rinehart, and Winston.

Kruse, K., & Keil, J. (2000). *Technology-based training: The art and science of design, development, and delivery.* San Francisco: Jossey-Bass/Pfeiffer.

Mager, R. (1997). *Preparing instructional objectives: A critical tool in the development of effective instruction* (3rd ed.). Atlanta, GA: Center for Effective Performance.

Merrill, D. M. (1997). Instructional strategies that teach. *CBT Solutions*, November/December, 1-11.

Reiser, R. (2001). A history of instructional design and technology: Part II: A history of instructional design. *Educational Technology Research and Development, 49* (2), 57-67.

Annotated Bibliography — Instructional Design

by Chris Davis, Baker College

Instructional design involves the determination of the content, methodologies, activities, sequencing, and assessment of learning. The instructional design process follows a recursive structure of analysis of learning outcomes, design and development of learning events, implementation, and assessment. The design process is driven by learning outcomes derived from long-term behaviors. These behaviors are assessed with measures that can be compared to performance criteria. This structure operates at programs, courses, and activity levels. This annotated bibliography provides a starting point to resources on instructional design, emphasizing program and course design.

Books

Diamond, R. M. (1997). *Designing and assessing courses and curricula: A practical guide.* San Francisco: Jossey-Bass.

This text provides a systematic, learner-centered approach to instructional design. While most books focus on course design, Diamond also addresses designing an entire program of study and how individual courses fit within this framework.

Dick, W., Carey, L., & Carey, J. (2000). *The systematic design of instruction* (5th ed.). Boston: Pearson, Allyn, and Bacon.

This book is considered the best single text on instructional design. A common textbook for graduate courses, it provides an overview and instructions for the classical instructional design process. This book is a great starting point for understanding instructional design.

Fink, L. D. (2003). *Creating significant learning experiences: An integrated approach to designing college courses.* San Francisco: Jossey-Bass.

Fink proposes a shift from teacher-centered to learner-centered learning environments to create significant learning experiences. This book provides a blueprint for both faculty and administrators about how to make that shift. As with other approaches, the process includes determining the learning goals, developing an assessment process to verify that the student has met those goals, and designing learning activities. Fink's approach is integrated and practical.

Gagne, R., Briggs, L., & Wager, W. (1992). *Principles of instructional design* (4th ed.). New York: Holt, Rinehart, and Winston.

This text serves as the foundation for all of the others in the area of instructional design. The concepts and ideas presented are still pertinent for instructional designers and also provide an understanding for the principles developed in more recent approaches to the instructional design process.

Mager, R. (1997). *Preparing instructional objectives: A critical tool in the development of effective instruction* (3rd ed.). Atlanta: Center for Effective Performance.

Mager pioneered the writing of learning outcomes in the 1960's, and his book is still the classic for this critical aspect of instructional design. All instructional design models start with learning outcomes, and this is the best book to address the development of learning outcomes specifically.

Reigeluth, C. M., ed. (1999). *Instructional-design theories and models: Vol. 2. A new paradigm of instructional theory.* Hillsdale, NJ: Lawrence Erlbaum.

This volume of essays covers the state of the art in instructional design theory. Articles from the major thinkers represent divergent theoretical perspectives on instructional design. While the text is theoretical, it still maintains a practical focus on application. The previous volume, published in 1987, provides the thinking of the 1970's and 1980's. This volume updates and expands the earlier work.

Wiggins, G., & McTighe, J. (1999). *Understanding by design.* Englewood Cliffs, NJ: Prentice-Hall.

Wiggins and McTighe label their approach to instructional design a "backward" design methodology because they begin design by identifying the desired results of the learning process. In practice, this follows the same general structure of the classic ADDIE instructional design approach. This book does provide excellent practical methods for analyzing the learning through the use of essential questions and for sequencing assessment and learning activities. A companion workbook is available.

Articles

Reiser, R. (2001). A history of instructional design and technology: Part II: A history of instructional design. *Educational Technology Research and Development, 49 (2)*, 57-67.

This short article provides an excellent historical review of instructional design theories and theorists. The article introduces the topology of the field from a historical perspective. Part I of the article focuses on instructional technology and is not required pre-reading for Part II.

Van Merriënboer, J. J. G., Clark, R. E., & De Croock, M. B. M. (2002). Blueprints for complex learning: The 4C/ID-model. *Educational Technology, Research and Development, 50 (2)*, 39-64.

The 4C/ID-model (four component instructional design) provides a structure for instructional design based on task-specific skills: learning tasks, supportive information, just-in-time (JIT) information, and part-practice. The model provides a framework for integrating these components and associated learning activities to support instructional design for learning complex tasks. The model is used frequently in the design of computer-based training.

Web Sites

Self Study Guide in Instructional Design. <http://www.id2.usu.edu/MDavidMerrill/IDREAD.PDF>

M. David Merrill is an influential teacher and leader in the instructional design field. This annotated bibliography provides a structured introduction and tour of instructional design. By following Merrill's advice in the guide, readers can develop a very thorough understanding of instructional design processes and approaches, especially instructional technology and computer-mediated learning.

Survey of Instructional Development Models. ERIC Digest. <http://www.ericfacility.net/ericdigests/ed411778.html>

This resource summarizes instructional design models from 1997. The article includes a taxonomy of models with references to key examples of each approach to instructional design. This is a great starting point for investigating approaches to instructional design.

Instructional Design and Learning Theories. <http://www.usask.ca/education/coursework/802papers/mergel/brenda.htm>

Brenda Mergel, University of Saskatchewan Educational Communications and Technology, provides an overview of the learning theories of behaviorism, cognitivism, and constructivism and their relationship to instructional design. The paper provides a very accessible introductory overview of these theories. The bibliography also contains links to additional resources.

Tips for Rapid Instructional Design. <http://www.thiagi.com/rid.html>

Sivasailam "Thiagi" Thiagarajan is a leading writer and instructional designer, especially in instructional games and activities. The resources from this page are tips for rapid approaches to instructional design. Traditional instructional design techniques require a great deal of analysis and development. Thiagi provides a model for how to develop a training session in seven days and produce a training video in one day. An essential part of his strategies is the use of templates for training and instruction. While these models are not ideal for rigorous instructional design, they do offer a methodology that might provide some structure in a crunch.

Problem-Based Learning. <http://chemeng.mcmaster.ca/pbl/pbl.htm>

This page provides a general overview of problem-based learning as a model for instructional design. The page includes links to two full-length books in electronic format: *Problem-based Learning: Helping your students gain the most from PBL* and *Problem-based Learning: resources to gain the most from PBL*. Both texts are free downloads written by Don Woods, McMaster University Chemical Engineering Department. Woods provides an alternative approach to instructional design that positions the question (problem to be solved) prior to the learning. These two texts provide a detailed explanation of this concept in the design of courses and programs, including design and implementation issues.

Organization

American Society for Training and Development (ASTD). <http://www.astd.org>
The leading organization for trainers and instructional designers in the United States. In addition to the national organization, ASTD has many local chapters around the country. ASTD has primarily a business focus, but the resources and networks are very valuable to professionals in the educational setting as well.

Section Seven
Program Assessment

Modules in this section:

Methodology for Designing a Program Assessment System

by William Collins, Stony Brook University and Daniel Apple, Pacific Crest

This module provides an overview of the methodology for designing a Program Assessment System (PAS). It introduces how to use the methodology. It should be read by anyone planning to design a program assessment system. Before beginning the design of a PAS, it is very useful to examine all of the steps in the design methodology to gain an understanding of the entire design process. In addition to presenting the complete methodology, critical steps faculty and administrators find particularly challenging are identified and briefly discussed.

Designing a Quality Program Assessment System

The methodology for designing a program assessment system is given in Table 1 found on the next page. While the steps of the methodology are listed in a sequential fashion, in most cases it is necessary to revisit and update previous steps while working through the methodology. The purpose of the steps can be broken down into five stages:

- specifying and defining the program (steps 1-6),
- establishing program quality (steps 7 and 8),
- designing annual program assessment (steps 9-11),
- constricting a table of measures (steps 12-15), and
- documenting program quality (steps 16-20).

Each of these stages is discussed.

Stage 1
Specifying and Defining the Program

As a program continues to evolve, it is important to step back and truly understand what the program is about. Stage 1 of the methodology focuses on the key aspects of the program defining and specifying components including the essence, goals, limitations, assets and important processes.

A significant benefit of designing and implementing a program assessment system is that it gives the stakeholders of the program the opportunity to clarify the identity of the program clearly and publicly. Through this action the stakeholders both claim ownership of the program and limit others from imposing an identity on the program. This benefit is realized through the straightforward, yet challenging act of stating the essence of the program (step 1). The essence statement should be a one-sentence description of the program at the present time in terms of the processes used and the products produced. Then building on the essence statement, identify the program stakeholders (step 2) and define the scope of the program (step 3). A key component of the

program specification is the identification of the current and future goals of the program (step 4). With a clear understanding of the goals, identifying the top products or assets of the program (step 5) and defining the processes to be used to accomplish the goals (step 6) is relatively straightforward.

Stage 2
Establishing Program Quality

The primary goal of a PAS is to enhance the quality of the program. In order to measure the quality of any program it is important to state performance criteria for that program (step 7). A strong criterion statement is stated clearly and concisely and supports one or more of the desired qualities of the program while suggesting at least one context for measurement. The objective is to identify 3-8 areas of the program that account for most of the quality of the program. The performance criteria will serve as the basis of the program assessment system by providing the framework for identifying specific attributes to be measured.

Writing performance criteria is one of the most challenging aspects of the PAS design process. In particular, many individuals have trouble seeing the connection between a quality, the meaning (or analysis) of that quality and how to express the meaning in the form of a written performance criterion. In addition, there is a common tendency to begin determining performance standards rather than focusing on identifying areas of quality in the program. It is important to identify key characteristics that determine quality for the products and processes. Using this list of characteristics, critical areas for measurement are identified and prioritized. Then the main areas of quality are clarified as statements (performance criteria) along with measurable attributes for each criterion (step 8). To facilitate writing quality performance criteria a detailed methodology has been developed *(see **Writing Clear Performance Criteria for a Program**)*.

Note, writing the performance criteria for a program parallels the same process of writing the performance criteria for a course or a learning activity.

Table 1   ***Methodology for Designing a Program Assessment System***

Specifying and Defining the Program

Step 1   Write a one-sentence description which captures the essence of the current program.

Step 2   Identify all program stakeholders and their interests.

Step 3   Define the appropriate scope (boundaries) of the program; what it is and what it is not.

Step 4   Identify the top five current goals and five future goals for the program; use a 3-5 year time frame.

Step 5   Identify the top five products or assets of the current and future program.

Step 6   Provide a description of key processes, structures and systems associated with the program which will help accomplish the current and future goals from step 4.

Establishing Program Quality

Step 7   Write clear performance criteria that account for most of the quality of the program.

Methodology for writing performance criteria:

1. Brainstorm a list of characteristics/qualities (and values) which determine program quality.

2. Check with other programs/stakeholders to determine if any key characteristics are missing.

3. Rank the top ten qualities for the future design of the program.

4. Select the critical areas for measuring; prioritize to just a few (7-10), reducing out highly related qualities.

5. For each quality, identify a set of 3-5 important aspects.

6. Write statements illustrating the performance expectation that produce these qualities by describing the important aspects of the performance.

Step 8   Identify up to three attributes (measurable characteristics) for each criterion.

Annual Program Assessment

Step 9   Self-assess the program for the previous academic year.

Step 10   All stakeholders should provide feedback (strengths, areas for improvement, and insights) about the performance program.

Step 11   Produce an annual assessment report.

Constructing Table of Measures

Step 12   Create the structure for a table of measures (see Table 2).
          Fill in the first two columns (criteria and attributes) with information from steps 7 and 8.

Step 13   Prioritize the attributes to the most significant through appropriately weight each attribute.

Step 14   Identify means for collecting data.

Step 15   Identify a key instrument associated with each chosen attribute to measure the performance reflected in the data collected.

Documenting Program Quality

Step 16   Determine current benchmarks and future targets for each attribute to document annual performance.

Step 17   Assign accountability (to an individual) for each attribute to assure targets for performance are met.

Step 18   Create an index for measuring overall success.

Step 19   Obtain stakeholder buy-in of the program assessment system through their assessment of the system.

Step 20   Annually assess the program assessment system.

Stage 3
Annual Program Assessment

An important aspect is to shift from thinking about doing assessment (planning) to implementing an assessment system. This is not an all-or-nothing process, and it is not necessary to wait until the PAS design process is completed before initiating assessment. Once the performance criteria have been identified, a pragmatic approach to implementation is to design an annual assessment report around the performance criteria. Begin by assessing the program for the previous academic year (step 9). The SII Method *(see **SII Method for Assessment Reporting**)* provides a useful format for this self-assessment. At this point in the process, it is important to include all of the stakeholders in the program assessment process (step 10). Complete the assessment by generating an annual assessment report (step 11).

Once you apply the performance criteria to the performance of the program over the previous year, the clarity of how to progress with the next step (designing measures) is enhanced dramatically. Further, the annual assessment report will serve as a model for annual reports generated in the future.

Stage 4
Table of Measures

The heart of the mechanism for measuring quality is the "Table of Measures" (see Table 2) that is a template for completing the PAS design process. It focuses on what really matters in the program, the measurable characteristics (or attributes) that align with the performance criteria (from steps 7, 8, and 12). An essential component of the process of building the Table of Measures is the act of prioritizing and weight the attributes to identify the most important while eliminating the non-essential ones (step 13).

For each attribute, determine if an instrument exists to measure performance (steps 13-15). Examples of instruments include: rubrics, alumni surveys, grants, publications, retention and graduation data, placement data, satisfaction surveys, and portfolios. If no instrument exists for a given attribute, then one must be built.

Stage 5
Documenting Program Quality

The final stage in the methodology focuses on the documentation of the program quality through the tracking of the quality of the attributes. For each attribute, it is helpful to make comparisons with benchmarks of current performance as well as to targets established for future performance (step 16). In addition, to share and distribute the responsibility for meeting targeted performance levels, it is important to assign the accountability for each attribute to a specific program member (step 17) and establish criteria for measuring overall success (step 18).

All participants and stakeholders involved in the program should be given the opportunity to provide assessment feedback (strengths, areas for improvement, and insights) (step 19) before full implementation of the program assessment system. In addition to improving the quality of the program assessment system, this helps to build commitment and trust which is essential for successful implementation of the system.

Assessment is a vital component to methodologies. Assessment provides the feedback mechanism which allows for building upon strengths and taking action to make improvements. It is important not to overlook the need to assess the program assessment system itself. Thus, a complete assessment system involves using various forms of assessment (formative, summative, and real-time) on all aspects of the program and the program assessment system itself (step 20).

Concluding Thoughts

The benefits to a program that are derived from a well-designed and successfully implemented program assessment system significantly outweigh the time and energy invested in the design of the system. Nevertheless, the design process can be an intimidating impediment to establishing an assessment-based program. The methodology for designing a program assessment system provides a clear progression of steps to assist even a novice in this endeavor. The end result will be an efficient program assessment system focusing on the key attributes that determine quality performance.

Table 2

Table of Measures

Criterion	Attribute	Weight	Means	Instrument	Benchmark	Target	Accountability

Writing Clear Performance Criteria for a Program

by Marta Nibert, Rhodes State College

Faculty Development Series

In the process of creating a quality program assessment system, all stakeholders need to collaborate in the creation of clear, concise performance criteria that can be used to guide assessment of the program. This module offers a series of steps that stakeholder teams can follow to generate high quality performance criteria for a program. These steps involve brainstorming current and future program qualities, identifying qualities that will have the largest bearing on the future design of the program, and selecting critical areas for measurement. Key findings are ultimately distilled into a finite set of readable statements that express the essential nature of the program being assessed, along with key indicators of how its success will be measured. These statements about performance of a program are the performance criteria for the program.

Role of Stakeholders

Accrediting bodies expect programs to involve their constituents (students, faculty, administration, alumni, and industry supporters) in the establishment and maintenance of the program objectives (ABET, 2002). Beyond the accreditation visit, these statements can be used to share program intentions with other faculty, campus administrators, student applicants, and potential donors. These statements have greatest meaning when they are used to align administrative and instructional decisions with program intentions.

Before a program can be implemented, stakeholders need to come to consensus about what the program is attempting to achieve and how that achievement can be defined, accomplished, and measured in specific "performance" (things that are done). These well-articulated descriptions become the measuring sticks for program effectiveness. They provide essential reference points to which all participants can return, time and again throughout the review process, to check on the clarity of their thinking and to ensure consistency in analyzing a program.

Writing Clear Performance Criteria for a Program

The writing of performance criteria for a program parallels the process used to write performance criteria for a course or activity. What is important in any of these cases is determining which qualities or characteristics are absolutely essential to the program, course, or activity in question. The work of identifying these features enables team members to then define the performance criteria that will determine how those program qualities will be achieved. In other words, if a key quality of the program is "commercially talented artists," the performance criteria statement should spell out specifically how that program quality can become evident. The following methodology will help assessors identify, verify, clarify, prioritize, and analyze these qualities. These preliminary steps will then be used to develop statements of performance criteria that incorporate the most important ideals that have emerged from this collaborative thinking-sharing-writing process.

Determining Qualities to Select for a Program

Many designers of continuous quality improvement emphasize the need for team effort to fully understand and appreciate a program or system (Scholtes, 1993, Productivity-Quality Systems, 1992) and stress the importance of buy-in from all key players (Badiru & Ayeni, 1993). Deming advocates the need for the inclusion of all classes of stakeholders in all these steps (Deming, 1982) and emphasizes the need for the entire team to brainstorm all the "knowables." In so doing , they can create a comprehensive or profound system of knowledge about the program, though there will always be "unknowables" which create system variance (e.g., the next year's enrollments, budget, political developments). Still, writing key performance objectives effectively demands that participants begin by reflecting on what is most essential to their program, bringing to the endeavor as much information and insight as they can.

Methodology for Writing Performance Criteria

Step 1 — Review previous design work.

In performing a program assessment, you will be creating your own design document that captures your work as you progress. After writing a one-sentence statement that captures the "essence" of your program, you will identify its goals and processes, as well as its scope and shareholders. With these documents in hand and with the collaborative experience of producing them behind the team, the participants will be ready to proceed to the steps outlined in this module.

Step 2 — Brainstorm a list of current qualities.

Next, the team's task is to brainstorm a list of characteristics that account for significant aspects of program quality. These qualities appear across products, processes, and other components of the program. Overall quality results from a set of specific program "qualities"—i.e., those things that characterize the program in a positive sense. The team should consider those aspects that (1) make the

Table 1   **Methodology for Writing Performance Criteria**

1. Review your stated program's essence, goals, scope, processes, systems, assets, products, results, and history.

2. Brainstorm a list of your program's current qualities; characteristics and descriptors that reflect what the program is all about, especially representing quality.

3. Brainstorm a list of your program's future qualities; characteristics and descriptors that reflect what the program will be about, especially representing quality.

4. Determine if any key qualities are missing by visiting with stakeholders and researching comparable programs.

5. Rank the top ten integrated current and future qualities for the program.

6. Analyze these qualities to pull out redundancy and overlap by renaming or pulling out duplicates.

7. Select and rank the critical areas for measuring performance to just a few (6-8).

8. Analyze the qualities by finding three to five aspects of each quality that characterizes what that quality really represents.

9. Clarify what each of these quality areas looks like through writing a clear statement of performance, called the program's performance criteria.

program unique and give it an identity, (2) are critical to the program's success, (3) match characteristics found in other quality programs, and (4) are attributes that stakeholders find special. These descriptions can best be captured in the form of adjectives or adverbs connected with nouns (e.g., dedicated faculty, research-based, empowering).

Additionally, assessors should explore stakeholders' perspectives, program resources, graduates, and program-related events to determine which features are most valuable to the program. It might be helpful to ask, for instance, "When recruiting students or faculty, how would you describe your program to them? How would you describe your program to someone at a conference?" Examine written materials about your program (e.g., marketing materials) to see what they say or imply about your program. The flow of information and insights from this array of resources will provide an excellent pool from which to select key ideas for writing performance criteria statements.

Examples:

innovative	community-based
scholarly	challenging
rigorous	highly desired graduates
applied	friendly
success-oriented	world-class faculty
open access	technical
responsive	adaptable
value-added	efficient

Step 3 — Brainstorm a list of future program qualities.

The next question to consider concerns the direction in which you would like your program to move. What key qualities would you like to see as an outcome of your ideal program in the future? What capabilities do you see in superior graduates or expert practitioners that you would like your program to emulate (Mattingly & Fleming, 1992)? How would you like to enhance your current program? Are there characteristics lacking in your graduates that are somehow imbedded in the very design of your program (Newble & Hejka, 1991)? What attributes would you like to build into your program for the future?

By determining the difference between the current and future status of your program, you can identify the areas that need attention. This type of analytically derived information will be invaluable to program leadership as they begin to map out future priorities of the program and of the institution it serves. The future program qualities that your team articulates, therefore, should reflect anticipated or perceived shifts; those changes should be reflected in planning. Brainstorm these ideas with your design team, remembering to include material from the "products" and "processes" your group has completed in the earlier phase of the program assessment system.

Examples:

state-of-the-art	student-centered
assessment-oriented	empowering
evidence-based	problem-based
fully inclusive	24/7 access
life-changing	transformational
diverse environment	resource rich
heavily endowed	well-funded
trend-setting	cutting edge

Step 4 — Determine key qualities that are missing.

Combine the lists from steps two and three to aggregate the collective qualities. Check the new listing to determine if there are any important characteristics/qualities missing or if any gaps exist. Investigate programs similar to yours (e.g., those of competitors, peers, and exemplars) and consider why they are viewed as being strong (or of high quality). Determine which of their characteristics you desire and decide if they are applicable to your program. It is extremely important to facilitate the participation of all stakeholders (such as board members, students, and representatives of the community) in this process. It is also important that the resulting set of qualities identified represents all critical areas of the program and captures the essence of it. Contact collaborative partners outside your program (e.g. funding agencies, peers who produce significant contributions to their professional organizations) and get their opinions and feedback. Ask them to feed back to you their perceptions about what is special about your program; ask them to express in their own words their perception of who you are and how you contribute to their efforts or serve their needs.

Examples:

highly selective	highly employable
heavily endowed	resource rich
learner-centered	job-ready graduates
high technology	high retention
community visible	

Step 5 — Rank the top ten integrated current and future qualities.

The next step involves the ranking of the characteristics you have just identified in the previous steps. Begin by selecting which qualities are the most important. This is an excellent stage in which to enlist the assistance of community and alumni advisory groups for validation. This is also a good point at which to cross-reference selected qualities with additional requirements, such as accrediting bodies, state regulator boards, certification examination criteria, community needs, and college initiatives and priorities (James A. Rhodes State College, 2002). Make a first pass at ranking the list by labeling criteria from low to high (on a scale from 1 to 5). Then, sort the scores. Next, starting at the bottom of the list, see if you can justify moving a characteristic higher up in the list. Move to the next highest ranked item and determine if it can be moved up. Two to three passes through the list will help ensure that no truly critical item is overlooked.

Step 6 — Analyze these qualities to pull out redundancy and overlap.

In this step, you need to double check for possible redundancy in your final list of qualities. Are all your program strengths represented? Additionally, check this listing against characteristics of other programs in your institution. Have you included anything that actually is covered by other programs or college departments (e.g. advising, marketing)? Are you still operating within your stated scope or boundaries? Do a perception check and ask if, collectively, the qualities (the program characteristics you have identified) cover every aspect of your program. In other words, do they fully describe the unique traits that make it what it is, that give it a special identity?

Examples:

heavily endowed	well-funded
resource rich	innovative
cutting edge	state-of-the-art

Step 7 — Prioritize qualities; select the top six to eight.

You now need to examine the special characteristics of your program in terms of your over-all institutional strategic priorities and initiatives. All aspects of your program (both academic and non-academic) should ultimately feed into student learner outcomes and be kept in alignment with the institutional mission (Higher Learning Commission, 2003). Are you still targeting the most significant areas? A program should select six to eight criteria. The number of criteria chosen depends on the length of time the program has existed and on its magnitude or complexity. In general, the longer or more complex the program, the greater the number of criteria it will need. One of the tools commonly utilized in continuous quality improvement systems is the "pareto" diagram, which arranges data into categories for easy visualization. Charting selected qualities with this tool can help create a holistic view of your chosen qualities (Productivity-Quality Systems, 1992). McNamara (2002) reminds program designers of the "20-80" rule, which claims that 20 percent of effort generates 80 percent of the results.

Deming says 85 percent of quality problems are due to system design; clearly identifying quality areas will enable all stakeholders to get more systematic control of the program (Deming, 1982).

Step 8 — Analyze the qualities to find three to five aspects of each quality.

What makes each of your qualities unique? Why are they important in defining your program? Analyzing each of the qualities, describe in different phrases what each one means. Ask what is meaningful or significant in a given area of performance or if other possible meanings need to be considered. What important things must exist for this program characteristic to be true? For instance, if you claim a quality of "computer literacy," is the institutional infrastructure in place to support it?

Examples:

Quality: student-centered

Aspects: student defines their own learning objectives,

faculty identifies student learning needs,

students are engaged in active learning, and

faculty and student assess student performance.

Quality: success-oriented

Aspects: needs are being met

outcomes produced

external affirmation

rewarding

minimal failures

Step 9 — Write the performance criteria as statements.

The performance criteria are thoughtfully expressed performance expectations that are mutually understood by all stakeholders. They demonstrate the importance of key performance areas to the overall effectiveness of your program. They delineate the specific aspects of a performance and describe how they are tied to a larger integrated performance. They also provide direction about what programs *specifically* need to do to satisfy the goals that have been previously set out in much more global terms. Performance criteria and qualities have a critical two-way relationship. The performance criteria you write must deliver the specific qualities that have been selected. For example, if you have specified that your program needs to recruit more students, the performance criteria need to spell out how that will be achieved.

Try to visualize the integrated performance that you are seeking. Now put together a sequence of steps or actions to get the job done, checking to see that the plan is coherent and fluent. Describe and then imagine putting it into a real context. For instance, is it reasonable to expect that you can increase student enrollment by 10 percent in the next year or by 15 percent in the next two years? Will your plan achieve the qualities you have earlier identified as being descriptive of your program's unique character?

Concluding Thoughts

The writing of performance criteria is facilitated by strong writing prompts that identify the qualities that matter for program effectiveness. Once these qualities are visualized and captured, the task of writing the performance criteria statements that flow from them becomes easier. Key processes and products can then be highlighted and made apparent all stakeholders. A roadmap for the design specifications for your program will emerge from this process. A systematic approach for measuring program progress will be presented in the next module.

References

Accreditation Board for Engineering and Technology (2000), Engineering Criteria 2000. <www.abet.org>

Badiru, A., & Ayeni, B. (1993). *Practitioner's guide to quality and process improvement*. London: Chapman & Hall.

Deming, W. E. (1982). *Quality, productivity, and competitive position*. Cambridge, MA: Massachusetts Institute of Technology.

Higher Learning Commission (February, 2003). *The criteria for accreditation and the operational indicators*. Retrieved June 1, 2004 from <www.ncahigherlearningcom mission.org/restructuring/newcriteria>

Mattingly, C., & Fleming, M. F. (1992). *Clinical reasoning: Forms of inquiry in therapeutic practice*. Philadelphia, PA: F.A. Davis.

McNamara, C. (2002). *Basic guide to program evaluation*. The Management Assistance Program for Nonprofits. Retrieved June 1, 2004 from <www.mapnp.org/library/ evaluatn/fnl_eval.htm>

Newble, D. I. & Hejka, E. J. (1991). Approaches to learning of medical students and practicing physicians: Some empirical evidence and its implications for medical education. *Educational Psychology, 11*, 3-4.

Improvement tools for educators. (1992). Miamisburg, OH: Productivity-Quality Systems, Inc.

Scholtes, P. (1993). *The team handbook*. Madison, WI: Joiner Associates.

Defining a Program

by Daniel Apple, Pacific Crest; Steven Beyerlein, University of Idaho; and Kelli Parmley, SUNY New Paltz

The following module describes the preparatory steps involved in designing a program assessment system—defining the program context. The ***Methodology for Designing a Program Assessment System*** provides an overview and is the first in a series of modules about program assessment systems. This module offers guidance for implementing the first steps of that methodology beginning with suggestions for assembling a team that will define the program. In order to obtain a clear picture of where a program is and where it should go, it is critical that these first steps be undertaken collaboratively with key stakeholders in mind. Next is a statement of the program's "essence" and scope followed by an exploration of current and future goals. The last steps to defining a program are to identify key assets and products (results) as well as the processes that contribute to the quality of the program.

Setting the Stage

In a fast-paced environment, the temptation may be to give these first steps little attention or to avoid collaborating with colleagues. However, defining a program sets the stage for designing the rest of the assessment system. With greater clarity and consensus about the program definition, the remaining steps in the assessment system design process become that much stronger. Clearly defining a program establishes a strong foundation for developing a complete program assessment system and is an important "bridge" between the present (who you are) and the future (what you want to become). Defining a program assists in linking assessment to other important campus processes including strategic and operational planning.

Assembling the Team

All members responsible for a program should be involved in defining the program. While the available resources and team size may affect the assembly and management of a team, getting many different perspectives serves to strengthen the process (of defining a program). A "retreat" environment provides an ideal setting that enhances the ability of participants to work through and develop consensus. In situations where assembling a team is not feasible, another strategy would be to assemble a smaller "core" group of individuals to produce an initial draft and then solicit assessment feedback from all program members. In smaller programs with only a few individuals involved, other strategies to get additional perspectives may be necessary. This could include collaboration with a related campus program or a similar program at a different institution.

Time should be set aside and allocated for the single task of defining the program. The location chosen for team members to assemble should be free from interruptions and distractions, preferably in a retreat setting or at least away from immediate work. Avoid the tendency to add additional time to a departmental meeting as it doesn't provide the necessary time and focus. Other things to consider include logistical items such as food, availability of lap top computers and printers, and comfort level of the physical surroundings. To help facilitate the process, provide a set of materials to participants in advance. Items to provide include existing descriptive program materials, materials from other programs, background on program assessment (including the Methodology for Designing a Program Assessment System), and guiding questions that will prompt thinking prior to getting together.

Step 1— Writing an Essence Statement

The essence statement is a succinct and targeted single-sentence statement that articulates the core values of a program. The statement should be comprehensive in that it represents the whole program, not a subset. The statement should also be written such that consideration is given both to where the program currently is as well as to where program participants feel it should be. Ask what is it that makes this program distinct or unique? What is it that we value in this program?

Step 2 — Identifying Program Stakeholders

Stakeholders are those individuals and groups who have a vested interest in a program. To obtain a perspective beyond those directly involved in a program, develop a list of stakeholders along with a description of their interest in the program. The following questions help to identify possible stakeholders. Who employs my students? What graduate schools do my students go to? Who funds my program? Who are my students and where do they come from (e.g. predominantly native freshman or transfers)? Who has linkages to my program (e.g. student affairs, education programs)?

Step 3 — Specifying Program Scope

Specifying the scope of a program both in terms of what a program "is" and "is not" establishes the boundaries of a program. While there is typically agreement about the core of a program, there are often gray areas where participants and stakeholders differ about the boundaries of the program. The more gray areas, the more difficult it is for a program to produce the quality it desires. Gray areas can be minimized by clearly specifying, in writing, the scope of a program. Focus on and include those items where there is agreement. Items outside the scope can be explored as part of strategic planning.

Step 4 — Listing the Top Five Current and Future Goals

Developing a limited list of programmatic goals as a collaborative activity not only provides the necessary foundation for assessment but also is part of the review processes for most accrediting bodies (Middle States (2001); Banta and Palumbo (2000)). When identifying goals, consider a timeframe of three to five years. Identify the top five program goals to accomplish, both current and future. For static programs, a longer timeframe (five years) should be used. For relatively new and rapidly changing programs, a shorter timeframe (three years) should be used. As program participants begin brainstorming goals and then refining and narrowing the list, the goals will often fall into the appropriate categories such as current (e.g., the upcoming year) and future (e.g., three years from now). The list of goals should include both student learning goals as well as broader program goals. Ideally, the goals should be specific, to minimize multiple interpretations; quantifiable, to enhance clarity and focus; and written with a clear direction and magnitude.

Step 5 — Identifying Top Five Products or Assets

All programs yield important "products." These products may relate to students or they may relate to other aspects of the program such as advising or curriculum. Programs may have assets that are distinctive, unique, and a core feature of the program. Assets, in addition to products, should also be given consideration as they likely require some form of regular assessment to ensure their quality. The list of products and assets should be important to the program and explicitly described. Identifying and prioritizing a program's products and assets will clarify, in later steps, the most appropriate measures and instruments for assessment.

Step 6 — Describing Key Processes

The prior step identifies the key products or assets of the program. However, there are also key processes that contribute to a program. Consider and describe the processes that will be needed to accomplish the goals established in Step 4. Begin by listing the processes associated with the program. Explain the processes as mechanisms (how they transpire) describing them from multiple perspectives to enhance the meaning. Be sure to provide an overview of the entire process. Identify three to five components for each process and write the description as a sequence that connects the components. Finally, descriptions should inform how the process connects to outcomes as well as identifies ownership and responsibility for the process.

Concluding Thoughts

Do not move on to the next steps of the assessment system design until there is closure to defining the program. Periodically revisit the program definition to ensure consistency with the later steps. Prior to each meeting or retreat, ensure that designated individuals are responsible for taking detailed notes on the work that is done. As soon as possible after each meeting, the work product should be shared with the team for peer assessment. An environment such as Blackboard™ or Web CT™ can be used to efficiently facilitate this process and be used as a central location for maintaining documents. While it is important to achieve closure and move on to the next steps, realize that the process for designing an assessment system is iterative, not linear.

References

Banta, T., & Palomba, C.A. (2001). *Assessing student competence in accredited disciplines: Pioneering approaches to assessment in higher education.* Sterling, VA: Stylus Publishing, LLC.

Diamond, R. M. (1998). *Designing and assessing courses and curricula: A practical guide.* San Francisco: Jossey-Bass.

Middle States Commission on Higher Education (2002). *Characteristics of excellence in higher education: Eligibility requirements and standards for accreditation.* Philadelphia, PA: Middle States Commission on Higher Education.

Identifying Potential Measures

by Kelli Parmley, SUNY New Paltz and Daniel Apple, Pacific Crest

Once performance criteria have been crafted and refined as explained in ***Writing Clear Performance Criteria for a Program***, you can proceed to match these with appropriate measures. Using examples from academic and non-academic functions, this module provides guidance in determining what is most important to measure in determining institutional effectiveness. Prompts are given for generating candidate measures, distinctions are drawn between direct and indirect measures, and common pitfalls are addressed in selecting measures for a program.

Generating Potential Measures

At the heart of a good program assessment system is knowledge about what is important to measure versus what is available or easy to measure (Nichols, 1991). In looking at performance criteria statements ask "What aspects of this performance are most important to measure?" For example, in the student centered performance criteria from Table 1 it is important that the learner is truly taking ownership for learning. One could survey students about their academic career plans. Another way is to consider "What would I ask someone else (e.g. students, faculty, alumni) to determine if this performance was met?" A third way could be to interview a stakeholder affected by the criteria such as parents of past and present students. However, as the focus of data collection shifts away from the primary participants cited in a criteria statement, it is vital to direct questioning so that data is not diluted with non-essential information. In selecting measures it is also important to not let historical measurements and existing data collection tools dictate what is most important to the program. Finally, performance measures should also be independent, thereby insuring that measures are not correlated. Another rationale for independence is that the cost of a measure is normally non-trivial and it is expensive to take multiple measurements on the same variation.

Indirect versus Direct Measures

Another critical aspect in identifying performance measures is to consider whether you are directly or indirectly measuring performance. Often times the aspects chosen for measurement act as a "proxy" for what you truly want to measure (Banta and Palomba, 2001). In other words, there may be high correlation between the measure and the actual performance. However, it doesn't mean that you're actually measuring performance. An example of this is perception or satisfaction. For example, in the "academically sound graduates" criteria from Table 1 one attribute might be student perception of their ability to analyze, synthesize, etc. However, while student perception is easy to measure, it is an indirect measure that is less important than actual performance skills for purposes of program improvement. Another example would be the "qualified graduates" performance criteria where one could choose to use a more readily available placement "rate" instead of placement "success." Placement success would more directly capture the aspects of placement such as whether it was a top choice by the student or whether it was because of the quality of preparation.

Common Pitfalls

Low Cost Data

Avoid being trapped by what is currently available or being measured, because often this data is not relevant to what really matters. Most people think any data will have value. Even when data is essentially free, there is the cost of analyzing and bringing meaning so that future performance will be enhanced. Use the process of program assessment to make decisions about what you will stop measuring as well as what you will start measuring.

Method Bias

There is a tendency to jump to instruments before you identify what you want to measure, the best venue for collecting this data, and the number of items that are really needed to characterize performance. Performance criteria should prescribe the measurement methods, not visa versa. Being tactical and precise in instrument selection simplifies data collection and insures the chosen measures are the most cost-effective.

Dilution

Often the prioritizing of the potential measures is not effective so what really matters does not get measured well while less important things end up getting measured more. When people write the performance criteria there are some attributes that are more important than others. One may actually capture 60% of the performance. More is not better. Every time you pick one, you're discounting the others. When you've got two potential attributes for measurement, ask if they are "close enough" to just pick one.

Historical Data

There is a tendency to continue to measure what was always measured, even though they may no longer be appropriate. As programs change, the attributes of the performance that should be measured need to be adapted and changed. Completeness and continuity of the historical record is meaningless if these data cannot be used to guide improvement efforts that flow from current performance criteria for a program.

Table 1   **Examples of Measurable Attributes**

Performance Criteria	Measurable Attributes
Academically sound graduates Scientifically literate graduates who are able to analyze, synthesize, and evaluate information in the areas of basic human communication processes, communication differences and disorders, and swallowing disorders, and who are prepared for doctoral study and/or professional careers.	research skills mastery of professional practice
Student-centered An enriched active learning environment where faculty, staff, and students focus on student's development through updated learning plans with personalized learning objectives, special needs, and continual assessment of student learning.	percent of currently accepted learning plans
Success-oriented A supportive community with the language, values, and expectations necessary to respond to the needs of students, refusing the accept failure and propagating significant accomplishments as well as consistently high performance.	graduation rate
Rich curriculum Offer a rich and diverse range of courses that span genres, historical periods, major authors, ethnic backgrounds across many Anglophone cultures exploring diversity issues in race, sex and economic backgrounds.	diversity
Qualified graduates Fully qualified graduates who are consistently accepted in graduate schools of choice because of their documented abilities to carry out independent laboratory work, undergraduate research, and effective problem solving.	placement success
Research (Office of Research) Extensive, wide spread research effort with collaboration among students and external researchers resulting in highly funded research projects and significant peer review journal articles and presentations.	number of faculty with the number of annual qualified publications research dollars
Service-oriented (Administrative Office) Consistently puts interests of others first, clarify clients needs, aligns with institutional needs, provides effective consulting and values prompt effective and conclusive response to clients perceived need.	satisfaction of clients

Grandstanding

The purpose of program assessment is continuous improvement. However, there can be a temptation to pick only measurable attributes that showcase current high performance levels, avoiding areas where performance needs improvement. Such a one-dimensional approach insures that the status quo is maintained, ultimately giving up long-term competitive advantages that result from regular attention to ongoing improvement.

Concluding Thoughts

At the heart of a quality program assessment system is the minimum set of measures that provide feedback on what really matters. Make sure that these measures derive directly from your performance criteria, are feasible to collect, meaningful to analyze, and are respected by the campus community. Selecting measures, like writing per-formance criteria, is best done as a collaborative activity involving stakeholders at all levels in the institution. By putting the spotlight on a minimum set of independent measures, involving multiple constituencies in interpreting measurement findings, and promoting broad-based dialogue about how to respond to these findings, an institution will be taking positive steps toward realizing its mission.

References

Nichols, J. (1991). *A practitioner's handbook for institutional effectiveness and student outcomes*. New York: Agathon Press.

Banta, T., & Palomba, C. (2001). *Assessing student competence in accredited disciplines: Pioneering approaches to assessment in higher education*. Sterling, VA: Stylus Publishing, LLC.

Writing an Annual Assessment Report

by Kelli Parmley, SUNY New Paltz and Daniel Apple, Pacific Crest

A mechanism that can sustain attention to continuous quality improvement and demonstrate accountability for external audiences is an annual assessment report. The challenge for program participants, once a quality assessment system is designed, is getting started. This module clarifies the purposes and uses of an annual assessment report and identifies a template for an annual assessment report.

Purposes and Uses for an Annual Assessment Report

Assessment systems have two chief purposes, improvement and evaluation. While the use of information for these two purposes requires a distinctly different mindset *(see Distinctions between Assessment and Evaluation)*, the process of measuring, recording, and reporting of information is common to both assessment and evaluation. An annual assessment report is a framework for reporting information for both improvement and evaluation. In the case of assessment, reported information is used to provide constructive feedback for purposes of improvement. Whereas with evaluation, performance is compared against a standard with the results being permanently and publicly recorded.

An annual assessment report serves two additional and important purposes. The annual assessment report is written with key program stakeholders as intended audiences. Therefore it can be used to communicate with these stakeholders in other processes such as budgeting, planning, recruiting, and fund raising. In the case of an academic program this could include multiple stakeholders such as students, faculty, alumni, and administrators. Lastly, an assessment system should be regularly assessed to ensure continuous improvement *(see Methodology for Designing a Program Assessment System)*. The annual assessment report provides the evidence necessary for assessing the assessment system by providing direction for improvement.

Components of an Annual Assessment Report

The report needs to be written with the program's multiple audiences (stakeholders) in mind. Therefore, the physical appearance of the report should be of publication quality (e.g., color, glossy print) similar to other professional annual reports. Table 1 presents a template for an annual assessment report. The following provides greater descriptive detail of components found in the template.

Packaging the Report

Front cover

The front cover of the report should clearly identify the program title, the year and list the names of the key program contributors (e.g., faculty). Complimenting this information is visual imagery (e.g., pictures, graphics, colors) that captures the essence of the program, its key processes or products.

Back cover

The inside back cover of the annual report should be used to list important activities and events (e.g., lecture series, brown bag lunches, alumni events) that are planned for the subsequent year. The back of the cover should include important contact information for the program (e.g., address, email, phone numbers) and list additional program participants (e.g., student workers, part-time employees, volunteers).

Providing Program Background

Inside front cover

The inside cover of the annual report provides important context for the report, and an important tool for communicating with stakeholders, by specifying the information from the first five steps of the assessment system.

Illustrating Program Quality

Interior pages

The interior pages should be printed front to back with each side devoted to an area of quality (performance criteria) identified in the "table of measures" of an assessment system *(see Methodology for Designing a Program Assessment System)*. These should be prioritized such that the first and second most important performance areas are captured on the front and back of the first interior page. The subsequent pages would address each of the remaining performance areas. One suggestion is to devote a page to assessment providing an opportunity to identify overall progress in implementing and assessing an assessment system.

Illustrating Continuous Quality Improvement

Format for interior pages

The page for each performance area should be divided to include five elements. These are found in the section "Design for a Page" of Table 1. The top accomplishments, additional accomplishments, and efforts allow those responsible for the program to convey a great deal of information about quality in that performance area, yet do so in a prioritized fashion. The top accomplishments should be significant contributions to performance in that area of the program. Each of those significant accomplishments should be thoroughly described based on evidence gathered (e.g., the attributes, means for collecting the data, and instrument vehicles in the assessment system). For a program with a newly designed assessment system, strong evidence may not be available, but does not prevent a program from writing the annual report. Use what evidence is available to describe the strengths of this accomplishment and its contribution to the quality area.

For any particular performance area there are additional accomplishments and efforts. These are less significant than the top accomplishments of the program, but indicate contributions to quality in that area. Additional accomplishments should be single sentences, while additional "efforts" would be stated briefly in phrases.

Lastly, each page should also identify short term and long term activities and plans for improving the program. In this section, care should be taken to avoid evaluation language and to emphasize opportunities for improvement. Identifying these activities and plans on an annual basis provides a clear linkage from one year to the next. The short term activities and plans should inform campus operational processes (e.g. budgeting and planning) and should be assessed in the subsequent year's annual report. The long term activities and plans should inform strategic and program planning processes.

Concluding Thoughts

A quality assessment report can be one of the most valuable activities all year. It helps the program recount all their accomplishments and provides the basis for direction in the next year. It provides clear documentation to obtain resources, internally, through the budget process and helps to obtain more resources externally through grants and development. An annual assessment report supports the strategic and program planning processes by clearly identifying long term activities and plans. Lastly, the accreditation, and other evaluation processes, become much easier because work is done on an annual basis.

*Table 1   **Template for an Annual Assessment Report***

Packaging the Report

Front cover
- Program title
- Slogan/phrase with special meaning
- Year
- Key program contributors
- Images that capture essence of program, key processes, and products

Inside back cover
- Schedule of activities and events of interest for the coming year
- Ways to get involved (e.g. open houses, presentations, social activities, celebrations, symposiums)

Back cover
- Contact information (who to contact for informal requests)
- List of program members

Providing Program Background

Inside front cover (carefully crafted for the audience):
- Program essence and scope
- Key features (processes/systems)
- Key assets (products)
- Goals (current and future)

Illustrating Continuous Quality Improvement

Interior pages (front to back):
- First page (immediately following the front cover) — most important performance area
- Second page (back of first page) — second most important performance area
- Subsequent pages — one page for each of the remaining performance areas
- Last page (before back cover) — continuous quality improvement (assessment)

Design for a Page

Performance area (specified at the top of the page)
  First page
  1. Top two or three accomplishments — paragraph with strong evidence and value articulated
  2. Top 10 additional accomplishments — single sentences
  3. Additional efforts
  4. Planned activities and improvements for next year
  5. Strategic plans for the next five years

Assessing Program Assessment Systems

by Kelli Parmley, SUNY New Paltz and Daniel Apple, Pacific Crest

The practice of continuous improvement not only applies to program performance, but also to the assessment systems that are used to assess programs. Assessment systems that are efficient and current are less time consuming to employ and are likely to yield more reliable data. As strategic planning processes shape institutional vision, mission and priorities, the assessment systems by which an institution's programs gauge performance and help direct improvement should be in alignment. Therefore it is crucial to annually review assessment systems with the goal of continuously improving the process. This module identifies the characteristics of a quality assessment system, provides a tool that assessors can utilize in assessing a program assessment system and how to effectively use feedback to develop an action plan for improving the assessment system.

What Makes a Program Assessment System a Quality Assessment System?

The process of assessing an assessment system begins with the same approach to assessing at other organizational levels or in other contexts; it involves a mindset where the actual level of quality is not of interest, "only how to improve it" *(see Distinctions between Assessment and Evaluation Module)*. Regular assessment of a program's assessment system, to ensure currency and alignment with institutional goals, is also consistent with the assessment standards of regional (Middle States Commission on Higher Education, 2002; Higher Learning Commission, 2001) and many professional accrediting bodies (ABET, 2002).

Table 1 identifies a tool for assessing a program assessment system. The columns in the table are structured for the assessor to provide the strengths, areas for improvement, and insights (SII) method to assess each element of the system. The rows in the table identify key criteria to use for assessing quality *(see SII Method for Assessment Reporting)*.

The essence statement, in contrast to lengthy, inspirational mission or vision statements, should provide an immediate sense of the core values of the current program. It should be concise, yet comprehensive and stated in a complete sentence.

The scope of a program is anchored in present performance and should clearly articulate the "core" of the program and its boundaries. Statements about what the program "is not" should identify what is outside the scope of the program and why "gray areas" occur.

The top-five current and future goals should represent a three to five year timeframe for the program and have enough specificity such that they indicate direction and magnitude. A teaching and learning center might identify "collaborative initiatives among faculty within and across disciplines and schools" as a goal. However, feedback might suggest clarification with respect to magnitude. Will the teaching and learning center be maintaining the level of offerings or increasing them?

The top five processes and systems of a program (e.g., curriculum design) should help contribute to the accomplishment of the current and future goals and produces the products, assets, and results. The distinction between the two is important for determining the performance criteria, which may be process or product oriented criteria.

The performance criteria, when present in a program, produce quality. For example, "Faculty provide proactive and developmentally based advising that is centered on students needs within a systematic framework." The performance criteria statement provides a concise statement in a specified context that is understood and valued by multiple stakeholders in that program.

Attributes (measurable characteristics) provide the means for helping to differentiate levels of performance for each criterion. There should be no more than three for each criterion, they should be measurable and significant. Examples of attributes for the advising performance criterion include (1) timely interaction with students (2) students graduate within four or five years and (3) students can effectively create a semester course schedule.

The attributes should be prioritized by the weights assigned to each. The weights should indicate the significance of that attribute to the overall program performance. In this regard they should add to one hundred percent, but no single factor should be less than five percent.

The means for collecting the data (e.g., portfolio, survey) should be a reasonable, cost-effective avenue for collecting the data in a timely manner.

An instrument is the measure of the data that is collected. For example a survey may be the means for collecting the data, but a satisfaction index would be the instrument for measuring satisfaction. Similarly a standardized test may be the vehicle for gathering data on student learning, but test scores are the instruments to measure knowledge. Instruments should be appropriate, valid, reliable, and accurate.

Benchmarks identify the current level of performance of a program, while future targets identify the level of performance the program is striving for. Future targets should have a clear relationship to the performance criteria. They should be based on performance (as compared to effort) and be attainable, yet challenging.

Accountability means that a specific individual (as compared to identifying a general title) is assigned responsibility for a factor. Responsibility should be distributed among program participants.

Using the Tool Effectively

The tool for assessing an assessment system is the means for an assessor and the assessee to increase the quality of an assessment system. Additionally, the tool provides a framework for structuring the feedback for assessor and assessee. The following tips can further assist in using the tool effectively.

1. An inter-disciplinary assessment review committee of five to fifteen people (from various disciplines across campus) should be established to assess a program assessment system.

2. Set up a time schedule where assessment systems are reviewed on a monthly basis with the full cycle of assessing program assessment systems occurring over a three-year period.

3. The program should identify areas in which it would most like feedback.

4. Based on the feedback priorities identified by the program, the committee should use smaller review teams of two or three people to assess. While providing additional (perhaps contrasting) feedback, be careful not to send mixed messages to the assessee.

5. Before beginning the review the team should read and analyze the criteria for assessing a program assessment system.

6. The review team should strive for feedback that is of high quality, not quantity.

7. Be careful not to use evaluative statements; there are no standards (good or bad) because the emphasis is how to improve.

8. Provide an opportunity to compliment written feedback with a face to face report.

9. The form should be used as an electronic template where feedback is recorded directly into the chart (versus hand written notes on a paper document).

10. The feedback should be very explicit and directive about how to improve; direction and assistance should be given, not platitudes.

Turning Feedback into an Annual Plan of Action

Using the feedback provided by the review committee the program participants can establish a course of action. Two to three percent of program's resources should be explicitly set aside for purposes of improvement. Within those parameters, the program participants need to "scope" the changes and address the basic question: What is a reasonable amount of change to make based on what was learned from the feedback?

1. Prioritize and choose the changes to be made to the assessment system based on which will leverage the most improvement.

2. Specify a detailed list of activities that must take place in order for a proposed change to occur.

3. The activities should be accompanied by dates for completion and an assigned individual who will be responsible for carrying out that activity.

4. Program participants should be updated on a regular basis, perhaps a standing agenda item on the regular program meeting schedule.

5. The changes made to an assessment system should be included in the program's annual reporting process as evidence of improvement.

Concluding Thoughts

An assessment system must be healthy, dynamic, and continually advanced for it to help the program's strategic plan to be aligned with the institution's strategic plan. Therefore the program should assess its programs assessment system once a year and invest two to three percent of its annual program resources for implementing program assessment and its improvements. The long term outcome implication for assessing the assessment system is greater "buy-in" from program participants.

References

Accreditation Board for Engineering and Technology, Inc. (2002). <http://www.abet.org>

Higher Learning Commission (20001). <http://www.ncahigherlearningcommission.org>

Middle States Commission on Higher Education (2002). *Characteristics of excellence in higher education: Eligibility requirements and standards for accreditation.* Philadelphia, PA: Middle States Commission on Higher Education.

Table 1   **Tool for Assessing an Assessment System**

Criteria	Strengths	Improvements	Insights
1. Essence statement • represents all of its stakeholders • is comprehensive • is concise • values are identified and appropriate			
2. Scope • clarifies what is outside the program's core • clarifies what the program does do • differentiates core aspects (current) from future aspects • clarifies why misconceptions can occur (gray areas)			
3. Top five current and future goals of the program • are specific • are measurable • are clear in direction and magnitude • represent a three to five year time frame			
4. Processes and systems • are descriptive • identify key processes • provide intent, direction, and connections			
5. Products, assets, and results • are explicit • are descriptive • are important • are obvious			
6. Assessment report • documents accomplishments • provides strong evidence • provides clear action plans • documents past year improvements made to the assessment system • presents a professional image			

Tool for Assessing an Assessment System

Criteria	Strengths	Improvements	Insights
7. Performance criteria • are concise • are free from jargon; understandable by multiple audiences • provide context • produce quality • are valued by multiple stakeholders			
8. Attributes *(measurable characteristics)* • are not too small • are not too large • are single dimensional • are measurable • contain appropriate units			
9. Weights • sum to one hundred • factors less than five are not included • are assigned an appropriate value • are aligned to a factor			
10. Means for collecting data • are cost-effective • are timely • are obvious • are reasonable • capture performance data			
11. Instruments • are reliable • are appropriate • are valid • are accurate			
12. Benchmarks and future standards • are related to criteria and factors • are based on performance as compared to effort • define level of success used for evaluation • are bench marked • are challenging • are attainable			
13. Accountability • is assigned to a specific individual (not just a title) • is assigned to all internal stakeholders • is distributed appropriately			

Pacific Crest

Faculty Development Series

Glossary

edited by Cy Leise, Bellevue University; Steven Beyerlein, University of Idaho; Marie Baehr, Elmhurst College; Mark Schlesinger, University of Massachusetts Boston; and Daniel Apple, Pacific Crest

accomplishment outcome	major work product or performance that transcends typical course requirements
action research	systematic, qualitative or quantitative exploration of processes as they unfold, frequently requiring attention to new information and changed conditions in the course of the exploration
active learning	learning by doing, whether individual or group focused
activity	structured use of limited time
affective domain	skills relating to intrapersonal behavior, attitudinal development, and emotional well-being
assessee	person whose performance, work product, or learning skill(s) is being assessed with regard to specific criteria he or she has set with the assessor
assessment	process of measuring and analyzing a performance or product to provide feedback to improve future performance or products
assessor	person who performs the assessment process on behalf of an assessee
attribute	qualitative or quantitative characteristic of a criterion
closure	stopping point at the end of a process, used for reflecting and reinforcing what has been learned, what issues remain, and where to direct future efforts
cognitive domain	skills relating to information processing, critical thinking, problem solving, and conducting research
collaboration	working together to accomplish a task to the mutual satisfaction of participants
competency outcome	level of knowledge and/or skills demonstrated as a result of a learning experience
concept model	construct that illustrates a concept; can be formed using language, physical objects, mathematics, or pictures
constructive intervention	interruption by a facilitator with questions or actions for the purpose of improving students' learning skills and /or work product
context	whole situation, background, or condition relevant to the use of a process, tool, or concept; pertaining to a particular event, personality, place, etc.
cooperative learning	working together to accomplish a task with specified criteria for personal accountability, individual skill development, face-to-face interaction, interdependence, and group processing
criterion	focus area of quality; (plural: criteria)
domain	hierarchical group of processes with supporting skills that apply to a large area of human performance (i.e. cognitive-thinking, social-interpersonal goal achievement, affective-emotional, and psychomotor-body control)

evaluatee   person whose performance or work product is judged against a set of standards established outside of the person's control

evaluation   process of measuring the quality of a performance, work product or use of a process against a set of standards to make a judgment or determination if, or to what level, the standards have been met

evaluator   person who renders or reports a judgement (conclusion) concerning the performance or work product of an evaluatee

evidence   collection of specific qualitative and quantitative data on attributes that relate to a performance or product

experience outcome   attitudinal alignment, value development, and/or connection with a particular context or community

facilitator   person who is in charge of pacing the activity and responsible for ensuring that the group best meets the criteria set out in the activity

factor   measurable characteristic of a criterion using a single scale

formative assessment   assessment performed by collecting and analyzing evidence at specific points within a process to determine what should be done to improve the performance in current and future efforts

growth   improvement in one's capacity for learning

guided discovery   learning through exploration and discovery where the instructor provides resources, objectives, criteria, and a set of carefully designed critical thinking questions

insight   something new, important, and significant that you now see clearer, or has greater meaning and understanding to you

instrument   specific tool used to obtain evidence

integrated performance synthesis of prior knowledge, skills, processes, and attitudes with current learning needs to address a new and significant challenge

knowledge   information, awareness, and understanding that can be readily accessed or constructed

knowledge table   collection of concepts, processes, tools, and contexts that make up or describe a particular area of knowledge

leader   common team role: his or her purpose is to insure that teams accomplish important goals in a timely and high quality manner

learning   acquisition of knowledge and skills and their integration into the existing knowledge base

learning outcome   change in knowledge base, skill utilization, beliefs, values, and behavior that occur as a result of learning

Learning Process Methodology   set of steps one can study to accelerate the construction of knowledge and to deepen one's ability to learn

learning rate	rate at which new knowledge is mastered
learning skills	aptitudes, abilities, and techniques used to acquire new knowledge, skills, and perspectives
learning to learn	improving skills so you can construct knowledge more efficiently and effectively
life vision	mental image of what you would like your future self to be
lifelong learner	one who can apply learning skills to new situations throughout his or her life
methodology	systematic study of steps that make up a process with the purpose of improving future performance in this area
mission	statement of purpose; the most important reasons to be in existence, strongly based on beliefs and value system
movement outcome	visible change in skills and/or processes demonstrated as a result of a learning experience
objective	general intentions at the beginning of a process
outcome	measurable entity (products, knowledge, skills, and attitudes) that can be documented as a measure of desired performance
ownership	being responsible and accountable with respect to achieving outcomes; can belong to an individual, a team, or an organization
peer assessment	assessment performed by a colleague or peer
peer coaching	assessment of a peer by a peer based on observations of performance
performance	carrying out an action or process; the work and actions you do; in the context of assessment, the action that is to be assessed
performance criterion	standard used to measure and assess performance during a learning activity
performance measure	basis for ranking a performance based on its quality
portfolio	collection of work products which demonstrate accomplishments, growth, and abilities in relation to defined areas of performance over a specific period of time
preassessment	assessment that takes place at the beginning of a process, used to determine the level of ability or preparedness
prerequisites	set of concepts that should be mastered before undertaking a new body of knowledge built upon these concepts
process	sequence of identifiable, ordered steps to ensure robust results
Process Education	educational philosophy focusing on improving students' performance skills and creating "self-growers"
professional profile	behaviors displayed by an expert

psychomotor domain	skills relating to body control
range	span that includes all the quality levels
real time assessment	assessment that occurs simultaneously with the process under study
recorder	common team role; his or her purpose is to regularly document team decisions and discoveries
reflective thinking	taking time to play back on an experience, process, or accomplishment with purpose of gaining new insights
reflector	common team role; his or her purpose is to make observations about team performance, interactions and dynamics
rubric	matrix (row and columns) of information of data; in the case of a measure to assess a learning skill, the rows represent levels of performance and the columns represent areas of performance
scale	means for determining the quality level of the evidence
self-assessment	assessing your own progress by thinking critically about your (learning) process or performance and the results of that process
self-grower	highest level of learner performance, having developed strong performance/learning skills; learners who are continually growing by using strong self-assessment skills to improve future performance
SII	assessment instrument which reports strengths, areas for improvement, and insights
social domain	skills related to interpersonal behavior, attitudinal alignment, and community connection
spokesperson	common team role; his or her purpose is to report to the class as a whole the discoveries documented by the recorder
standard	level of performance that is determined as the minimum level for success
summative assessment	assessment performed by collecting and analyzing evidence at the end of a process to bring closure to the process
theme	implicit or recurring idea throughout a course or experience
tool	any device, implement, instrument or utensil which serves as a resource to accomplish a task
training	specialized instruction and practice to become proficient in doing something
way of being	set of behaviors, actions, and use of language associated with a particular discipline or knowledge area

Alphabetical Listing of Modules